W9-AEW-583

6.00

41- 23896 APR 15 96

IDEAS FOR THE ICE AGE

Also by Max Lerner

IDEAS ARE WEAPONS

IT IS LATER THAN YOU THINK

FOR

Bruce Bliven

journalist and friend in any age

31186

Foreword

This is, in one sense, a companion book to my earlier volume, *Ideas Are Weapons*. I have sought here to go somewhat further in the exploration of the history, the meaning, and the uses of our contemporary ideas. But while there is this continuity, the present volume will (I hope) stand by itself as the record of one American's approach to those revolutionary events and forces of the past few years that have burst the bounds of our social forms, our international organization, our received ideas. While the essays cover a wide area, I trust that they have the inner unity of a point of view.

In its focus, then, this book is a study of the varied aspects of a revolutionary era. We are in the midst of a revolution whose scope is not national but world-wide; a revolution in which every nation must participate willy-nilly, because to the captain of every boat on a stormy ocean the choice is not whether he will allow the storm to approach him, but whether he will ride the storm or be ridden by it; a revolution which has been forced upon us; and a revolution which is not yet completed but is ours to complete.

Our role in such a revolution has four aspects, which I have used as the major divisions for grouping these essays. In the struggle in which democracy and fascism are wrestling for the ownership of the future, we have the task of winning that future and planning its organization. We have the problem of retraversing the course of the Western mind and selecting out those elements of a usable past on which the beliefs and ideals of our time are based and which, when strengthened and extended, can assure us a livable future. We have the problem of acting decisively in the international crisis. And we have the problem of strengthening our home front, and finishing the unfinished business of democracy.

Since the focus of this book is on the tasks of a revolutionary era, its mood is not a gentle one. The essays reprinted here represent the larger part of my writing energies over the past two years, while perhaps a fifth of the book goes a few years further back. If the reader remembers that those years have been the harsh age for our civilization, he will understand the grimness of feeling which is reflected both in the title and in the contents.

That grimness is not bleakness of mood, nor is it despair and defeatism of purpose. It is rather what I have several times in the book characterized as the "tough-minded" viewpoint. We may as well understand that there has been no age in modern history which has been so deeply betrayed by those who should have been its leaders, and so desperately a victim of its own accepted ideas. And we had better confront also another fact. Because of our errors of commission and omission in the past, we stand—even under the best outcome we can envisage—on the threshold of an ice age, in which we shall have to fight and endure, steel our will, nourish our patience. The one thing that can be said for the catastrophe that has overtaken our world is that catastrophe too has its social uses. It may awaken slumbering energies, solidify a sense of men's comradeship in the nation and the world, evoke the qualities of great leadership. The Czechs, the British, and the Russians have shown that a nation great in prosperity may be even greater in adversity. The Americans, entering now on a war and on a revolutionary struggle whose end they cannot foresee, will (I have no doubt) show the same quality.

But despite this harshness of outlook, I do not believe in any fatalist doctrine. I believe that history has imperatives within which we must work; but within those imperatives of economic planning, political centralization, administrative strength, scope for leadership, a fabric of world organization, the future may be totalitarian or it may be toughly and nobly democratic. I have asked repeatedly in these essays: "Who owns the future?" The answer is for us to hammer out.

But we shall not be the ones to hammer it out successfully unless we keep certain things in mind. First, that democracy must not be conceived in such terms that by definition it is too weak to survive. In a recent radio debate with Lawrence Dennis, I found him trying to force on me a definition of democracy as a system of pressure groups, checks and balances, and weak leadership. Obviously it is to the interest of the fascists in our midst to have us adopt such a conception. But those who believe in democracy must not fall into the trap. They must understand that democracy, if it is to be an effective social and political system, must have a dynamic—whatever it is that makes it sharp and strong and gives it the swing of an upward arc. Second, that a democratic dynamism will involve the use of many means which we are asked to call "totalitarian" and thus to surrender to the dictators—planning, military might, executive power, an administrative elite—but which are as compatible with democracy as with totalitarianism. As Ralph Barton Perry has put it, "The problem for a democracy is how to be total without being totalitarian." Third, that there is an organic relation in any social system between its foreign and domestic aspects, and that a democracy which is effective in world affairs can and must finish its unfinished business at home. Fourth, that we are lost unless we can fashion a fighting faith in which we believe with an intense conviction—a fighting faith that is deeply anti-fascist only because it is even more deeply humanist and democratic.

These are the ideas with which we can fulfill our revolutionary era. They are the ideas which can, I think, tide us over the harsh period ahead of us, and serve after the war as the basis for world reconstruction under American leadership.

Contents

PART ONE

Who Owns the Future?

1

The War as Revolution

I. THE BREAKING OF NATIONS

IT WILL be hard for America to prepare its armed forces to face the contingencies of the war. But it will be even harder for us to prepare our thinking for the new world we shall have to live in. Harder because, while the might of the German military machine has now become the prime tangible in the world, the framework within which it has come to operate with such success is a framework of intangibles, elusive to our urgency and unpleasant to our prejudices. Harder, too, because we think, as we live, by the last moments of the clock, and our outlook today has a panic quality that is the enemy of thought.

The thrust of the Nazi columns has left its trauma not only on the European consciousness but on the American as well. We are like someone who wakes out of an anesthetic sleep in a strange room, enclosed by unfamiliar walls, and wonders whether the spectral shapes around him are nightmare imaginings or terrible realities. Clinging to the radio, hoping against hope as we listen to the sickening bulletins, we attempt to exorcise the horror. But it will not away. These are not ghosts—this brutal power of the Nazi war machine, this pervasiveness of a new system of ideas, this dynamic will of the German governing group, these new barbarians come to sweep away the empires of our minds. We shall not for a long time restore ourselves to the tranquillity we once owned.

One of the results of the almost fantastic disintegration of country after country before Hitler's drive to power has been the bewilderment and disillusionment of the American people. Nor is it hard to see the basis of our mood. Those whom we have always thought the border guards of our civilization have been routed like so many wooden soldiers. The old landmarks are gone: the radicals have become conservative, the reactionaries of the world have

3

become its revolutionists. Yet here lies our greatest danger. If we yield to bewilderment and hysteria we have three-quarters lost the battle. Now as never before we must know what we believe in, what America stands for, what the imperatives are which will determine our actions. The world in which we live is facing an era of wars, civil wars, and revolutions. Only a new tough-mindedness in the service of a set of fervent convictions can possibly rescue us from what seems the common doom. Only thus will we master the dimensions of the battlefield which has become our world, and act in it with the economy that makes survival possible, so that we may live in it with the grace that gives life meaning.

And first we must understand that the war, which seemed during its first eight months a good deal less than a war (remember the quips about the *Sitzkrieg?*), is in reality, and has been from the beginning, a good deal more than a war. It is the military phase of a complex of changes and tensions in Western life so vast as to amount to a revolution. One difficulty in estimating American opinion on the war lies in the fact that the Great Debate has been couched wholly in terms of intervention or non-intervention. "Are you warmongers?" the non-interventionists hurl at the interventionists when they plead for armaments for Great Britain. "Would you rather send your guns or your sons?" the interventionists hurl back. In such a debate everything depends of course on the reality and immediacy of the Hitler threat to America, and on whether Hitler can be ultimately appeased and will stay appeased.[1] What each side tends to forget, however, is that neither intervention nor non-intervention in itself ends the problem; and that the effect of helping Britain or not helping Britain, of going to war or not going to war, depends upon the nature of the forces active in the world today, the forces which have conditioned Hitler's rise and shaped his victory thus far. The Great Debate has been carried on wholly in terms of immediate program. But, at the risk of being called academic, I say that analysis is even more important than program. If your basic analysis is right, you can shift your immediate program with the shift of events. But if you shape a program blindly, without reference to the major currents in the world, you drift helplessly with every change.

---

[1] See "Hitler's American Dream," below, p. 175.

We must recognize that what is happening today is something very close to a world revolution. It is not the sort of revolution that Marxists have for a century envisaged. Theirs was a revolution from below, led by a disciplined and class-conscious group. But that revolution missed fire. It had its chance on a world scale, and it may have its chance again in another generation. Right now, however, the revolutionary wedge has been driven by a new group working from above—a praetorian guard in every country operating in what Lenin would have called "a revolutionary situation" —using the leftist methods of propaganda, violence, and class war, taking advantage of the contradictions of capitalist economics but for ends far removed from the ends of the left.

We speak of Hitler's triumph, and we should err monstrously to underestimate the greatness of Hitler's role. Hitler will take his place in the succession of praetorian leaders who shaped world history, from Alexander and Attila and Genghis Khan through Napoleon. He may well rank as the outstanding instance of a man who, knowing no ruth, gave history the shape of his will; and who took not one country or even one continent but the whole world as his stamping-ground. Rauschning has written convincingly of Hitler's megalomaniac outlook. He represents the triumph of an insidious intelligence, an unbridled imagination, a steel will, in a world that did not know its purposes and did not organize its forces. Yet knowing all this we must not too easily succumb either to the great-man theory or to the devil theory of history. Hitler has been able to do what he has done because he has been active in a situation ripe for him.

We have been told time and again that Nazism is a revolution. Rauschning has said it, Dorothy Thompson has said it, Peter Drucker has said it, Thomas Mann has said it, Archibald MacLeish has said it. Rauschning calls it "the revolution of nihilism" and MacLeish "the revolution against." They are of course right. Nazism is revolutionary. But it is not the revolution I have in mind when I speak of the war as the expression of a world revolution. Nazism is a bastard revolution. It is a revolution enforced from above by the will of a man and a group of adventurers around him, enforced by terror and accepted through fear. But—and this is the important thing—it is a revolution that has been accepted for want of a better one. It is a premature and destructive organization of revolutionary forces that might have had, and may still have, an alternative organization.

What are these forces? The first is the result of our incapacity to organize world peace after the last war. We made a political settlement, but it was frustrate because it did not provide an economic settlement as well. We left a Europe of fragmented nations, incapable of joining together economically because of their national rivalries, yet incapable of surviving without thus joining together. The Europe of the past quarter-century has been a Europe of international disorganization, capitalist collapse, liberal helplessness, tory sabotage. Thus the way was left open for someone to organize Europe by sheer unqualified force. Whether he will succeed in keeping Europe organized after his conquests is another matter. For the present it is enough to point out that European disorganization has been an element in the revolutionary complex.

Closely related to this has been the failure of the nation-state as a viable economic unit. We live in a time which may be described generally as a time of the breaking of nations. But there is a specific sense as well in which this term applies. Even if Hitler can be stopped, the day of the nation-state is over. Hitler has often been compared to Napoleon, and the present period to that of Europe under the French imperium. The analogy is not without force. Nevertheless, though particular nations fell under the hoofs of Napoleon's cavalry, the nation-state as such was not one of the victims. In fact, the Napoleonic period represented one of the high points of national development—the completion of the feudal break-up which opened the path for the fully developed nation-state. Nor do I believe that the historical analogy between the present period and that of the barbarian invasions is from this angle a wholly apt one. The barbarian tribes broke up the top-heavy structure of the Roman Empire but for centuries could not replace it with anything—not until the emergence of the nation-state. For me the most interesting comparison is that between the present period and the fifteenth and sixteenth centuries, which saw the break-up in Europe of the small feudal unit and the rise of the nation-state. The small nations that remain after the present war, whoever wins it, will become economic satellites of large and powerful empires or will have to combine with other small nations, not into a diplomatic bloc, but into a working economic and administrative community. It is significant that even before the start of the Hitler *Blitzkrieg* there was talk of a real Anglo-French Union, and that the proposal was being seriously considered when Reynaud was forced out by the Pétain clique.

And what was true of these two great nations is even truer of the small ones. Our generation and the next will witness the transition from the present nation-state to a new form of economic empire-state. We are entering on an epoch of imperialism in which, even under democratic auspices, the surviving economies are likely to be not national but continental or even hemispheric economies. The European continent may constitute one such economy, the British Commonwealth another, the Soviet Union still another, Japan may be the center of a Far Eastern economic constellation, and the Americas may, if they have the luck and courage, constitute a Western one. That at any rate is the possible picture unless Hitler is able to push on and absorb Russia, sweep the Japanese Empire within the Nazi orbit, and drive a wedge between the United States and Latin America, thus smashing the Monroe Doctrine. In such an event we should have something much closer to a single Hitler world economy. But what I have sought to indicate is that even if Hitler is unsuccessful in plunging the sword of his hopes up to its hilt into the world, the sovereign nation-state is a dying form.

What has brought about this lack of endurance in the nation-state? The economists say it is the rise of economic nationalism, and there can be no doubt that there is an element of truth as well as of irony in the fact that the extension of nationalism from the political and cultural into the economic realm has meant the death-knell of nations. Yet it is truer to say that it is not the reaching for national economic self-sufficiency but the failure to achieve it which has resulted in international chaos. It has become impossible in the world today to cling to an anarchic and unplanned economy and still survive.

And this leads me to the third revolutionary element—the thrust within each national economic unit toward centralized economic power, state intervention in all the major decisions of the industrial structure, in short, toward planning as an economic imperative. Germany's war preparation began crucially with Hitler's first steps in reorganizing the German economy on a basis of planning. The really dangerous German propaganda is Hitler's propaganda by deed, his demonstration that planning can raise the national income and maximize economic effectiveness, even though by inhuman methods and for inhuman ends. And not the least potent factor in the German military campaign has been such a co-ordination of German war units as could be achieved only by a planned military machine that was part of a planned economy, and only by the discipline of a group habituated to the technique of planning. The English under Baldwin and Chamberlain were under the illusion that they could win the war and carry on "business as usual" under the anarchic conditions of an unplanned capitalism. They are now hastening to correct their error; yet it must be remembered that planning is a matter not only of intention but of practice and habituation as well. Unless the English war machine can work smoothly as part of an English economy brought to its maximum productive capacity through planning, aided by American economic reserves, there is no hope for England.

The fourth revolutionary force is the great development in war technology and war administration. Both Germans and Russians have had the daring to liberate themselves from the conception of war as combat, and have adopted the logical implications of war as a machine process. What delight Veblen would have taken in pointing out the way in which the machine process has now rounded out its dominance over modern life! But there are other revolutionary elements in warfare which the machine has made possible: the old technique of surprise given a new meaning—*Blitzkrieg;* the old technique of complete concentration of fighting power given a meaning that extends it to all the national resources—total war; and the old technique of propaganda given a new insidiousness in the form of the fifth column. I have pointed out above the extent to which it would be dangerous to separate war techniques from the economic planning of which they are an organic part. It is notable that in both realms Germany and Russia have been explorers, but that in both also Hitler has carried further what Russia began. And it is also worth noting that the revolution in warfare applies not only to the conquest of power but to its consolidation as well. The whole problem of keeping conquered peoples in subjection is changed when rebel forces find that they must confront the airplane and tank concentration that was hurled at Belgium and France.

Fifth and finally, there has been a psychic revolution in the outlook of men and women throughout the world. This has proceeded from two sources: the failure of unplanned capitalism to make use of productive capacity or to distribute its proceeds so as to provide employment and decent living standards; and the bearing of our new insight into the irrational in people upon the problem of democratic effectiveness. To the unemployed, to WPA workers, to those living on or just below the margin of elementary decency, political democracy and civil liberties may well be made to seem empty forms. And those who understand the irrational depths in men will recognize that the tensions and dissatisfactions produced by collapsing economies may well be exploited for the benefit of political adventurers and the creation of new empires.

II. THE ATTITUDE OF THE INTELLECTUALS

Almost twenty-five years ago Randolph Bourne wrote an essay on "The War and the Intellectuals" which in the bareness of its logic and the cold passion of its language stands out from the mediocrity of the war writings. It was published in a little magazine called the *Seven Arts* and summed up what was in Bourne's generation the best and most generous effort of the left. The intellectuals, Bourne said, were plumping for the war; they had been betrayed by the philosophy of pragmatism. But the true intellectuals could have no traffic with the war; the real choice was between the war and American promise. Bourne was ignored when he was not vilified. He died at the age of thirty-two before he could see the harvest of the dragon-teeth that the intellectuals, in their acceptance of the war and all its implications, had sown.

The role of Bourne and those whom he attacked in the last war is worth our study.[2] Many have argued from it that since Bourne was proved right by what happened after 1933 his position must be the right one for 1940. Every generation of thinkers tends to act negatively in terms of its experience in some analogous situation within its memory. It carries over from its previous experience a sense of the mistakes it once made and wants to rectify them. What

---

2 See "Randolph Bourne and Two Generations," below, p. 116.

we forget now is that the intellectuals of the first World War were the Wilsonian generation of liberals who felt that they had finally come into power after the long, lean post-Civil War years. We think now of that Wilsonian generation as composed of idealists. Actually its thought was saturated in pragmatism. As Bourne pointed out, John Dewey and Herbert Croly and Charles Beard and Walter Lippmann were followers of the Wilsonian war policies because they felt that it was better to swim with the current and thus retain some influence than to remain frustrate outside the current. They sought—to shift the figure—to manipulate the great forces of history, to ride the whirlwind and command the storm. The whirlwind and storm were too much for Wilson and his brain trust. The Allies were unable to organize the peace, and America found itself implicated in their failure. The Wilson group had talked to the people in idealistic terms but acted pragmatically. The result was a deflation of the pumped-up idealism which left the post-war generation with a sense only of how stale, flat, and unprofitable were all wars and all attempts to organize a peace.

What attitudes have the survivors of that generation taken toward the present war? Lippmann writes for the New York *Herald Tribune* with something like his old mixture of pragmatism and idealism; Dewey is scarcely heard from; Beard is isolationist; the *New Republic,* most savagely attacked by Bourne, has sought for years to find atonement for its sins in the first World War by isolationism in the present one, and has been jolted out of its position only recently by the *Blitzkrieg;* Dos Passos has clung to his ironic sense of withdrawal; [3] Hemingway fought fascism in Spain and is now reported to be finishing a novel in Cuba; [4] Lewis Mumford and Waldo Frank, who stood with Bourne during the first war, have swung into the vanguard of interventionism today; MacLeish, who once admired Hemingway and Dos Passos, has swung with them. Yet it is not these movers and shakers, going off in divergent directions, who will count decisively in the American future. Many of them are still smarting under the intolerable humiliation of having once been taken in, and the attitude of our isolationists today is not so much a reasoned view as it is a licking of wounds.

[3] This is apparent, in the form of isolationist overtones, even in *The Ground We Stand On,* published in 1941.

[4] This later appeared as *For Whom the Bell Tolls* (1940). After its publication Hemingway went to China as war correspondent.

What will count is the generation now coming to maturity. Everything they have learned from the "lost generation," from the war novels and the historical post-mortems and the Nye committee reports, leads them to suspect the stakes, the purposes, the costs, and the consequences of intervention in another war.

I do not blame them. I cannot join in the present cry of my own generation against the cynicism of the college-age generation, both within and outside the colleges. I think that in a national crisis a disbelief in the basic premises of their culture on the part of young people is dangerous, but I can understand its sources. How can we expect them to be anything but cynical considering the mess we have made of the world we are handing on to them; considering that we have never given content, in terms of their lives, to the concepts of democracy, liberty, the career open to talent? Just as in the last war the carry-over of attitudes led the young generation to one form of mistake, the overcalculation of what they could do to control world forces, so the carry-over of attitudes in our own time has led to the opposite mistake—a disbelief in all international action by America so deep as to add up to a suicidal inaction, a skepticism of values so intense as to add up to a form of nihilism.

I have spoken thus far as if there were a single strain among our intellectuals and that younger group which generally follows them. That is of course not true. There has probably never been a period in our history when a deeper cleavage existed between, let us say, college faculties and college students on a major issue of social policy.[5] And this reflects a split among intellectuals in general which is especially serious on the left. In one camp are the "deadly-parallel" anti-interventionists, both of the middle and the younger generation. Without any particular party affiliation, they cling to a common desire not to be fooled again. With them are the Communists, who, until August 1939, acted as if a European war would find them cheering American entrance, but who now bask in the good fortune of having been swung by the course of events back to a line where they can once more quote John Reed's "This is not our war." [6] With them stand, ironically, the Communist-baiting

---

[5] This is less true now (1941) than it was a year ago, when this essay was first published.

[6] Since this was written the Communists have again, with the Nazi invasion of Russia, swung over to the interventionist cause.

Trotskyists and Socialists, at least the majority groups among them.
Since I am speaking only of intellectuals I omit the Coughlinite and
Nazi elements in the anti-interventionist camp.

In the other camp, favoring intervention through war or measures short of war, are most of the non-Communist groups that were
formerly for collective security, the left-wing New Dealers, including many who spoke with scorn of collective international action
a few years ago, the intellectuals of every political persuasion who
plead for intervention in moral terms because this is to them a war
between two diametrically opposed conceptions of human destiny,
and those independents on the left who believe that their only
chance of continuing to work in the direction of a collectivist democracy lies in preventing a Hitlerized world. Again, since I am
speaking only of the intellectuals, I omit the pro-British industrial
and financial groups and the hysterical patrioteers.

The Hitler revolution has found American intellectuals, as it
found intellectuals elsewhere, unprepared to understand, to resist, or to transform it. In Germany and in every country which the
Nazis have annexed, the republic of scholarship and letters was
the first victim, and in every instance it became the satrapy of the
conquerors. I am not prepared, however, to conclude that the ineffectiveness of intellectuals and the division among them betray
a deep core of decadence in our culture. Our thinkers still exhibit,
even in their disunity, a fierceness of belief which is the best mark
of a continuing vitality. The fact is that almost the only resistance
that Nazism has thus far encountered has come from the intellectuals and the workers. In Germany, in Austria and Czechoslovakia,
in Spain and Norway and France, this resistance was undermined
by capitalist sabotage, treason in high places, middle-class passivity
and bewilderment. But the intellectuals themselves, who formed
the heart of their country's culture, showed no decadence—only a
heroism which may still be an earnest of vital cultures yet to come.
The Spenglerian gloom with which so many of our thinkers have
spoken of our decadence is something the enemy delights in. If
we really believed it, there would be nothing, either for the intellectual or for the common man, left to fight for.

But the intellectuals cannot help to control the present or shape
the future by clinging to the past. It is not their function today to
exemplify those who cling to outworn economic, political, or ad-

ministrative forms, even though they use such terms as "Western
culture" or "the great tradition." Only to affirmations will our
young people respond, and only if we seek to organize the future
can we achieve or deserve their allegiance. Nor can the intellectuals
be effective unless they move beyond the materialism which has up
to now kept both the capitalists and the left arid, unless they recognize in men a desire for the heroic that cannot be summed up as a
response to self-interest or even class interest, a desire to link themselves with the fate of something larger than the individual atom
in a society.

Whatever the intellectuals may accomplish for our culture in
the future, they cannot accomplish it by themselves. The "illusion
of centrality" informs many of the recent calls to arms sounded by
intellectuals. There is an underlying assumption that if our thinkers determine their share of the guilt in the victorious march of
fascism they can then proceed to convert themselves and remedy
everything. This assumption underlies the recent writings of
Frank,[7] Mumford, and MacLeish. But intellectuals cannot by themselves shape history. When they have become effective in the past, it
has been because they have linked themselves with the rising energies of new classes and new elites. For while intellectuals must not
follow the mass, they dare not alienate themselves from the mass.
They must discover the healthy lines of direction in their culture
and work with the people along those lines. Their objectives today
must be socialism in economics, democracy in politics, planning in
administration, humanism in culture. But to achieve these they
must become again, as they were in Milton's day and Voltaire's and
Jefferson's, organic parts of the life, the thinking, the striving of
common people. If they fail here, they are lost. They are lost in the
sense that they are reduced to an elite of the spirit competing for
mastery with other elites which do not have their purposes or their
scruples but which know how to make themselves a part of the life
of the people.

There can be no doubt of the strength of the German elite or of
the effectiveness of the administrative revolution it has accomplished. Our own elite has shown that it need not be deficient in

---

[7] For a discussion of Frank's position, see "The Daedalian Vision of Waldo Frank,"
below, p. 161.

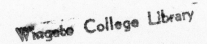
Wingate College Library

this respect. "Brain trust" furnished a term of contempt which measured the fear that the business men felt about their effectiveness. Our intellectuals have already shown that they can move into the realm of government, master the techniques of law and engineering and production and administration, and compete even in these areas with the men of action. The French and British experience has now shown conclusively that the business elite as such is through, that it cannot be trusted to run a government for democratic purposes with any measure of success. In Britain it was the Baldwins and Chamberlains—the business men in government—who messed things up, and today England has turned to an aristocrat like Churchill and to labor intellectuals like Morrison, Bevin, Attlee, Laski, Cripps. It may be too late for Britain. But America has more time, and it need not be too late for us. The British did not discover until their backs were to the wall that there was a revolution going on in the world, that only a revolutionary reorganization of democracy could cope with it, and that the intellectuals on the left, with the labor forces, would have to be the vanguard of this reorganization. How long shall we wait before we make the same discovery?

The intellectuals cannot afford to wait until the discovery is made by others. They must understand that in a world in which things are moving very fast in some direction survival is for those who push things in a direction of their choosing. That means that they must rid themselves of the last residues of ivory-towerism. That is the real meaning and validity of Archibald MacLeish's recent (June 1, 1940) *Nation* piece on "The Irresponsibles," although Mac-Leish might have added that the intellectuals have been forced into an ivory-tower irresponsibility by every pressure within their social structure.[8] We have moved far from the time when Julien Benda

---

8 This has since been reprinted in book form. The best criticism of MacLeish from the interventionist left is Harold Laski's "Letter to MacLeish," published in the *New Republic* for September 2, 1940. Along somewhat similar lines is the following statement which I wrote at the time in answer to an invitation from the *Nation* editors:

"My comment on Archibald MacLeish's deeply felt and eloquent article must take the form of what the lawyers call a plea in confession and avoidance. Most of the scholars and writers of America richly deserve the drubbing they get from Mr. Mac-Leish. But if they have been irresponsible, the responsibility for that is not wholly, in fact not principally, theirs. And why? Is it not because the defense of our inherited culture has up to now been carried on as part of the defense of our inherited eco-

could get a wide response for his book *La Trahison des Clercs* (in English *The Treason of the Intellectuals*). What Benda called treason was the abandonment by some intellectuals of the detachment of the medieval clerks or clergy and their mingling in the battles of the day. What we call treason now is not the political activity of intellectuals but their withdrawal from politics and the fact that they were not realistic enough fighters.

---

nomic and social system? The scholars have been encouraged and in many instances even coerced to choose pure science as their model because otherwise their scholarship, if it were really put into a form which would reach the people, would be dangerous. And the writers have been encouraged and even coerced to take pure art as their model because otherwise their writing, if it really took sides and manned the intellectual barricades, would be dangerous. Dangerous, I say in both cases, to the established order of corporate capitalism. Mr. MacLeish might easily have broadened his indictment. In all fields we have sent experts out into the world without a knowledge of values, and we have sent philosophers without a grounding in social fact. This cleavage is not merely the result, as Mr. MacLeish surmised, of the natural process of specialization. It is, as Thorstein Veblen long ago pointed out in his book on *The Higher Learning in America,* a consequence of the tenacious defense of corporate capitalism by the men who have controlled our universities, our press, our research foundations. I want to make it clear that I regard the present tendency, represented not only by Mr. MacLeish but also by Lewis Mumford and Waldo Frank and others, to put the primary blame and responsibility for our present chaos upon the intellectuals, as not wholly without merit. It is true that our intellectuals have failed. Nevertheless, I do not consider that this analysis reaches to the core of the problem of world chaos today. Mr. MacLeish speaks of Hitlerism as a 'revolution against.' He is in the main right, although I believe that he, as well as Rauschning and others who speak of the revolution of nihilism, does not make enough allowance for the fact that to many millions of people it is poverty and insecurity that represent the real nihilisms. For them even Hitlerism has an affirmative psychological appeal. Even a 'revolution against,' if it is to succeed, must have deep roots in a preceding social chaos. And Hitler's revolution has these roots. Hitler's revolution is only the outward expression of more basic revolutionary forces at work in the world today. . . . Above all, these revolutionary forces proceed from the failure of the democracies to refashion their economic and social institutions so as to bring them into line with the democratic creed and with the basic drives in men.

"In short, if the intellectuals failed, their failure happened long before the rise of Hitlerism as a world movement, and long before their failure to recognize the threat that Nazism carries for all cultures. It was the basic failure to see that the incapacity of the democracies to change our social system by democratic and humane methods would necessarily leave the field open to the brutal changes of totalitarianism. And the blame for this earlier failure, if we are at this late date to play the game of apportioning blame, must lie not only with the writers and scholars but with those other men who have held positions of power in our economic and political world. No matter how greatly we exhort them, writers and scholars cannot by themselves defend or change social institutions. Mr. MacLeish mentions Thomas Mann, yet the possession of a Thomas Mann by Germany did not change the course of events there. Mr. MacLeish talks of our having split in two the earlier man of letters; yet the one country where the man of letters has continued into the modern time—France—has also not been exempted from the common doom. Mr. MacLeish mentions Milton and Voltaire. Yet both of them were effective because their courage and their vision as men of letters were linked with the rising energies of new classes

It is upon the intellectuals and the common men that the real burden of the democratic struggle against minority power and social incompetence has in the past fallen. In this struggle they have together evolved an outlook on life which has been dangerous to the holders of economic power, but which has been the only continuing guarantee of democratic survival. The partnership has been on the whole an uneasy one. The intellectuals have had a sort of Olympian attitude toward the people, and the people have responded by an anti-intellectualism which has made them the prey of the demagogues of the right. But even this uneasy alliance has been given a rude jolt in the past quarter-century. The intellectual has gone on believing that he can enlist the support of the common man for their mutual interests on the plane of logic and reason. He has gone on believing that all he has to do is to map out in his mind the outlines of the good society, and that the common man will then proceed through free thought and free suffrage to enact that society into reality. He has finally found, of course, that in thinking thus he has all along been living in a dream world. The common man discovered that he was not getting his *quid pro quo,* that the principles of civil liberty and intellectual freedom which meant so much in the realm of absolute values were in his world only so much rhetoric. His claims and expectations had been aroused by the promises implicit in the universals of liberal democracy, and now these claims were less and less being fulfilled. The gap between rhetoric and actuality was too monstrous to be tolerated. The sheath of rationality, thin enough at best in any group and at any time, was now worn completely through; and the way was opened for the irrationals which are always latent in political life.

---

to a common fight against old classes and dying cultures. The writer's power to defend and change cultures is never great unless it is similarly linked with expansive and not merely with defensive forces in a culture. What this means is that if we are to meet the 'revolution against' represented by Hitlerism we must do so militantly and aggressively, with a revolutionary democratic force that challenges Hitler's revolutionary totalitarianism, with a revolutionary affirmative force that challenges Hitler's revolutionary nihilism. We cannot do this merely by defending our culture and our intellectual freedom. If we restrict ourselves to defense, we have three-quarters lost the battle already. Scholars, writers, and men of letters alike must today not only defend our system; they must also help transform it. In transforming it, the writer can have an important role. But let us not overestimate that role, and let us not ignore the fact that it will be frustrate unless it is linked with revolutionary social energies in labor, in the professions, in responsible business groups, in science, in politics."

No historian will ever write adequately of our epoch unless he sees clearly the dual chords of the irrational upon which the political adventurers of that epoch were able to play. A revolutionary situation brings to the fore first of all the active irrationalism of change and dislocation, of the drive to power, the release of resentments, the wreaking of vengeance. But once the new power structure has been created, a second and more passive set of irrationalisms comes to the fore—a desire to be ruled, to submit, to have done with the intolerable uncertainty of change, to yield, to adjust oneself to the inevitable. Much has been said of the capacity of Hitler and Goebbels to imbue the German people with their own fanaticism. Undoubtedly there has always been a group, whether storm troopers or parachutists, which has followed the Führer like a band of drugged assassins. But the more important hold that Hitler now has over the Germans and may still acquire over other peoples is his capacity to evoke their desire for submission and their weariness of struggle.

If the intellectuals of our time recognize what has happened in this psychic revolution, they will rid themselves of the myth of the reasoning man. They will understand that since ideas are weapons in social struggles, their own ideas cannot be merely chaste logical constructions but must be part of the deep emotional currents of their time. They must discard the fear they have thus far felt for the mass mind. They must understand that the kind of society they want will not be achieved unless, in company with the mass of ordinary people, they are willing to enter the struggle for state power.

"War," wrote Bourne, "is the health of the state." It is perfectly true, of course, that in wartime state powers are maximized, national cohesiveness is more easily achieved, and dissident opinion is stamped out. Yet for the intellectuals to argue from this that they can never have any traffic with war or with a state in wartime is for them to abdicate effective leadership at the very crisis period when leadership is most needed. Whatever may have been true in the past, it is true today that state power can build, crush, and rebuild the elements of the world. We must face the implication of this for intellectuals, whether we have war or whether we have peace.

We need not justify war or celebrate it in order to recognize the function it has played in history. War has always been a part of the revolutionary process, has always been a phase of rapid social change. War never solves any problems, but war often removes the obstacles which stand in the path of their solution. War can overcome the crystallized inertia of the past, as it has done in England, where the sort of social revolution that has now taken place would have been impossible except for England's peril. Social catastrophe of any sort may have a cleansing and unifying effect, and for intellectuals to shut their eyes to these facts is for them to shut their eyes to history and politics. We can no longer go on believing in the liberal notion of the unaided final triumph of the idea. Nor can we sit back passively and bask in the long historical perspective. In describing this war we cannot continue to use phrases like "a war between two imperialisms," which have lost every bit of real meaning they once had and whose effect is to pave the way for the only imperialism in the world that offers any great danger today—that of the Nazis. Nor can we indulge in the wishful fiction that if we let this war run its course and meanwhile preserve our chaste intellectuality, it will be followed by a real class war in which we can finally participate and which will lead to socialism. All the conditions out of which democratic socialism may yet emerge are in the world today. But if we are to bring it forth we must vie with Hitlerism in organizing the revolutionary forces of the world. Ultimately America will have to play its role in organizing the world of the future, and there is no nobler effort on which American intellectuals can choose to spend themselves.

We had better understand that there is a triple war going on in the world today; first, the military war, which can be seen; second, a civil war in every country, much of which is unseen because much of it consists of secret efforts by the enemy to win over powerful groups in our culture and gain the victory without fighting for it; and, finally, the war within each person. This last is the most important war that is going on today—the war between the fascist and the democrat in every one of us. It is in this war that our intellectuals have a special task of leadership. But they cannot fulfill it unless they confront the realities of all three wars.

III. AMERICA AND THE NEW WORLD

Once America was the New World. And other peoples had to adjust themselves to the new conditions we had created. But a still newer world has been in the making ever since 1917. In it the initiative was first taken by the proletarian forces of the Russian Revolution, which managed to do the right economic things for the right ends through the wrong political means. Later the initiative was taken from them by the German National Socialist revolution, which managed to do at least the partly right administrative things through the wrong political means and for the catastrophically wrong ends. Meanwhile the rest of Europe and America, instead of moving on to a democratic socialism which would do the right things in the right way for the right ends, trembled and marked time. And because of what the others have done and we have failed to do, there is now a new world. America must either take the lead in organizing and transforming that new world or adjust itself to it by some process of appeasement and imitation.

Are we, therefore, part of the Old World? We need not be, fatally. Human history is a curious affair, with no straight-line advance in it and few finalities. It looked, after 1917, as if the field were clear for a revolution of the left, the world over. But a small group on the right in Europe sized up correctly how fluid the situation still was, estimated the resources of strength it could draw upon in terms both of money from above and of hatred and despair from below, gauged with an uncanny exactness the slumberous smugness of the established order and the fatal splits on the left, and then struck with sharp successive blows at the citadels of power. It replaced a red socialism as the dynamic force in history by a black pseudo-socialism.

The energies by which history moves from one epoch to another have puzzled our thinkers and eluded the grasp of minds like Machiavelli's, Marx's, Lenin's, Spengler's, Veblen's. There are, however, certain things we know. That men can on the whole move forward we know, even if we reject the easy Victorian optimism about progress. That they can slip back we also know—slip back into barbarism for long stretches of time. We know that at different times in history the dynamic role has shifted from one geographic area to another, from one racial stock to another, from one class to another, from one nation to another. My premise is—and I think it can scarcely be denied—that the world revolutionary situation is still as fluid now as it was in 1917 or in 1933, perhaps even more so. And my plea is that America must above all avoid sinking back into the passivity of the Old World, must once more play its part in shaping a new world.

Whether we shall ever have a chance to play that part depends to some extent upon the capacity of Hitler's empire for consolidation and advance. Western thought, in blinders, has all too long assessed Nazi strength as it once sought to assess Soviet strength—by the norms of a capitalist market economy and of a liberal-rationalist intellectual outlook. It must now shift to the cold judgment of survival capacity through a controlled economy, a confident elite, and ruthless organizing genius.

In the short view the picture is, for us, a dark one. The possession of the Low Countries and France and the recent settlement in the Balkans have placed in Hitler's hands vast economic resources that will give him for some time to come the edge in what is, in essence, a war of factories. His difficulty is that it takes time to reorganize the conquered peoples and restore their economic capacity—more time even than it took to conquer them; and time is the one thing he cannot afford to let Britain have. I do not say that there is any immediate chance of Hitler's defeat. Only a British-Soviet-American alliance could compass that, and such an alliance would be politically feasible only after it had become too late from a military viewpoint.[9] I do say that Hitler must for several years to come face economic chaos and potential famine in the territory he has occupied but been unable to organize. And he must face this in particularly acute form so long as the British keep proving that their island fortress is from a military viewpoint tenable, and so long as the British navy maintains from that island fortress its blockade against continental Europe.

That is the basic reason why Hitler must, through war or peace, break British resistance. Those who argue, as Lindbergh does, that America can offer honorable peace terms in Europe do not reckon with this fact. Nor do they reckon with other facts. The Nazi economy is unstable as a capitalist economy unless the surplus profits continue to be absorbed in armament production. And even if this were not so, Hitler's Napoleonic dream would keep him moving

---

[9] Since this essay was first published, the Nazi invasion of Russia has brought us closer to such an alliance. It is possible that the above statement was too pessimistic. But until America enters the war, the alliance is only potential; and our failure to enter thus far must be the warrant for allowing the statement to stand.

on. Unless, then, he can break the British blockade he cannot ward off famine in his territory, reach the Latin American products that his people need or the markets that his capitalists need, or fulfill his own megalomaniac vision.

The capacity of Hitler's empire to survive must therefore be assessed in long-run rather than short-run terms. And in the long perspective the picture looks, for us, not nearly so dark. Hitler has not yet won completely. If Britain, with the increasing aid of American factories, can manage to hold out against him over the span of several years, then Hitler will face problems of increasing tension within his own empire. The economic contradictions the world over which made his rise possible will begin to operate against him. Unless he wishes to face panic conditions among his people he will have to turn a good deal of the productive energy of his economy to food and other necessities instead of to war machines. If, as is likely, he chooses to maintain a decentralized administrative system in which France, Holland, Norway, and the rest remain as economic units rather than to attempt to weld them into a single continental economy, he faces problems of persisting nationalism which may prove fatal to him at his first moment of weakness. But his crucial difficulty is that before long he must come to a reckoning with his capitalists, when they confront the question whether they will continue to allow the state to forge into armaments their mounting accumulation of profits. And then Hitler will have to face the alternative of unused capital surpluses with their attendant unemployment, or an effort at outright socialism with its attendant class struggles.

The best single request that we could address to the fates would be this: that Hitler should have to face, as we have had to face, the internal problems of his own economic and political system; that, once he had reached the limits of appeasement and easy conquest, he should face these problems not only within Greater Germany but within Germany itself, without resounding diplomatic triumphs or continued military victories or easy religious persecutions to divert attention from the real problems.

The aim of American policy should be dual: to join with others, outside the limits of actual warfare if possible, in drawing this iron circle of necessity around Hitler, so that he will face the consequences of the revolution he has started; and meanwhile to take the

lead in organizing the rest of the world on the basis of a real democratic revolution of our own. In the end, even partial success in
the second aim would cut the ground from under Hitler's revolution.

In this effort we must first of all know our potential allies. They
are Britain (but only the new Britain of the Churchill-Labor government), the rest of the British Commonwealth (and what still
untapped resources for democratic expansion are there!), the Soviet
Union, China, Latin America. This offers a daring perspective, but
only daring perspectives are worth anything in this hour of crisis.
It means the attempt to reconcile diverse and even hostile national
traditions and social systems, linked only by common danger and
common opportunity.

Does this present an impossible task? I can only say that if it is
impossible, nothing short of it is possible. The very scope of the
perspective is one of the essential things about it. Nothing will succeed now except what would formerly have been deemed grandiose.
One thing that Hitler will have accomplished is to have forced us
to change the scale of our international thinking and planning. We
must today in America think in terms of India and Australia, of
Russia and China, of Canada and Chile. Realists have laughed at
Clarence Streit's plan because it covered so much ground. They
were wrong. Its fault was that it did not cover enough ground.
It was Europe-centered, and within Europe it was democracy-
centered; and European democracy crumbled under Streit's fingers
even as he wrote. And internally it worked on too formal a level,
mapping legal structures, seeking to preserve the status quo instead
of to transform it.[10]

If we abandon our piddling pragmatisms and our formal world-
democracy patterns we may be able to face the central fact of
America's relation to the new world. The fact is that if we do not
take the lead in organizing the new social order, it will be left for
Hitler to organize. I do not accept the Beard thesis, echoed now by
Lindbergh and whoever is behind him, that every effort on the part
of America to play a world role must be frustrated. Beard, as a historian and a democrat, speaks out of the bitterness of disillusion-

---

[10] For a fuller discussion of Federal Union see "If We Own the Future," below,
p. 58.

ment with his former Wilsonianism; Lindbergh, ignorant of both history and politics, speaks only out of a vague dislike for democracy and an even vaguer pan-Aryanism. I should not juxtapose their names if it were not that the argument against an affirmative American foreign policy comes both from advocates and from enemies of democracy within America.

It is not a valid argument. If it is based on the failure of Wilsonianism in foreign affairs one might reason similarly that because of the failure of Wilson's New Freedom the New Deal, which is to a great extent patterned after it, should also be abandoned. I urge a bold American leadership in world affairs for the same reason that I urge a bold American effort toward a democratic collectivism at home—because laissez faire in both areas has proved catastrophic. But in foreign policy, as in domestic, half-measures are the very devil. It would be better to leave things alone in both than to tinker with both irresolutely. If we are to act at all, we must make it clear that America is very much on the offensive. We must make it clear that we accept, without any illusions as to its difficulties, the necessity for doing what we can to organize the phalanxes of democratic effectiveness and human dignity everywhere. Those phalanxes will not organize themselves. They need the assurance of action along with what is still potentially the strongest economic unit and the freest political unit in the world.

I am not talking now of a world federation or of a military alliance. Those are not the realities today, although they may become so when the world is in either a much better or a much worse state. I am talking of close economic co-operation, of friendlier cultural relations, of a unified morale. Out of these may flow eventually that common foreign policy which alone can "stop" Hitler, in the sense of enclosing him within the necessity of moving from the grandeurs of war to the realities of his own economic and social system. In such a task we shall not be alone. "The peoples of Europe," declared the *New Statesman* in London, "know . . . that the French capitulation has closed an epoch of history and they ask themselves anxiously, 'Is the battle now between Hitler's New European Order and the Old British Empire?' Or is it, as they desire but hardly hope, between the lords of the Third Reich and the protagonists of European revolution? On the answer to that question hangs the issue of the war and the fate of these islands." But beyond the outcome of the war and the fate of Britain, the same question is being asked now, ever more articulately by the peoples of the whole world, about Hitler's New World Order and America as a revolutionary force.

Britain, with its back to the wall, has already carried through a more far-reaching transformation toward a revolutionary democracy than would have been thought possible a year ago. That does not mean the change has gone its full length. Labor is still on the margin of power rather than at its center. Economically the government exercises strategic controls but has not yet learned how to plan. There is still the paradox of more than three-quarters of a million unemployed when every man and woman is needed for the national effort. The forces of appeasement are still in the Cabinet. What England needs is the encouragement of our aid and the challenge of our own democratic forces to go further. The British dominions will follow the lead of Britain and America, and we may for the present be in a better position to co-ordinate their economic efforts and strengthen their morale than even the British. China needs little enough aid to go on with its amazing resistance to Japan, but it needs that little very much.

The central problems are the Soviet Union and Latin America. Toward the latter we have made all manner of obeisances—although not always of the right sort. Toward the former we have preserved a frigid hostility. I do not want to argue at this point the abstract question of whether all the totalitarianisms should be lumped together. In concrete terms every plain American and Englishman and even Mr. Roosevelt and Mr. Churchill know that the enemy of democracy today, the dangerous expansive force in the world, is not the Soviet Union but Nazi Germany. And they should know also that if they succeed in throwing Stalin completely into the arms of Hitler the democratic effort in the rest of the world is either wholly lost or can survive only after generations of protracted war and chaos. If we make our plans without Russia we shall find it in the end against us. If we followed our vision and not our blindness there would be today in Moscow side by side with Stafford Cripps an American envoy who could talk the language the Soviet ruling group would understand, and would lead the way in sinking mutual distrust in the common danger. This is not a counsel of political cynicism. It is a plea for a perspective toward America's position in a hostile world that will recognize that hostilities are relative. The real cynicism is that of the people on the comfortable right who want America to act on a world scale against the combined powers of German and Russian imperialism; or of those on the extreme left who counsel a proletarian class revolution in America that they cannot compass, and failing that would let the workers be destroyed by Hitlerism everywhere; or of those on both left and right who, through their isolationism and desire for appeasement, would surrender America, along with the rest of the world, to the ruthlessness of those who know what they want.[11]

I have said that America must assume a world leadership in economic co-operation, cultural relations, humanist morale, a common anti-Nazi foreign policy. But America is an abstraction. What sort of America? And who in America?

In answer here I can only briefly indicate the steps we must take to give leadership to the world by example. (1) Aid to Britain, to the full extent of our factories and our economic man-power. This aid should be and can be "short of war," and we need not worry about Hitler's interpreting it as an act of war. He could not hate us more than he does already; and whatever we do he will wage against us the fullest war of which he is capable. (2) A vigorous prosecution of the national defense effort, but not under the slogans of business and profits as usual. A defense program can succeed only if it moves in its basic direction toward a socialized economy, and if it provides for the indispensable requisites of a planned military machine which is an organic part of a planned economy. (3) A management of this defense effort which provides for labor's rights by giving labor an important share in the administration, as Britain has done. (4) A realistic attitude toward the question of national unity, civil liberties, and fifth columns. (5) A heroic collective effort to grapple with the problem of unemployment and insecurity through a program of government spending for living standards as well as for armaments, and through new strategic controls of the economic system. (6) Continued progress in the administrative revolution which has already put within our grasp a better apparatus for economic con-

---

[11] Since the Nazi invasion of Russia, American policy toward the Soviet Union has been grudging in its recognition of a common anti-Nazi cause, and eloquent with lack of enthusiasm.

trol and planning than any other democracy has—if we know how to use it. (7) A policy toward Latin America which has some chance of success. Here especially much more analysis is required than space permits. I can only say that the President and the State Department do not yet seem to have recognized that we cannot move toward a hemispheric economy of the Americas unless we strengthen governments, such as those of Mexico, Chile, and Colombia, which are genuinely democratic, and put pressure upon the others to give greater scope to their internal democratic forces. The ruling groups in most Latin American countries lean toward Hitler more than toward us. It is plain people for whom Roosevelt has become a symbol of a fighting democratic world force. (8) A vigorous fight against the groups within America who would appease Hitler, and a recognition that appeasement abroad is closely linked with reaction at home. (9) Pressure on the home front to extend the New Deal effort.

1940

2

Letter on Democracy[1]

D EAR FREDERICK SCHUMAN: When you showed me your exchange of letters with Lawrence Dennis, I felt that the letters raised issues so striking that they ought to be published.
I am adding now a few notes of commentary as one who disagrees
sharply with both of you.

My differences with Dennis are, of course, more profound than
my differences with you. For Dennis's values scarcely differ from
those of fascism. To be sure, he now talks of "socialism" where
earlier he was a good deal franker. I can only explain the change
by the need for protective coloration in an American climate of
opinion still too harsh for fascism. I cannot go along with your bland
view that the differences between the two are "irrelevant." If socialism and fascism are the same, then millions of blasted lives have
had no meaning.

For Dennis to say socialism and fascism are the same is a matter
of strategy (I can well understand why he is "not one to boggle over

---

1 Some words of explanation may make the context of this letter clear. Frederick L.
Schuman wrote to Lawrence Dennis about the latter's book, *The Dynamics of War
and Revolution,* and Dennis wrote a letter in return. When I saw the letters I asked
the writers for permission to write an answer to both, and, with their consent, arranged
for the publication of all three in the *Nation,* where they appeared under the title
"Who Owns the Future?" For the purposes of this book it was impossible to reprint
the other letters, but their tenor and argument are implied in my answer.

Dennis's thesis is that capitalism has lost the dynamic that once gave it strength
and with it the possibility of survival; that the triumph of a socialism organized under
the single-party state is inevitable; and that the current efforts on the part of America
to resist Nazi military expansion are doomed to ultimate failure because a post-war
reaction will bring the (to him not undesirable) triumph of fascist forces in America.

Schuman believes that some form of Caesarism is inevitable and that it may as well
be American as otherwise. He calls for militant American action to fight Nazism and
establish the conditions for an American world imperium, but is skeptical of our
ability to organize resistance effectively because of a paralysis of will which he considers characteristic of Western capitalist democracy in its present phase. For further
comment on a somewhat similar point of view see my criticism of Henry Luce's editorial "The American Century," in the chapter "The People's Century," p. 53.

27

definitions"). For you to say it, however, is sheer confusion and blindness, unpalliated by your allusions to Spengler's Caesarism. The distance between the two is deep and wide and black as the pit. You say all this is "morals" and "ideology," and that they are intangibles that are brushed aside by the imperatives of history. And yet you were one of the first to say that Stalin's invasion of Finland would in the end be disastrous for Russia's cause, even in Machiavellian terms, because it did not reckon with the moral intangibles of policy. And your letter and Dennis's are drenched with emotional and moral terms—"cowardice," "irresponsibility," "decadence." I believe with you in the strategic factors of history. Yet, forgetting the enormous differences between socialism and fascism for the masses everywhere, for their living standards and their freedom—even in terms of strategy your insistence on calling all collectivism "Caesarism" is fatal.

Why so? You know how wholly I agree with you on the need for sending full aid to England, regardless of the risk of war. But I don't see how you expect people to follow you if the moral and ideological aspects of Nazism are unimportant. Men do not willingly die to have a choice between Tweedledum and Tweedledee.

Nor do they willingly die in a hopeless cause. As soon as you admit Dennis's thesis that fascism (your "Caesarism") is inevitable, he has the draw on you, shooting with both barrels. By embracing the "inevitability" of Caesarism, you render hopeless our common cause of aiding England in order to keep Nazism from America, and our common cause also of creating a democratic dynamism which will make America's role at home and in world affairs a great one. Not only will Americans be confused about what they are fighting for, but they will know that, whatever it is, it doesn't stand a chance. That's "wave of the future" talk you are both giving us. And the mere fact that it is couched in the grandiose phrases of Spenglerism rather than in the Smith English of Mrs. Lindbergh doesn't change its effect on the middle-class American mind. For that mind has always been a bandwagon mind. Dennis says the American faith is faith in a perpetual land boom, and that's a good sentence—just close enough to the truth to be brilliant. Relying on a land boom means hoping to get in on the ground floor of a "good thing." And if you tell the American people that the stars in their courses are fighting for fascism, they'll want to be with the stars in their courses.

There is room and to spare within the dynamic of history for the strong democratic state which is *not* Caesarism—which is, in Lincoln's phrase, neither too weak for survival nor too strong for the liberties of its citizens. Neither of you in his letter has made the emergence of this sort of democratic state part of the campaign of history. Yet democracy is the great force in the world today, whether as dream or as reality—greater than capitalism, which was once a force, or liberalism, which has never been a real one, or communism, which has too eagerly thrown its strength away, or fascism, which once it goes down the skids will go fast, or internationalism, which may yet emerge as a great force.

Oh, I know that there has been more drivel talked about democracy than about anything else in our universe. And I know that crimes have been committed in its name. But these are signs of vitality. You don't imitate a shadow, and you don't speak in the name of a nullity. One of our heritages from Marxism is to think of democracy as the shadow of a substance—capitalism—which is disintegrating. But ours will be a ghastly blunder if we do not recognize that democracy is substance as well as dream. It is something to die for, to live by, to give our talent and energy to extending. If that sounds insubstantial for us, it is real enough for the Indian peasant who in his hut in Bolivia or Chile has a yellowed picture of Roosevelt on the wall, for Chinese coolie and intellectual alike, for the British common man and Frenchman and Hollander and Pole and Norwegian who are staking their lives on democracy's being real. Of course, we have the duty of being tough-minded, if we are to survive. But especially if one is tough-minded one will know how to value a dynamic force as powerful as the idea of a society in which men can shape their own destiny, and rise to their full height, and be comrades, and not be pushed about. Let's agree that God is on the side of the big battalions. But those battalions won't be worth a wooden pistol unless they are fighting for an idea that can somehow be made real to them.

What has so far limited us in doing this with democracy? Dennis says "capitalism"; you say "decadence." I agree more with Dennis here, but as usual he has stopped short where I want to go on. It is capitalism thus far uncontrolled by the democratic forces of the people that has betrayed us, nationally and internationally. Dennis is wrong when he calls our whole economy stagnant. By public spending and lending, by the control of saving and investment, by anti-trust action such as is now being used to beat down prices, by trade-union organization, by planning, by a whole array of strategic controls, our economic system can be made to live and work for the mass of people more efficiently than the enslaved economy of the Nazis that Dennis so greatly admires. The "land boom" is already on the way to becoming an organized system of controls. We have plenty of knowledge of what to do with our economic machine. The snags lie not in economics but in politics—in the realm of class resistance and press distortions and in the realm of power.

So when you ask, Why don't Americans have the will to fight the Nazis? I accept neither your answer that it is because they are cowardly and decadent, nor Dennis's that it is because they know there is nothing to fight for. My answer is that democracy in its fullest extension is what there is to fight for. The people are not decadent, nor cowards, nor fools. To be sure, they have been duped and doped by Congress and press. It is taking them long to slough off an isolationism deepened by the experience of the last war, but they are doing it—just as fast as they are being allowed to do it by the barons of opinion and the lords of appeasement and their Congressional isolationist liegemen. For the people cannot convince themselves that democracy is in as much danger from the Nazis as you and I know it is. They are waiting also to see whether Britain means its democracy genuinely, for India and its own workers as well as for the Empire; and they are being confused by the talk of the "inevitability" of a Nazi triumph. They are waiting also to see whether we, in our labor policy and our defense policy, really *mean* democracy at home. Given this set of obstructions, the wonder is that mass opinion is not more confused than it is. Let us not go reading the sickness of Spengler into a culture which, at the end of a decade of depression and world crisis, is stronger than it was at the beginning.

But I agree with you when you say to Dennis that there are imperatives in history working in the direction of some form of internationalism. I believe completely that the chief "revolutionary" aspect of the present period is that it marks the breaking of nations. The small state, politically "sovereign" but economically helpless, will survive only as part of a larger economic unit and only as it surrenders part of its sovereignty to some federal system. The large states will have to do the same if their world is to be kept from chaos. But what kind of federal system? You mention Lenin, Wilson, Hitler, and Clarence Streit all in the same breath. That is why we must talk of more than mere world federation. It must be democratic world federation, just as our internal socialization must be democratic socialization. And the two can be achieved only in connection with each other, as part of a single campaign.

Where shall we get the will to do both? Ultimately I agree with you when you say that the future belongs to those who are willing to do "the job." But what job? I think the job is to use the fullest resources of the machine process on the economic plane, the administrative process on the political, and the élan of the democratic idea on the ideological. And then the job is to smash Nazism, carry through the civil wars against it wherever it has gained power, organize the world on a working economic basis, and carry through a social reconstruction which can keep with the people the essential decisions that affect their lives. That job only a democratic dynamic can accomplish. If the job, however, is only the conquest and retention of power and the maintenance of "order" through coercion, it will be done—at least temporarily—by fascist gangsterism (Caesarism) fighting for naked power and loot and a place in a new social hierarchy. If we choose the first, as you and I do, it is because we know men can be tough-minded yet passionate with belief, because we know that there can be spunk and steel in them as well as fear and indecision. We know that under great leadership they can do the "impossible"—that is, extend the limits of achievement to the utmost by gauging rightly the boundaries of social and historical possibility. If you don't believe that, what's the use of calling on the democracies, as you do, to resist Nazism?

Dennis wants to get the will for his job from an elite. I think I know the assortment of primitivist business men, high-powered advertising-agency executives, adventurist priests, demoniac salesmen, and intellectual muscle men that would comprise that elite, if and when. And because Dennis scorns democracy, he thinks your whole idea of internationalism is a pipe dream. He is for the single-party state. There is where his totalitarianism centers. You let him get away with it, by speaking of the inevitability of "socialism" as "military totalitarianism resting on a dynamic faith." If you are saying what you seem to be saying, Dennis's way seems to me much simpler and more logical. Poor Streit: you put a big burden on him if you think that his plan or any like it is going to hold together a pack of totalitarian wolf-states, each with its own brand of military socialism worked out. Internationalism, in any sense in which you mean it, is possible only where the constituent units, by the inherent nature of their economies, their political systems, their ideologies, do not have the imperative drive for further expansion. If the principle is going to be military totalitarianism at home and economic imperialism abroad, then Dennis's party-state will win out. What you will have will be the "socialist" (Nazi) party organized in every nation and on every continent, using national machinery and traditions where convenient—how ingeniously Dennis and his friends could work out an ideology for an American Nazism—but using the international Nazi party line and the Nazi spirit to cement the various national units.

What a heavenly city that would be! The single-party system, the state monopoly of conscience, the purging of dangerous thoughts, the Aryanization of science, the robotization of the common man, political Alcatrazes dotting both our coastlines, the administrative machinery of the nation one vast FBI. I don't have to draw this picture for you who have for a decade been our most brilliant and persistent exposer of the barbarism as well as the danger of Nazism. I implore you, since our ends and values are so similar, to look to your means. The Dennises are not your comrades, although like you they talk the language of Machiavelli, Marx, and Spengler. They are the polite forerunners of the barbarians whom you so rightly see as undertaking "the job" in our country if we do not. You say you are "bothered" by them not for moral reasons but because they won't be able to finish the job. I confess I am much more "bothered" by what they'll do, whether they botch the job or finish it: what they'll do with this America of ours, which is not merely landscape and fields of corn and skyscrapers and mines, but a living culture that we call democratic and humanist.

Dennis seems much less bothered by the barbarians. He thinks that "men of brains and good impulses" will share power with the Himmlers and Streichers and Coughlins and McWilliamses. Perhaps, with each of us, our dream of a "new order" is, after all, only a projection of the picture we have of ourselves in it. Let us leave him with his dream, sitting for the moment in his "ivory tower," writing for his "limited public," until the barbarians do with him what in Europe they have done with the Strassers and Rauschnings and other "men of brains and good impulses" who have cleared the way for them.

But you don't belong in an ivory tower. Most thinkers have some pet frustration, some feeling of having been an unheeded Cassandra. Nevertheless, our job is to fight—in marketplace and statehouse, in schoolhouse and factory—for the world we wish to help fashion. And in that fight we are, as thinkers, not alone. We have the people as allies. In Spain, in Czechoslovakia, in Poland, in Norway, in Holland, in England, they have shown a knowledge of the meaning of the struggle and a desperate heroism in waging it. They have been betrayed by the capitalists, the politicians, the generals, the diplomats. But in the face of all that they have not let us down.

1941

Democratic Ends and
"Totalitarian" Means

1

O NE may say about the history of political ethics what Matthew Arnold said about the history of literature: that it contains alternate periods of creation and concentration. A creative period may be described as a period of flux in standards, of the dissolution of the old and its replacement by the new under the impact of history. It does not necessarily follow, however, that, in a period of concentration, change and the creative energies are absent; they are present, but are directed toward the elaboration of standards already sketched out in a more or less shadowy manner. Our present age is in this sense a creative one. To be sure, as in all periods of rapid and drastic change, the creative work is carried on at the edge of the abyss, with the ever-present danger that man and what he is fashioning will be hurled down the precipice toward the primitive and even the bestial. But that is a risk from which men have never been wholly immune.

What remains is of enormous importance: that a period of this sort does give those of us who believe in a democratic dynamism the chance to rethink the implications and reshape the outlines of our democratic values under the conditions of today. It also puts us under the necessity of modernizing our armory of means in order to enable those end-values to survive and to become more effective.

Ends and means in politics are not constants that have had some mysterious traffic with the eternal and come away with their mortality rubbed off. No age has a pipeline to the infinite. After many a summer dies not only the swan but also much of the equipment both of ends and of means with which any culture must fit itself out in dealing with the physical and the social world. This is not out-

right relativism in ethics. Despite what we have learned from anthropology and history (perhaps because of what we have learned)
we can see that there is a framework of outer limits for systems
of ethics—limits imposed by man's nature and the nature of society. But within this frame the world of politics and ethics is a
dynamic world, ever in the pangs of change, ever showing new faces
to the man of thought and to the man of action alike.

It is, on the whole, healthful for us—even in times of crisis like
the present—to keep our sense of the relative and the tentative in
this area as in others. Ends are, in reality, never such in any literal
sense: never the end. They are, in Tennyson's image,

> that untravelled world whose margin fades
> For ever and for ever when I move.

But that does not make them any the less worth pursuing, although
we should never delude ourselves about their complete definiteness. Few Americans have paralleled Justice Holmes in his wisdom: he once wrote that his last words, when he should die, would
be, "Have faith, and pursue the unknown end." If ends are rarely
sacred and never precise, it is even truer that means must be kept
from becoming ends in themselves and tyrannizing over our lives.

Here, as elsewhere, our task is neither to submit blindly to archaic
categories that we call ends nor to make fetishes of encrusted habits
that we call means. Our task is rather to face the campaign of history with high purpose and soldierly courage, and also with tough-
mindedness and flexible resource, and wrest what victories we can
for the sort of world we wish to fashion, knowing all along that the
victories will be neither complete nor final, and that the world
we desire with such desperate assurance will some day seem faintly
musty and a fit study only for the scholars. To survive, men in societies must always believe with a fierce tenacity. But to keep their
human sanity in the midst of survival, they must submit their fighting faiths to the scrutiny of history and science.

But to go on with ends and means: we venture here into a difficult terrain, yet the venture is worth undertaking if for no other
reason than that the destinies of our culture may depend on our
undertaking it, individually and together. Moreover, we have recently had a fund of incomparably rich experience in the pageant
of the rise and fall of nations, and perhaps there has been enough

movement and stir in recent social thought to give meaning to that experience.

One difficulty with what our culture has done about this in the past is that it has carried on its thought and action in different compartments. Thurman Arnold was not far wrong when he drew the basic distinction in our time between the "right-thinking man" and the "organizing man"—the first patterned by the folklore of our culture, the second by ingenuity of action in his march to his goals. Each has gone on his appointed way in bland disregard, if not in open contempt, for the other. That is probably one of the evidences of that dislocation of ethics from reality which indicate the need for ethical change in an age of great change. Yet it may also point to one of the roots of the prevalent disbelief which is the cause of so many modern laments on the part of the believers.

A striking example of this dislocation may be found in the history of Machiavellism. Despite the persistent eyebrow-raising and finger-pointing that every century has directed at Machiavelli since the Church first placed its ban on his writings, the men of action in both church and state have followed his precepts, and a remarkable list of discerning commentators have in their grudging way admitted his insights into the springs of human action and the shaping forces of history. One is at a loss to account for the paradox, unless one were to say that there is something of Machiavelli in each of us, and that we know it deeply, although we cannot square it with our received values. Hence the attraction and repulsion he exerts. By hating him openly we absolve ourselves for acting in the pattern that he laid out.

But the most destructive element in our heritage from the Machiavelli controversy has been the artificial differentiation we make between ends and means. There are supposed to be two points of view—one, that the ends justify the means; the other, that to use the wrong means corrupts and defeats the ends. Such ideas seem to me puzzling and baffling, as do, for example, the apologies of the *New Masses* and the *Daily Worker* for the departures from traditional Marxian political ethic that the Stalinist realism has demanded. I have also sought, although without much resulting nourishment, to graze in the serene pastures of Aldous Huxley and Gerald Heard and those others who think in the categories of the timeless, and who say that to resist force with force is to start by becoming the captive of what you are opposing. But, I still ask, if the end does not justify the means, then what does? To hold that the means is self-justified, or that there is some autonomous moral force in it, would be to fall prey to the most mechanistic of philosophies. Means are always justified—if they are justified at all—by their ends, as these ends are acquired from their cultures, rationalized by their metaphysics, explained by their motivation; and ends are always fulfilled by their means. In a real world, such as ours, means are always a bit grimy and sweat-streaked, like the present war or the Presidential campaign of 1940. If, to use a phrase that may be Mr. Winston Churchill's greatest contribution to political literature, the "blood, toil, tears, and sweat" that they carry along with them are to be justified at all, only their purposes can justify them.

It is, of course, crucial to acknowledge that ends do not justify any and all means; or, to state it more precisely, that given ends do not provide a clear and unlimited field for means. Nor for that matter can any given means effectively serve all ends. Means and ends are thus integral to each other—but only to a limited extent, since they are not integral in any one-to-one relation. There is no one path for democratic survival, any more than there is one path for achieving socialist values. Ends and means are integral in the sense that, given certain ends, certain means are excluded, although the area that is left is broad enough for the heart's content, broad enough for flexibility, realism, effectiveness. They are integral also, and this is even more important, in the sense that, given democratic ends, a certain quality and temper are necessarily implied in whatever means are used. Thus, ends are dependent on means for fulfillment, means are dependent on ends for implication. While neither gives a wholly clear field to the other, there is room in each to build significant structures of values and to develop rich resources of method.

2

But, you say, while this may be a deceptively simple way of reaching, in the ivory tower, solutions which prove dust in our mouths in the marketplace and statehouse, how about the irreconcilable conflict between democracy and dictatorship? In what way can your analysis be of the least help in telling us the extent to which we

can use totalitarian means for democratic ends? Do not democratic
ends, whatever they may be and whatever the differences we have
about them, exclude immediately the whole range of totalitarian
means?

Let me say first that this question which is uppermost in the
minds of all of us today is undoubtedly the prime question of political ethics in our age. I call it the prime question because so many
of us have been disillusioned in that liberalism which believed in
the final triumph of the idea, unaided by force and organization.
One of the roots of hopelessness today, more important even than
our experience with the ruthlessness of power-drunk men who knew
what they wanted, is our experience with the men of good will who
willed the ends of democratic survival but did not will the means.
And that is why it has been good to hear the voices of some of our
spokesmen recently assert that democracy is worth dying for.

But in the very heat of our protest against the irresponsibles
and the ineffectuals, there is a still, small voice within us whispering all sorts of disquieting questions. After all, it says, this is not a
matter of stoicism, of the noble Roman who would rather die than
have the dignity of his soul debased. After all, every culture in
the act of disintegration has—as Spengler points out gallingly—
given birth not only to the ineffectuality of cowardice and flight
but also to the ineffectuality of stoicism. It is good to have men
ready to die, at need, for their country and its values. It is even
better to provide them with the means whereby they will be able
to live for their country and extend its values. And does not this,
the still, small voice asks, does not this involve the use of totalitarian
means in a world like ours, which is already half captured by the
totalitarians?

And would that not defeat your democratic ends from the very
start? To fight fascism you must wage total war, and is not total
war itself fascist? To build a defense for democracy you must somehow eliminate the fifth columns, but does not this mean suppression, and does not suppression mean the scrapping of civil liberties? To keep capitalism from falling apart you must enclose it in a
steel web of governmental control, and set its mechanisms to work
according to the blueprints of some economic plan; and are not government control and planning either communist or fascist, but

certainly totalitarian? To reconstruct Europe ⟨
ful war, you will have to impose democratic ⟨
totalitarian peoples, and are not the words "imp⟨
racy" incompatible? To run such a Europe and su⟨
will need continentally integrated economies, world ⟨
international air forces—and are not Hitler and Claren⟨
cousins under the skin? To act for survival in our own country ⟨
during and after the war crisis, you must have leaders with a g⟨
for dramatic decision and followers with a gift for unity of purpose: but is that not the *Führerprinzip?* To turn out the planes we
shall need during the war or the goods we shall need after the war,
you must have an administrative elite who cannot be chosen by the
people because the people are not qualified to judge them: but is
not the idea of an elite a fascist idea? To furnish the cement for an
integrated social system we shall have to add to the eighteenth-
century bill of individual rights a twentieth-century bill of social
duties; and Lewis Mumford, in his *Faith for Living,* has already begun to translate into language for the layman this revolt of the
counter-romanticism of the society against the eighteenth-century
romanticism of the individual; but is not this emphasis also a totalitarian one? Harold Lasswell has written an able book which he
calls *Politics: Who Gets What, When, How.* Must not a climate of
opinion in which the word "gets" thrives so mightily be replaced
by one in which the word "gives" has some place in the definition of
politics? But is not that too the romanticism of the state, and therefore totalitarianism?

3

I have put all this in the form of a sequence of questions in order
to point up the dilemma of political ethics today as most of us conceive of it. The trouble is that we have lumped together the images
of what the totalitarians believe, what they are, and what they do.
Totalitarianism calls to our mind a group of men with singleness
of purpose and ruthlessness of method. It calls to our mind also a
value-system, nihilistic though it may be. It calls to our mind a
related ideology or idea-system, even though some people contend
that this ideology is wholly rationalization, in the nature of after-
thoughts. It calls to our mind a social structure and a set of going

...ial institutions. And it calls to our mind a set of techniques of war, government, and administration. When we say "totalitarian means," we think of the whole constellation of what I have just mentioned.

We should not, of course, even say "totalitarian means" because of this danger of confusion. The term would not have been used in the title of this essay if it were not that the problem ordinarily presents itself to us in this form. The totalitarians have sought deliberately to encourage us to think of them within a broad frame of reference. They want us when we think of planning to think of them, when we think of leadership to think of them, when we think of decisiveness of action to think of them, when we think of the plenary use of power to think of them. Also, they have recently been encouraging us when we think of revolution to think of them; and the sad thing is that so many have been innocent enough to be taken in. The beginning of wisdom in this whole matter is to draw a distinction between a set of values, idea-systems, and social institutions which are thoroughly impregnated with the totalitarian spirit, and a set of economic and political and administrative techniques which may be and are neutral. There is, to be sure, a whole range of totalitarian means which are not neutral: the single-party system, the monopoly of conscience, the systematic use of terror. If these have not been contributed to politics by the totalitarians, they have at least been brought to a high degree of perfection by them. But we will be foolish if we allow our horror and contempt for these to carry over and infect our attitude toward techniques which rightly belong in our own cultural heritage, techniques which totalitarianism has exploited first and now claims for its own monopoly.

To call these techniques ethically neutral is not necessarily to say that they are shorn of all ethical significance. The bomber plane, the timetable war, and the systematic use of propaganda and espionage do not lack moral connotation, although it is a negative connotation because they are death-giving rather than life-giving. Yet which of us does not believe the truth of Churchill's dictum about the British air force, that "Never in the field of human conflict was so much owed by so many to so few"? A labor leader named Walter Reuther is today [1] making headlines in America be-

---

[1] December 1940.

cause he has a plan by which we shall be able in six months to turn out five hundred of these death-dealing machines a day. We applaud, and rightly. We fervently hope it can be done, because the plane, for all its connotations of death, is ethically neutral. In the service of those who are seeking the triumph of totalitarian ideals, it takes on overtones of totalitarian ethics. In the service of democratic defense, it takes on democratic overtones. What is true of war techniques is even truer of planning and administrative techniques, of leadership and *expertise,* which—taken out of their totalitarian context—are neutral enough to serve our uses if we have uses to which we wish to put them.

But, you say, this is the blackest sort of opportunism, arrant Machiavellism brought up to date. You rip things out of one context and put them in another, and then you grin as blandly as the Cheshire cat during her feat of disappearance. But I know that government and society are not matters of mechanism, not collections of replaceable and standardized parts, but organic growths. I know that as organic growths there can be in them no reckless displacement of parts, and that even transplanting and grafting are dangerous things.

The fact is that fascism has only a bastard claim to most of these techniques of decisiveness and survival. Most of them are the developments of modern industry and science and administration which we have been betrayed into neglecting, or which we have used, but organized badly. Nevertheless, they are part of the heritage of Western science and Western development. The military technicians tell us that even to war there is nothing essentially new that the fascists have contributed, except the precision of their organization and the ruthlessness of their purpose. The fruits of science are the products of the free spirit of inquiry under the democracies. The administrative arts come from Taylorism in industry, from business management, from the European civil services, from the *ad hoc* contrivances of the New Deal administrative revolution. The techniques of planning are an amalgam of corporate practices under capitalism, the engineering mentality, and some of the social vistas of Marxism: it is significant that the important suggestions toward a planned war economy in America now have come from engineers like Morris Llewellyn Cooke and labor leaders like Philip Murray. And the psychological insights that the totalitarians have displayed on their road to power—insights into the nature and the social role of myths and symbols—have long been known to the democracies. The greatest name here is that of Sigmund Freud, who died, as he lived, hating the Nazi uses to which his insights had been put.

It is not, then, opportunism to make use of these products of our own enterprise and our own civilization. They are the heritage of the Western tradition, a birthright to which we have thus far not laid adequate claim. It is not we who are the eclectics, who rip things out of their context. It is the fascists. If we have the wit to understand the uses of the products of our own culture, and the boldness to apply them as means toward our own democratic ends, we can do so with the assurance that we are but completing the organic process of our own development.

How then has it happened that we still tend to think of these techniques as totalitarian? To answer that question adequately one would have to rewrite, in a way in which it has not yet been written, the history of the modern centuries in the Western world. And I suspect the clues to such a rewriting would be somewhat as follows: that out of the growth of science and technology came the development of industrial potentials broad enough as a base to allow for several alternative systems of class relations, of social institutions, of legal and political systems, of ideologies, to be built on it; that the organic growth from the past was a system of individualist capitalism and a system of liberal democracy, each contributing its energy to the rest of the social structure, those energies sometimes fusing, sometimes in conflict; that another organic growth was the sovereign nation-state, built on the two polar principles of plenary power for the state and unlimited natural rights for the individual; that as these various systems developed, the divergent elements in them, which had lived more or less tolerably at peace with each other, began showing ever more clearly their contradictions. Democracy, which had flourished in a period of expanding capitalism, found itself hemmed in during the period of a contracting capitalism, while capitalism found itself more and more afraid of the threats of control implicit in majority rule. The sovereign nation-state, in the face of this jealousy of its powers, became a government of limited rather than of plenary powers, and became less and less able to deal with its problems; while its own jealousy for its sovereignty prevented it either from forming the economic combinations that would enable it to live in peace with other nations, or from building the federal structures that could have kept down aggression at its very start. Within this framework the totalitarian states came into their own. Reckless outlaws, severed from the organic roots of the past, they had at once a clearer vision of what was required for success and a more uninhibited will to use what was required. The field was open for them, and they exploited their opportunity to the full.

That, in brief, is the story. It is not a story of creativeness on the part of the fascists, unless we describe as creative the streamlined gangsterism that operates within the interstices of an ineffective social structure. It is not one of superhuman efficiency on their part, although they have been at pains to create that myth. Actually the economic and administrative wastage under the Nazis, resulting from their elaborate superstructures of bureaucracy on bureaucracy and from their use of coercion as an incentive, is ghastly. There is no question of revolutionary inevitability about their system: in any meaningful sense of the word "revolution," a system which continually narrows rather than broadens the base of power is fantastic. What they have done has been to take advantage of a situation which, because of our inability to make the necessary adjustments, had become unstable enough to be called a revolutionary situation. In it their dynamism has until recently been rampant and unopposed. The problem for us is whether it shall continue so.

And I submit that the answer to that problem lies in no small measure in the extent to which we can recapture for our own democratic uses the ethically neutral techniques which are organic outgrowths of our own past, which we have up to now heedlessly neglected, and which are not only compatible with the democratic spirit but necessary to its extension.

4

It is possible to indicate here only in the briefest fashion the problems of ethics and politics raised in five typical areas: First, how a democracy can wage total war against fascism, as England is doing so successfully today, and still remain, in every ethical element that counts, a democracy. Second, how a democracy can deal with the problem of fifth columns realistically and even relent-lessly, and yet without any vigilantism on the part of either the people or their officials. I cannot say that we have as yet solved this problem, but I think it fair to say that the missing elements in the solution are not ethical but political. Third, how a democracy can explore the range of strategies of economic control, on the princi-ple that the organization of the flow of goods and income is the prime matter of state concern, more crucial even than police, mili-tary, and taxes; and on the principle also that the strategies adopted must not aim at drastic change for its own sake. Fourth, how a democracy can build up an administrative bureaucracy to whose technical expertness full scope is given, but whose members are not above the law, which is the expression of the social conscience. And fifth, how a democracy can join its economy with others on a continental scale without taking on the ethical patterns of imperial-ism; or how it can join its political structure with others on a plane of world federalism without crushing the chances of free social experiment in the insulated chambers afforded by the nation-states.

This, in outline, is the task of the social invention of our future. That task will have to be done in a collectivist fashion, in the best sense of collectivism: pooling our social intelligence and our social courage and our social will. It will involve the shattering of many myths as to who constitute the elite of our society. The national de-fense effort has already shown, in both England and America, that the common man as worker has as much to contribute in technical competence and political imagination as have the elite of business and the army, if not more. This is not an attempt to cry down the notion of elite groups. They are crucial, and especially so in a de-mocracy, where they can be continually revitalized by a genuine attempt to keep the career open to talent. I am only seeking to say that here, as elsewhere, we shall have a good deal of dislocating to do to our thinking. But one thing must be clear: we cannot afford to let the totalitarians take the credit of alone giving scope to talent. In a society where there is a free flow of talent because the career is genuinely, and not just mythically, open to it, even huge admin-istrative obstacles and difficult problems of means and ends can be overcome. In a society which has become the stationary state, every administrative molehill will become a mountain.

The same applies to leadership. We have made the mistake of

surrendering the concept of leadership to the totalitarians, as though it were unworthy of the democratic spirit. When we think of leaders we think of tyrants; when we think of followers we think of sheep. This is a ghastly error, and we have paid for it. Yet it is an error that is not irremediable. We have in recent years turned up in England a leader who can be compared in imagination with Disraeli and in boldness with Cromwell. And in America we have turned up a leader who will be discussed by historians on the plane on which we discuss Jefferson and Lincoln. This is no inconsiderable achievement. It is notable that these have been the very men most under attack on the ground that they have sought to use totalitarian methods in a democracy. It is, I think, a measure of their stature that they have seized in the quick way of leadership the ideas that have been set forth here. But it is also a measure of their stature, and of the safety with which democracies can use the methods of decisiveness and plenary power, that they have at no point placed themselves outside of the state, as have the fascist leaders. We need to extend further the gift and the art of leadership in a democracy, as well as the art and the gift of followers. For only in a democracy can leaders have humility, and only in a democracy can followers have dignity.

And only in a democracy can the natural processes of growth absorb new economic and political means in the service of ends which are as old as human decency and as ever-renewed as man's essential fellowship with man.

4

Economic Empire and Monopoly State

I F OUR social theorists have the wit, they have in their world the materials for a new and great age of social analysis. I take Guenter Reimann's important book [1] as an earnest of not impossible great works to come out of our time, some of them perhaps by men who are today still obscure. It sometimes happens with social catastrophe, as with personal tragedy, that it liberates in any age those energies that have been dammed up by habit and stagnation. The agonies of our generation may well have a therapeutic effect upon our thought.

If you want personal experiences or journalistic color or the easy answers, you will not find them here. Reimann's book is not a broadside against the Total State. It does not have the jejune and repetitive stickiness of the books on why France fell, or the Frank Merriwell cheeriness of the books on why England held. It falls in the category of the long-perspective books. Their principal cost is that you must pay the admission price of getting accustomed to a somewhat arduous Olympianism on the part of the writer. There comes to my mind one of the greatest of such books, Veblen's *Theory of the Leisure Class,* and—when I first read him—my bewilderment at one who shattered my world yet remained aloof. Reimann has the deliberate manner of Veblen, although without the bitterly ironic overtones of the latter. And once you pay his admission price, the reward is great. For there are all manner of good things in this suggestive, compressed, and essentially dense analysis. I say "dense" for lack of a better word because Reimann cuts through the surfaces and, deep as he drives his analysis, there are always depths

---

[1] Guenter Reimann, *The Myth of the Total State,* New York, Morrow, 1941. This essay appeared as an introductory critique in Reimann's book.

beyond that are suggested. In an age of popularization I welcome an author who is not content with presenting just so much of a subject as you can see through, but gives you the refracted meanings and the partial and oblique illuminations.

Reimann's central topic is one of the three or four major subjects of political inquiry of our day—the nature of the new power-formation in whose shadow we live. He calls it the "Total State," and it is a good enough term although I could have wished that he had chosen one more indigenous to American usage. I should prefer to call the Nazi state a "Monopoly State"; and I am strengthened in my leanings by Reimann's first-rate analysis of its origins in the huge national trusts of Germany, and the manner in which the creature-state swallowed its own creator-monopoly by becoming the biggest monopoly of all. The Monopoly or Total State, how and whether it could have been averted, how it arose and was given scope for triumph, how it can be fought and perhaps transformed—these are matters of some moment to us. Reimann approaches them with freshness, and yet he does not break his continuities with past thought. He knows that we must use new intellectual tools to take apart and reveal the meaning of a new world, But he knows also that in fashioning the new tools we can learn from the old. We have been witnessing recently the fragmentation of Marxian and liberal thought by the sheer packed-up dynamite of events. We are having to reassemble the pieces in new formations and build them somehow into the structure of our thought. And Reimann is one of a small group who are doing that, with his eye for the economics of power and the politics of economic interest, his preoccupation with the old and new aristocracies, his concern about imperialisms and the transfer of power from one world-center to another, and with what is viable and what is no longer able to function in our world.

He does well, I think, to start his book with the powerlessness of the Old Conservatives to save their world, and to end with the powerlessness of the New Conservatives to consolidate another. The quality of toughness that is common to the thinking of men as diverse as Lenin, Pareto, Mosca, and Spengler comes from their willingness to face the decisive relation of ruling group to cultural survival. Reimann has given us here one of the shrewdest analyses of aristocracy in the contemporary literature of political science. He understands that the weakness of the British aristocracy was not limited to the British. "There were too many Chamberlains in power when Hitler made his often announced *Blitzkrieg* attacks," he says, in answer to the position that it was the accidental deficiencies of individuals or nations that counted; and yet his theory of the lack of will of the Old Conservatives and the blindness of their habit-response might have been stronger if he had found room in it to differentiate between men like Chamberlain and Churchill, Hoover and Roosevelt. The difficulty is increased when one considers that Reimann makes the Old Conservatives basically rentiers, and that both Churchill and Roosevelt belong in that class.

Despite this criticism the concept is a suggestive one, and leads to some good insights: that Spengler's thought, for example, may be best understood when we see it as expressing the sense of fatalism of the German Old Conservatives in the face of the new forces; that "in the critical period when he had to act quickly or perish, Conservative Man could only function on the outmoded patterns of the past"; that liberal thought, with its motifs of order and pacifism, took its color from a business civilization for which war assumed ever more destructive aspects; that even the labor movements of Western countries had become those of a labor aristocracy which had the same social premises and final stakes as Conservative Man. Reimann has come upon a concept for which he will be remembered. Yet I wish he had given it greater precision of outline. Sometimes he seems to mean by Conservative Man the international bankers, sometimes a broader rentier class, sometimes the drive toward security and the elements of the population dominated by that drive, sometimes merely (or so much as) the principle of stability in a culture.

To call the new ruling groups in the Total State the "ersatz aristocracy" was a happy inspiration, yet its merit goes beyond the verbal. More clearly than other recent writers Reimann sees that while the Nazis have found a way whereby their Führer can apply the principle of "divide and rule" to his tripartite bureaucracy of business, army, and party, they have not by that fact given the new aristocracy any stability. It is ersatz because it can develop no autonomous strength and permanence: its obedience to the leader must at every stage be renewed. It is good to have, for once, a pluralistic approach to the problem of the Nazi ruling group that has so troubled our thinkers ever since the communists called the Nazi State the last mask of capitalism, while another group saw in it the coming of the middle class to power, and still another a classless "State of the masses." Reimann shows well that there are three groups, each performing a specialized function, and all of them in the end manipulated by the leader. And, as against Burnham's single-barreled thesis of a "managerial revolution," I tend to agree with Reimann that the managers form the weakest of the bureaucracies in the Total State, with the shakiest of positions.

Yet I should like to add some caveats and qualifications of my own. Whether, as Reimann seems to imply in this book as in his earlier *Vampire Economy*, there is a big revolt potential among the business men and the managerial bureaucracy, depends upon how long Hitler has to consolidate his power. Given the premise of world military success and a long enough period in which Hitler can play off one ruling group against another, the basic psychological change among business men on which Hitler counts may take place. Moreover, if the leader's capacity to checkmate each group by the others is as mechanically perfect as Reimann makes it, then his power would seem to be in internal terms relatively secure, and might afford the State the principle of stability it needs. I doubt both the neatness of the analysis and the security of the power. There are strains in a Total State other than the bureaucratic disease itself: strains implied by the very fact that the leader must be four-fifths juggler and manipulator. The problem of succession of power is not avoided in the Total State, and is all the more acute because it is not institutionalized. The problem of distribution of power among the leader's lieutenants is maximized. And once victories in the field have given way to even a few defeats, the strains on the administrative machinery are more likely to cause collapse than in a democracy. Finally, I wish Reimann had done more with the relation of the party to the State, and had dealt with the question of whether the Total State is in essence a Party-State.

That he does not do so may be partly explained by the fact that he approaches political theory primarily as an economist. While this precludes a sharp analysis of the nature of State power and function in the Total State, it gives greater strength to the treatment of the origins and conditionings of that power. After this book no one will be able to talk of the decline of British power or the rise of the Nazis without talking of the decline of international finance and the clash between international and national monopolies. The latter distinction is especially good and, to my knowledge, has never before been so clearly developed and with so much implication. The author shows well how the Nazis turned the limitations of their position on the world market into an element of strength; how they used national monopolies to build up their power within Germany and then to break down the world economic order outside. There is a brilliant suggestiveness even for American readers in his linkage of generals and industrialists in a military economy, and in the interaction of the steel and chemical trusts with diverse lines of national policy. Yet here too I may be allowed some queries. Was the decline of the international economic order quite as inevitable as Reimann implies? The imperatives of our financial history march through these pages very much like George Meredith's "army of unalterable law." Were the only alternatives to an unworkable system of international trade and finance the unrealistic proposals of the liberals for patching it up, or the plans for a United States of Europe, which also failed, presumably of necessity? This is important because by killing off the alternatives to a Nazi economic imperium, Reimann leaves us with a rather blank prospect for the future even in the event of military victory. It may be that the function of analysis is to tell us what to expect rather than what to do; but it is not unusual that new alternatives for action open up new perspectives of thought.

I come finally, among the main themes of the book, to the old imperialism and the new. The old was tied to the rentier spirit at home and opened backward regions to competitive exploitation; the new is tied to the spirit of militarist expansion and turns the whole Western world, including Europe itself, into a backward area for exploitation by the Total State alone. The old imperialism was linked with the international market and the international division of labor; the new depends upon the open door at home for armament industries and the reduction of conquered countries to a state of pre-industrial vassalage. I should make these sections of the book required reading for the tired socialists and the professional liberals who see little to choose between the conflicting imperialisms in the present war. And better than anyone else Reimann shows the naïveté of Lawrence Dennis's dream of a world of co-ordinate "socialist imperialisms" which would have room for an American fascist empire. For the essence of the imperialism of the Total State is not that it drives toward making itself economically self-sufficient, but that it drives by inherent necessity toward a world imperium.

Because his analysis is so subtle on this score I am disappointed that Reimann was led out of his way, in his next-to-last chapter, into an attempt to equate the Nazi and Soviet Total States. I have the advantage, as he perhaps did not have, of writing this comment when open war between Germany and Russia has undercut our easy assumptions of the identity of the two systems; at a time also when, whatever the ultimate outcome of Hitler's invasion, the morale of the Russian people thus far in their struggle against him casts doubt upon an analysis which would imply widespread popular hostility to the Soviet regime. This section of the book lacks the hard-headed character of the rest. I agree that there are large areas of identity between the political methods used internally by the two dictatorships. And we stand in need of a good book on them. The trouble, however, lies in the fact that the main body of this book is concerned with analyzing the economics not of the Soviet State but of the Nazi State in relation to the rest of the world; so that the later section on Russia, whether true or not, comes as an almost complete non sequitur.

There remains the discussion of the chances of tomorrow. Here, despite Reimann's detachment, I cannot help feeling that he has allowed a not unimportant element of wishfulness to seep in. I find him too insistent, for example, that Hitler cannot possibly unify Europe and survive the economic strains that that would involve. He proves adequately that it would mean the economic ruin of the conquered countries. But I see no reason why they could not be kept either agrarian or industrial satrapies within a Nazi world empire, without the danger that the competition of their goods on the world market would threaten the Nazi power. An essential premise, of course, is that the Nazis should have monopolized the total military power in the world; another premise is that they should have worked out indirect controls for preventing industrial capacity from being converted into political or military power. But both premises are certainly within the realm of possibility. I should myself see the economic weaknesses of a Hitler world imperium in the internal drives toward a more complete socialism, with resultant class conflict and geographical fragmentation.

Despite his valid criticisms of a mechanical Marxism, some of the Marxian habits of thought find their way into the book, and give it what hopeful tone it has. I know that Reimann prefers Hobson to Lenin in his analysis of imperialism. Yet the dialectic has left some of its residues here. The book is a good study in paradoxes —of conservatism breeding revolution, and of revolution seeking to become conservative and find its principle of stability. But it is also a study of contradictions that go beyond literary paradox. "In so far as the Nazi 'revolutionist' succeeds in his aim, he simultaneously nullifies his purpose." "All authoritarian rulers are prisoners of the system they have created. They cannot abdicate or change it without arousing forces they cannot control." We read of an imperialism that must move forward, but if it does, moves toward its destruction; of the promises of the rulers of the Total State that must be made, yet cannot be fulfilled. This is heartening, and, in particular instances, true enough. Yet one cannot depend upon it as a method of analysis. Reimann is so good in his analysis of past and present that one wishes that he would face the future without benefit of the method of basic contradictions. Even without them there is room for action, and to action we must ultimately appeal.

1941

5

The People's Century

THOSE who say that either capitalist imperialism or nationalism is dead had better read Henry Luce's editorial "The
American Century." [1] It was published originally in *Life*
in February 1941, but since then its persuasive power has been
prodded by double-page-spread ads in some of our papers. Mr. Luce
overwrites and Mr. Luce must go through all sorts of literary heroics
before he says his say. Yet the piece as a whole has in it so much
conscious and unconscious candor that it goes beyond Mr. Luce
himself and becomes one of the important documents of our time
—a symbol of what is strong in America's present position and a
portent of what is dangerous in it.

Mr. Luce's thesis can be stated briefly: America has become the
most powerful nation in the world, with the greatest prestige.
Let us live up to our role, win the war not to help other nations but
to help ourselves, become the senior partner with England of a
combination which will establish its hegemony over the world, control the world sea lanes and world trade, send out technicians to
develop the world and educators to teach it and food cargoes to
feed it and ideals to inspire it. This is to be the American Century,
both in power terms and in spiritual terms. Not only does Mr.
Luce see money flowing into the coffers of American business:
from Asia, for example, "four, five, ten billions of dollars a year."
He also sees what is, in effect, a *pax Americana* established over
the world, with the franchise of American citizenship extended as
the Romans once extended Roman citizenship to those who were
worthy. And he sees us also as assuming a new American Burden. "It
now becomes our time to be the powerhouse from which the ideals
[of civilization] spread throughout the world and do their mys-

---

[1] Henry R. Luce, *The American Century*, New York, Farrar & Rinehart, 1941.

terious work of lifting the life of mankind from the level of the beasts to what the Psalmist called a little lower than the angels."

It is easy to be snippy about this and easy to be merely negative. I don't propose to be either. I take Mr. Luce seriously, partly because he is a man who has shown himself to be intelligent and resourceful, partly because he has, as a baron of opinion, power that can shape not only purposes but instruments as well, mainly because he speaks for a new capitalist-conscious group, most of them younger men, who do not fear the war but regard it as an opportunity. The liberals have made the mistake of shouting "imperialist" at Mr. Luce and letting it go at that, as they have consistently made the mistake of identifying criticism with truth and negativism with finality. Mr. Luce has the merit of being tough-minded; in his own way he is a radical—one willing to follow through the implications of his position. Only an approach as radical and as affirmative as his, if from different premises, can hope to grapple with him. We cannot afford to leave it only to the Luces of our country to plan our future with a hard and yet imaginative realism.

There are whole areas of agreement which I can pass over with a few words. It is true that we are living in a time of troubles that presents a wholly new environment; true that isolationism is impossible; true that America must have an affirmative world policy and assume world leadership; true that we must co-operate with Britain in winning the war and shaping a peace. Because Mr. Luce sees this I prefer him infinitely, though our purposes are as far removed as the four corners of the winds, to men like Burton Wheeler and John Flynn, who, though they inherit the populist attitudes, are more dangerous than the tories, because their aims are more noble but their world just as musty and archaic.

But here I part company with Mr. Luce and so many others who feel that the war is the dark tunnel that must lead into the air and sunlight of a paradise of American-dominated world capitalism. Every person has his own private apocalypse. Mine is not that of American heroes sprouting from mounds of Standard Oil or du Pont profits, or of American culture being pumped out over the world from powerhouses located on the MGM lot in Hollywood or the Time and Life Building in New York. Nor do I fancy the corporate muscle men—the advertising-agency executives and high-pressure publicity people—who will form the legionaries of the *pax Americana* and the praetorian guard of our power in each country.

My quarrel with Luce lies in the adjective "American" in his phrase "the American Century." As he uses it, the adjective embraces both too much and too little. Too much because, despite his repeated excoriations of our "deceits and self-deceits," he uses the nationalist symbol of American culture to signify the power of a single strain in that culture—that of the capitalists and their allies. Too little because, in world terms, "American" is only metonymy for "democratic"; and what has given us our strength and prestige is the reality of our living standards and our freedom, however relative—the promise of our democratic life.

Mr. Luce is curiously careful in talking about democracy. He talks of it mainly as a myth and catchword—"the brassy trumpeting of majestic words." If democracy is only a majestic word for Mr. Luce, then for all his boasted realism he is politically bat-blind. As I write, word comes of the overthrow in Yugoslavia of a Nazi-oriented government by a mass movement so deeply felt that it even reached the army and the church—a mass movement whose dynamic force was an identification of national freedom with the democratic cause. Some months ago the same thing happened in Greece, some months before that in England. What dynamic except that of democracy does Mr. Luce think we can use to win a war which the Nazis have already converted into a civil war in each country? What other common language is there that will unite nations as diverse as China and Greece and England in a war against heavy odds?

Mr. Luce says ours is a "revolutionary century." If that is not merely a "brassy trumpeting of majestic words," what does it mean? It can only mean that there will be a succession of revolutions in our century that will set the framework for the power-structures of the future. They may be revolutions on our side or against us. The revolution of the Yugoslavs is the first of a series, and it is on our side. Mr. Luce doesn't like the prospect of messy revolutions. The Revolution of 1776, he assures us, was accomplished by "gentlemen and men of common sense." I shall not argue over his history, but I suspect strongly that the revolutions of the future will not all be gentlemanly affairs. I doubt whether Poland will ever throw off its Nazi shackles in a gentlemanly fashion after what the Nazis have done to the Poles.

Let us not flinch from it. We cannot expect to have been blind for so long to the revolutionary situation in the world to have let the Nazis get the jump on us, and to put a quietus on it all by aid to Britain, Union Now, and a consortium of Anglo-American capitalists. To say we are in a revolutionary situation means that the revolutionary situation must bear its fruit. It will not somehow disappear because we win the war. We cannot put the lid down on it. We shall have to fulfill it, and we shall have to let other nations fulfill it.

This does not mean blood and violence in every nation. For those nations which today have democratic forms and traditions, like the English and Americans and, in their own way, the Greeks and the Chinese, this must mean and has already to an extent meant what Harold Laski calls "a revolution by consent." Despite Mr. Luce's vicious paragraphs about the first two Roosevelt administrations as representing stages toward our own form of National Socialism, the whole past decade has been deeply revolutionary in America although within a constitutional framework. In other countries, where the people must overthrow their leaders to achieve freedom, war and violence will go hand in hand.

But what will these people be fighting for? Their own freedom and equality in an international community, or the privilege of sharing in an American Century? Mr. Luce must wear unusually opaque social blinkers if he thinks they will fight for the latter. Why should they exchange the projected New Order of the Nazis in Europe and the Far East for the New Order he has in mind? Why should they pant for the privileges of forming provinces in this new imperium?

Let there be no mistake. We do not have, as a workable alternative, the prospect of beating the fascists and then, like Cincinnatus, returning to our national plow. That would be a more catastrophic provincialism than any we have been guilty of. But is an American imperium over the world our only alternative to that?

It is not. There is an alternative that can combine democratic dignity with firmness. We shall, of course, have to use an iron hand, both in the war and in the years immediately following it. Whatever else the future may hold, its military and economic methods will be like nothing before them; they will involve planning, state power, economic regionalism, a new role for the technicians and the managers. But there are ways and means of using these necessary methods.

Ours must be a people's century. It must involve the leadership not just of America and England, but of a *democratic* America and England. It must involve democracy now, and not at some future time, in our diplomacy and foreign policy. It must involve a democratic military force and organization of the armament industries. It must involve democracy now in regional agreements with Latin America. And it must involve finally a federation of nations in which, if we are leaders, we are leaders among equals, with their consent, pooling our resources of wealth and intellect and will with theirs.

Unless we can achieve a people's century for all nations, it will not have room in it for the democratic efforts and dreams that make us proud to be Americans.

1941

6

If We Own the Future

1

THE "paralyzing abstractions" about the war, for which Justice Frankfurter has found the right phrase, are almost equaled by the abstractions about the peace after the war. Some people cling prayerfully to the conviction that any peace, no matter under whose auspices or at what price or how badly planned, must be somehow good. Others feel that the world will have been desolated by war beyond reconstruction, and that no sooner is the cycle of depression, reaction, and war ended than it is begun again. Both generalizations express a desperate insecurity. They bring to mind A. E. Housman's comment about the scholars who prepare editions of classical manuscripts and who "use their texts as a drunkard uses a lamp-post: not to light him on his way, but to dissimulate his instability."

Even in this dark period of the war, with the Germans near Leningrad and the Ukraine half overrun, with all of Central and Western Europe under Nazi exploitation, and with America still unable, like a bound Gulliver, to shake itself free and rise to its war strength, we can without fantasy glimpse some perspectives of an enduring peace. We can assert that a substantial measure of reconstruction is possible, provided we do not promise more than we can accomplish. But we must see also that the post-war period will be as arduous in its way as the war period, and that it will require fully as much along the lines of a new technology as the war period—only this time it must be a technology of political and economic invention, and not of death.

That is, if we have a post-war period. It is not defeatism to envisage the real possibility of a German victory. If the Nazis should win it will be not our post-war plans but Hitler's that will be relevant. The answer to the question "Who owns the future?" must thus condition all thinking about the peace. If the Nazis own it, the role of America—whether or not we have taken part in the war itself—will be that of a satrapy rich for despoilment by a monopoly world state. The conditions of conscience and intellect, the loci of power, the living standards and cultural norms in such a satrapy need no underlining.

But if we own the future our planning for the peace takes on reality. And as I write we have a good fighting chance to own the future. It is now the beginning of the third year of the war. The Nazi invasion of Russia, so fiercely resisted and, thus far, with an almost unconjectured efficiency and determination, has brought the war to a new phase. For the first time since the collapse of France the conditions exist for creating a two-front war, although except in the air they have not yet been taken advantage of. For the first time Nazi military casualties have been enormous, the powerful Nazi machine has bogged down in Russian mud and morale, and Hitler has had to make use of his full resources. For the first time it is possible to think of gaining a continental foothold for a land war against the Nazis in conjunction with the air, sea, and ideological war. And, what is much more directly relevant from the present viewpoint, the ideological unity that existed in anti-Nazi circles before Munich can now be re-achieved, and Russia brought back, as England has been brought back, to be a responsible partner in international organization. To have America, the British Commonwealth, Russia, and China acting together in the war is of not negligible importance in building a consensus broad and strong enough to carry the burden of a peace settlement.

2

In working toward such a settlement, the first essential is an immediate offensive, both military and ideological, under American leadership. As for military action, it is impossible to predict when we shall find release from the expeditionary-force taboo that has paralyzed our potential effectiveness in war. But an ideological offensive is more possible. I am not now referring to the much-mooted question of a statement of war aims or peace terms. It is possible to claim too much for the effects of such a statement in itself, and to be either deluded by its too facile verbalisms, as in the case of the Wilsonian credo of the last war, or diverted into fruitless quarrels over territorial settlements and the status of colonies and minorities. Apart from the dramatic character of the meeting of Roosevelt and Churchill on the high seas, the actual eight-point declaration they agreed on has, thus far, proved something of a dud. I am thinking rather of a different sort of offensive: for America to show by example that democracies are capable of a decisiveness of will and action in war, and to give by word and deed a picture of a not impossible new world that a democratic people envisages after the war.

Thus far we have done the first in only a middling fashion and the second hardly at all. There are those who start with the premise that democracy as a system is inherently incapable of either. But even among others there is a tendency to fall back for an explanation of our failure upon a mystical theory of democratic paralysis of will, generally accompanied by an apocalyptic vision of an inevitable world imperium that will supplant democracy. It is hard to analyze mysticism or argue with the apocalypse. I am skeptical that it could be shown, despite Spengler's volumes or Toynbee's or Berdyaev's, that any period of history or any people was richer or thinner in some inherent will-stuff. Paralysis of will is a reality to be reckoned with, but it is much more likely to be the result than the cause of social institutions. The real problem of the failure of will lies in the blocking of communal action by group fears and cupidities, as has been shown in the case of the men of Munich and the men of Vichy. The real problem of the success of will lies, as Graham Wallas long ago pointed out, in an effective communal organization of it.

The matter is worth some elaboration if we are to be clear about the conditions of an ideological offensive. Group interests and habituations are today responsible for much of the failure of the American will. The American financial and management groups have shown will enough and planfulness enough in their own narrow grooves, but thus far they have for the most part been unable to redirect either will or planning into broader channels. They are fearful of the war because they have learned that drastic social changes come in the wake of wars. They are fearful of war production because to be successful it involves the expansion of productive capacity, and they do not see how there will be post-war markets for that expanded capacity without a redistribution of income to make higher living standards possible. They sense that a successful war economic effort involves the dynamiting of the blockages that their monopoly position has thus far interposed against maximum production. To be caught in a dilemma means to be paralyzed in will. And the business groups are caught in a dilemma: they are fearful of losing the war to the Nazis because they know that Hitler's world has no room for the individual entrepreneur and room for monopolies only if they are Nazi monopolies; but they are also fearful of winning the war because it would mean that they would assume unaccustomed functions and burdens in an unpredictable social order.

The labor groups are not very much better situated. They too are the prisoners of their habits of action and thought. Their perspective in action has rarely gone beyond their shop and union and only in very recent years beyond their industry. Their perspective in thought has been until recently summed up in the simple axiom that if we will only take care of American domestic affairs, our foreign affairs will take care of themselves. In the last months an increasing number of them have been jolted by events into abandoning this insularity. I pick industry and labor because of their power and because they form relatively homogeneous political forces. What is true of them is even more true of agrarian thought and of the middle class. If the American Congress is today at all representative of the middle-class mentality, then its ignorance of world realities is kin to its ignorance of our own economic environment and fear of its change.

I cannot leave this part of the analysis without a word about the progressive tradition. The progressives have in the past formed the spearhead of the attack on laissez faire in domestic policy; yet they also have, as much as any other group, fallen victim to a strain of thought in foreign policy which in its way runs parallel to laissez faire. It is a strain that cannot be described merely as isolationism, but is rather a belief that a world role for America, however desirable, is from the start doomed as the sheerest adventurism. The progressive tradition has been guilty of a fatal neglect of world perspectives, of military technology, of world economics, and power politics. Among its first-rate thinkers I count a few striking exceptions: Veblen, notably in the far-ranging scope of his institutional comparisons and in the startling pre-vision of German fascism contained in *Imperial Germany and the Industrial Revolution;* Brooks Adams, who was—as Matthew Josephson has pointed out in *The President Makers*—one of the intellectual fathers of Theodore Roosevelt's foreign policy, but who also saw things never dreamt of in T.R.'s philosophy; Justice Holmes (accepted in liberal circles, although more a conservative than a progressive), with his blending of martial and humanist values; Lincoln Steffens, who started the hegira of American intellectuals to Moscow, muckraked Europe as well as America, made revolutions and wars his stamping-ground, and fathered the genre of the war-correspondent's autobiography; and, of course, although not perhaps a first-rate intellectual figure, Woodrow Wilson.

What is required for an ideological offensive, then, is something more than a flagellant exhortation to ourselves to undertake it. There must first be a shift of emphasis in our own thinking —a shift that we may not make until it is forced on us by a present catastrophe to our cause. This means a new realism in financial, managerial, labor, and middle-class groups alike, subjecting their group interests to an overriding national interest which they see as depending on decisive action and conviction on an international plane. It means some solution of the persistent problem of ideological blockage by a powerful minority strategically placed in the opinion industries. It means a greater decisiveness in the administrative and policy-making agencies of the government, particularly in the State Department. It means a more daring leadership on the part of the President, which is not confined to verbalism and gestures, important as they are.

It means also the further development of a nucleus which already exists for intellectual direction on the international plane. I am thinking here of the remarkable instances we have of the genus foreign correspondent, whose illusions on foreign affairs were shorter-lived than those of other people because they were subject to an occupational therapy they could not escape; of some government administrators who have understood the meaning of economic strategy in totalitarian war; of a few editors and even a handful of professors who have been lifted by the occasion to the plane of militant eloquence; of an honorable roster of men of letters who have discovered that literature has social roots and responsibilities; of a sprinkling of columnists and radio commentators; of a handful of social thinkers who have seen that the development of technology has burst social forms and institutions all over the world and that America is not exempt; and finally of a small group of political refugees who have learned their lessons in the bitter school of dictators and who are of incalculable importance not only in bringing to us the chastening experience of Europe, but even more in serving as a bridge over which in turn our influence can be directed toward the liberation of their enslaved peoples.

Even among some of these groups, precisely because they have required hardness and sophistication of thinking, there is a tendency toward ideological weariness. Dorothy Thompson, for example, who has shown a more sustained if erratic sense of awareness than most of her craft, writes in a recent column containing a crisp call to American action and headed "Now Is the Time." "Ideologies are not important in this moment. The ideology that wins the war will rule the world." One can agree with the second sentence without accepting the first. In fact, one could invert the second sentence and reach a truer first sentence: that the ideology that rules men's minds today all over the world will win the war.

That sets the task for the thinkers, publicists, administrators who must be the staff officers in the ideological offensive. I can understand why they should today be showing some signs of weariness. The obstacles and frustrations are immense. We call for opposition to Nazism all over the world, yet we set an example ourselves of cautious and interested watchful waiting. We preach resistance and practice appeasement. We hope for rebellion in the subject countries of Europe without creating conditions for it by decisive action and by deliberate and planned use of the short-wave and other instruments of idea-warfare. We train an army in ways of fighting without providing for the educational effort that will make them know what they are fighting for. It seems almost that it is the wrong people—those not in power—who have the right ideas, while the right people—those in power—have either no ideas or all of them with a fine impartiality. But that means merely that the war of ideas, like all wars, requires resourcefulness and strength and patience.

But on the assumption that we can stir ourselves to leadership, what is the armory of ideas that we require for this war? Quite summarily these: that democracy has in it untapped strength and unused expansibility, both in waging a war and in reconstructing society afterward; that the peace must be approached in the spirit neither of vengefulness nor of forgiveness, but of determined planning for more feasible ways of running a world; that economic settlements are required fully as much as political; that there must be definite steps toward a federal world structure of some sort; and above all that we do have a picture of a new world to guide those who are fighting and hearten those who are enslaved.

3

What sort of picture, and what chance has it of becoming reality? The beginning of wisdom here is to understand that there are at once imperatives and permissives in world change. Without the smugness that goes with the belief that whatever has been must be, or the delusion that we can effect whatever we have willed, we must be wary of the uses to which the myth of inevitability is being put against a democratic future. There are American intellectuals who seem to have studied the social myth in Sorel and Hitler, and learned for propaganda purposes the hypnotic effect of the persistent theme of the "doomed cause." We must understand that the future is at once limited and, within those limits, richly variable.

Let me take first, as an instance, the economic structure of the post-war world. I do so mainly because the problems of economic reconstruction are the most difficult of all and condition the solutions in the other areas. It is not necessary here to premise a rigorous determinism that technology exercises over economic forms. Technology, both of industry and of warfare, has been, to be sure, the prime mover in the present world revolutionary upheaval: Hitler's legions have merely given a particular historical twist to that upheaval. And it is true that the levels of industrial technology and energy-supply that are within the world's reach are such as to make new types of economic organization at once possible and necessary for reasonably full exploitation of our resources. Nevertheless, the only imperatives are those of integration, planning, maximum utilization. What will be the modes of integration, the techniques and purposes of maximum utilization, the auspices under which planning is carried out, will depend upon the polity that controls the world and the ethos that informs it. Politics and ethics are thus, within a framework set by technology, creative forces which have an effect even upon economic forms.

Is it true that the present economic organization of the world's resources, trade, and finance is doomed and must give way to drastically new procedures? The thesis is by now familiar: that the world economy has been organized around the norms of international access to the exploitation of resources in backward areas, the international gold standard, international finance, the international division of labor, and organization of the world market by competition and cartels; that in this scheme England has had a position of dominance since the eighteenth century, although more recently America has at some points supplemented and at others replaced it; that England has owed its dominance to getting the jump in industrialization, and to its position as a carrying and investing nation and as a colonial power; that with the diffusion of industrialism England has lost the advantage of its early start, and with the growth of economic nationalism its functions not only as manufacturing center but also as carrier and investor have been on the wane; that the movement toward economic nationalism has destroyed the structure of economic internationalism; that managed currencies and state trade monopolies have destroyed the gold standard and international trade; and that national monopolies have cut the ground from under international monopolies. In short, that the world economic order as we have known it in the heyday of world capitalism has been doomed for some time; that America's attempt after the first World War to assume leadership in patching it up proved a failure; and that whatever else happens in the future we shall never see the return of the old order.

Thus the argument in its most general form. It has little to do with the political sympathies of those stating it. Parts of it will be found in books whose intellectual assumptions are as diverse as Jerome Frank's *Save America First*, Lawrence Dennis's *Dynamics of War and Revolution*, Guenter Reimann's *Myth of the Total State*. Nor can the argument be dismissed. For myself I find in it more realism than in the free-trade internationalism of, say, Lionel Robbins's *Economic Planning and International Order*, or of the economic group around Secretary of State Hull. But while I find strength in the general direction of the analysis, I cannot go with some of the implications for the future that have been drawn from it. For one thing, though the galled jade of Britain wince, our American withers are unwrung. To say that the day of British world dominance is over does not carry the necessary conclusion that nothing can be salvaged from the international economic order over which Britain presided, nor does it mean that the conditions that have thus far given America a favored economic position and an increasing world leadership have ceased to operate. To say that state trade monopolies must play an increasing role in the world order does not mean that only the monopoly state can survive; nor does it mean that the expansion of that monopoly state into a world imperium by conquest and submission, by force, fraud, and propaganda, is necessary in order to fulfill the possibilities of a world order.

4

How can we fulfill those possibilities without the monopoly state and the world imperium? I can answer this best by a sequence of rather summary propositions.

First, there is much in the past that we shall have to scrap. Whatever world economic organization emerges after the war will not only have to utilize existing technology to the full and accept its imperatives: it will have to accept also the obsolescence of many of the received assumptions and mechanisms of world economic intercourse, and will have to understand that many of the new assumptions and mechanisms have come to stay, and are not merely part of the fascist thrust at power.

Second, America's role in the post-war world cannot be placed under the same tent-roof with that of England. I am not arguing now against economic collaboration between America and Britain: I should even be in favor of immediate economic union, as a first step toward a post-war world economic structure. But what I am concerned with now is America's strength and the chances of America's tomorrow. Unlike Britain's, our world position proceeds from our vast productive power, our resources, our technology. It does not and need not in the long run proceed from our rentier or investment role, nor our carrier or colonial role, nor our vast and essentially meaningless storehouse of gold. What gives America a great potential position of leadership in the world is thus what makes it also the prize fatted calf as a potential victim of a Hitlerized world. These strengths of America are inherent rather than adventitious. Neither the accidents of time nor the logic of history can wipe them out. They can be frustrated only by an actual transfer of world power to a single monopoly state which is not our own, or by our own stupidity in wasting our strength.

Third, there is little doubt that America could, if it wished, achieve an American economic imperium over the world after the war. If, as seems Mr. Roosevelt's assumption thus far, the Nazis can be beaten without extensive participation by America in a shooting war, America will be in a sweet and pretty position. With the other powers—Britain, Germany, France, Russia, Japan—exhausted, with our own strength unimpaired, with our military productive capacity at its peak, we could cash in on a new economic imperialism that would give us the role in the future that Britain has occupied in the past. Something like this, although not so nakedly put, is implicit in the imperialist groups whose immediate outlooks are as diverse as those of the "American Century" group and "America First" group. I shall discuss later the costs and the implications of such a policy. For the present I want only to point out its reality as one of our alternative post-war choices.

To be successful in an "American century" we should have to adopt many of the features of the monopoly state. But national monopolies under the monopoly state are the best way to organize production under modern technical conditions only when there is fear of using, or no will to use, other techniques.

It is to the use of these other techniques that my *fourth* proposition is addressed. They would involve an extension to a world plane of the price and market controls, the credit and investment strategies, and the planning mechanisms with which the crisis democracies have been experimenting for a decade. This means, in contrast to the view of the American imperialists, that we must see the American role in the world not as the powerhouse of a national finance capitalism but as the powerhouse of world-wide industrial productivity under democratic controls.

Fifth, we must move toward a strongly built world economic framework. Here we approach the question, so much mooted now, of the comparative merits of a co-ordinated world structure with a single power-alignment at the center, as against a set of co-ordinate regional economic blocs operating within a very loose world framework. I do not believe this question can be settled before we have a clearer picture than we can get now of the political complexion of the post-war world. A world in which America, Britain, Germany, Russia, and Japan all remained as strong powers, and in which an indecisive issue of military operations had led to a temporary standstill-peace, would be one in which regional economic blocs were the logical order of the day, and in which world economics would become a jockeying for strength and position in preparation for the next war. A world in which Germany were alone victorious would be a world dominated by a single ruling economy and state, with no room in it for economic regions. A world in which the anti-Nazi powers, including America, Britain, and Russia, emerged victorious would be a world under the economic leadership of those powers, with America having the major role of leadership, but it would also be a world with room in it for the principle of economic regions. I see no incompatibility between the principle of a world economic order under the leadership of a victorious entente and the existence of economic regions within that order.

For, *sixth*, the real choice is not between economic regionalism and a central economic authority, but between two sorts of regionalism. The basic distinction is between a competitive regionalism and a co-operative regionalism. Regionalism would be vicious, as nationalism has been vicious, if it aimed at self-sufficiency for the purposes of military strength, and if it was organized around units preparing for the ultimate test of world power. There has been a good deal of loose talk about regional economic blocs, some of it calculated to nourish the strength of the Nazi dream of world power. For the hope of being the center of a regional bloc is held out to-day to powerful economic groups in America as the hope of *Lebensraum* for an expanded economic imperialism; and the fact is that such an imperialism would either have to be subordinate to Nazi world power or sooner or later clash with it. And even assuming that these co-ordinate regional imperialisms were possible, it would still be true that they would involve as correlatives a set of monopoly state structures internally. Economic regionalism would be safe only if it were democratic; and it could be democratic only if it were a co-operative part of a world framework with a central economic authority democratically administered. Given this assumption, however, regionalism is highly desirable, since it could aim at the planning of resources within units economically more effective than the nation, and more manageable and institutionally more homogeneous than the world-unit. It is a tragic thing that Europe was never able to unite economically, that all the plans for a United States of Europe came to nought. What its adherents failed to see was that a united Europe was possible only within a less chaotic world economic framework than could be achieved at the time. But even without European political union a loose form of economic co-operation could be worked out on the European continent within the larger confines of a world economic set-up. And the same holds true for the British Commonwealth, for a Pan-American economy, for an East-European bloc including Russia, the Balkans, and the Near East, and for a Far Eastern bloc centering in China.

Seventh, this would involve an international economic body at the center with considerable powers. Its task would be to provide adequate controls for whatever policing and setting of uniform standards had to be achieved in the world economy. This might involve access to, allocation of, or internationalization of basic raw materials that could not be found plentifully within each regional bloc; monetary and foreign exchange controls of such a sort that America's possession of the world's gold would not form a stumbling-block to trade; minimal tariff standards and other regulations for trade between regional units; loans and investment policy; the movement of labor; the regulation of the manufacture of and trade in harmful commodities.

This sounds unduly ambitious, but I do not intend it so. We should be proceeding by the principle of organic growth—by enlarging the scale and scope of the efforts that have already been made and the experiments that have already been tried, whether they have been the innovations of the democratic countries or the totalitarians. We have our own experience to go by—the regulatory devices within our own economy, the economic agreements within the British Commonwealth, the work of the International Labor Office, the work of the Bank for International Settlements, the task recently begun by the Economic Defense Board under

Vice-President Wallace, the economic war co-operation of America with Britain, with Russia, with China. We have also what we can learn and adapt from the experience of the Soviets and the Nazis.

We have suffered from two weaknesses. Our very sense of the doom of our international economic system has taken the strength out of the movements to apply more effectively the controls inherent in it—controls intended to equalize trading power and make economic competition more effective. But also our sense of fear of the totalitarian systems, of barter trade and exchange controls and state trade monopolies, has led us to turn our faces stonily against whatever elements of merit they possess. We have here paralleled on a world scale the mistakes we have tended to make within our own national economy: we have not taken our system seriously enough to make it work (as witness what remained for Thurman Arnold to attempt it enforcing the anti-trust laws), and at the same time we have feared the challenge of the new economic systems to such an extent that we have fought the planning idea and surrendered most of the planning techniques to the dictatorial regimes. Both these faults are marks of a basic lack of confidence in our ability to shape our economic future. With that confidence we could strengthen what was practicable in what we have, and borrow techniques to correct the defects.

Eighth, within the regional and national economic units would lie the primary areas for economic planning and controls. Here we shall have to push further in America the anti-depression price and production strategies; here we shall have to continue the economic mechanisms intended to secure our people against want, and project those policies to a larger plane. Within America and within the economic region of which America forms part, we shall have to achieve guarantees of minimal living, housing, and health standards; we shall have to use our resources for whatever rehabilitation of housing and transport may be required; we shall have to point the way to Europe and other regions not only to replace what the war has destroyed, but to use the opportunity of the destruction itself to launch new programs of architectural planning.

The immediate post-war period will be economically a difficult one, because of economic demobilization and the need for gearing our industries once more to peacetime uses. Some of our industries will have been expanded beyond their normal peacetime capacity, others will have suffered from disuse. The important thing here is not to aim merely at a return to the *status quo ante bellum,* but to use the expanded capacity of particular industries, like steel, aluminum, magnesium, hydro-electric power, as new norms for the rest of the economy to aim at. Our agricultural industries too, whose production is being stepped up now for the purpose of supplying our allies and winning the war, will have the task of helping feed a desolated Europe, a ravaged Russia, a prostrate Asia; and even with new technologies it can retain its manpower afterward to supply a home market which higher living standards have created. In doing all this we shall also be able to raise the living standards in Latin American countries, buy more of their products and find there more markets for our own goods. The whole nature of the picture I have tried to draw implies a mutuality of relation between the three levels of nation, region, world; and it implies also that economic health or sickness will communicate itself from one level to the others.

To those who may ask how we shall be able to create economic order in and apply planning techniques to transnational units when we have not been successful at a national level, there can be no adequate answer. Undoubtedly America and England would both be in a better position to confront a post-war world economy if they had learned the arts of planning first within their own boundaries. I admit the force of the objection, and it makes me skeptical of the probabilities of any brave new economic world in the post-war period. Yet what I have sought to sketch as being in the realm of possibility is in no sense to be thought of as a paper scheme. It can be achieved only in step-by-step fashion, and only in building on what we already have. But there are certain assets to be placed on the probability side. A war economy necessarily involves the utmost in economic planning if the war is to be won; and if the war is, as it is likely to be, a protracted one, there will have been by its close a considerable habituation to the techniques of planning, both in America and in England. These habituations will have been strengthened by contact with the military and economic planning techniques of the formidable Nazi enemy whom we shall have been fighting, and of the impressive Soviet power which the strange logic of history has now made our ally. Moreover, we may well find that we can resolve difficulties on an international level that we have been unable to cope with on a national. That is, after all, the essence of the possibility of wartime planning in a capitalist democracy.

This would not be the first time in history that this sort of paradox was resolved. Progress is no straight-line affair. History often moves by crooked and circuitous routes. The imperatives of national planning have, in the democratic capitalist state, come up against formidable class and ideological resistances. It would not be unthinkable that the cause of national planning should be aided by the very fact that on a transnational level the imperatives were stronger and the resistance not so tenacious. Nor would it be unthinkable that the problem of making economic planning compatible with political democracy should be eased when a regional and international economic co-operation had lessened national rivalries and directed attention toward something other than the armament industries.

5

I have been speaking thus far of economic reconstruction and new construction. But that implies similar thought and creativeness on the political level. And so I turn to the question of the nation-state and national sovereignty, and to the movement for a federal world structure.

Let me start by saying that the primary task of government in the next century will be to make the new techniques of economic planning democratic, just as the primary task of economics must be to make the old techniques of political democracy efficient. And in seeking the conditions of democratic planning an ounce of history is worth a pound of abstraction. Every new political form carries within it the potentials for destructiveness and liberation. The nation-state was, at the time of its emergence, a revolutionary form of centralism. The power which in the feudal system had been both diffused and rigid became in the nation-state centralized and yet more flexible. The nation-state came thus as a potentially progressive force. Yet almost at the beginning it was pushed too far in the absolute monarchies. A century and more of struggle not unpunctuated by violence was required before the nation-state could become a democratic instrument—before it could thereby liberate the industrial and cultural potentials of its people.

But now the nation-state has once more proved inadequate to the new strains imposed on it. We seem to be groping for something like a continental state, on a scale large enough so that the problems of economic resources, markets, military strength, can be met. And within that we are groping for the political machinery of economic planning. The new form of state has already shown a tendency to be pushed to a reactionary extreme in fascism: *Lebensraum* has been linked not with the valid concept of units large enough for effective governmental action in the economic realm, but with conquest and the racial idea, and planning has been applied on the fullest scale only by the monopoly states. Yet the continental state and the planned economy may still have their democratic phase ahead of them. When that is achieved, the industrial and cultural potentials thus opened up are exciting.

A word of warning in this connection: I have several times written elsewhere that we live in a time of the breaking of nations and that the day of the nation-state is over. I have been assured that I am wrong, and one of my students has even shown me with scholarly thoroughness in statistical terms that the number of nation-states had been increasing rather than decreasing up to the present war. I have never had any intention of denying this. In fact, the very increase of nation-states, and the fragmentation of Europe that has resulted, have been at once symbol and concomitant of the weakness of the nation-state. For its weakness lies in the gap between its internal cultural tightness and the external imperatives of military power and economic effectiveness. Nor do I think that our own time will see the death of the nation-state. I say merely that its heyday is past, and that increasingly we shall be moving away from it to new political forms.

In its rise the nation-state developed the political ideology of sovereignty. The concept fluctuated between the sovereignty of the kingship and the sovereignty of the people, but the essential of both was that the sovereign power was complete and indivisible. Actually, however, far too much stress has been placed upon the concept: the important thing, as Harold Laski has suggested, is the variety of uses to which the concept has been put in the practice of the state, in order to bolster class rule and break up any attempt to challenge it.

But another difficulty with the sovereignty concept has been that for most states, recently, sovereignty has been an illusion. The distance has been a great one between the fictive sovereignty of a state like Rumania or Denmark and its capacity to maintain it in military and economic terms. Clinging to their phantom sovereignty, the small states were thus reduced to the diplomatic manipulation of their relative weaknesses, and were finally forced to cling to a neutrality that was at the mercy of the first great power that chose to break it. In the end they were annexed or crushed.

That is why I find it difficult to be much impressed by those who fear that the nation-state must surrender part of its sovereignty in the future, whether it forms part of a regional economic bloc, or a world economic framework, or a federal world state. Something of a pother was raised in England and in Eastern Europe by a leading article in the London *Times* for August 1, 1941, suggesting that Britain could not undertake to guarantee the integrity of the small nations of Eastern Europe, and that their fate was linked with Germany or Russia. For the thesis as stated, there can be no defense: given the tradition of the *Times*, it was mainly to be construed as an attempt to get out from under certain international obligations. Nevertheless, the tone of righteous indignation with which the leader was greeted by those speaking in behalf of "the rights and independence of small nations" was less than candid and less than realistic. If Britain and America were to assume a protective role, the sovereignty of the small nations would to that extent be qualified, just as much as if the Soviet Union were to assume a protective role. The solution is likely to lie, as I have suggested, in a pattern of regional economic collaboration within a larger pattern of world economic control, all this—as I shall suggest—within some framework of world federation.

But this too would involve a qualification of sovereignty. It has for some time been recognized that the weakness of the League of Nations lay in the unwillingness of the member states, particularly the great powers, to surrender any of their sovereignty by applying or subjecting themselves to the sanctions of the League. But as for the small nations, how can they be conceived of as losing anything by the partial surrender of what they never had fully? It is somewhat reminiscent of the surrender of the individualism of the worker when he receives a Social Security card, or of the trade-unionist when he makes himself subject to the findings of the National Labor

Relations Board. The truth is that the small states, and large as well, will have to surrender part of the fiction of sovereignty in order to get more of the reality of free national action.

Surrender it to what? I am convinced that the answer lies in an approach, some time in our century, to a federal world state. The federative principle, whatever its weaknesses for a country like America, has obvious advantages for the policing functions of a world state. It means the possibility of strictly delegated and limited powers, but with power enough at the center to perform the necessary functions. In this sense there is an essential soundness of direction in the various plans for Federal Union, along with the boldness of their conception and the fervor of their promotion.

If then there are still doubts in the minds of many about Federal Union it is due not to the federal structure itself, but to its other characteristics. One of the fatal objections to the League of Nations was that it was being used as a convenient tool for Anglo-French domination of the post-war period. There are grounds to suspect that Federal Union would be a similar instrument for Anglo-American domination. Though it is not decisive evidence, the character of the groups supporting it is of interest. While there is a sprinkling of labor support in England, there is almost none in America; and in the latter country the prestige of the movement derives from the support given it by the financial elite and their journalistic and political spokesmen who are pro-British in the war and for an "American century" after it. When I attended a New York meeting of Federal Union, I thought for a moment that I had blundered into a joint convention of the National Association of Manufacturers and the Willkie Republicans.

The fact that "Union Now" has recently become "Union Now with Great Britain" is not one to allay these fears. If such a union is intended to bring us into the war on Britain's side, which I happen to favor, I can only answer that there are no shortcuts to the war decision, which must be made openly and out of a fullness of conviction of American leadership and the American people. If it is intended to supply a cadre for world order in the immediate post-war period, I must again agree that America and Britain are the logical countries to assume that leadership. But I must add that they cannot build a structure of world order as the exclusive members of a club choosing later members by the process of cooptation. The requirements of internal democracy which a nation must fulfill before it can qualify for membership in Federal Union contain a narrow emphasis on the forms of political democracy. The emphasis should be rather on the temper of institutions, on the democratic aspirations of the vast mass of people, on whether the regime is making genuine efforts toward internal political liberty. By such a standard it should be possible to include China, Mexico and other Latin American countries, in addition to America and the members of the British family of nations. Nor, on the same principles, should the door be closed to the Soviet Union.

But even such considerations are still too formal to reach to the heart of the matter. My basic quarrel with Federal Union is that, to the extent that it provides for a world centralism, it is thinking in terms of a deliberative rather than a functional authority. And this, I think, not only strips it of its utility for the future, but is even a misreading of the spirit of the American Founding Fathers, from whom Federal Union derives so much.

The American Constitution, with its emphasis upon separated powers, and with its conception of government as a sequence of legislation, execution, and construction, is a poor model for a world state which will have to tackle problems more difficult than any in modern history. The essence of government today is to be found in an amalgamation of the consultative, the technical, and the administrative. That is true even of American national government: the measure of our capacity to survive has been our capacity to move away from our earlier Congressional government and our later government by judiciary toward a newer executive and administrative process. What is true of the American national state must be even truer of the world centralism we are envisaging. It will have difficult problems to deal with—of the recognition and support of constitutional governments in the defeated countries, of the supplying of a devastated and famished Europe and Asia with the means of sustaining life and rebuilding industry, of the rebuilding and replanning of whole cities and areas, of the movement of industries and the repatriation of peoples, of international policing, of trade and colonies and foreign investments. And in this context the emphasis of Federal Union upon an international legislative assembly, with its membership carefully distributed among the constituent nations, is something short of realism. Our recent experience with Congress should have indicated the failure of parliamentary decision in the problems with which modern governments are chiefly concerned.

I have said that the essence of modern government lies in a fusion of the consultative, the technical, and the administrative. An application of that principle to the federal world state would mean that the tasks I have described would have to be accomplished not in the forum of a world assembly, but by mixed commissions including political representatives of particular class and functional outlooks, technical advisers in the economic, military, labor, educational areas, and competent, trained administrators. This would provide at once political power and responsibility, technical *expertise*, administrative realism. I should be willing to trade the entire proceedings of a world assembly for even a small portion of these.

Nor need these be mainly paper constructs. One of the heritages of the era of constitutional government has been a reliance on the power of words on paper to constitute a polity. Woodrow Wilson's League of Nations group suffered from the same itch for Constitution-making, for the structural as contrasted with the organic. Less important than a ready-made Constitution is the succession of steps from where we are now, through economic cooperation with Latin America, war co-operation with Britain, Russia, China, the setting-up of an economic general staff not only for the war effort but for the post-war effort as well, the transition from the present "phantom" governments of the vanquished states in London and the economic and military missions in London, Moscow, Washington, Chungking, to the mixed commissions I have been describing, the institutionalization of these makeshift arrangements until they become an organic part of the national governments concerned and therefore of the world state. A Peace Conference there will have to be; but we must not depend on it to take more than a few preliminary post-war steps. The creative work will have to be done outside the feverish atmosphere of a Peace Conference, vulnerable as it is to every pressure and intrigue.

That means that we shall have to envisage a transition period between the end of the war and the effective functioning of the new world economic arrangements and political mechanisms. In that transition period the nations that have the economic power, the political prestige, the moral strength in the world will have to take the pragmatic leadership. They will have to solve the enormously difficult problem of finding or setting up governments in the defeated countries with which they can deal, a problem serious enough in nations like France and Rumania, but almost insuperable in Germany itself. Ferrero has suggested, in his recent *Reconstruction of Europe,* that the European powers faced the same problem after the Napoleonic wars, and that it was the genius of Talleyrand that found the solution. However that may be, the test we shall do best to use is not merely legitimacy in the line of pre-Hitler succession, but the extent to which the government has the confidence of the large majority of its people, the extent to which its members can point to genuine anti-fascist and pro-democratic behavior in the past, the extent to which they can combine firm and realistic action with strength enough to brook an opposition.

In all that I have said the accent has been on a pragmatic effectiveness within a democratic framework. That was, I think, the spirit of those who founded our government. They used the best wisdom of their time in an approach to the problems of their time. We cannot be content with reverting to their political forms in our approach to the problems of our time. It will be better for us to borrow their spirit than their solutions.

6

There remains the question of the auspices under which all this can be accomplished. That they must be democratic is a first principle. But one does violence to the term by speaking of an "American century," or dreaming of a British-American condominium over the world. Democracy is a world force, capable of liberating still untapped productive and moral energies all over the world. A democratic post-war world would mean one which put into power in every nation, and at the world-center, those groups that best understood and expressed the felt needs and the possibilities of the culture.

There has been a good deal of talk, and not all of it unjustified, of the gap between have and have-not nations. To move from the fact of possession to the fact of social function is as necessary in the international as in the national sphere. Similarly one can draw a parallel between the movement within a nation away from the manipulation and exploitation of scarcities to the fullest expansion of productive capacities, and the similar movement in the international sphere. The democracy of the future will mean the sort of national and world government which allows for these directions. And this must mean a transfer of governmental function to the groups which have the technical skill and the knowledge of the industrial and administrative arts, the groups that are untrammeled by the vested ideas that have not worked in the past and unblinded by disabilities of social vision, the groups which are willing to convert into general living standards and cultural potentialities the goods and services whose production they organize.

Without an effective transfer of social function and political power to these groups and their leaders, the present war against fascism will not finally have been settled.

1941

PART TWO

The Voyage of the Mind

1

---◆◆◆---

Machiavelli and Machiavellism[1]

1

WE LIVE today in the shadow of a Florentine, the man who above all others taught the world to think in terms of cold political power. His name was Niccolò Machiavelli, and he was one of those rare intellectuals who write about politics because they have had a hand in politics and learned what it is about. His portraits show a thin-faced, pale little man, with a sharp nose, sunken cheeks, subtle lips, a discreet and enigmatic smile, and piercing black eyes that look as if they knew much more than they were willing to tell.

There is little we can say for certain about his early years. He was born in 1469, of a family that was part of the small and impoverished gentry of Florence. His father, a lawyer, tried desperately to keep his family from slipping down into the ranks of the middle class. Niccolò must have had the sort of boyhood that most children had in the homes and on the streets of Florence in the *quattrocento*. He steps onto the threshold of history in 1498, already a young man of twenty-nine, only a month after the execution of the friar-politician Savonarola, who had dominated the last decades of the dying fifteenth century in Florence. At that time Machiavelli got a minor job as secretary to the Second Chancery—an office he was to hold for fourteen years.

He was what we should call today a brain-truster and bureaucrat. He loved his job as idea-man for some of the stuffed-shirt Florentine politicians. And because he was so good at it, the stuffed shirts came to regard him as someone on whose shoulders they could place the burden of administrative work—the man who got

---

[1] This first appeared as the introduction to my Modern Library edition of Machiavelli's *The Prince* and *The Discourses*.

papers drawn up and orders sent out and correspondence carried on and records kept. In due time—since Florence like the other Italian city-states in an age of intrigue depended on skillful diplomacy for its survival—they broadened the scope of his work and sent him on diplomatic missions. In the course of a decade he visited as envoy every important city-state in Italy and several of the courts outside Italy. He sent back reports which may still be read for their tough understanding of diplomatic realities. Invariably he acquitted himself well; he met the movers and shakers of the world, and the narrow horizon of the Florentine expanded into the vistas of the European state-system.

It was thus that Machiavelli was in a position to become the first modern analyst of power. Where others looked at the figureheads, he kept his eyes fixed behind the scenes. He sought the ultimate propulsion of events. He wanted to know what made things tick; he wanted to take the clock of the world to pieces to find out how it worked. He went on diplomatic missions, organized the armies of Florence, carried through successfully the long protracted siege of Pisa. Yet always he was concerned with what these experiences could teach him about the nature of power. In an age of portraiture it was natural that he too should be a painter, but his subjects never knew they were sitting for him. He studied Pope Julius II, the secular princes, the *condottieri;* above all he studied Caesar Borgia, the Duke Valentino, who came closer to embodying the naked ideal of power than any other person Machiavelli had met. There was in Machiavelli, as in Savonarola, an intense and searing flame, but it was a secular flame, and the things it fed on were not such things as religious dreams are made of.

A man like this might have lived out his days, tasted somewhat of power, known what it was to run a state from behind the scenes as an underling, and died leaving behind him some excellent diplomatic reports, a few plays, and some polished verses in the style of the time. But Machiavelli's destiny was different. The petty dynasties and bourgeois merchant princes who ruled the Italian city-states played their fateful game of chessboard diplomacy all through the fifteenth century until finally in the sixteenth it led to disaster for all of them. This is not the place to review the succession of maneuvers by which France, Spain, Germany, and the Papacy vied for supremacy over Italy. When, after the League of Cambrai, a split developed between France and the Papacy, Florence adhered to its basic alliance with France. When Julius II drove the French from Italy, Florence was lost; and not even the new citizen army that Machiavelli had trained could withstand the combined force of the Pope's prestige and his Swiss mercenaries. One of the conditions of the papal peace was the restoration of the Medici in Florence. And so Machiavelli, who had always been stanchly republican and anti-Medici, found himself in 1512 at the age of forty-three a dejected liberal without a job in a world that had come tumbling down about his ears.

He tried to make his peace with the Medici, but to no avail. There was a witch-hunting atmosphere in Florence, and everyone was suspect who had ever been identified with the liberal cause. Two ardent young republican conspirators had evidently made a list of those on whom they might rely for aid, and Machiavelli's name was on the list. He was arrested, drawn by the rope, tortured. But he was plainly innocent, and finally was released. He slunk off to a small farm near Florence, and for the next fourteen years until his death his letters are full of fervent pleas to be reinstated in the favor of the Medici and the Pope, plans to recommend himself to them, strategies by which his abilities could be brought to their attention. It is, as so many commentators have pointed out, neither a pretty nor a graceful picture. Yet we must reflect that Machiavelli out of office felt himself a vessel without use. The letters he has left us during this period, for all their bitter pride and the unbreakable gaiety of their style, show that reinstatement in office spelled for him nothing less than a return to life.

Ironically, it was this period of his disgrace that represents the high point of his creative power. The enforced leisure compelled him to fall back on himself. Finding himself after fourteen years deprived of his job, he felt shut in like a bird in an iron cage. The result was his books—his solitary song. More and more he retreated to his study and his mind. From them came *The Prince*, the *Art of War*, *The Discourses*, the *History of Florence;* various plays, among them a first-rate comedy, *Mandragola;* poetry, stories, biographical sketches. The civil servant, the politician, the diplomat, the military organizer had become a man of letters *malgré lui.*

There remains only the final ironic act. In 1527 the papal armies were defeated and Rome was sacked by the soldiers of Charles V.

At this the popular party in Florence overthrew the Medici and for a short time restored democratic government. Machiavelli had hurried back to Florence, eager to regain his post as secretary. But he never stood a real chance. *The Prince,* circulated in manuscript, had made him enemies; the small dull men who had it in their power to dispense office feared his brilliance and his wit. Mercifully Machiavelli fell sick and never learned that the final vote of the Council was overwhelmingly against him. Before the news came he was dead. And so a man who had hoped for the ultimate glory of being restored to the Florentine civil service died, leaving behind him nothing but the memory of a few books he had written in his exile.

2

There is a famous letter from Machiavelli to his friend Vettori, the Florentine ambassador at the Papal Court in Rome, in which he describes the tenor of his life on the farm, and the relief that he finds among books in his study.

On the threshold I slip off my day's clothes with their mud and dirt, put on my royal and curial robes, and enter, decently accoutered, the ancient courts of men of old, where I am welcomed kindly and fed on that fare which is mine alone, and for which I was born: where I am not ashamed to address them and ask them the reasons for their action, and they reply considerately; and for two hours I forget all my cares, I know no more trouble, death loses its terrors: I am utterly translated in their company. And since Dante says that we can never attain knowledge unless we retain what we hear, I have noted down the capital I have accumulated from their conversation and composed a little book, *De Principatibus,* in which I probe as deeply as I can the consideration of this subject, discussing what a principality is, the variety of such states, how they are won, how they are held, how they are lost. . . .[2]

It was the period of the great humanist revival of ancient learning. The books Machiavelli read were the traditional Latin authors and (since he probably did not know Greek) the Greek authors in Latin translation. And as he read there came crowding back into his mind the varied experiences of his life; and out of the fusion of reading and experience came new insights into politics, at first

[2] I use here the translation made by Ralph Roeder, in his *The Man of the Renaissance.*

jotted down in the shape of notes which eventually formed themselves slowly into a vast book.

That book was not *The Prince*. There are clear indications that Machiavelli started to write what afterward became *The Discourses,* planned on a grand scale. But as he wrote in his study, things were happening in the world outside. There was a new Pope in Rome, a new regime in Italy; the Pope was carving out a new state in Italy and placing his nephew Giuliano at its head. What more natural than to wish to influence this new prince and recommend oneself to his favor? Perhaps one could once more thus have a hand in world affairs, and—who knows?—set in motion a train of forces that might arrest the decadence of the Italian communes and free Italy from the invaders. But *The Discourses* were too vast to finish quickly, and their form was far too sprawling for the purpose. And so, carving out of *The Discourses* certain sections and ideas, Machiavelli proceeded to recast them in the form of a short treatise, *De Principatibus*. Eventually the title was changed from the Latin abstract to the Italian personal, *Il Principe*. The book was written in 1513 at an almost white heat, in what was probably only a few months. Dedicated to Lorenzo de' Medici, it was presented to him and by him neglected and forgotten. It was, however, circulated in manuscript during Machiavelli's lifetime, surreptitiously copied and corrupted, and achieved an underground fame. Since his death it has been one of the half-dozen books that have done most to shape Western thought.

What gives *The Prince* its greatness? It is not a great formal treatise on politics. It is bare of any genuine insights into social organization as the basis of politics. It has very little passion in it —so little that, because the final chapter crackles and glows with Machiavelli's fervor for the unification of Italy, some commentators have suggested that it is not an organic part of the book but was added as an afterthought. It has been pretty well proved, moreover, by recent scholarship that Machiavelli's pamphlet on princes is not even original in form. It is part of a whole traditional literature on princes that stretches back to the Middle Ages. The structure of the book, its division into chapters, and even some of the chapter headings follow the conventional form of what has been called the mirror-of-princes literature: the discussion of how to rule conquered territory, what advisers a prince should rely on, how he should conduct himself among the intrigues of diplomacy, whether he should depend mainly on fortified castles or entrenched camps in warfare.

But the intellectual spirit that pervades the book is quite another matter. Here we are in the presence of something little short of a revolution in political thinking. The humanists who had written books about princes had written in the idealistic and scholastic medieval tradition; they were ridden by theology and metaphysics. Machiavelli rejected metaphysics, theology, idealism. The whole drift of his work is toward a political realism, unknown to the formal writing of his time.

I say unknown to the *formal writing*. That does not mean it was unknown to his time. Machiavelli was expressing the realism that characterized the actual politics and the popular ethos of his time. Take, for example, some sentences from the famous eighteenth chapter, "In What Way Princes Must Keep Faith." The Achilles myth of the centaur, he writes, teaches us that we are "semi-animal, semi-human" and that "a prince must know how to use both natures. . . . A prince being thus obliged to know well how to act as a beast must imitate the fox and the lion, for the lion cannot protect himself from traps, and the fox cannot defend himself from wolves. . . . A prudent ruler ought not to keep faith when by so doing it would be against his interests, and when the reasons which made him bind himself no longer exist. . . . It is not, therefore, necessary for a prince to have all the above-named qualities, but it is very necessary to seem to have them." When Machiavelli wrote thus he was not creating a new ethos, whatever we may think of it; he was expressing the ethos of the late *quattrocento* and the early *cinquecento* not only in Florence but in the whole of Italy. Machiavelli was, in short, the child of his time—neither better nor worse than the contemporary intellectuals, politicians, diplomats, and civil servants.

He was able, using the traditional humanist literary forms, to pour into them a realistic political spirit which his age was acting on but which had never before been so well expressed in political thought. He had the daring to turn against the whole idealistic preoccupation of the humanists. He had the clear-eyed capacity to distinguish between man as he ought to be and man as he actually is—

between the ideal form of institutions and the pragmatic conditions under which they operate.

But if we have come close to his greatness here, we have not wholly succeeded in ensnaring it. There have been other men who have expressed the consciousness of their period. They have in very few instances achieved the highest rank in the history of ideas. And while those who content themselves with seeing Machiavelli thus in the context of his time may succeed thereby in countering the charges made against him of being a sort of anti-Christ who had created a new immorality, they do not thereby get at the roots of his greatness. To take a further step in our analysis, we must see that Machiavelli, while he expressed the ethical consciousness of his time, was also a good deal ahead of his time in other respects. He lived in a period when economic growth had gone so far as to burst the bonds of existing political forms. What gave the city-states of Italy their Renaissance grandeur was not some mysterious flowering of the humanist spirit at the time. It was the fact that with the opening of the East by the crusades, the break-up of the manorial economy, and the growth of trade and handicraft manufacture, the cities of Italy found themselves strategically placed with respect to the world trade routes. There followed what amounted to a communal revolution in Italy and a reorganization of the government of the Italian city-states under democratic and guild forms. The expansion of the economic power of these cities went on apace into the end of the fifteenth century. By the time Machiavelli came to the maturity of his powers, a sharp contraction had set in. The expansion had gone as far as the political limits of the communal organization allowed.

If the Italian city-states had been able to adjust themselves to the needs of an expanding economy by resolving their rivalries and joining in a united political structure, Italy might have been spared the two and a half centuries of humiliation and cultural aridness which followed the fall of the communes. Elsewhere, however—in France, in England, in Spain—the expansion of political forms kept pace with the economic expansion. Machiavelli lived in what, with our historical perspective, we now see to have been the beginnings of the Western nation-state system. As we know it, he was himself only dimly aware of it. He was in no sense an articulate nationalist, and the fervor of his national feeling has probably been overestimated by commentators. But two elements were historically to enter into the composition of the Western nation-state. One was national unity and the idea of a common tongue, common culture, and common economic limits. The second was a realistic concentration of power at the center in order to break down divisive barriers. Machiavelli only dimly foresaw nationalism, but he very clearly expressed the second element—the use of power from the center, the methods by which unity could be achieved.

Therein lies the importance of *The Prince* in the subsequent history of the Western world. Machiavelli wrote a grammar of power, not only for the sixteenth century, but for the ages that have followed. Read *The Prince* today and you will be struck by the detonations which its sentences set off in the corridors of our experiences with present-day rulers. Machiavelli seen only in his historical context does become intelligible; but his greatness does not emerge until we see that when he wrote his grammar of power he came close to setting down the imperatives by which men govern and are governed in political communities, whatever the epoch and whatever the governmental structure.

The Prince has become, for better or worse, a symbol of a whole body of literature and a whole approach to politics. Just as in literature and art we must always face, under whatever names, the polar conflict of classic and romantic, so in the history of political thinking we have always faced the polar conflict between the ethical and the ruthlessly realistic. *The Prince* is part of the world's polemical literature because it places itself squarely in the ranks of realism. It brushes aside, with an impatience in which Machiavelli scarcely cares to conceal his disdain, the tender-mindedness of reformers and idealists.

There is in all of us, along with the ethical and normative strain, a strain of hard-headedness and of the acceptance of the frame within which we have to work. One can trace it back to Aristophanes and the way in which he always deflated contemporary dreams and illusions by getting back to the essential limits of the human animal. And in every generation since his the young men have been divided between the pursuit of some passionate ideal and the hard-bitten inquiry into how things actually get accomplished in a real world. It is to that pole of our political thinking that *The Prince* gravitates. As long as this strain remains in political thinking, so long will *The Prince* be found to have expressed in undying prose its intensity and its temper.

3

Very few who talk of *The Prince* have ever read more than a few sentences in it. But fewer still have read the work of Machiavelli which, without having the same éclat in history as *The Prince,* is nevertheless the saner, the more rounded, the more comprehensive work. I refer to *The Discourses*. It was the longer work on which Machiavelli was engaged when, because of political opportunism, he made a sudden sortie to finish *The Prince*. He came back to it later. He seems to have worked on it intermittently for the better part of a decade. It bears to *The Prince* much the same relation that Marx's *Capital* bears to the *Communist Manifesto*. It is the considered, comprehensive treatise. Outwardly a commentary (unfinished) on the first ten books of Livy's *History of Rome,* it is actually a set of *pensées,* loosely gathered together into a book—reflections on politics which use Roman history as a point of departure. It is clearly not a book which ever had a chance for real fame. The very people who have written most about *The Prince* seem to have neglected *The Discourses,* and for the most part very few seem to have read it. When we talk of Machiavellism, it is *The Prince* we have in mind. And that is perhaps as it should be. But when we talk of Machiavelli, we must have *The Discourses* in mind as well. For if we are to judge a man it is fairer to judge him by the book into which he sought to put his whole system of politics rather than by the pamphlet which he dashed off to win a friend and influence a personage.

Scholarship has not done well by *The Discourses*. The scholars pay lip service to it as the larger frame of reference within which *The Prince* can be understood. Yet having done so, they go on to talk of *The Prince*. Its structure is difficult and fragmentary. Precepts drawn from Livy form the chapter heads. There are whole sections that might easily be cut out to improve the book. A good editor today, receiving such a manuscript, would probably ask the author to cut it down to one-third and pull it together a bit. Yet once read, *The Discourses* stay in your mind as an impressive intellectual experience. And once you have read them, whatever impression you have formed of Machiavelli through reading *The Prince* is rather drastically changed.

What was the intellectual tradition that lay back of *The Discourses?* In the case of *The Prince,* it was the mirror-of-princes medieval and humanist literature. Felix Gilbert has suggested in a recent article, and I think the suggestion is a sound one, that research into the literature of "the good state," both in Italian and in Greater European thought, might yield exciting results for an understanding of *The Discourses.*

However that may be, what are the basic ideas of *The Discourses?* I should say the following: first, the superiority of the democratic republic to every other political form; second, the ultimate reliance of even despotic and authoritarian regimes on mass consent; third, the primary political imperative of cohesiveness, organic unity in a state, stability, and survival; fourth, the great role of leadership (which Machiavelli calls the role of the lawgiver) in achieving this cohesiveness and survival; fifth, the imperative of military power in insuring survival and the need for putting it on a mass base (he felt that war was essential to the state); sixth, the use of a national religion for state purposes, and the choice of one not for its supernatural validity, but for its power as a myth in unifying the masses and cementing their morale (Machiavelli's count against Christianity, like that of Nietzsche after him, was that by glorifying humility and pacifism and the weaker virtues it dulled the fighting edge of a state); seventh, the need in the conduct of even a democratic state for the will to survive, and therefore for ruthless instead of half-hearted measures when ruthless measures were necessary; eighth, the idea—later to be found in Vico and in our day in Spengler— of the cyclical rise and fall of civilizations due to decadence and corruption and the reinvigoration of the new.

This is, of course, only a sampling of the vast riches to be found in *The Discourses.* It is not a single-themed, monolithic book, such as Marx or Mill wrote. It has a catholicity and vastness of resource which will make it yield different discoveries for every reader and on every reading.

This is not the place to discuss the themes I have mentioned. I want only to say that if *The Prince* is great because of its intensity, *The Discourses* are great because of their variety; if *The Prince* is great because it is polemical, *The Discourses* are great because they have balance; and if *The Prince* is great because it gives us the grammar of power for a government, *The Discourses* are great because they give us the philosophy of organic unity not in a government but in a state, and the conditions under which alone a culture can survive.

4

"The authentic interpreter of Machiavelli," Lord Acton has written in his erudite preface to Burd's great edition of *The Prince,* "is the whole of later history." In the same essay he strings out a remarkable series of quotations from the great writers and statesmen of the past three or four centuries which show the impact that Machiavelli had on the European mind. The history of that impact may be called the history of Machiavellism.

It is clear that one element in the denunciation of Machiavellism was the use of that symbol as a weapon of the Counter-Reformation. Machiavelli was utterly secular in his thinking. And when the Church, in assuming the aggressive against the religious reformers, sought something that could be set up as a secular Devil-symbol in contrast to the ethical teachings of religion, it easily found what it sought in Machiavelli's writings. At the same time also the symbol could serve to brand with infamy the methods that were being used to set up and consolidate the new nation-states of Europe, the power of whose sovereigns was one of the great threats to church power. And so the Church statesmen who had at first accepted *The Prince,* then ignored it, finally decided to attack it. Under Leo, Clement, Paul III, it was tolerated. But under Paul IV, in 1557, a generation after the Florentine's death, Machiavelli was put on the Index. What is somewhat ironic about this is that the Church princes, like the secular princes, were among the principal followers of Machiavelli's precepts. As Lord Acton points out, the arguments used to excuse the massacres of the religious wars were drawn from Machiavelli.

There is another important element in the history of Machiavellism—so far, at least, as the English-speaking secular world is concerned. Machiavelli entered our consciousness largely through the Elizabethan drama. Wyndham Lewis has written a provocative, although erratic, book with the title *The Lion and the Fox.* It takes its point of departure from a fact that had been long known to scholars—that the figure of Machiavelli dominated the imagination of the Tudor dramatists. The meeting between Italian Renaissance culture and the Tudor mind contained an element of shock arising from novelty. The English were, like all cultural borrowers, at once attracted and repelled by the Italians. Moreover, Tudor drama was enormously sensitive to world currents. The result was that not only were there, as Meyer has pointed out, some 400 direct references to Machiavelli in the Elizabethan literature, but the Machiavelli figure, whether directly or indirectly, dominates it as does no other. Iago was drawn from Machiavelli, as was Barabas. Webster, Massinger, Ford, Marston, Ben Jonson, Shakespeare— they were all fascinated by the image they constructed of subtle cunning, of treachery, of the gap between outward seeming and inward being, all of which they thought of as Machiavellism. To the Tudor imagination, which has in turn so influenced our own, Machiavelli was the symbol of the decadence, the corruption, the unfathomable depths of Renaissance Italy. It was probably due to the fusion of the influence of church and state that Machiavelli became associated in the popular mind with the Devil himself. "Old Nick" became an epithet equally applicable to both.

It may therefore seem surprising that Tudor England had scarcely read Machiavelli at all. *The Discourses* were not translated into English until 1636, *The Prince* until 1640. The Elizabethans got their knowledge of Machiavelli from a French book attacking him, Gentillet's *Anti-Machiavel*. And Gentillet gave only enough of Machiavelli to distort him, and not enough to make him either comprehensible or human. This should not surprise us. It is the essence of a symbol that its outlines should be shadowy. What has first been sifted through the intellect is unlikely to ensnare the imagination. Had the Elizabethans really read *The Discourses* and *The Prince,* they would no doubt have been more just to the author, but their drama would have suffered and one of its type figures would have had to be scrapped. By the time the translations were made, it was unfortunately—or shall we say fortunately?—too late to affect either their intelligence or their art. The symbol had become fixed.

I have spoken of various historical reasons why the Elizabethans should have responded to the Machiavelli symbol, and Wyndham Lewis adds the fascination which the diabolical holds for the Puritan genius in every age. Yet we come closer to the core of the truth when we remember that the Elizabethans had the same perverse and feverish preoccupation with the theme of death. And, I am inclined to guess, for much the same reason. It *unmasks* the human animal. But for this very reason Machiavelli became the subject of attack from still another source—the seventeenth- and eighteenth-century absolute monarchy. To be sure, we have a long roster of despots—benevolent and other—who are reputed to have drunk in Machiavelli with their mothers' milk and were known as "Machiavellistae." But we must remember, so black had Machiavelli's reputation become that if you wanted to hit at a monarch, you had only to start a whispering campaign to the effect that he ruled according to Machiavelli's grammar. The supreme irony was that Frederick the Great of Prussia, while still a young man, wrote a refutation of Machiavelli. As Frederick's later career showed, Machiavelli had adumbrated the methods of the benevolent despots only too well. His offense had been only to unmask them, to lay bare to the world the mechanisms of power which were behind the authority of the ruler. Voltaire encouraged the young prince to write his treatise; but his comment on Frederick in his *Memoirs* is delicious:

If Machiavelli had had a prince for disciple, the first thing he would have recommended him to do would have been to write a book against Machiavellism.

But if Machiavelli was a butt and a tool in the Age of Reason, he came into his own in the nineteenth century in the age of the new nationalism. Men rediscovered Machiavelli the liberal, Machiavelli the democrat, Machiavelli the nationalist patriot. In Germany, during and after the Napoleonic wars, the intellectuals rediscovered Machiavelli, and turned their fine gifts of scholarship toward him, with the characteristic result of a spate of Machiavelli studies. The leader was Fichte, who made an analysis of Machiavelli part of his famous *Address to the German Nation;* and Hegel, who following Machiavelli made a cult of the state, taught that "the course of world history stands outside of virtue, blame, and justice." And in Italy Cavour and the leaders of the Risorgimento found in Machiavelli their ideal symbol. What both the Italians and the Germans sought in him was what they needed for their movements

of national liberation: the stress on cohesiveness, the pursuit of
the main chance, the prime virtue of political survival. The Germans took from him the concept of *Staatsräson*—opportunism justified by reasons of state policy; and in the field of foreign affairs,
Realpolitik.

In country after country the rediscovery of Machiavelli seems to
have had an almost magical efficacy in stirring latent national energies. And to complete the history of Machiavellism, I need only
point out that for the collectivist movements as well he became
an evocative figure. H. G. Wells, in what is one of his really first-
rate political novels, *The New Machiavelli,* dreamed of a "strengthened and perfected state" that blends Machiavelli with English
Fabian humanitarianism. Both Lenin and Mussolini did their
work in the shadow of the Florentine. And Rauschning, in his
Voice of Destruction, which recounts his conversations with Hitler,
asserts that Hitler ranks Machiavelli with Wagner as among the
influences shaping his thought and that he used to keep a copy of
The Prince at his bedside.

5

It has become a truism to point out that Machiavelli is the father
of power politics. Whether a truism or not, it is still true. Machiavelli, as ambassador and administrator, could not afford to do any
wishful thinking. If he did, the penalty was swift and merciless—
failure. Which may not be a bad idea as a school for political theorists. But to say that he was the father of power politics may have
curiously erroneous implications—as if we were to say that Harvey
was the father of the circulation of the blood. Power politics existed before Machiavelli was ever heard of; it will exist long after
his name is only a faint memory. What he did, like Harvey, was to
recognize its existence and subject it to scientific study. And so his
name has come to be associated with it. And in our time, when
Japan seeks to crush China, when Italy pounces on Abyssinia, Germany on Austria, Czechoslovakia, Poland, both on Spain, Russia on
Finland, when England gambles for its imperial position with the
destinies of small nations, we cry "Machiavelli."

To be sure, Machiavelli's role is not wholly innocent. His grammar of power brought a whole new world to consciousness. With
one of Molière's characters, the princes of Europe became aware

that all their lives they had been talking prose. And the awareness led them to perfect their prose. Frederick, Richelieu, Napoleon, Bismarck, Clemenceau, Lenin, Stalin, Mussolini, Hitler have gone to school to Machiavelli. But by bringing the world to this awareness Machiavelli did what every creative figure does. We might as well blame Shakespeare because, by creating Hamlet, he has intensified the agony of the indecisive and divided liberal.

Machiavelli has also been accused, and it is true, of being the father of the martial spirit, of propaganda techniques, and of the totalitarian spirit. But here again he anticipated things latent in the very texture of society and the state. A reading of *The Discourses* will show that his thinking fathered many movements, democratic as well as dictatorial. The common meaning he has for democrats and dictators alike is that, whatever your ends, you must be clear-eyed and unsentimental in pursuit of them and you must rest your power ultimately on a cohesive principle.

May I venture a guess as to the reason why we still shudder slightly at Machiavelli's name? It is not only the tradition I have described. It is our recognition that the realities he described *are* realities; that men, whether in politics, in business, or in private life, do *not* act according to their professions of virtue; that leaders in every field seek power ruthlessly and hold on to it tenaciously; that the masses who are coerced in a dictatorship have to be wooed and duped in a democracy; that deceit and ruthlessness invariably crop up in every state; and that while the art of being ruled has always been a relatively easy one, the art of ruling ourselves is monstrously difficult. Machiavelli today confronts us with the major dilemma of how to adapt our democratic techniques and concepts to the demands of a world in which, as never before, naked power politics dominates the foreign field and determined oligarchies struggle for power internally. It is not an easy dilemma to resolve. And in a sense, just as the seventeenth- and eighteenth-century monarchs hated and feared Machiavelli because he had exposed their authority to the world, so today we hate and fear him because he has exposed our dilemma and made it visible to ourselves and the world.

Let us be clear about one thing: ideals and ethics are important in politics as norms, but they are scarcely effective as techniques. The successful statesman is an artist, concerned with nuances of public mood, approximations of operative motives, guess-work as to the tactics of his opponents, back-breaking work in unifying his own side by compromise and concession. Religious reformers have often succeeded in bringing public morale closer to some ethical norm; they have never succeeded as statesmen. Even in the theocracies of Savonarola in Florence, Cromwell and the Puritans in England, in our own New England colonies, the men of God, when they came to power, learned to play the game of power. The only difference between them and others is that, since they had a certitude of having a pipeline to God, they did not have to reckon at all with the uneasy factor of their conscience. The most destructive imperialisms of the world have been those of men who have elevated their preferences to the pinnacle of moral imperatives and who have then confidently proceeded to impose those imperatives on others.

Today, as in Machiavelli's day, our world has become a collection of principalities struggling for survival, maneuvering for position, fighting over spoils. The scale is bigger but the proportions are the same. The strong men have come forward in every state, using the rhetoric of mass interest and national glory to extend their power and entrench their class. The first law of internal policy is to hold on to power; of external policy, to extend your imperialism.

Let it be said that Machiavelli in his day blundered as we are doing in ours. He could not make up his mind whether what he wanted was a democratic Florence or a unified Italy. I think he must have felt, when he wrote *The Prince,* that democracy would somehow follow if unity were achieved. There are some today who feel the same way about the attempts in Europe to achieve continental integration, whether by the imperatives of England, Germany, or Russia. There are others who feel that no integration is worth the candle if democratic rights and human decencies are scrapped in the process. In Machiavelli's writing you will find both attitudes, but more often the first.

This raises sharply, of course, the interminable question of ends and means. Machiavelli would, I think, shrug his shoulders at the whole problem. He himself, he would say, was an observer of politics. And as such he would find it irrelevant to impose his own ethical patterns on the torrential flow of world history. It is for that very reason that Machiavellism, after everything has been said about it, fails to be an adequate philosophy for a way of life. Men are not only observers, not only participants; they are also valuing individuals. Without judgments life loses its hierarchical quality of being a choice between preferences. And losing that, it loses its savor.

Machiavelli sought to distinguish the realm of what ought to be from the realm of what is. He rejected the first for the second. But there is a third realm: the realm of what can be. It is in that realm that what one might call a humanist realism can lie. The measure of man is his ability to extend this sphere of the socially possible. We can start with our democratic values, and we can start also with Machiavelli's realism about tough-minded methods. And we may yet find that an effective pursuit of democratic values is possible within the scope of a strong and militant state and an unsentimental realism about human motives.

1940

2

The Mind and Faith of
Justice Holmes

THIS is perhaps not the time to be thinking of someone who seems so removed from military technology and power politics and the totalitarian outlook as does Justice Holmes. Yet I must confess shamelessly that I have just finished reading through the body of his published work—the speeches, essays, letters, judicial opinions—with a view to making a book of selections of these that will convey some sense of the whole man. And I have come away from Holmes, as have so many others, with a feeling of new strength.

Of the recent events which have put us in a position to reappraise Holmes's meaning, I shall not deal with his magnificent exchange of letters with Sir Frederick Pollock. But there is the Supreme Court revolution, which has put Holmes's role in our constitutional history in a new perspective. And there is the war, bringing an intellectual climate to American life in which much of Holmes that once seemed strange now wears an aspect of immediacy. These two trends in our internal and external affairs, which seem unrelated, cross in Justice Holmes's personality. We have tended in the past to separate Holmes the judicial craftsman from the Holmes who fought in the Civil War and retained throughout his life, as a fighting faith, an almost mystical sense of dedication. But since Holmes was more than anything an integrated person it will be well to seek the principle that joined his mind and faith.

It is well recognized among the lawyers that the new doctrinal directions of the present Supreme Court spell a return to Holmes. Five years ago those who followed the New Deal constitutional crisis were overcome by a sense of sadness at what seemed the decisive defeat of the Holmes tradition. The Court majority, dominated by the humanism of Justices Van Devanter, McReynolds, and Butler, and expressing itself in the intellect and style of Justices Sutherland and Roberts, was not only turning its face stonily against the American future, but even against the best past of the Court itself. But today when the Court assembles for conference the true Chief Justice is the image of Holmes that all but one or two of its members carry in their thinking. Rarely has a more certain defeat been followed by a more complete triumph.

What was there in his thinking tough and enduring enough to survive the bleak years of our history that his judicial career spanned? All his life as a judge he fought an unequal fight against the blindness and smugness of those who had it in their power to shape American action. He had no self-pity about it and never saw himself as a martyr. Yet his confident manner cannot conceal that there was no time at which he could, in the crucial cases, rest on the knowledge of a clear majority behind him. Even in his twenty years on the Supreme Court of Massachusetts he was on the dissenting side in the cases involving social issues—municipal coal and wood yards, the woman suffrage referendum, the great labor cases of *Vegelahn v. Guntner* and *Plant v. Woods*. He was no novice at lonely fighting when, in 1902, he came to Washington and the United States Supreme Court at the age of sixty-one. He smiled at the idea of himself as a reformer, and yet there was so much in him of the judicial craftsman that there could not help being a good deal of the judicial innovator. For one who, as he wrote Pollock, had "broken his heart in trying to make every word living and real," it was a bitter thing to read the slack and stupid notices, whether of praise or disapproval, that greeted his appointment. "If I haven't done my share in the way of putting in new and remodeling old thought for the last twenty years then I delude myself."

The Supreme Court, when he joined it, was one of the worst in our history. The two great antagonists who had given it, in the eighties, some measure of greatness—Justices Miller and Field—were gone. With the exception of Harlan and White, the men on it were mediocre minds against which Holmes measured his own with assurance. At the beginning he was caught up in the excitement of the cases that came before him. But soon what was essential in his nature found that it could not stomach what was essential in the nature of the majority. And so he hung up his pennon, without fanfare but unmistakably, in the Lochner dissent in 1905. It was the case in which the Court had invalidated a New York statute establishing a ten-hour law for men in bakeries. Holmes did more than dissent. Like an archaeologist he dug beneath the subsoil of the majority opinion to reveal the buried cities of Herbert Spencer's intellectual universe. He laid bare the moral imperialism by which five judges sought, under the guise of the legal doctrine of freedom of contract, to impose a body of economic thought and a structure of economic power on the majority of the people. With the Lochner dissent, it is often said, a new jurisprudence was born in America. That is to say, the fight was no longer confined to the Court: it was in the open. More and more Holmes used his dissents as brief manifestoes to rally the armies of future judicial change. From most of his colleagues he ceased to hope for much. "I am very hard at work again," he writes Pollock in 1925, "preparing small diamonds for people of limited intellectual means."

Did he understand the social forces that were transforming America? To an extent he did—not with the sharpness and precision of a Brandeis, but in a large and loose way of his own. As early as 1893 he had taken the trouble of trying to find out what it was that labor wanted. He tells Pollock of presenting himself at the house of a labor leader and asking what he would like if he could have it. "Organization, the eight-hour law, and the Swiss referendum seem to be his particular objects." But in the main he stayed clear of direct contact with social movements. He accepted the "felt needs" of his day as the givens of his society. He accepted labor unions, although his own economics told him they had but a limited scope, because he saw them as part of historical development. By trying to fight them, he said in a *Harvard Law Review* article in 1894, the courts were "flying in the face of the organization of the world which is taking place so fast." But it is important to note that he felt the same way about combinations of capitalists as of workers: hence his unwillingness, in the Northern Securities opinion which so outraged Theodore Roosevelt, to dissolve the railroad holding company which Morgan and Hill had formed.

In his economic views, in his politics, in his philosophic vision and his personal tastes, he was not a reformer but a conservative. One could put together from his various writings a sizable pamphlet in defense of conservatism. He was against whatever seemed crotchety, over-urgent, excessive. That was one reason for his anti-socialism. About Debs and some of the other defendants in the sedition cases in 1919, he wrote Pollock that they were "poor fools whom I should have been inclined to pass over if I could. The greatest bores in the world are the come-outers who are cock-sure of a dozen nostrums. The dogmatism of a little education is hopeless." When he was weak in his judicial opinions it was generally because of some economic theory he cherished. Holmes was no technical economist as he was a technical lawyer and, although he was a brilliant amateur at anything he turned his mind to—whether metaphysics or Greek tragedy or *Tristram Shandy* or the history of etchings—he did not have the discipline or the competence to support the magisterial assurance with which in economics he made and destroyed theories.

In *Plant v. Woods*, on the Massachusetts bench, he marred a brilliant dissent by adding as an afterthought a little exposition of the wage-fund theory, in which he argued that trade unions merely took the wages out of the pockets of one worker and put them into the pockets of another. In 1904, in his Northern Securities opinion, he interpreted the common law doctrine of restraint of trade so literally that he carried over with it the petty economy of England at the time the doctrine was born. "We must read the words before us," he wrote, "as if the question were whether two small exporting grocers shall go to jail." The fact, however, that Morgan and Hill were not exporting grocers, but represented a vast concentration of economic power, was the essence of the case. Men who had the power that these men had felt themselves above the law. Hill was quoted as saying after the adverse decision that now he would have to sign two certificates instead of one. In 1911, in the Dr. Miles Medical Co. case, the Court held a resale price maintenance agreement invalid. Holmes dissented, on the ground that competition in the market had little to do with determining prices; that prices were determined in our minds by the "equilibrium of social desires." There are some who would agree with his flounderings in the bog of Austrian marginal-utility theory; but someone might have pointed out to him that neither the Constitution nor the common law had enacted Eugen von Böhm-Bawerk's *Positive Theory of Capital.*

I have set down some of these shortcomings in Holmes's thinking —and there are others as well—as a necessary personal corrective to the overwhelming emphasis of his opinions, which emphasis was on constitutional freedom for social experiments that the majority wanted. Although all his fights were along the judicial front, their consequences were to be found in the daily lives of ordinary men and women and children. He fought for equal bargaining power for workers—"the equality of position between the parties in which liberty of contract begins." He fought against yellow-dog contracts. He fought for the power of Congress to legislate through the commerce clause against "the products of the ruined lives" of children. He fought for state workmen's compensation laws—the right of the state to shift to employers the cost of "the pain and mutilation incident to production." He fought for the right to experiment with laws against labor injunctions "in the insulated chambers afforded by the several states." He fought for state minimum wage and hour laws, and for the right of Congress to provide for minimum wages for underpaid scrubwomen and nurses. He fought for state laws creating funds to guarantee bank deposits, regulating chain stores, regulating trucking. He fought for a broad enough view of the commerce power to provide for federal control of slaughtering and meat-packing. He fought for adequate tax programs and saw taxes as the necessary price we pay for civilization. He set himself against the creation of a separate judicial caste: he insisted that judges were citizens just as others are and not immune from the income tax; that judges could not suppress newspaper criticism by holding summary contempt proceedings; that judges could not overturn state judicial decisions on matters of the common law by the "subtle fallacy" of a federal common law that was only "a brooding omnipresence in the sky." He fought for adequate governmental power both in peace and in war. And yet he fought also, even in wartime, for freedom of speech and thought, freedom especially "for the thought that we hate."

This was his humanism. He had a tenacious sense of privacy, and did not welcome the thought of having his biography written. But his biography had already written itself: it was written into the whole record of the social struggles of the country during the half-century of his judicial career, from 1882 to 1932. It was the half-century in which a predatory capitalism came to the peak of its power and passed into its decline, the half-century in which it used constitutional law to protect its position. How did it happen to fall to this aristocratic conservative to lead the minority of bar and bench in the struggle against the oppressive forces of American life?

The answer is that Holmes viewed the struggle in legal terms. He was a legal craftsman with a sense of the limits of his craft as well as its possibilities. We have learned that an economic ruling class must, to capture power, first change the laws in its direction; and then, to entrench itself in power, it must shut the legal system tight and make it static, to preclude a transfer of power to another class-alignment. Every economic ruling group must create, then freeze, the body of legal rules that validates it. Holmes's whole conception of law was of a moving, living thing: he fought those who would freeze the law for their economic interest as fiercely as those who would freeze it for their love of logical symmetry. He had come to the law with a thirst for something that was bigger than a profession. It was for him the record of a civilization: law was a calling that showed life as an art. He saw himself as a factor in the long inevitable process of legal change moving with the long inevitable process of social change, part of the army whose "black spearheads" he saw "stretching away against the unattainable sky." And because of this vision he would not allow that conscription of the legal Constitution to the uses of the economic Constitution for which the majority of his brethren on the Court panted. He has often, by his eulogists, been coupled with John Marshall, and there is some similarity in their conceptions of effective governmental power. But the differences between them are even greater. Marshall in his day brought the legal and economic Constitutions together; Holmes in his day sought to drive a wedge between them.

It was with this end in view that Holmes developed the judicial doctrines on which his greatness in the law will always rest. They may be grouped under three headings. First, the doctrine of judicial tolerance of legislative and administrative action. His very first Supreme Court decision in 1903, in *Otis v. Parker*, the case of a

California provision prohibiting margin trading, sounded that note, and it was his continuing theme. A study of Holmes's verbal strategy, such as Kenneth Burke might make, would reveal the persistent use of the double negative. While his brethren said that the government could not do a certain thing, and their critics insisted that it could, Holmes said merely that we could not say that it could not. Second, the doctrine of judicial restraint: the judges have no concern with social policy, which is not theirs to make, and must therefore minimize their use of the judicial power. And third, the doctrine of judicial relativism: that absolutes were to be avoided, whether they were called "liberty of contract" or "police power," "property" or "freedom of speech"; that all legal questions were questions not of eternal truths but of degree; and that the judge's function was to study each particular case and determine whether it fell on one side of the line of judicial trend or the other, whether the ends sought were within the scope of government action and the means not "manifestly absurd."

But all these doctrines, whether social or legal, flowed from a central source in Holmes: the sense he had of America as a going concern, which was in turn part of his sense of life as a going concern. Holmes had a naturalist philosophy, along with his rationalism. He could not play at system-making because all along he knew that his system was part of nature, not nature part of his system. He knew, as he several times put it, that he was in the universe and not the universe in him: that it was only when we came to recognize that we were not God and had not dreamed the world that we were mature. His comment on Hitler might well have been, if he had lived to comment on him, that he was still adolescent enough to believe he was God. And because Holmes saw himself thus, the deepest strain in him was a strain of respect for the natural forces of life and the long campaigns of history. Because there was risk in all life, he could not read certainty into law: hence the standard of liability he adopted was the "external standard" often called the "harsh" and "Draconian" doctrine of liability not according to motive or fault but according to the reasonable consequences of your act. Because there was experiment in all life, he saw the Constitution, too, as an experiment with which it was not his job to meddle. In America as a going concern there was room not only for the organizing genius of a Hill (whom Holmes frankly admired) but also for trade unions, not only for capitalist development of our resources but also for legislative control of capitalism. Holmes had a streak of Darwinism in him. His eye was on survival: a fact had to validate itself by showing its capacity to survive as a normal part of civilized living; when it did it was not his business to use the law to crush it.

It will be clear from this recital that the Supreme Court is today in every area following the doctrinal lines that Holmes laid out. But why did Holmes have to wait so long for his vindication? It was because his doctrines of tolerance for the organic forces of social life were of no avail until the crucial issue of power had been settled outside the Court. I do not know any evidence that Holmes himself ever saw this. Yet he was none the less performing his function in preparation for the struggle outside the Court. His function was to keep open the channels of judicial tolerance and restraint, to keep the principles of constitutional flexibility alive for the crucial test. That test came with the Great Depression, the New Deal measures taken to cope with it, and the constitutional crisis that followed. How that crisis was resolved is not part of our inquiry now. But it is worth noting that the weapons that the Brandeis-Stone-Cardozo minority used during the crisis were weapons fashioned by Holmes; and that even before the appointment of the new Justices by Mr. Roosevelt, when the Court retreated (with the shift of Chief Justice Hughes and Justice Roberts) the retreat was in the direction of Holmes.

Holmes wrote of Montesquieu that he was buried under his own triumphs. That is in a sense true of Holmes himself. For thirty years his dissenting opinions were national events; he has been the judge most closely studied in the law schools; he has so long set the pattern of liberal legal thought that his attitudes have become liberal commonplaces. Yet we must remember that of the leaders of the present Court, Chief Justice Stone was for years his partner in dissent; Justice Frankfurter was his friend and disciple and is his prospective biographer; Justices Black, Douglas, and Jackson are the devoted admirers of his judicial principles, as they are also of the Brandeis economic philosophy.

In 1891 there appeared in Boston a slim and chaste volume of *Speeches* by Holmes. The two themes of the speeches, the Civil

War and the calling of the law, disparate as they might seem, had a similar note of high enthusiasm running through them. "In our youths our hearts were touched with fire. It was given to us to learn at the outset that life was a profound and passionate thing." Thus runs one of the speeches on the Civil War. And in a speech on law as a profession, "I say . . . that a man may live greatly in the law as elsewhere . . . that there as well as elsewhere he may wreak himself upon life, may drink the bitter cup of heroism, may wear his heart out after the unattainable." And these ideas with which he bound his early life together were cut from growths reaching even deeper into the soil of his past. There were two ancestral strains in him: the Puritan and the intellectual aristocrat. "I am enough of a Puritan," he said in a speech, "to conceive the exalted joy of those who look upon themselves only as instruments in the hand of a higher power to work out its designs." The "higher power" for Holmes the intellectual aristocrat had ceased to be God and had become, under the influence of Darwinism, the great natural forces of life; but there was still in him a sense of surrender to them.

The experience of the Civil War, in which he was three times wounded and in which he lost some of his best friends, was the maturing force in Holmes's life. Despite a strain of sentimentalism and some sloppy passages ("Such hearts—ah, me, how many—were stilled twenty years ago") his Civil War speeches are on the whole characterized by grace and a restrained warmth and his usual flashes of phrase: they are easily, with Lincoln's, the best war speeches in American literature. From these speeches one may trace four themes of his thinking that merge in his views on both law and war: that life is risk, that our fate depends often on a throw of the dice, and that law must allow for this aleatory element; that life is battle, and the best meaning of effort comes out under fire; that one must be a good soldier, with a sense of honor and a "splendid carelessness of life" in a cause; and that a fighting faith is the ultimate in the meaning of life. Always Holmes sets these values over against the values of comfort, of utility, of materialism. This appears in perhaps his greatest speech, "The Soldier's Faith," delivered on Memorial Day, 1895. "War is out of fashion, and the man who commands the attention of his fellows is the man of wealth. Commerce is the great power. The aspirations of the world are those of commerce." It is heartbreaking to read this and other pleas against materialist values, made in the eighties and nineties to a generation that had converted the victory against an exploitative slavery into the triumph of an exploitative capitalism.

Holmes believed in war for a variety of reasons: because it transcended the material interests, because it merged the little individualities of men in a common goal, because it was part of the principle of struggle which he saw at the core of life. "I hope it may be long," he says of war, "before we are called again to sit at that master's feet. But some teacher of the kind we all need. In this snug, oversafe corner of the world we need it, that we may realize that our comfortable routine is no eternal necessity of things, but merely a little space of calm in the midst of the tempestuous untamed streaming of the world, and in order that we may be ready for danger. We need it in this time of individualist negations, with its literature of French and American humor, revolting at discipline, loving flesh-pots, and denying that anything is worthy of reverence, in order that we may remember all that buffoons forget. We need it everywhere and at all times. For high and dangerous action teaches us to believe as right beyond dispute things for which our doubting minds are slow to find words of proof. Out of heroism grows faith in the worth of heroism. The proof comes later, and even may never come." With those who doubted the worth of the effort, Holmes would not argue. It was a matter of basic belief. "You must begin by wanting to." Nevertheless he was disturbed by the growing skepticism of martial values. "War is out of fashion," he says in his 1895 speech. And in a letter to Pollock in 1923, "From time to time I meet young men from both sides of the water who profess to think patriotism an empty superstition or even a noxious humbug. But it strikes me as little more than an example of experimenting in negations—now in vogue."

There is much in these speeches of which the liberal mind today will disapprove. "I do not know what is true. I do not know the meaning of the universe. But in the midst of doubt, in the collapse of creeds, there is one thing I do not doubt . . . and that is that the faith is true and adorable which leads a soldier to throw away his life in obedience to a blindly accepted duty, in a cause which he little understands, in a plan of campaign of which he has no notion, under tactics of which he does not see the use." Here is a highly poetic sense of the value of war, a sense of blind obedience which approaches the religious *credo quia absurdum*. But this was a strain that ran through the whole of Holmes's life. "We live by symbols," he said in his speech on John Marshall, in 1901. And, speaking of the power of Marshall's thought in the future, "It is all a symbol, if you like, but so is the flag. The flag is but a bit of bunting to one who insists on prose. Yet . . . its red is our life-blood, its stars our world, its blue our heaven. It owns our land. At will it throws away our lives."

There was mingled in Holmes's attitude to war the love of honor ("the power of honor to bind men's lives is no less now than it was in the Middle Ages"), the sense of the mysterious in life transcending reason ("we have shared the incommunicable experi-ence of war; we have felt, we still feel, the passion of life to its top"), the dedication to a larger end beyond the individual life ("our only but wholly adequate significance is as parts of the unimagina-ble whole. . . . Even while we think that we are egotists we are living to ends outside ourselves." "To act is to affirm the worth of an end." "If I were dying my last words would be: 'Have faith, and pursue the unknown end' "). For all the vaunted skepticism of his thought, there was a vein of passionate belief in him, which time could not affect, nor the ebbing memory of the battlefields. At times this reached an apocalyptic height which makes bad lit-erature as it makes bad thinking. At times also it was mingled with an aristocratic belief in blood-inheritance which we do not today share ("a price well paid for the breeding of a race fit for headship and command").

Yet Holmes did not idealize war. "War when you are at it is horrible and dull." Whatever the romantic notion of it, he knew, "the reality was to pass a night on the ground in the rain with your bowels out of order and then after no particular breakfast to wade a stream and attack the enemy." There was one amusing incident that he relates in the Pollock volumes in which he was attacked as a jingo because his "Soldier's Faith" appeared in print, by co-incidence, in the midst of the Venezuela affair with England. ("Fancy my speech of last Memorial Day being treated as a jingo document! . . . It seems to some of the godly as if I were preach-ing a doctrine of blood!") But there was none of the jingo in Holmes. His doctrine went beyond any sense of nationalism to the

roots of his view of life. His speeches run a nimble gantlet between militarist and humanist values. A decade ago the American
reader might have dismissed them summarily as being far too close
to the militarist. But a generation that has seen democracies go
down through pacifism and passivity, through the smug assurance
of wealth and the denigration of both fighting and faith, is in a
position to take this phase of Holmes as seriously as his judicial.

As he grew older, Holmes must have found it painful to stir up
the old memories of the Civil War. "I hate to read of those times,"
recurs in several letters. Yet he continued to reject any sentimentalism about the sanctity of human life. "Every society rests on the
death of men," was one of his favorite remarks. "If you don't kill
the weakest one way, you will kill them another," he adds in a
letter to Pollock in 1922. There was a toughness in his thinking
which derived from the tradition of Hobbes, Malthus, and Dar-
win, and from the memories of the war. "I hate to discourage the
belief of a young man in reason," he writes to his young Chinese
friend, John Wu, in 1921. "I believe in it with all my heart, but I
think that its control over the actions of men when it comes against
what they want is not very great. A century ago Malthus ran his
sword through fallacies that one would have thought must die
then and there, but men didn't like to believe him, and the hum-
bugs that he killed are as alive as ever today." And in a 1926 letter
to Wu, he writes that he does not believe that "man always is an
end in himself. . . . We march up a conscript with bayonets behind to die for a cause that he doesn't believe in. And I feel no
scruples about it. Our morality seems to me always a check on the
ultimate domination of force. . . . When the Germans in the late
war disregarded what we called the rules of the game, I don't see
that there was anything to be said except: we don't like it and shall
kill you if we can. So when it comes to the question of a *corpus
juris* the ultimate question is what do the dominant forces in the
community want and do they want it hard enough to disregard
any inhibitions that may stand in the way." And elsewhere, "Behind every scheme to make the world over, lies the question, What
kind of world do you want?" And almost as if following up this
question of his own, twenty-five years later (1920) in a letter to
Pollock, "Between two groups that want to make inconsistent kinds
of worlds I see no remedy except force."

I have said enough about Holmes on war, and quoted enough from him, to indicate where this phase of him met and crossed with his judicial phase. Because his judicial career happened to coincide with a humanitarian movement in American life, the humanitarian aspect of Holmes has been greatly overemphasized. Holmes brought to the problem of law as he brought to the problem of war a profound—whether we think it wrong or right— sense of the limits of the individual life and the immensity of the forces of nature and history. He brought to both a toughness of approach that accepted death and danger and force as integral parts of life. He saw the fulfillment of the individual life in effort and battle, in which the individual spends himself for something larger than himself; and he saw the fulfillment of law in creating a framework broad enough to allow the forces of life to fight it out for dominance. He saw in America as a going concern a far-flung movement for the expansion of economic rights for the common man, for governmental control of property and contractual rights. He knew that this movement could not be stopped without breaking the fabric of civilization: he was unwilling therefore to deny it the garments of law. But he did as he did on naturalistic and historical grounds, not humanitarian. And he knew that at any moment it might be necessary to use force and bloodshed to preserve the right in the future to continue this struggle within a legal framework. When that time should come he was ready not only to accept war as a necessary evil, but even to celebrate it as fulfilling the social meaning of the individual life. If ever there was a legal thinker who sought to give law a basis in majority power movements, and a democrat who sought to give democracy a naturalist base, it was Holmes.

One phase of his thinking remains to be considered: what happens to law and to democracy while a war is being waged? It should be clear from what has been said that Holmes would make every effort to find room in the Constitution for adequate war powers. He had occasion to write the opinion in the Emergency Rent cases, in which the emergency rent laws enacted during the war for the District of Columbia and for New York were up before the Court. Holmes upheld them, using reasoning broad enough to include any other instances of the use of adequate national war power.

"That the emergency declared by the statute did exist must be assumed," he wrote in *Block v. Hirsh,* "and the question is whether Congress was incompetent to meet it in the way in which it has been met by most of the civilized countries of the world." This was a significant way of phrasing it. John Quincy Adams long ago said that while the peace power of the American government was closely contained within the constitutional provisions, the war power "is only limited by the usages of nations." Holmes's remark is strikingly parallel to this conception. Here is doctrine broad enough to meet the constitutional requirements of a democracy like ours in a world in which the techniques of total warfare have become imperative.

On the question of executive power Holmes was of a somewhat divided mind. In the case of *Moyer v. Peabody,* in 1919, he took a broad view of the powers of a state governor under martial law, holding as a general proposition that in a time of public danger the executive process may be substituted for the judicial, and that so long as the executive can show good faith he cannot be held to account for his actions afterward. This is about as far as the Court has ever gone in opening the way for emergency executive power, and it may prove crucial if in the future a situation arises threatening civil war. I am leaving out of account now, as not directly in point, Holmes's dissent in the Myers case, where he sought to limit the President's power of removing executive officers, and by implication sought to limit his role as administrative chief. I happen to believe that Holmes was wrong in that case and Taft right; but as he was not dealing with a problem of power in time of danger, he was less directly concerned with the demands of effective government.

It is fairly clear that the present Supreme Court will follow Holmes's lead in upholding a program of adequate war powers for the President and Congress. But the most delicate problem in wartime is governmental power over speech and conscience. This is the area in which some of Holmes's greatest opinions were written, and some of his most enduring doctrines expressed.

His principal contribution here is the "clear and present danger" doctrine. Holmes developed this in the Schenck case, the first of the Supreme Court decisions under the Sedition Act of 1917 and 1918. It does not make free speech an absolute value. But it fixes this test for speech that may be suppressed: "whether the words are used in such circumstances and are of such a nature as to create a clear and present danger that they will bring about the substantive evils that Congress has a right to prevent." Thus the stress is laid not upon the words themselves, nor upon their indirect consequences, but on their immediate relation to a context of war danger. Holmes held Schenck guilty and, in an unfortunate opinion that disturbed him greatly and is undoubtedly one of his worst decisions, he held Debs guilty. But in the Abrams case he insisted that the words presented no clear and present danger; and his dissent there is perhaps the most brilliant and most impassioned utterance of his career. It is here that he asserts that there can be no survival value in a government that does not provide for a competition of ideas in the market. And in his Gitlow dissent he goes further. After holding that Gitlow's "Left Wing Manifesto" had "no chance of starting a present conflagration" he adds: "If in the long run the beliefs expressed in proletarian dictatorship are destined to be accepted by the dominant power in the community, the only meaning of free speech is that they should be given their chance and have their way." There are few clearer instances of Holmes's belief that the function of government is to give expression to the struggle of life.

In the Schenck, Abrams, and Gitlow opinions Holmes developed a doctrine as well calculated as any in the history of crisis democracy to safeguard both the individual and the social values of intellectual freedom during wartime without unduly jeopardizing the strength of the state. The "clear and present danger" doctrine, of course, will not do the job by itself. It needs an absence of general hysteria and the presence of a great Supreme Court before it will work well. But thus far both conditions are fulfilled in the American scene.

It may seem to many inconsistent that Holmes should have been willing to expand the government's power to deal with economic and military problems in wartime, yet limit its power to deal with dissenting thought. But if we remember that in both cases he is thinking of the needs for long-range survival, the paradox is resolved. In the first case there is a fateful life-and-death struggle of wills between one community and another; in the second case there is a health-giving struggle of ideas within the community.

There are many things in Holmes that I am skeptical of, and some that I dislike. Perhaps the greatest weakness of his thought is a fault-line in it between a pragmatic skepticism that denied the force of "general propositions" and an idealism that often approached the mystical. He could never quite make up his mind whether he was a devil's disciple or a captain in the phalanxes of the Lord. Holmes himself saw this. "The men who teach us to disbelieve general propositions," he wrote Wu, "are only less valuable than those who encourage us to make them." And again, "We must be serious in order to get work done, but when the usual Saturday half-holiday comes I see no reason why we should not smile at the trick by which nature keeps us at our job." It was part of his uniqueness that he should not only make the attempt of welding his mind and his faith in a semi-mystical naturalism, but that he should also have the saving humor to see where the cracks showed. If he did not wholly make philosophical ends meet, he has given us one of the surest fusions of militancy and rationality to sustain us in the fighting to come and guide us through the peace that will follow.[1]

1941

---

[1] For some further discussion of Holmes, the reader may wish to consult three earlier essays of mine in *Ideas Are Weapons* (1939), pp. 54–69.

3

Randolph Bourne and Two Generations[1]

1

RANDOLPH BOURNE was not during his life one of the great ones of the earth. He did not move among the powerful, he was not consulted in their councils. He was a lonely figure, thirsting within his own small circle for recognition and love, and his thirst was not slaked. The total span of his writing was only seven years, from 1911 to 1918. He published in this period three books of essays and studies, all of them minor. The work on which his importance rests was not published in book form until after his death, and some of it has not been collected yet. He died at thirty-two. After his death a legend gathered around him; but even in our time I can testify that when I have mentioned his name to college students I have been met by a blanker stare than usual.

Yet there are few American writers of our century whose thinking goes as deeply as his to the dilemmas of intellectuals faced by war crises. He wrote sensitively and passionately for his own war generation, and was either abused or ignored. I want to write of him as one whose mind and work deserve study by our war generation. I do not accept for our time some of the conclusions he reached for his own time. But his premises have dignity and his philosophy has strength. And even an opponent will find that his own convictions taste sweeter if they have survived the chastening ordeal of being tested against Randolph Bourne's thought.

---

[1] This was first read as one of the Stafford Little Lectures at Princeton University in 1940. Later, in revised and expanded form, it appeared in *Twice a Year*. The quotations from Bourne's letters I have in some cases taken from the published letters as they have appeared at various times in *Twice a Year*. In other cases the extracts are published here for the first time.

2

Bourne grew up in the New Jersey town of Bloomfield, where he was born in 1886. On his father's side of the family there were Congregational ministers; on his mother's side lawyers. It was a restricted Puritan world in which Bourne was raised. One may guess that his later critical essays, with their blasts against Puritanism in American literature, had their origin in his boyhood memories. And there is among them an essay of his on "The Social Order in an American Town" which parallels in many ways Veblen's analysis (in *Absentee Ownership*) of the American country town. But there is another facet to Bourne's inheritance. The Protestant tradition from which he came, like that of Emerson and Channing and Parker, has been one of America's creative forces, with its sharp interior sense of criticism and revolt, and its feeling for the local community as the unit of a culture. Bourne was to show that for all his rebellion against Bloomfield and its middle-class stuffiness and triviality, he cared about social roots in a local soil. There is an essay of his on the Italian settlement at Bloomfield; and when later he had become interested in German city-planning he wrote a letter to the editor of his local paper, suggesting a town plan for Bloomfield.

The fact that Bourne was a hunch-back was to dominate his whole life. I have seen extracts from his boyhood diaries that are striking in their intensity and perceptiveness. He went to school and high school at Bloomfield, read with the absorption of a boy shut off from play, took long walks, listened to music, steeped himself in the piano. His family had but little money and so he had to postpone going to college after high school. He did secretarial work, became a musical proof-reader in a pianola factory, a piano tuner, an accompanist. Finally in 1909, at the age of twenty-three he entered Columbia with advanced standing. Rarely, I think, has anyone become a student in an American college more eagerly or with better preparation for it.

We have descriptions of him at that time by some of his classmates. He was a familiar figure on the campus—hunch-backed yet walking with a quick and eager stride, a large head, "a long sensitive Gothic face, with heavy features, a deformed ear, musician's hands" (Paul Rosenfeld). By the testimony of all, there was about him an

unforced cheerfulness. There has been a good deal of sentimentaliz-
ing over Bourne's deformity. His own attitude about it was, at least
outwardly, normality itself. He did not ask for sympathy nor yet
was he aggressively reticent about his body. He took it as a fact,
something to study and understand and talk about as he might
have talked about any other trait in himself and its consequences
for him. He wrote one of his *Atlantic* essays on this subject, "The
Philosophy of Handicap."

Yet in his own mind Bourne brooded a good deal over his fate. I
have read several hundred of his manuscript letters. They rank
high with any American letters in their sensitive self-delineation
of a mind. They alternate between joy and despair—revealing at
times the insolent strength of one who knew his own powers, more
often an agonizing sense of insufficiency and an awareness of himself as a bundle of conflicting desires. It is little wonder that he
loved Rousseau's *Confessions* ("so frank, human, sensitive, sincere.
I found myself feeling so much of him, saying at nearly every page,
'Yes, that is what I would have felt, have done, have said' "), and he
loved Tolstoy also. There are passages in his letters, particularly
about his desires and frustrations in relation to women, that are
not unworthy to be compared with the confessional insights of both
of the men he admired.

About the comradeship of men and women [he writes in a letter from
Paris to Mary Messer dated December 28, 1913], I have a few such wonderful woman friends that I begin to think that perfect play of idea and
appreciation is making an ideal real—when up springs eternal, insati-
able desire, the realization of which, inhibited to me, sets the old problem recurring poignantly, and makes me wonder whether Shaw's preface
to "Getting Married" is not the profoundest and wisest word on the
matter ever written. It is a subject to make one's thoughts, indeed, go
round and round without satisfaction, and particularly when one is a
man, and a man cruelly blasted by the powers that brought him into
the world, in a way that makes him both impossible to be desired and yet
—cruel irony that wise Montaigne knew about—doubly endowed with
desire. Give him then an extreme fastidiousness of idealism, and you
have a soul that should satisfy the most ironical of the gods. Encase that
soul, which is myself, in Puritan morality, and you produce a refined
species of spiritual torture, which is relieved only by the demands, appeals, fortunately strong, of philosophy and music, and heaven-sent
irony which softens and heals the wounds. But, to complete the job,

make him poor and deny him the thorough satisfaction of the higher appeals, deny him steady work and thus make easy the sway of desire, and you force all his self-impelled action, all his thinking and construc- tive work, to be done in hampering struggle with this unrealized desire, which yet—another irony—colors all his appreciation, motivates his love of personality, and fills his life with a sort of smoldering beauty. This is a complete, if perhaps too dark picture. But like many things in life, both it and the other side are true.

And again to Alyse Gregory, on November 19, 1916:

Having led the experimental life, and sifted and sorted, I feel that I know now exactly what I want. It is all as far away as ever, with only samples to tantalize my memory and impede my clean delivery of my- self over to the present. Love, fame, joy in work, would bring, perhaps, the resources for the freedom that I want to move about in and yet have a center and a hearth. All my problems are interwoven; if I had one solved, it seems as if they should all be solved. Of course, it seems to me that the key to all of them is love, and the deprivation the one impediment to blossoming. At least, I should give anything in the world for an opportunity to test this theory. Is it Greenwich Village that is the poison, or is it the times that produce the type of fair and serious and life-denying woman, who in the name of a career and her pride and the sacred independence of woman destroys not only you but her- self? The philosophy that you are not a man but Man, and therefore, in spite of your sympathy, personal quality, and contribution, really only a lustful Being who wants you to cook for him—this is the philoso- phy that has succeeded in poisoning all my days and my work. I am inclined to doubt whether man's wrongs to women are so much greater than woman's wrongs to men. We certainly have a peculiarly acute mechanism for suffering.

But the letters I have quoted date from Bourne's post-college days. Columbia itself was almost idyllic for him. He blossomed and grew in his few years at college, luxuriating in his friendships, sedu- lous about his rooms at Hartley Hall, preparing tea for visitors, matching his mind against other students in a discussion club, rifl- ing the minds of his teachers, reading consumingly. Of the faculty he liked Robinson, Beard, Dewey, Woodbridge, Giddings, Shot- well. He disliked John Erskine and President Butler. In his *History of a Literary Radical* there is a satirical sketch of the first called "The Professor" and of the second called "One of Our Conquer- ors." He could be waspish as well as genial, and it was best for anyone to get out of the savage path of his wit. He could sharpen a sentence until all that was left of it was its destroying edge. His reading in this period, as mentioned in his letters, gives us a sampling of the intellectual diet of the pre-war years: the Jameses—William and Henry—Lowes Dickinson, Chesterton, Maeterlinck and Bergson, Nietzsche and Dostoievsky, Arturo Giovannitti, Spingarn, Edward Alsworth Ross. Columbia was a free and joyful place for him. Again and again in his later letters, he speaks of it with the nostalgia of a man who remembers that he was once part of a "beloved community." Royce's phrase was one of Bourne's favorites.

One day in 1911, when Bourne was in his junior year, Professor Woodbridge suggested that he write an answer to an article in the *Atlantic* denouncing the younger generation. Bourne did, his article was accepted, and led off the issue. Other articles of his followed, and he became a frequent *Atlantic* contributor, developing a "quality magazine" style with lucidity and a sort of lulling grace, but without strength or individuality. His essays were published in 1913 in a volume called *Youth and Life*. There are some good things in the volume: an essay on "The Two Generations" which speaks sharply for the young to the middle generation, and one on "The Dodging of Pressures" which is a subtle analysis of the tensions within each group making for standardization. They verge on one side on the homiletic—yet Bourne was able to freshen even homilies with his sense of immediacy; on the other side they verge on the manifesto. Bourne had almost overnight come to fill one of the most dangerous of all roles—that of a professional spokesman for the young.

One can see now something of what had happened. Bourne, having come late to college life, was more articulate than his fellows. Columbia, more nearly than any other American university of the time, was the cross-roads of the world, with students from countries in Europe and the Far East where youth counted for something in intellectual and cultural leadership. They set Bourne to thinking in similar terms for America—America whose cultural barrenness under the heavy hand of the old contrasted so with his beloved community at college where the young reigned. And so Bourne came to see in terms of the conflict of generations what could more fruitfully be seen as the clash between pecuniary and non-pecuniary values. His eagerness had led him to blur his analysis. And it was not long before he conceived a semi-contempt for these perfectly turned-out articles with their phosphorescent and harmless sentences about the generations. But not so harmless was a note struck in one of the essays, "For Radicals." Bourne used the term "radical" rather than "socialist." The latter was for him too exclusively political. He wanted a radicalism that ran the whole course of a culture, and in which politics and economics were but parts of the whole.

There are two striking things about his writing at the time. One is his quiet confidence in a League of Youth to remake the social system. The other is a psychological subtlety in his essays—their scalpel-skill in laying bare both the energies and the inhibitions of the young, the conflict of loyalties as between their class origins and their social conscience, the desire for revolt and the experimental life and the desire for comfort. It was not some easy arrogance that gave Bourne's voice on the eve of the war a note of authority for his comrades in youth. If they devoured his articles and recognized his authority it was because he stirred them to protest and yet saw inwardly what stood in the path of revolt.

But Bourne's chief worry as his college days came to a close was personal: a job and a start on a career. There are in his letters repeated self-questionings as to whether he could get either. He had hurt many with the slightly poisoned darts of his mind. What reason was there to think that the wounded ones would help him to a start? He wanted a post teaching literature or an editorial niche somewhere from which he could try out his ideas. Then came the award of the Richard Watson Gilder Fellowship for travel abroad. Bourne was giddy with delight. At last he should be able to see Europe, meet its great ones, observe its masses, study at its universities. He finished his work at Columbia in 1913, with both a B.A. and an M.A., and set off for Europe. The horizons of Bloomfield and of Hartley Hall were expanding into those of the cultures of Europe.

3

Bourne did the *grand tour* with a vengeance: a few weeks rapidly through Belgium, Holland, and Germany with a college friend who left him at Munich; then a week alone in the Tirol and northern Italy; three weeks at Lausanne; a short stay in Wales, then long ones in London and Paris; then a swing through France, and again through Germany and Italy. He saw Europe with a trembling eagerness not to miss anything, and to crowd everything into a single *Wanderjahr*. He walked about the streets of European cities unashamedly with a map in his hand. His letters, for all their revealing of one who was determined to "do" Europe, are fresh in their summing-up of national character and acute in their observations on some of the great names that Bourne encountered, such as the Webbs, Havelock Ellis, and Graham Wallas. To Bourne and many of his American generation Europe was a relief from what seemed the stuffiness and inertia of their own country. They did not have about Europe in 1913 the sense of impending catastrophe that we from our historical vantage associate with that doomed moment. They had rather the sense of Europe as a laboratory for new social and economic constructions—social democracy and town-planning and municipal government in Germany, the militant suffrage movement and Fabianism in England, syndicalist power in France and Italy.

We must remember that Bourne's college generation grew up with vague aspirations toward socialism in economics and liberation in culture. It was the generation of Walter Lippmann, John Reed, and Heywood Broun, of Van Wyck Brooks and Max Eastman; of the New Poetry, the Little Theater, and the New Freedom; of the Wobblies and of labor-capital violence, of Arturo Giovannitti's poems and Mabel Dodge's salon. The year in which Bourne sailed for Europe—1913—was also the year in which a Hoosier named Charles Beard published *An Economic Interpretation of the Constitution* and a Massachusetts Brahmin called Brooks Adams published *The Theory of Social Revolutions*. The muckrakers, who had filled the decade just preceding with the clangor of their journalism, had by 1913 failed but had left their tradition as a heritage. The youngsters felt they had to go further and deeper. They were beginning to call themselves "socialists," or as Bourne did, "radicals." Some of them were pacifists. They organized socialist societies in the colleges, and asked labor leaders and socialist intellectuals to address them. But it was all, for Bourne at any rate, a vaguish affair. His essays in *Youth and Life* sought to blend the idealism of Royce's beloved community with the pragmatism of William James's pluralistic universe. One finds cropping up in both his Columbia and his European letters the word "sociological" in a sense that seems curious today. For us the word has a ring of academic barbarism, yet Bourne's letters may remind us that once it promised to expand the horizons of the human mind instead of cramping life within filing-cases. For Bourne the word connoted the revolt against individualism in society and against the ivory tower in literature and art. It included loosely within itself all the gropings toward collective living that Bourne's generation was making. And one may suspect that socialism, radicalism, sociology, and revolution were mingled in Bourne's mind as a sort of epiphenomenon—a glowing and visionary flame nourished from logs that were somehow only conceptual.

That was one reason why his European trip turned out to be important for him. Europe forced him to think through many of his fine Columbia phrases. It was a corrosive to his vagueness. He had to face the question of the tactics of social change.

Fabians [he writes to Alyse Gregory from London on October 11, 1913] have made Socialism rather respectable here, and I enjoy talking with them, but I am far more desperate than they and welcome any aggressive blow, any sign of impatience with the salvation of society by our self-appointed leaders of church and state. England is one succession of fearful strikes, and our fond theory of the triumph of orderly trade-unionism slowly levering up the working-class to a position of comfort and influence is daily knocked into a cocked hat. . . . It is difficult to see that capitalism has been one whit weakened by all the struggle.

Bourne had discovered that Fabianism was not enough. Yet the same Bourne wrote that the books of the English liberal John A. Hobson were "the most convincing basis for Socialist economics I have seen." He read Henry James's *Princess Casamassima* and reported that it was "a superb novel with wonderful radicals in it." He regarded G. B. Shaw as "one of the great prophets of the day." And while he was beginning to suspect the political Fabianism of parliamentary socialism and to supplant his former economic Fabianism with leanings toward syndicalism, he could still write that the imperative American need was a score of socialists in Congress. Bourne was evidently wrestling in his mind with the core problem of revolutionary as against parliamentary methods for social change. He had not resolved the problem, but he was storing up concrete observations of strikes and political action, and was seeking out the new and militant voices in Europe.

But the Bourne who was groping toward international socialism was still very alive to the subject of differences in national character. His European letters are filled with dangerous observations on Englishmen, Germans, Frenchmen, Italians, Swiss. I say "dangerous" because they were largely on the intuitive level. Bourne was seeking to reconcile Bergson with socialism. At Columbia he had written that Bergson's "idea of intuition" is nothing mystical, but simply our ability to "perceive the qualities as well as the quantities of things." And in pursuit of qualities he constructed a sort of hierarchy of national preferences. He loved the Swiss best and the English least, and placed the other nations in between, with the French well toward the top. In discussing the English, however, he generally quarried his intuitions from the solid rock of the English class relations. He was filled with an almost joyous bitterness about the English capitalists, the English governing class, the imperfections of English democracy.

One may guess that Bourne's acidulous *aperçus* into the English character were possible only because of the curious relation that England bore to his thinking. When Bourne wrote about the English he was criticizing relatives, and a man is never so savage in criticism as when his loyalties are engaged. England was for Bourne a projection of America—more outside of himself and therefore to be seen more objectively. But his criticism of English capitalism was in essence a criticism of all capitalism, including the American. He speaks in one of his letters of having "a sense of social guilt quite analogous to my Puritan ancestors' personal guilt; and this guilt cannot be wiped out by the simple operation of being personally 'saved.' " And in another letter:

I don't see [he wrote from Paris on March 13 to Alyse Gregory] how anybody with a social conscience who has once had his eyes opened to things can ever get adjusted to things, without feeling like an accomplice in great crimes.

It was this tortured religious sense (it is worth noting that Bourne felt an affinity for Dostoievsky) that formed the psychic roots of much of the adventure of self-criticism that Bourne's generation in America took part in. Never before had an American generation been so critical of its own culture.

It was partly by contrast with his sense of the exaggerated individualism of American life that Bourne felt attracted to the new movements he found in Europe toward collective living. Everywhere in Europe he sought this. It was in France particularly that he thought he had found it. In one of his most striking letters from Paris he sets down the longing of mind and spirit which made him seek at the time in Europe for what was probably not there—or if there, only in beginnings:

The world universal [he wrote to Mary Messer from Paris, February 7, 1914] seems to begin to take form as social; your spiritual man is my social man, vibrating in camaraderie with the beloved society, given new powers, lifted out of himself, transformed through the enriching stimulation of his fellows—the communion of saints—into a new being, spiritual because no longer individual. This malady that we are feeling today is an exhaustless social *hunger,* thwarted and unsatisfied by the chaos of a society split up into separate, mutually uncomprehending groups. . . . What the primitive man had easily, through the compactness of his society, and what every compact group gets easily— the exaltation of the individual by concerted social expression of the common desires, ideas, and ideals—we are reaching out for with great pain and striving, thwarted and perplexed by the barriers of class, codes, institutions, which have served their little local purpose and now straddle the ways along which we are feeling for a complete social consciousness, which must eventually raise the whole world to a Kingdom of Heaven. . . . This leaves me with a wonder at the means; I never see clearly the process by which this spiritual is to be discovered and cultivated. But translate this "spiritual" as social, and everything becomes clear to me. I see the social movement with all its manifestations— feminism, socialism, social religion, internationalism, etc.—slowly linking the chains of social consciousness, and thus transforming the individual persons, the individual group, lifting them to a higher level, giving them a more abundant sense of sympathy and unanimity. . . .

Here Bourne strikes the mood of all his striving in those pre-war years. In France he hailed the work of Jules Romains and the new movement of *unanimisme* among the poets and novelists, deriving from Zola, with whom the collective protagonist was supplanting the individual hero. And from this the step was a logical one to a possible international community based on social justice within each country and a transnational relationship between the workers and other functional groups.

But Bourne glimpsed this vision at a time when the war which was to crush it for generations to come could no longer be averted. He was making his *grand tour* of a Europe just about to enter on a cycle of wars, revolutions, counter-revolutions, and wars again. The Europe he was seeing was the Europe of the Red Week in France, the Dublin strike in Ireland, the general strike in Italy, the armament race, the diplomatic jungle. It was the Europe out of whose class tensions and irrationalisms Pareto was constructing the counter-Marxian and anti-humanist theory in his *Mind and Society*, the Europe that was enacting Sorel's "social myth" of the cleansing sanctity of violence, the Europe in which Spengler was writing *The Decline of the West* and Lenin in Switzerland was gathering in his notebook materials for *The State and Revolution*. Bourne did not see the reaches of thought that these men saw. He has a remarkable account in one of his letters, in July 1914, of living through the general strike in Rome. It had, he wrote,

Enough elements of a revolution to give me a very good idea of the beginnings of one. . . . I began to wonder whether I liked being in the midst of a foreign revolution. . . . One of the interesting features was the hysterical demonstration of the bourgeoisie on the third day of the strike, when they formed a procession that marched down the principal business street and cheered frantically as from one balcony after another the Italian flag was somewhat tremblingly unfurled.

Bourne was beginning to see that nationalism was an explosive force that could be used against labor and internationalism. What he did not see—what none of his generation saw—was that nationalism could be used thus against labor on a scale which would make out of nationalism itself an international movement.

For the moment, however, Bourne saw only the relation between nationalism and war. Three weeks after the letter about the general strike Bourne was writing to his mother from Dresden that the streets were filled with cheering patriotic crowds and that Austria had declared war. Two days later he found that the threatened general war would keep him from seeing the Socialist Congress at Vienna. And on August 25 he was on the boat for America, writing:

The wheels of the clock have so completely stopped in Europe, and this civilization that I have been admiring so much seems so palpably about to be torn to shreds, that I do not even want to think about Europe until the war is over and life is running again.

He had had his *grand tour* and had learned deeply from the spectacle. But how expensive a spectacle it was to prove for the world—and for himself!

4

Bourne came back from Europe with a long black student's cape that was to be his distinctive badge until his death. He came back to an America beginning to work itself up to a pitch of war fever and that had no place for such as he, but an America that was to occupy his mind and energy and whole being in the four years of life that remained for him. He tried at first not to think too much of Europe and the war. He took rooms in New York City, in a model tenement on 31st Street, far east. He sought out his friends. But the old magic had gone out of his relations with them. He had alternate bursts of energy and of despondency. He still served tea and had on his Tuesday afternoons a sort of salon where his friends could meet and talk intimately for talk's sake. He tried getting a teaching job but he was thought too dangerous. What he wanted most was editorial work. But the old muckraking magazines were gone.

I wish [he wrote to Alyse Gregory from Paris, April 10, 1914] there were to be some forum when I get back to America, from which I could preach some disagreeable truths to my countrymen.

There was one such forum which had just got started when Bourne returned—the *New Republic,* subsidized by Willard Straight but built around the dominant personality of Herbert Croly. Bourne tried his hardest to become one of the editorial group, along with Lippmann and Francis Hackett and Walter Weyl. But the best he could get was a retainer to do some reviewing and occasional articles, and the ornamental role of Contributing Editor.

The material he specialized in was education. It is hard for us, in these days when John Dewey's reputation is embalmed in jubilee volumes, to think ourselves back to a time when his educational ideas were living and—it seemed—revolutionary weapons. Yet that was true, and to no small measure as a result of Bourne's ardent discipleship. He threw himself into the polemics raging around progressive education, and he was a dangerous opponent to en-counter. His *New Republic* articles and others were gathered into a volume called *Education and Living,* and, in 1916 he published another volume on *The Gary Schools.* His plea was the pragmatic plea of re-uniting education with life. "By closing off the school," he wrote, "and boxing up learning, we have really smothered education."

But he did not confine himself to education. These years from 1914 until America's entrance into the war evoked his best literary criticism; and there are some, like Van Wyck Brooks, who claim for Bourne a high rank as critic. A volume of his critical essays appeared after his death as *The History of a Literary Radical.* They established him, I think, as one who, had he lived, would clearly have become one of America's great critics in the sociological tradition, a true forerunner of Vernon Parrington. His book reviews tended always to be critical essays on the social roots of a man's thinking. They were radical in the sense that they were unsparing in the application of the critical canons they chose. Not that Bourne lacked a breadth of sympathy: his essay on Cardinal Newman had in it generosity and appreciation. But the main direction of his mind was more exacting. "At the present time," he wrote, "it is of no use to wield one's weapons *for* art; one must simply turn them *against* what is hostile to art." To do this as a literary critic he had to become a critic of our social institutions—our business ideals, our Puritanism, our capitalism, our spurious melting-pot cant, our social-settlement attitudes, our flabby sentimentality, our folksiness, our genteel values. His attacks on the Philistines among novelists and critics, in whose number he included W. C. Brownell and Stuart Sherman, had a joyful abandon. He was, in a sense, an American Matthew Arnold, with a touch of Nietzsche's "gay science," who had studied Veblen and delighted in him. His writing, like Veblen's, was ironic; and I am using the term here in Bourne's sense of irony —as flowing from a democracy of the literary realm in which no idea can plead privilege or immunity from a drastic deflation.

What held together Bourne as educator, literary critic, and social critic was his vision of a possible American culture. He had caught at Columbia a glimpse of a culture in which the individual had dignity because the group lived collectively. In Europe this perception had deepened, but Europe had gone off on a war madness, and in revulsion Bourne turned to America again. For him the war was more than a war of imperialisms—it was a crime against the culture he had envisioned and meant to help enact. But Bourne was no longer the professional spokesman of youth. The war years matured his thought. He spoke now not as one of the rebel young, but as a mature American seeking to evoke in America the resources that would bring it to maturity.

This was the cry that others of Bourne's generation took up: *America must come of age.* Bourne was himself groping for a concept of American culture as distinguished from the American nation or the American state—a culture that he summed up in one of his finest phrases, "the effort of reason and the adventure of beauty." Still using the instrumentalism he had learned from James and Dewey he hoped, for all the frank destructiveness of his writing, that Americans would be able to use their institutions as instruments for fashioning a new society. Here was a Bourne very different from the Bourne who mocked Fabianism as not being revolutionary enough. And he knew of this contradiction himself. He had once seen, in a flash of self-revelation, that here lay the paradox of his career and thinking.

I wondered [he wrote in a letter to Alyse Gregory from Cilmery, September 8, 1913] what perverse fate has imposed on me a philosophy so cross-grained, so desperately unpractical as mine of scorn for institutions, combined with a belief in their reform.

But across this writing and thinking of Bourne, however perverse and paradoxical, the war threw an ever-longer shadow. As America became more embroiled with Germany, and patriotism mounted, Bourne thought he saw his own culture going the way of Europe's. He turned to fight that drift with every resource of his powerful mind and caustic pen. And he had to pay the price. Increasingly he found the *New Republic* columns closed to him. The *Dial* too, for which he had been doing some writing, now rejected him. Another editor returned one of Bourne's articles on a politically harmless literary subject because he did not approve of Bourne's views on the war. There remained only a new magazine called the *Seven Arts;* and for this, month after month, Bourne now wrote a series of biting, brilliant articles against American entrance into the war. They were later gathered by James Oppenheim into a small volume, *Untimely Papers.* Upon them his reputation as a social thinker is likely to rest.

In this period occurred the great crisis in Bourne's life. His attitude toward the war led to a break with many of his friends, among them the man whom he had always revered and whose disciple he had been—John Dewey. To signalize the break Bourne wrote one of his most acid essays, "Twilight of Idols." What a personal wrench this involved for him I can only guess—I have seen no letters of his referring to it. But I do know that intellectually it meant breaking with a philosophy in which he had grown up. He felt increasingly isolated. He was denounced as pro-German, trailed by federal officers. There was one incident at Woods Hole when he was arrested by secret service agents, his bag searched, and some scribbled notes for a poem mistaken for a code description of the coastline. He could not be silent about what was happening to others as well: he spoke out bitterly against the treatment of conscientious objectors. But he was ineffective. He had misjudged completely the culture in which he lived. He had never believed that the whole country— liberal and conservative, labor and capitalist—could be so wholly caught up in the war fever. Eventually he saw that he stood almost alone. His little figure with the long dark cape and the quick step became a symbol of his alienation from the main forces of American culture which he thought he had understood. In September 1917, even the *Seven Arts* had to suspend publication because its subsidy was withdrawn. Bourne had scarcely enough to live on. For over a year he was completely silent, so far as public writing went. He gave up his rooms and went to live with some friends who loved and cherished him. There he died on December 22, 1918—of pneumonia, six weeks after the Armistice, at the age of thirty-two.

Death found him in the midst of writing a treatise on *The State*, which he left behind as an unfinished fragment of some twenty or twenty-five thousand words, and which forms part of his *Untimely Papers*. It was his last effort to understand the nature of the forces which had snuffed him out, as they had snuffed out his vision of a humanist society.

5

It is the Bourne who wrote "The War and the Intellectuals" and the other essays in the same *Seven Arts* group, and the "Unfinished Fragment on the State," who claims our attention today. His attack on the liberal intellectuals of his day and on their role in bringing America into the war was one of the most scathing in American political literature. Bourne was pacifist in his deepest convictions; he was also a democrat in the truest cultural sense. The war crossed his grain on both counts. He takes at their word some of the more self-conscious intellectuals, that they had willed American entrance into the war and had persuaded the democratic mass.

They are right [he says in "The War and the Intellectuals," June 1917] in that the war certainly did not spring either from the ideals or the prejudices . . . of the American people, however acquiescent the masses prove to be. . . . The nerve of the war feeling centered, of course, in the richer and older classes. . . . The intellectuals, in other words, have identified themselves with the least democratic forces in American life. They have assumed the leadership for war of those very classes whom the American democracy has been immemorially fighting. . . .

In a letter to Van Wyck Brooks, on March 27, 1918, he elaborates on this. What the intellectuals have done, he says, is to give their reactionary opponents a rationalization for the war; but the real control of the war will be taken over by the reactionaries who pull the strings of power. The liberals have, he says, led us into

a hateful and futile war, with a fatal backwash and backfire upon creative and democratic values at home. . . . The difficulty with the liberal is that so far he has felt that he could ride two horses at once; he could be a patriot and still frown on greed and violence and predatory militarism; he could desire social reconstruction and yet be most reverent toward the traditional institutions. . . . Somehow in the liberal attack upon the unsocialized beast, liberalism has accepted—in what I believe to be the vain hope of conscious guidance and control— almost every program that the bigoted unsocialized patriot has demanded.

But why have the intellectuals acted thus? Here Bourne's answer runs not in terms of class interest but of the sway of ideas. The liberals have, he says in his essay "Twilight of Idols" (October 1917), acted under the impulsion of the instrumentalist philosophy of John Dewey and his school. This essay is one of the most poignant pieces of writing in our political literature, for the break with Dewey was a painful one for Bourne.

What I come to is a sense of suddenly being left in the lurch, of suddenly finding that a philosophy upon which I had relied to carry us through no longer works.

The instrumentalist philosophy as applied by the liberals to the war he describes as follows:

It is only on the craft, in the stream, they say, that one has any chance of controlling the current forces for liberal purposes. If we obstruct, we surrender all power for influence. If we responsibly approve, we then retain our power for guiding.

Well [answers Bourne], it is true that they may guide, but if their stream leads to disaster and the frustration of national life, is their guiding any more than a preference whether they shall go over the right hand or the left hand of the precipice?

What follows, then? Has Bourne broken wholly with instrumentalism? Here he makes a distinction:

Dewey's philosophy is inspiring enough for a society at peace, prosperous, and with a fund of progressive good will. . . . Where institutions are at all malleable, it is the only clew for improvement. But . . . it depends on a store of rationality and is effective only where there is a strong desire for progress.

And, of course, the war—as Bourne saw it—would blot out both rationality and the desire for progress.

In the light of this analysis, what did Bourne advise doing? Although he spoke out for conscientious objectors, he was not one himself. He knew too well the power of the state, enhanced in wartime, for him to counsel a direct confronting of it. What he proposed was a sort of passive obedience.

Let us [he wrote in "A War Diary," September 1917] compel the war to break in on us, not go hospitably to meet it. Let us force it perceptibly to batter in our spiritual walls. . . . Those who are conscripted will have to be broken in on. If they do not want to be martyrs, they will have to be victims.

And in "Below the Battle" (July 1917) he tells the story of a young artist friend of his who does not want war and who through a passive and grudging submission will be not above the battle but below it. But the result, Bourne sees, will be cynicism—"an appalling skepticism of youth."

6

"The war—or American promise: one must choose. One cannot
be interested in both. For the effect of the war will be to impoverish
American promise. It cannot advance it." Thus Bourne in "A War
Diary," and in these sentences we reach the heart of his outlook.

It is not, as Bourne presents it, a wholly integrated outlook. He
tended to approach problems of social theory as an essayist—
through indirections, through tracing in one essay after another a
personal psychograph. To get at the structure of his thinking one
must piece it together, block by block, from his essays and letters,
all surcharged with an intensely personal emotion. Yet the structure, what there is of it, is there.

It has, for its base, three principal lines of thought. One is
Bourne's cultural outlook. Here his code phrase is one taken, as if
by a special ironic twist, from the *New Republic's* Herbert Croly
—"the promise of American life." But while the phrase is Croly's,
the content is Bourne's, taken from the whole odyssey of Bourne's
life and thought, his travel in Europe fused with his hope for
America. The second is Bourne's class vision—a growing proletari-
anism which made him feel that the struggle to fulfill the American promise was wholly an internal struggle within American life;
that it was a struggle between the possessing classes and the functional classes; and that it could be carried on without a primary
concern for what happened in Europe. The third is Bourne's theory
of the relation between war and the state.

This theory Bourne expressed most fully in his "Unfinished
Fragment on the State," written in the winter of 1918 just before
his death. It was written as a treatise rather than as another essay.
Its form is rigid and severe. "Government," it starts, "is synonymous
with neither State nor Nation. It is the machinery by which the
nation, organized as a State, carries out its State functions." It was
as if Bourne, isolated and frustrated, finding his anti-war essays ineffective, had given up the attempt at month-by-month persuasion
and protest, and had decided to dig deep into political theory in
preparation for the long struggle to come after the war. Yet I am
inclined to think that the impulsions of this treatise were more
personal than its outward form would indicate. I cannot help feeling that Bourne was dissatisfied with the level on which his thinking

had rested. Up to 1917 he had accepted Dewey's philosophy. It had failed him. But his protests against it would be ineffective unless they came from a counter-philosophy as deep and integrated as Dewey's own. And here Bourne could find no one to lean on, even if he had wished to. No one but himself. He could draw on Veblen's *Imperial Germany and the Industrial Revolution*. He could draw on Simon Patten's *Culture and War*. He could draw on Beard's *Economic Interpretation of the Constitution*. But he would have to use them for his own purposes, and the final product would have to be his own.

What Bourne might have achieved in this respect if he had lived we can only guess at. The "Fragment" is a brilliant beginning in what John Chamberlain has called ironically "grand political theory." But only a beginning. Bourne's whole training had scarcely fitted him for grand political theory. His natural language was the language of literary and social criticism. When it comes to political concepts he handles them as a brilliant amateur, but still an amateur. Bourne was groping toward a Marxian theory of the state as an expression of the class relations of production, but there is no evidence of any intimate acquaintance with the Marxian literature, on either economic theory or state theory. He was dealing with material involving the clash between idealist and materialist theories of politics, yet there is no indication that he knew the work of either Engels or T. H. Green. He was dealing with the nature of power, force, and violence, yet there is no mention of the tradition that had wrestled with these problems in the modern state from Machiavelli to Sorel. He was dealing with the knotty question of why men fought and what fighting did to them, yet there is no indication that he was acquainted with the work that had been done on mass psychology. Bourne's "Fragment" has insights that go deeper than the work of the formal academicians. Yet as it stands those insights are not integrated.

But even as it stands Bourne's "Fragment" must be regarded as one of the notable American attempts at a theory of the state. It is part of a tradition that began with Madison's papers on class theory in the *Federalist,* and that extends through Turner's theory of the frontier and the work of J. Allen Smith, Charles Beard, Herbert Croly, Walter Weyl, Vernon Parrington. Which is to say that Bourne sought his theory of the state in a study of American history and an attempt to discover the shaping forces that produce a politics and a culture. There can be little doubt that it was Beard's *Economic Interpretation of the Constitution* that gave him his starting-point, for the larger part of the book is an attempt to apply Beard's class approach to the later reaches of American history.

But if Bourne is giving us Beard, it is Beard with a decided difference. And that difference is contained in Bourne's emphasis on the strength of the state. Here was something not to be found in Marxian theory, which has always underscored the viability of economic rather than political constructions. Nor was it to be found in the thinking of the American progressives on which, in the main, Bourne drew. It was related rather to a strain in contemporary German thought. We know that Bourne had read John Dewey's *German Philosophy and Politics,* and Thorstein Veblen's *Imperial Germany.* He may have read, or perhaps only dabbled, in some of the contemporary German thinkers whom the war had for the first time revealed to Americans. But there can be little doubt that he saw, more clearly perhaps than any other American except Thorstein Veblen, the toughness of state power, once granted its roots in class interest and tenacity, in traditional acceptance, in psychological allegiance. One of the revealing passages in the "Fragment" deals with the attack, in the decade of 1904–1914, upon the capitalist control of the American state—an attack made by T.R., by the muckrakers, by the Wilsonian idealists.

These [the possessing] classes actually had little to fear. A political system which had been founded in the interests of property by their own spiritual and economic ancestors, which had become ingrained in the country's life through a function of 120 years, which was buttressed by a legal system which went back without a break to the early English monarchy, was not likely to crumble before the anger of a few muckrakers, the disillusionment of a few radical sociologists, or the assaults of proletarian minorities.

The propertied classes, Bourne continues, bided their time until "the exigency of a war, in which business organization was imperatively needed."

The mass of the worried middle classes, riddled by the campaign against American failings, which at times extended almost to a skepticism of the American State itself, were only too glad to sink back to a glorification of the State ideal, to feel about them in war the old pro-

tecting arms, to return to the old primitive robust sense of the omnip-
otence of the State, its matchless virtue, honor, and beauty, driving away
all the foul old doubts and dismays.

Here in these passages one gets the essential quality of Bourne's
state theory. The reverence for the state was a primitive tribal feeling. The state itself, rooted in this feeling and buttressed by legal
institutions, was an instrument of class power. That instrument had
been challenged in America by a nascent proletarian and agrarian
democracy. Upon that democracy the dominant class had imposed
a Constitution, formulated in its own interest; and it had fortified
itself by a party system it could manipulate and corrupt. Its own
failure as an economic ruling class, however, made the prestige of
its state a shaky affair. When war broke out, therefore, this class
welcomed it for reasons of class interest, just as the middle class
welcomed it because of (here Bourne delighted to use a phrase of
L. P. Jacks) "the peacefulness of being at war." Thus the state was
again strengthened. "For war is," Bourne repeatedly asserts, turning the German conservative thought to ironic use, "essentially the
health of the state."

It is a melancholy experience to read the "Fragment" today—
melancholy because so much of it is profoundly right and profoundly disturbing. There can be little doubt that Bourne and
Veblen, almost alone of their generation in America, saw the roots
of totalitarianism in the modern state. Bourne set those roots in a
psychological soil of what he called the "gregarious impulse." In
terms of contemporary psychology that now sounds archaic, and
one must remember that Bourne wrote before the reception of
Freudianism in America. Yet if one overlooks the terminology there
still remains a residue of validity in his analysis.

Just as in modern societies the sex-instinct is enormously over-
supplied for the requirements of human propagation, so the gregarious
impulse is enormously over-supplied for the work of protection which
it is called upon to perform. . . . All human progress . . . must be
carried against the resistance of this tyrannical herd-instinct which
drives the individual into obedience. . . . There is in the feeling
towards the State a large element of pure filial mysticism. . . . The
chief value of the state in wartime is the opportunity it gives for this
regression to infantile attitudes.

But Bourne does not stop with this psychological analysis, however faulty. He goes on to a class analysis of the state in wartime.

War becomes almost a sport between the hunters and the hunted. The pursuit of enemies within outweighs in psychic attractiveness the assault on the enemy without. . . . A white terrorism is carried on by the Government against pacifists, Socialists, enemy aliens, and a milder unofficial persecution against all persons or movements that can be imagined as connected with the enemy. War, which should be the health of the state, unifies all the bourgeois elements and the common people, and outlaws the rest.

Is this true, as Bourne sees it, only of a particular type of state? Here his answer is difficult, but I shall try to present it. War is, as he sees it, the inevitable function of a *state-system.*

It is States that make wars and not nations. . . . War, as such, cannot occur except in a system of competing States which have relations with each other through the channels of diplomacy. War is a function of this system of States, and could not occur except in such a system. Nations organized for internal administration, nations organized as a federation of free communities, nations organized in any way except that of a political centralization of a dynasty, or the reformed descendant of a dynasty, could not possibly make war upon each other. They would not only have no motive for conflict, but they would be unable to muster the concentrated force to make war effective.

What Bourne seems to be saying is that war is an integral part of the Western system of dynastic states, including the capitalist democracies.

7

I have quoted at some length from Bourne's "Fragment" because it is difficult to convey both its variety and its contradictory qualities except through quotation; but also because Bourne alone, of those who opposed America's entrance into the war, did so as part of a reasoned analysis that sought to pierce to the heart of the problems of psychology, class relations, and political power that were involved. I do not propose here to inquire how valid Bourne's reasoning was for his time. I am more concerned to inquire how valid it is for the dilemmas of our own generation. If in this section I emphasize my points of difference, it is partly because I have already by implication indicated my sympathy for many of the positions he took with respect to his own generation.

In the first place, Bourne seems never to have reconciled his view that war is an inevitable and functional part of the state-system with his efforts to keep America out of the war. For America was, by Bourne's own analysis, part of the very state-system out of which the war had arisen, and would therefore have to be part of any war that sprang so deeply from the tensions of that state-system. We may guess here that Bourne did not see this so clearly when he wrote the *Seven Arts* essays, and that his sweeping abstraction on this score when he came to write the "Fragment" was an attempt to console himself for his defeat and to explain it to himself as having been inevitably in the cards from the very beginning.

At this point one who wishes to follow Bourne's thought is faced by a dilemma. Let us say, on the one hand, that he accepts the thesis of the inevitability of war and its complete class and dynastic character. It would follow that the only way to abolish war or to prevent American entry into it is the way of revolutionary overthrow of the class state and the establishment of the classless state, both nationally and internationally. But here we are faced by the fact that the very state power of which war forms the health is capable of crushing not only resistance to war but class revolution as well. This has been demonstrated in the whole of recent Western history. In the one state where a revolution looking toward a classless society was successful, the Soviet Union, it has succeeded in abolishing neither war nor ruthless state power. If anything, the Marxian state has turned out to be even more dynastic, more centralized, more determined to suppress cultural variants and minority thought than what Bourne called the "reformed descendant" of the dynastic state—capitalist democracy. And where, after the Russian Revolution, proletarian revolution has threatened the capitalist state, it has reverted to the more primitive dynastic state, using all the instruments of technology and planning both in war and in industrial control, to put complete state power at the service of feudal objectives. Thus assuming Bourne's thesis of inevitability, one comes out in the end with either revolutionary frustration or totalitarianism.

Let us now make the opposite assumption—that by conscious effort short of revolution one can resist the state and transform its character. This is to take an instrumentalist approach, for which Bourne excoriated the intellectuals of his generation—and for which the intellectuals of our own generation are being similarly reproached by followers of Bourne. I have indicated the extent of my sympathy for Bourne's attitude at the time, and my admiration for the savage grace of his writing. Yet Bourne's position was by no means completely thought out. It was not the instrumentalism of the Lippmann-Croly-Dewey group that was at fault: it was the lack of realism within their instrumental approach. They did not understand that war must not be embraced as an instrument of national policy merely as a way of gaining a strategic position in the organization of peace. It must not be used unless the objective international situation is such that to do anything else would be catastrophic. And even then it must not be used for the negative ends of making the world "safe" for anything, whether democracy or capitalism, but only for affirmative ends of forward movement in class relations and economic welfare within America and in the world at large. Any instrumentalism, in short, is bad or good depending on whether its purposes are dynamic or static, its outlook realistic or complacent, and whether it has at its disposal some means for enforcing its purposes and enacting its vision.

Judged in these terms the intellectuals of Bourne's generation could scarcely stand up under the acid analysis to which he subjected them. Where their ends were not static they were vaguely idealistic, running in terms of open diplomacy and a League of Nations. They made the fatal mistake in their perspective of looking toward the further extension of European nationalism and the further fragmentation of the world; and they misunderstood completely the irrational character of political action, which Bourne in the end glimpsed. And, in terms of means, they sought to enact their purposes through the sheer force of their ideas, rather than through the retention of state power and the building of an ever-strengthened class and national base for that state power.

In our own generation, we have a world situation dominated by the rise of totalitarian state techniques more complete and ruthless than any that Bourne could contemplate, in the service of an ideology more barbaric than any within the range of Bourne's experience. The Nazi power today, because it has already conquered the greater part of Europe, because it is organized to exploit class tensions and personal insecurity in a world revolutionary situation, threatens directly the American nation and its political and social framework, both from without and within. If America were to preserve a strict neutrality, there can be little doubt that British resistance would be easily broken, and we should have to face alone the prospect of either fighting or appeasing a Nazi-dominated world. In such a context the withdrawal of America into its own shell could mean only, adopting a phrase from Nietzsche that Bourne liked to quote, "a detour to suicide." Granted that war itself cannot advance social purposes or enrich life, one might cite against Bourne the remark I have quoted from him above in discussing his literary criticism: "At the present time it is of no use to wield one's weapons *for* art; one must simply turn them *against* what is hostile to art." Bourne wrote this in a period that seemed too bleak for literature; we live today in a period of incomparable bleakness for the whole human spirit. If it is too much to hope that the war against Nazism will advance democratic living, one can at least pursue it to hem in what would otherwise utterly destroy the chance of democratic living.

What has intervened between Bourne's generation and ours is a change of world perspective so complete as to make the earlier outlines unrecognizable. The state, whose power Bourne feared so, has multiplied its power many times. The dynastic state has become the totalitarian state. And the totalitarian state has fed not upon the readiness of its opponents for war, but upon their unreadiness. Bourne made the ghastly error of thinking so completely in absolutes that he lumped all states together with respect to the nature of their power. I say "ghastly" advisedly, since the absolutist tendency shared by Marxian and liberal schools alike to think of the state as a single abstraction left us unprepared for the emergence of totalitarian states, the range of whose powers went far beyond that of even the most illiberal democracies. And because men did not see how different in kind was the totalitarian state from our own, they were unprepared either to see its threat or to resist it. Bourne, as I have said earlier, foresaw the psychological basis of totalitarianism; and he foresaw also that it could grow out of the tensions of the Western state-system. What he could not see—what even most of our own generation did not see—was that there were two lines of direction in the Western state-system: that one was in essence anti-democratic and anti-humanist (Veblen saw this in his *Imperial Germany*); and that the other would become so only by not fighting (as Belgium, Holland, Norway), or fighting too late and badly (as France).

And because Bourne was an absolutist, he was misled in his class analysis, arguing that the worst fate that could befall the working-class in a capitalist democracy was war. Actually the destroyed working-classes in the former European democracies would be alive today if they had understood that not to wage a war against an anti-proletarian as well as anti-humanist enemy like Nazism was the surest way to destruction. There is nothing in Bourne's theory of the relation of class structure to war which explains why the British working-class consistently fought the Baldwin-Chamberlain appeasement policy, why it finally forced a reluctant bourgeois government into war, why it was willing to join in a government with a tory like Churchill when the British ruling classes were finally forced to a vigorous prosecution of the war. Nor could his theory explain why British labor leaders see in the successful issue of the war the only chance for the liberation of labor in other countries as well, and the only chance for the extension of democratic socialization.

For the fact is that Bourne, in his hatred of war and his insistence on viewing it only as "an upper-class sport," failed to take account of the possibility that in the Western state-system the fate of the lower and functional classes might be just as surely tied up with the use of war as a defensive instrument as the fate of the possessing classes. And by premising a one-to-one correspondence between the control of state machinery and the control of economic power, Bourne left out of account the continuing fight that the functional classes in a democracy have been making to gain and retain control of the state machinery. There is nothing in his thinking that would prepare us for the administrative revolution that has already taken place in the American state, and the rise of a new bureaucracy whose allegiance is not given primarily to the owning classes.

It is in his affirmations that Bourne's abiding importance will lie —his affirmation of the necessity for safeguarding liberty of expression and cultural variants, whatever the internal pressures toward centralized power. Bourne's writing will serve to remind us how easy it is for a democracy at war to turn its ferocity inward, against the friends rather than the enemies of the culture. This happened in France at the outbreak of the present war; yet the current example of England shows that it need not happen generically in a democracy at war. And from the viewpoint of civil liberties, for a country like America today, the great danger comes not from our own economic difficulties—considerable as that danger is—but from the impact of the Nazi ideology upon our insecure groups. Given the crushing of that ideology, we shall still have the chance to raise our living standards and guard our civil liberties. Given a Nazi triumph that chance will vanish, and even the terrorism that Bourne witnessed and that loomed so large in his experience will seem like a halcyon period in comparison.

8

Bourne did not think through to the utmost reaches of his problem. Who in his time did? Who has in our own time? He thought in many respects, I venture to say, further than anyone in his generation. His has been called the "lost generation" because the war came athwart its promise and its unfolding. We may or may not accept Bourne's conclusions for our day. But if we learn from him that the question of war or no war cannot be accepted negatively, that it must ultimately be referred to the question of what will preserve and extend the creative groups in American life, ours will not be called the lost generation.

1941

Franz Kafka and the
Human Voyage

Genius, wherever it crops up, is a strange and solitary plant; nor have we in literature had so many instances of it that we can afford to neglect one as authentic as Franz Kafka. There was about his genius a lonely and almost nihilist quality. It seems to have come from nowhere, to belong to nothing, even perhaps to lead to nothing. Kafka is part neither of the humanist nor of the anti-humanist tradition into which we have come increasingly to divide the recent intellectual history of Europe. Yet unmistakably his books have left a scar upon our consciousness.

During his lifetime Kafka made no great noise in the world. He never sought recognition and never received it. He was born in 1883 of a Jewish tradesman's family of Prague. He grew up, sensitive and unhappy, in the shadow of his father's dominant personality. The memory of that (as we learn from his famous "Letter to My Father") and the sense of inadequacy that went with it were to haunt and cripple him for life—make him set impossibly high standards for himself, make him reluctant ever to call a piece of work finished or to surrender a manuscript for publication, obsess him (as Thomas Wolfe was later to be obsessed) with the search for a father and for justification before him. He studied law and became a functionary of the Austrian bureaucracy in the workmen's compensation division. Here in an office he spent his days; his evenings he spent with the writing which he loved so and which so tortured him. He joined no movements, whether literary or political, and seemed more absorbed with the tempestuous voyage of the human spirit than with the turbulence of Europe in its chaotic war and post-war phases.

The last years of his life were broken by sickness and the search for health. His relations with women were troubled: he never married; twice he broke off his engagement; and only at the close of his life did he find some peace in such a relation. He died in 1924, at forty-one, of tuberculosis, leaving instructions (fortunately unfulfilled) that his manuscript writings be burned. There is a photograph of him (why is it not in any of the American editions?) showing a sensitive, dark, sloping face, sharply chiseled features, and piercing eyes that arrest the whole attention, and hint at the firmness and the skepticism, the unflagging humor and the questing passion for belief that give his writings their quality.

Since his death Kafka has become a force in our writing. Yet everywhere his influence has been confined to the smallish literary groups and their magazines. Talk of him there and you get as response the subterranean intensity of the early Christian fathers, wrapped often in incommunicable symbols. This catacomb Kafka is not healthy: it means the blocking of the channel that might connect him with the large body of potential readers; it means also that those who are left are forced often into uncritical acceptance and elaborate commentary—the cult and the canon.

For that reason the recent publication of American editions of two of his major works is something of an event. Kafka published during his lifetime some stories and sketches comprising one of the six volumes of his collected works in German. The rest appeared posthumously under the ministering hand of his friend and executor, Max Brod. The three great novels fill three of the other five volumes. The remaining two contain further short stories (Kafka was a master of the short story in a form almost wholly alien to the Anglo-French-American tradition), parables, *pensées,* journals, letters, and even an act of an unfinished play.

Of the novels *Amerika,* written on the eve of the first World War and for some years available in England, is now [1] first made available to American readers, with an introductory essay by Klaus Mann. The second, *The Trial,* written during the World War, was published here in 1937. The third, *The Castle,* written just before Kafka's death, was published here about a decade ago but now appears in a new edition,[2] with a prefatory "Homage" by Thomas Mann. All three are the Edwin Muir translations, which deserve in

[1] Norfolk, Conn., New Directions, 1940.
[2] New York, Alfred A. Knopf, 1941.

their own way the tributes that have been paid to Proust's translator; for Muir can convey the formal tensions of Kafka's style because he understands the inner tensions of his thought. The new prefaces by the Manns manage to be at once appreciative and acute. And the publishers have made the books handsome to look at. I have, however, a serious quarrel with them. All three of Kafka's novels were left unfinished. But the definitive German edition by Brod adds fragments of the unfinished chapters which are of no little value. The new American editions should have included them. The lack is only partly made up by the inclusion of several of these fragments of *The Castle* in the excellent *Miscellany* [3] of writings by and about Kafka. One further note for those who may wish to venture on Kafka: a volume of his short stories, *The Great Wall of China,* has been published in England; other stories have been translated, notably "Metamorphosis" in one of the issues of *transition* and "In the Penal Colony" in a recent issue of *Partisan Review.*

Kafka is a philosophical and religious novelist. I mean this in a central and not marginal sense. He is not a novelist who happens to be dealing with these themes or, as Muir points out, chooses to use religious characters. Kafka was absorbed with certain problems from an angle which made it impossible for him to treat them except through fiction, allegory, parable. He was a philosopher groping for a form rather than a novelist groping for a theme. It is fairly clear that the writing of these novels was, as their reading may be, an act of religious exploration. I use the term religion, of course, not in the sense of an institutional creed or a body of received dogma, but of a system of personal belief transcending experience— the sense that Carlyle meant when he said that the most important thing about a man was his religion.

But while the themes are grand themes, Kafka does not attack them in a magisterial way. He approaches them indirectly, through stories that, for all their oppressive nightmare quality and their overtones of allegory, wear an aspect of innocence. *Amerika,* for example, is in form almost a picaresque novel—a twentieth-century *Roderick Random.* It seems to be only a loose episodic narrative of what happens to Karl Rossman, a German boy of sixteen, when he sets out to make his career in America—his meeting on ship-

---

[3] *A Kafka Miscellany,* New York, Twice a Year Press, 1940.

board with a stoker, his adoption and abandonment by a rich uncle, his adventures in a country house, his career as elevator-boy in a hotel, the misfortunes that befell him through two rascally knights of the road who later settled down in a ménage with a fabulous mistress, his employment by the "Nature Theater of Oklahoma." *The Trial,* less loosely wrought, is the story of Joseph K., who finds himself accused of a crime he did not commit and the nature of which he cannot even discover. He tries to get a hearing, deal with an advocate, find allies, reach the higher judges. He never succeeds. But he gets a warning of his sentence from a sermon preached in a cathedral to himself as a one-man audience; and in the end he is stabbed to death by two officials of the court.

The protagonist of *The Castle,* K. (note the progressive attenuation of name), comes to the village thinking he has a summons from the castle to act as surveyor. But he receives from the castle only denial or evasion. He spends his energy on successive stratagems and devices for getting near the officials of the castle, particularly one called Klamm. There are adventures with women, with village inhabitants and castle retainers, with K.'s two assistants; there is a harrowing story within a story; there is a comic note of high diplomacy in the alliances and alignments K. seeks to form in order to get even the smallest foothold in the village. In the end, Max Brod tells us, Kafka planned to have K. wear himself out in his efforts; but as he lies dying, a messenger arrives from the castle to say he can stay in the village on temporary sufferance.

Many a critic has tried his hand at interpreting the allegory. I do not intend to do that here. But some things may be said summarily. Kafka is dealing with the largest themes of the fate of man in a world whose meaning stretches beyond his experience. His starting-point is the inadequacy of the empirical and the rational. The purpose of life becomes thus an endless quest for the meaning of life. The quest, whatever its form, is always a quest for an organic relation with something beyond ourselves. It may be, as in *Amerika,* only Karl's desire after his expulsion from the Old World (he had been seduced in Germany by a servant-girl) to find roots in a new world—a job, a career, a home, independence—and thus fulfill himself. It may be, as in the cathedral scene in *The Trial,* a desire to find what lies beyond the door of our unique personality. Joseph K., dissatisfied with the rational routine of his life, was "accused"—a marked man. He haunted the court where lay his fate, yet he could make no connection with it. K., in *The Castle,* also wanders beyond his accustomed locus; he wants a connection with Klamm, even of the slightest and humblest. Even the agonizing rebuffs he receives do not make him think of retreat. His search for roots in the village, for a place near the castle, seems to come from a fatal inner necessity.

But with the sureness of the necessity there is also the sureness of failure—absolute failure in *The Trial,* failure relieved in *The Castle* only by the grimly ironic concession at the end. The quest must continue, but the one certain thing about it is the massive inaccessibility of the goal. I do not believe, as some of his critics say, that Kafka was content with this; that he resolved it with the old liberal cliché of Goethe and Tennyson that meaning lay in process rather than in end, in the search for the grail rather than the grail itself. Kafka was bitter. And anyone who does not read his bitterness in his novels and stories misses, I think, half their quality. But the paradox from which grew bitterness yielded by the same token inexhaustible material for a sort of cosmic comedy. I have already mentioned the attempt to reach God by power politics. Kafka's attitude toward God was that of the Greeks who constructed an entire theogony but retained in it human frailties. Klamm, the chief man of the castle, looks like a paunchy bourgeois and has barmaids as mistresses. The court officials in *The Trial* are old, wheezy, and generally decrepit; the attendants are lecherous and sadistic. The whole theme of bureaucracy as part of the cosmic is a persistent one in Kafka, no doubt because of his own experience in Austrian administrative officialdom. On shipboard, in the hotel, in the "nature theater" (although this is a genial and careless bureaucracy), in courtroom, village, and castle, red tape is king. Man is caught in a mechanism not of his own contriving—a mechanism, moreover, whose operations are gallingly slow, inefficient, and even accidental. In fact, by a wild irony in this regime of order and law, it is accident that is decisive. Despite the oppressive anxiety of Kafka's protagonist to fulfill his quest and come to terms with his universe, despite his desperate straining to make even the slightest headway, he is hopelessly entangled in a network of casual incidents. The most irrelevant act may lead to the widest consequences; the trivial is canonized.

This is, of course, the stuff of dreams: and the most obvious thing about the Kafka world is that it is a dream world. There hangs over it the heavy blanket of anxiety that we know from our own dream existence. Will the protagonist make it? Will he, after roaming through corridor after corridor, find his way off the ship?—the passage that leads back to the living room of the country house? —the key that opens the door of escape from Brunelda's apartment? —the door, among all the myriad doors of the tenement house, that leads to the courtroom?—the way out of the cathedral before his name is called and the sermon starts?—the path in the snow that leads back to the inn before night falls? This nightmare world has also its comic aspect, and there is a Chaplinesque music-hall quality to Kafka that has several times been noted. But the other aspects are more persistent. As in a dream, events follow each other with the phantasmal logic of illogic. Granted the premises, the details have a certain cogency: but the premises are outrageous. Time plays tricks: K. starts out in the morning from the inn toward the castle; in a few hours, night comes and it is dark. Space plays tricks: the more K. presses toward the castle, the farther away it seems to move. There are changes of identity. In fact the whole Kafka universe seems to illustrate the principle of discontinuity. You go from A to C without having passed through B.

The uncertainty is underscored because Kafka's protagonist moves throughout in an atmosphere of intrigue and conspiracy. There is a crazy quilt of plot and counterplot, but with a wild subjectivism in it all: the dangers and malignancies that beset the path of Kafka's protagonists you see only through their own eyes. Kafka means you to see that subjectivism. In *The Trial,* for example, although Joseph K. is under arrest, he is not under detention. He is out on a sort of psychic bail, goes about his daily tasks in the bank and reports to court only from an inner necessity. And yet his world, like the world of K. and Karl Rossman, is none the less full of enemies and obstacles, like that of a savage in the jungle of his fears. In fact, the most important thing is that the enemy is never localized, and enemy and goal are one. The castle and the court are not only inaccessible; they carry on in their own remote and complicated way a campaign not to be reached. And the very allies that Kafka's protagonists hope to use in attaining their goal turn out to wear the badge of the enemy-goal. One gets a hint of Emerson's Brahma:

"When me they fly, I am the wings"—except that this is pursuit rather than flight. What we seek with is part of what we seek. What we fight with is part of what we fight.

This sense of being involved in a dualistic world is a strong sense in Kafka. It is to me even stronger than the feeling of the alienation of the individual from his world which the critics have tended to stress. Loneliness is the great fact of our mechanized life and has become one of the great themes of our literature; yet it will not do to see Kafka as a Sherwood Anderson writing another Winesburg no matter how cosmic. Kafka's protagonists are not lonely because their social system is deadening: they are lonely because they are caught midway between a good and an evil whose contradiction there is no way of resolving, although each is part of the other. Max Brod has pointed out that Kafka was not tender-minded enough to think there is a synthesis for this polarity. His God is like the Jehovah god of the Jewish tradition, at once terrible and desirable. Kafka's religion is thus far from the religion of consolation. He offers no cheap and easy endings, no safe harbor for the human voyage. It is rather a religion of unceasing exploration. It is, to be sure, heavily laden with a sense of guilt and a sense of determinism, both of which go back to the Greek tragic conceptions. The scene in *The Trial* in which the executioners come for Joseph K. and find him waiting for them and link their arms in his moves swiftly and with a sure fatality. Yet this is not characteristic. More so are the scenes in *The Castle* in which K. holds his intricate and casuistical conversations with Olga and with the various functionaries on how things work in the castle. It has often been pointed out that Kafka was influenced by the Chassidic movement, and there is throughout the books that feeling for the folk-mind and its inherent symbolism which characterized the Chassidic revolt against theological hair-splitting. And yet there is also an enormous amount of hairsplitting in the unwearying discussions in Kafka of the ways of God to man. Kafka was God-drunk; but in his intoxication his subtle and powerful intellect did not stop working.

It seems curious that a writer with preoccupations of this sort should be today one of the great influences in our literature. The reason lies, I think, in the state of that literature. We seem to have come to a dead end. Among the younger writers the emphasis has been social, the method realistic. And Kafka challenges both. He goes beyond the problem of man facing his society to the problem of man facing himself and the unknown and inaccessible within him. He belongs thus in a sense to the tradition which, in Freud's words, has sought to explore the "psychology of the depths."

Yet always in his own way. For his is not the emphasis upon the irrational which is true of the Freudian group. What he has done has been to give the tradition of rationalism a new twist so radical as to transform it. Since the seventeenth century our thinkers have believed that to suppress the barbarian in man and thus make civil society possible, men must enter into a "social contract"—a compact with each other to preserve the fabric of civilization and make law and order possible. But for Kafka social constructions and even social reconstruction are not enough. His protagonists are seeking always not a compact with man but a compact with God. Hence it is not surprising that, as I have mentioned, so many of the speeches in Kafka seem exercises in ratiocination. Compacts are legalistic affairs, and Kafka's characters want to get their precise bearings in the universal frame of things. Yet whatever their mode of speech, what they are driving at—and what Kafka is concerned with—lies beyond rational and irrational, in the realm of the non-rational.

Similarly with Kafka's method. Realism as a method has been run to the ground. While I do not agree with MacLeish and Van Wyck Brooks that literature must nourish national morale, I do agree with Philip Rahv that the cult of experience in our literature has worn thin. What Kafka does is to stand realism on its head. He recognizes that the fictive world must somehow be made real, and that this depends upon great particularity of detail. But he applies this precision of method to a world of his own creating which has no correspondences to the world of our daily experience. Kafka has often been spoken of as an "abstract" writer. But that is to miss the whole point. He does not see his truth, as the abstract artists do, in generalizations and geometrical abstractions. He is nothing if not concrete. He loved Dickens, and there is something of Dickens in him. His people are so highly individualized as often to reach the comic.

This combination—realism of detail within a framework of symbolism—is Kafka's peculiar gift to fiction. The American tradition contains nothing quite like it, and even for distant resemblances we must go back to Melville's *Moby Dick*, with its allegory of evil, and to Hawthorne. One may answer that most good writing today has overtones of symbolism. And that is true, even in the naturalistic fiction of Steinbeck, whose tortoise crawling across the road in *The Grapes of Wrath* is not only a tortoise but the whole mass of plain people. But there is a distinction between a novel with symbolic overtones and a novel whose essential material is symbolism. Or perhaps it is better to say that Kafka writes on several planes at once, and the planes are interconnected. One plane is that of real people doing and saying workaday things but in a dream world; the second plane is that of symbols and of the allegorical framework that furnishes a logic for the otherwise illogical actions of the people; the third plane is that of the philosophical and religious implications of people and symbols together. Justice Holmes in one of his letters to Pollock spoke of Laurence Sterne writing in a room with mirrors. Similarly one can speak of the multiplane writing of Kafka, whose mirrors are more likely to be the mirrors of meaning while Sterne's were all too apt to be only verbal mirrors.

It is this genuine complexity of Kafka and the enormous earnestness of his meaning that keep his art from becoming—what much expressionist art has tended to be—an escape from the ugliness of social reality. Not that Kafka was much of a social thinker. I can agree with Harry Slochower that there are some acute insights into the nature of the social hierarchy in Kafka, but I cannot agree that they go much beyond isolated insights. It is the complex and the non-rational and symbolic in Kafka's vision that have so deeply influenced the younger writers, including Julian Green, Rex Warner, Dylan Thomas, W. H. Auden in his most recent phase, and the *New Directions* group. To many perhaps Kafka will prove a good escape from the current social weariness; to many he will offer what Spengler so uncannily foresaw in his term "the second religiousness." Kafkism is not in its inherent nature any sort of ivory tower-ism. It is not art for art's sake. It goes beyond the social but it remains within the problematic; and the problems of human belief and human destiny that it plots out are as worthy of exploration as almost any in our time. A book, Kafka wrote in one of his aphorisms, must be the ax that breaks the frozen sea within us. For the younger American writers he may himself prove to be that ax.

1941

PART THREE

America's Hour of Decision

1

In the Time of the Great Debate

Continentalism and World Leadership

IT LOOKS as if America has begun its Great Debate on foreign
policy. Compared with the urgency of the issues being discussed in homes, colleges, factories, farms, drugstores, and filling-stations all over the country, the Senate debate on neutrality in
the fall of 1939 was a piddling and superficial affair. Hitler's *Blitzkrieg* against the Allies has left its impact as well on all discussion
of American foreign policy. Already, only a week or two after the
publication of the two books [1] under review, there is a slightly archaic flavor to both of them.

Charles Beard has never stated his argument against American
intervention in foreign wars more persuasively than in this present
little book. It is in form an elaboration of the chapter on foreign
policy in *America in Midpassage;* in basic economic philosophy it
is a distillation of his earlier book, *The Open Door at Home.* But
the lines of analysis are more sharply drawn, the thrust of the argument more powerful, the lash of the ironic words more stinging.
Like Veblen, Beard has grown more an ironist as he has grown
older. Unlike any other writer today on foreign policy, he achieves
the effects of a fierce polemicist by the methods of a detached historian.

On its face his present book is a historical study of three strains
in American foreign policy—"continental Americanism," "imperialism," "internationalism." He is savage in his analysis of the founders of the imperialist policy—Mahan, T.R., John Hay, Henry

---

[1] Charles A. Beard, *A Foreign Policy for America*, New York, Alfred A. Knopf, 1940.
Raymond Leslie Buell, *Isolated America*, New York, Alfred A. Knopf, 1940. This
review appeared at the end of May 1940, just after the beginning of the *Blitzkrieg*
against the Low Countries and France.

Cabot Lodge. He is less openly belligerent but none the less unsparing in dealing with the internationalists—Wilson, Elihu Root, Frank Kellogg; Nicholas Murray Butler and James T. Shotwell and the Carnegie Foundation group; Quincy Wright and Harry Gideonse and the other academicians. He is tenderest of all in his treatment of the continental American strain, for whose genealogy he conscripts Tom Paine, Washington, Jefferson, Madison, Monroe, John Quincy Adams, Clay, and Seward. And his closing chapter, phrased as a note on the persistence of continental Americanism despite the inroads that imperialism and internationalism have made upon it, is in reality a strong plea for a self-contained policy that will stay between our two oceans.

Quite aside from one's agreement or disagreement with Beard's conclusions, one cannot help admiring the techniques of his analysis. More than any other man he has carved out an approach to the problem of foreign policy on the historical plane which will have to be reckoned with. His skill in making history serve his argument is superb. Yet I for one must confess that while I began his book wanting very much to be convinced, I finished it unpersuaded: I came to pray and remained not to scoff but to doubt. One reason perhaps is that I have never believed that the wisdom of the Founding Fathers with respect to the issues of political policy in their day must necessarily be our own wisdom in our day. The isolationist Senator ranting over the radio about Washington's farewell address is a long way removed in insight and intellectual integrity from Charles Beard writing about the wisdom of the Founders' hands-off policy with respect to Europe; nevertheless Beard's argument is not more relevant than the Senator's.

Jefferson, for example, was an isolationist, an agrarian, a states' rights man, and a philosopher of democracy. Of these four only Jefferson the democrat has survived with any real relevance for us; and I am as little convinced by Jefferson's arguments about American isolation as I am by his arguments about states' rights and the superior virtues of the American farmer. The changes since Jefferson in transportation and communication, in war technology and propaganda and in the whole world climate of opinion, put upon us the task of rethinking the whole problem of our relationship to Europe. To be sure, Beard rejects both for Jefferson and for himself the label of "isolationist." He wants world trade and he wants world intellectual commerce. Yet since he feels that American power to underwrite either is negligible, I can see little point to his recognition of American world ties. As rhetoric it is important; as logic and in its practical consequences it is empty. Except for semantic reasons I do not see why "continental Americanism" is a better term than "isolationism."

Perhaps if Beard came out of his historical corner into the contemporary daylight, if he exchanged his ironic indirections for a direct confronting of the issues of an agenda for American foreign policy, we should lose the unique flavor he adds to the Great Debate. Yet I cannot help wishing that he and others would confront four major questions. First, what stakes do we have in the outcome of the present world struggle? Second, what would be the cost—in terms of the impact on American civil liberties and the American economic and social system—of a policy of intervention? Third, what in similar terms would a policy of isolation or "continental Americanism" involve? Fourth, what would be the impact of American intervention or non-intervention on the structure of world peace and social organization?

It is to the last of these questions that Beard primarily addresses himself. The nub of his position is contained in his closing pages. Continentalism, he says, does not seek to make a hermit nation out of America. It merely recognizes "the limited nature of American powers to relieve, restore, and maintain life beyond its own sphere of interest and control." It recognizes "the hard fact that the United States, either alone or in coalition, did not possess the power to force peace on Europe and Asia, to assure the establishment of democratic and pacific governments there, or to provide the social and economic underwriting necessary to the perdurance of such governments." And from there Beard's argument moves to the conclusion that America must concentrate its energy and intelligence in "overcoming the grave economic and social crisis at home."

If the Beard thesis is to be met, it must be met on these two fronts: America is incapable of insuring peace and democracy for the world; America must make democracy work within its own borders. This Raymond Leslie Buell seeks to do in his *Isolated America*. Buell's book is an impressive compendium of information and analysis, historical and contemporary, on practically every issue now being discussed in the Great Debate. He carries over into his book all the occupational skills and the occupational hazards of one who has been research director and later president of the Foreign Policy Association, and has more recently conducted the Fortune Round Table. His arguments are buttressed by so many facts and figures, names and dates, and references to the monograph literature as to leave the ordinary reader lost in a maze of detail. Buell lacks the depth of insight and the mastery of style that Beard possesses; he possesses a capacity for a researcher's intellectual round-up that Beard lacks. His book is not, as some might judge from its title, a plea for isolation. The title is ironic. And while the book is never brought to sharp focus so far as the basic question of intervention or non-intervention is concerned, the drift of the argument is undoubtedly toward interventionism. In Beard's classification, Buell would belong to the Wilsonian internationalist school. In Buell's analysis, Beard would be classed as a pleader for an isolated America.

But questions of terminology aside, how does Buell confront the two basic arguments I have mentioned? To the argument that America has never succeeded either alone or in coalition in imposing world peace or in organizing world democracy, Buell's answer is a plea in confession and avoidance. He agrees that our past efforts have failed. But he insists that the primary blame for the failure rests elsewhere than on the shoulders of the internationalists. First, there was our failure before we entered the last war to indicate clearly and forcefully on what terms we were entering and what would be our conception of the structure of world peace afterward. To supply this lack, Buell devotes the latter part of his book to a post-war program premised either on an Allied victory or a German revolution following Hitler's refusal to accept the American program. At the present time it all sounds weird and unreal. Second, Buell puts the major blame for the American failure to follow up Wilson's Versailles position on the isolationists and Republican diehards in America who sabotaged Wilson's work. Finally, he points to the fantastic international fiscal policy we have followed since the World War. His reasoning is persuasive. Nevertheless, the question persists whether the intrigues of European politics, the nature of the American party system, and the *mores* of

American capitalism do not make the recurrence of the sort of post-war split we had in 1919 hard to avoid for the future as well.

On the question of setting our own house in order, Buell's answer is more forceful. He points out in perhaps the best section of the book that the American continental economy does not exempt us from containing within our own country the same seeds of religious hatred, democratic disillusionment, economic struggle, and potential fascist revolution that the European social system contained. And he goes on to argue that a Nazi victory in Europe and Asia will strengthen these elements of inner cleavage and that the attempt to deal effectively with our economic problems will be an almost hopeless one. Even in the past few days I have had occasion to witness the effects of the impending Nazi victory over France upon people of all classes in America. There is in each of us an inner struggle between a desire to believe in democracy and a disquieting doubt about it. This is especially true among the young, the unemployed, the marginal income groups, the declassed in our society. A Nazi victory would tend to resolve this inner civil war into a victory for the anti-democrat in every man. It has already in that respect cast its shadow before. I do not myself agree with the implications of Mr. Buell's economic analysis, which are that American survival depends upon re-establishing the conditions of a free world market and loosening many of the governmental controls over the economic system in our own country. I agree far more with the basic Beard premise that if America is to survive it must be through a planned economy. Nevertheless, under the conditions of a Nazi victory, such a planned economy is in America more likely to be directed by a fascist personnel toward fascist objectives than a democratic personnel toward democratic objectives.

It has been said by several reviewers that the two books cancel each other and that we are left with no hope. I do not agree. It may well be, of course, that France and England will crumble so rapidly before Hitler's war machine that the whole question of American intervention will within a month's time be academic. If so, there is not much further to be said about either book. But if the Allies can hold out long enough to make American industrial aid on a large scale effective, then we are faced in this hour of decision by a cruel dilemma. On the one hand, if we give the Allies strong enough aid to constitute more than an expression of sympathy and moral support, we thereby transform our industrial system into a war economy with all the consequences that this carries for civil liberties, repressive legislation, and the bogging down of the New Deal reform program. On the other hand, if we adopt the attitude of continental Americanism (our hearts are broken over what is happening in Europe but we can't do anything about it) we face the desperate prospect of having to rebuild our economy and transform our social system within a world framework dominated by Nazi power, Nazi philosophy, Nazi prestige.

The dilemma is cruel, but not impossible to resolve. If we keep our eye on the main objective, which is American democratic survival, we must extend aid to the Allies if they are not already beyond the reach of aid. But in doing so we must not delude ourselves into thinking only in terms of a war between Right and Wrong, or that we are likely to be easily successful in reorganizing the world after the war. Second, we must be fully aware of the danger to free thought, a free labor movement, and progressive reform which even further economic intervention would entail. If we recognize these dangers, we may be able to minimize them.

What neither book has is a comprehension that both the effort to meet the Nazi threat (Buell) and the effort to build democracy at home (Beard) must be pursued in a framework of world revolution today. Neither writer has in this respect dug far enough under the surface of events, or seen that Nazism is not so much in itself a revolution as it is the expression of manifold revolutionary disturbances all over the world, including America—a revolution in the viability of the nation-state, a revolution in the internal economies of all nations leading to planning imperatives of one form or another, a revolution in war technology and war organization, a psychic revolution on the part of the masses of people everywhere.[2] The question of American foreign policy is only a prelude to the more basic questions that we shall have to confront, whether Germany wins the war or is stopped, whether America participates or stays out. No intelligent program of American action can be formulated until our intellectuals and our statesmen have made the attempt to understand the nature of the contemporary revolution. If

---

[2] This is elaborated in "The War as Revolution," above, p. 3.

we do not succeed in understanding it, we may just as well dig in
and wait for the Ice Age to come.

1940

The Daedalian Vision of Waldo Frank

I WRITE during Europe's hour of decision, while Nazi planes are
strafing the populations of the Low Countries and the bursting
bombs are spelling out the pattern of generations to come. If
Waldo Frank's premise in his new book [3] of the moral chaos of the
world needed confirming, this staccato accompaniment would
furnish it. Yet for all its note of passionate urgency the book might
have been written as well when the Junkers rained death over
Guernica during the Spanish war, or when Mr. Chamberlain
stepped from his plane at the Croydon airport bringing peace in
our time; and it will be read just as well a decade from now, whatever the issue of the war. For Mr. Frank has written the only kind
of tract for the times that is worth the ink and paper it costs—one
with a long-range philosophy about men's purposes and men's
motives.

Much of the aridness of today's discussions of American foreign
policy derives from their failure to formulate these basic philosophical premises. All the schools of thought from immediate intervention to extreme isolation bandy about a common body of
data about military strength and strategy, economic resources,
moral contrasts between the contestants. Everything depends on
what tricks you play with this well-worn material. Thus far, very
few who have discussed the war have gone beyond this threshing
of the dry straw of argument. Which of the many spokesmen for
one school or another has really sought to discover those springs
of human action and currents of world history which alone can
give meaning to all the empirical arguments? In this crisis, as never
before, the questions we must ask of our intellectual leaders when
they profess to guide our action go deep to the bases of society and
history. Are they thinking of the war as a self-contained entity or
as a symptom of something much more comprehensive? Are they
aware that the world is in the process of revolution? What do they

---

[3] *Chart for Rough Water*, New York, Doubleday, Doran, 1940.

conceive to be the nature of that revolution? What are their ideas of how democracy must reorganize itself to survive? What do they think have been the origins of Hitlerism and what the sources of its strength? What do they think of the rational and irrational in man? What view do they hold of the human animal—not Hitler but *Homo sapiens?*

It is because Mr. Frank has the courage and insight to face some of these questions that I find his book exciting. Those who have followed his intellectual career will recognize in this book all the master-themes of his thinking—the attack on empiricism and rationalism, the passionate striving for wholeness and for the moral springs of creativeness, the mysticism and the religious strain, the criticism of American life and the evocation of American leadership and cultural maturity. From *Holiday* to *The Bridegroom Cometh,* from *Our America* through *The Rediscovery of America* to *In the American Jungle* Mr. Frank has never failed for a quarter-century to urge all these themes. What he has done in this book is to gather them together, compactly and very much foreshortened, and apply them to the world crisis today and America's role in it. The book will prove irritating to many. It is shrill, and what will seem the note of urgency to some will seem hysteria to others. Its high seriousness, rarely tempered by a saving humor, often becomes pedantic and sometimes downright funny. It struggles with a mystical vocabulary more likely to be encountered in commentaries on the Rig-Veda or the Upanishads than in discussions of contemporary public problems. Yet we would be wrong to set too high a store on the verbal commonplaces of most of our books, where the language has been worn smooth because the thought has been worn empty. Mr. Frank is one of those writers who tries to say more than he can. But no one can afford to dismiss the body of his thought smugly because the whole of it has been an attack on American smugness. This book is no exception, nor has anyone the right to criticize it who does not bring to it as radical an approach and as thoroughgoing a philosophy as Mr. Frank does.

Its argument runs somewhat as follows. There is nothing so empty as the American boast of uniqueness and the condescension implied in "Thank God, we live in America." We are not isolated from Europe but integrally related to it, "the focus and fulfillment of ways and means of the whole West." We are part of its "great tradition"—Hebraic—Greek—medieval—which recognized the individual as a person with roots and a vision extending beyond himself. We are part also of the Western religion of materialism that has grown up to humiliate Europe and threaten American survival—the shallow religion of industrialism and the machine, of things and reason and pragmatisms in which are linked Rousseau and Marx and John Dewey, Stalin and Chamberlain and Roosevelt. Fascism, which has a life-cycle of its own, is also implicit in us, and the guilt for it rests heavily on our own intellectual spokesmen who have fashioned a religion that includes things and excludes the spirit, that includes rationalism but leaves life out. The roots of fascism are deep in the psyche of the common folk, who, finding their strongest emotions dammed and frustrated in our sort of world, turn their energies into hate—and submission-channels. War is not in itself good or bad but may have its delights; far worse than war is a disgusting peace which is in the end only an anarchy of small wars, and which because of our inertia and cowardice allows fascism to conquer without facing a serious challenge. We must recognize that we are in the midst of a revolution. We must make that revolution creative—in our education, our cultural criticism, our political parties, our whole consciousness. Elsewhere, in a recent *New Republic* article, Mr. Frank had added to this general exhortation a more specific one: "With every ounce of our economy, of our political prestige, we should make ourselves *non-belligerent* allies of the Allies." Yet his book deals with the long-run rather than the immediate, and with the analytic rather than the programmatic. It insists that, whether or not we become directly involved in the war, we can save ourselves from barbarism only through a "collective conversion" to a new "synthesis value." Only thus can we take the leadership in releasing men's emotions once more, and making them persons in the context of a religion.

The merit of Mr. Frank's book is that it dares deal greatly with a great theme. Its complexity lies in the multiple role Mr. Frank essays of being at once religious prophet, moral exhorter, fashioner of new myths, social analyst, historian of ideas, political polemicist. The weakness of the book is that the apocalyptic vision that gives stature to Mr. Frank's prophetic faculties does not give equal stature to his abilities as a social and political analyst. If I may myself use the language of myth (a great temptation, once one is steeped in the book) the daedalian vision of Mr. Frank on his moral heights becomes an icarian collapse as his creature wings soar through the real air of social thinking over the real earth of social institutions.

And this brings me to my quarrels with Mr. Frank. The first is with his theory of history. He considers technologies, economies, and social institutions as the products of states of consciousness, rather than the other way round. His whole theory of history seems to be idealist-Hegelian. He sees world history as a succession of states of consciousness—call each of them "religion," "ethos," what you will—operating through a dialectic that is never made clear, and hurling up out of its mysteriously changing depths economies, states, wars. I should have thought we had gone beyond this view and seen it for what it is: the attempts of intellectuals to make themselves the center of the historic process by making their ideas and dreams and symbols the prime movers in life and its final creative principle. Given Mr. Frank's view it is hard to see what dynamic there is that causes the shifts in these religious visions, what gives them life and death, growth and decay, what makes some survive and pushes others under. Spengler at least, who was as passionately anti-materialist as Mr. Frank and as wedded to the organic principle in history, gives us a cyclical theory which, whatever you may make of it, does present a framework for historic changes. Lacking this, Mr. Frank finds himself compelled to fall back on the concepts of sin, salvation, and the regenerative force of conversion, all of them rising somehow from the depths of the individual conscience.

This raises the question of materialism. I do not say against Mr. Frank that the material is all. I think most of us have outgrown such notions if we ever had them. I do say that technologies and their organization, natural resources, geography, population, condition the outer limits of cultural creativeness, and that the interplay between these changing frames and the psychic drives of the people working and living within them has conditioned human history. I say that the emphasis on living standards and on the release of the ordinary man from economic exploitation is and has been a healthy thing in Western culture. Mr. Frank has some harsh things to say of the materialism of Steinbeck's *Grapes of Wrath*.

"The economic humiliation of the Joads by their exploiters," he writes, "is as nothing compared to their spiritual humiliation by the author." I have met this brave doctrine before, and I know its easy harmonies, which will be welcome in the ears of that depersonalized creature the Associated Farmers. It was Spengler, in his *Prussian Socialism,* who spoke of the common materialism of socialism and capitalism, calling socialism the capitalism of the masses, and capitalism the socialism of the Stock Exchange. What remains when you have thus disposed of both is the "spiritual" socialism that Spengler glorified and Hitler exploited. I do not deny the seeds of destruction in Western culture. But I say that it is the breakdown of our economies that has produced our moral breakdown rather than the other way round, which is the way Mr. Frank puts it. What has been wrong with the West has not been its materialism as such, but its mechanical nature, unrelieved by any frame of values reaching beyond it; and not materialism as such but the social organization of our material means. This is crucial, for if Mr. Frank is right we must pass through a collective conversion and on the basis of that reorganize our society; if I am right, our chief task is to go further in the social organization of our technologies, and on the basis of that give direction to men's work and release to their emotions.

That is why I quarrel also with Mr. Frank as intellectual historian. A man has the right of course to attach the term "great tradition" to whatever strain in the history of ideas he pleases; but he must make his choice persuasive. For Mr. Frank the great tradition is the mystical-religious tradition of the West, and correspondingly the rationalistic tradition is anti-Christ and the eighteenth century the century of sin. But why this desperate turning against rationalism, like that of a man who breaks the windows because he finds the air stuffy in the room? Mr. Frank says the centuries of reason have wound up in pragmatism and materialism. But I answer that the centuries of religious exhortation have wound up in the Sunday-sermon pages of the Monday morning newspapers. The great tradition in Western thought is for me the humanist tradition, which includes both the rationalist strain and the religious-ethical, the empiricist and the myth-making. These two should not be separated: the greatness of each is the facet it turns to the other that makes the other possible. Together they add up to that dream of a spaciously ordered society in which men will be able to turn in on themselves because they have learned to control their environment, in which the individual can explore the mysteries of life because he has mastered the arts of collective survival, and in which the Joads will explore the soul that lies beyond bread because the bread has been achieved. As against this tradition there is the anti-humanist strain, which divides the world into those who are far more than men and those who are far less, the daemonic and the subhuman.

Let me make it clear that I go along to some degree with Mr. Frank, as I go alone with his comrade-in-arms Lewis Mumford, in their irritation at the rationalistic complacencies of our liberals—and our conservatives too. We are not, as Thorstein Veblen never tired of pointing out, merely lightning calculators of pleasure and pain. There is far more under the crust of our culture than is dreamt of in our philosophies. We have premised a wholly rational man and have surrendered all the rest of him to our Hitlers and Goebbelses for exploiting. Yet there is a vast difference between recognizing the irrational and celebrating it. And my basic quarrel with Mr. Frank is that I do not believe we can achieve salvation by calling for it, or by a masochistic lashing of ourselves for our sins. Nor do I think we can achieve it by conversion. The ordinary man is no better and no worse than he is, and if he has strayed from the path it has not been for want of theologies and clergies and exhorters. In fact, if one wished to locate the intellectual tradition in which the tone and intensity of Mr. Frank's book could best be duplicated it would be the German. It needs some explaining that the very nation in which the idealistic currents of philosophy ran strongest was the one that has most completely succumbed to fascism. The methods of religious conversion in politics are methods used most effectively not by those whose values are Mr. Frank's but by the call-of-the-blood crowd. Anyone reading Rauschning's *Voice of Destruction* will see how effectively the Nazis have conscripted the apocalypse to their uses.

But I do not argue that because an idea may be turned against you it should not be used. We shall get nowhere by becoming the prisoners of our fears. Even though it is true that we may be destroyed by beliefs, it is also true that we shall not survive without beliefs. What I argue, however, is that beliefs in a humanist society must be organic parts and end-results of social reconstruction; they cannot precede it. We shall not recapture them by looking backward to a great tradition, whatever its nature, but forward to a revolutionary democracy which can cope on its own ground with the revolutionary character of Nazism. Our young people today seem almost to have lost their capacity for belief. If they recapture it, it will be not because we exhort them to faith but because we show them through effective action that our values are worthy of belief. That involves a program of action at home in America, to which I should wish that Mr. Frank had devoted a far larger portion of his book than the few pages toward the end. It involves also a sense of the real stakes we have in what is going on in Europe. Yet these objections have to do with immediate policy. And Mr. Frank's book should be criticized on the level on which it was written—the evaluation of Western history and culture which alone can give meaning to immediate policies.[4]   1940

---

[4] In the *Saturday Review of Literature* of June 13, 1940, Waldo Frank wrote a sharp reply to this article under the title of "The Mind of a Liberal." In placing me in the category of liberals paralyzed by their intellect and incapable of seeing the need for effective anti-Nazi action, I fear that he misread the intent and content of my essay. In the issue of July 15, 1940, an ironic letter by Charles Beard appeared querying what both Waldo Frank and I were driving at in our quarrel and asking each of us for a direct program in words simple enough to be understood. I append my reply as a useful supplement to the article above:

Sir: Are you sure it was Charles Beard who wrote that letter? I seem to remember a book by Mr. Beard called *The Discussion of Human Affairs*, published (if I can recall correctly—I do not have it with me now) in 1936, and lambasting the people who make the discussion of human affairs over-simple and over-rigid. Human societies, Mr. Beard tells us in that book, are very complex, very tangled, and our thinking about them must not too rudely break the web. Was that the same Charles Beard who now calls for simplicity, like any business man asking an intellectual to reduce his ideas to a page?

Mr. Frank's book was not about programs but about ideas; hence my review of it was also a review about ideas. If Mr. Beard wants to know what I think America should do concretely, he will find it in my review of his own book and Mr. Raymond Leslie Buell's in the *New Republic* [reprinted in this volume under the title "Continentalism and World Leadership"]. However, I am perfectly happy to give Mr. Beard my five-point program for America today:

(1) Help Great Britain to the full extent of our capacity;

(2) Face the realities of the war, understand that it is an outgrowth of a revolutionary situation, and that we shall not mend the world until we have fulfilled in our way these revolutionary forces;

(3) Adjust our thinking about government and economics in the light of the new revolutionary situation;

(4) Reorganize our national defense as part of a vast effort of economic and administrative reorganization, so as to have a collectivist democracy;

(5) Make democracy work at home, thereby fulfilling the aspirations of our young people, and insuring our national survival.

2

Notes on the March of Fascism

An American Yankee at Hitler's Court

O N JUNE 8, 1933, in the office of a professor of American history at the University of Chicago, the phone rang. "This is
Franklin Roosevelt. I want to know if you will render the
government a distinct service. I want you to go to Germany as
Ambassador." And thus William E. Dodd came to leave the classroom where he was turning graduate students into teachers, and
the study where he was writing of the Old South, to journey into
the jungle of Nazi Germany.[1]

If the record of our times were not so keyed to the tragic, it might
be read as first-rate ironic comedy. Here was a Germany in which
there had just come to dominance a power-drunk fanatic, a ruthless
activist who knew little of history and hated democracy; and the
man we sent to him to represent American interests was a retiring
scholar who lived wholly in the world of ideas, who felt (like a
Plato turned Gibbon) that the historians should become kings and
who, in the quality of his democracy, was perhaps the last pure
Jeffersonian to be found in America.

I do not say that Dodd was a bad choice for the job. The President could have done, and on occasion did, a good deal worse. For
Dodd was no banker-minded appeaser, intent on wangling a few
financial concessions from the Nazis and paying for them with
American self-respect. Nor was he a State Department career man,
almost as contemptuous of democracy in his own snobbish way as
the Germans in theirs. Nor was he a diplomatic adventurer who
promised more than the American government could deliver.

He was a man of transparent honor and integrity. He was utterly

---

[1] *Ambassador Dodd's Diary: 1933–1938*, edited by William E. Dodd, Jr., and Martha
Dodd, New York, Harcourt, Brace, 1941.

scrupulous. He was nobody's fool. But in Hitler's Germany he was helpless—not because of himself, but because of the conception of policy in Washington which his choice as Ambassador reflected. For the Roosevelt government evidently felt that Germany could still be wooed away from Nazi barbarism and brought back to the relative decency of its past. And so it chose as Ambassador a scholar who had once studied in Germany and was linked to the best traditions of that past.

It did not work. And this diary, which the Ambassador (being a historian) conscientiously kept as a record of his experience, gives the detailed account of the many big and small ways in which it did not work. Like Sir Nevile Henderson, Dodd might have called his experiences the *Failure of a Mission*. There is an undercurrent of failure in all the diary entries, from the time when Dodd saw that the "incidents" involving Americans in Germany would continue despite formal Nazi apologies to the time when he gave up his mission and returned to his Round Hill farm in Virginia, having incurred the bitter rage of the Germans and the hostility of Sumner Welles and the controlling group in the State Department.

And yet, wholly unlike Henderson's failure, Dodd's had about it something of a moral grandeur. Although he had made the mistake of underestimating both the strength and the ultimate ferocity of the Nazis, he had never once really compromised with his own democratic principles.

If he was doomed to be ineffectual, at least he never trimmed, was never shabby in his words or actions. He hated everything anti-democratic, in America and in Germany alike. He had the attitude of the Jacksonian frontier toward pomp and display. He hated embassy politics and early infuriated the career men. He had an ascetic feeling about lavish expenditures, and in his diary the trifling instances of his Catonian disapproval of parties with wine and bejeweled women and low-cut gowns may be found side by side with the great issues of international policy and the colossal inhumanities of the Nazi State.

Above all, he had the courage of one who, on the side of democracy, was something of a fanatic himself. A few months after his arrival he took the step of refusing to appear at the Nuremberg party festival of the Nazis. He made speeches about democracy and slavery in American history, diplomatically correct and yet pointed enough for those who cared to draw analogies. It was part both of his strength and his weakness as Ambassador that, as he confronted the Nazi regime and its true meaning finally dawned upon him, he could not remain quiet. There was some merit in being the naïve Jeffersonian set down in the most powerful monopolist state in the world.

It is important to note that this sense of the true meaning of Nazism did not dawn on him for a long time. When he first met Edgar Mowrer, he felt he was "almost as vehement, in his way, as the Nazis." For a while Dodd thought of Foreign Minister Neurath as better than the rest; for a long time he clung to a faith in Hjalmar Schacht, the Minister of Economics, and a belief that he represented the German moderates. The diary reflects what appeared to be the splits between Hitler and some of his lieutenants: Dodd never knew—as perhaps we shall never know—whether those splits were real or part of a deliberate Nazi strategy to win time and concessions from the democracies.

More tragic is the sense one gets from the diary entries of the lack of any sort of working agreement between the various nations as to how the Nazi menace was to be met. Not only were the democracies hopelessly split in conception and policy, but there was one point at which the Soviet envoy was completely isolated and no one spoke to him. But most tragic is the sense one gets that Dodd, like the other envoys, was aware in detail of what was going on—how Germany was rearming and what its ambitions were—and yet these detailed insights never added up to the overwhelming sense of danger which might have led to action.

The diary has been receiving a good deal of publicity because of the remarks in it about prominent people like William Randolph Hearst, William C. Bullitt, and Senator Wheeler. Those entries are anything but flattering. Mr. Hearst appears as an active supporter of fascist power in Europe. Mr. Bullitt is depicted as a meddler who, at the very time he was accredited as Ambassador to the Soviet Union, was doing his best to argue the French out of the Franco-Soviet pact.

But Senator Wheeler comes off worst of all. In an already famous passage (page 212), Dodd speaks of a party at Rexford Tugwell's house where "a certain well-known Senator," angry at President Roosevelt and influential with Huey Long, was present. "He talks like a National Socialist. He would stop trade with Europe. He advocated German domination of all Europe, our domination of the Americas, and Japanese domination of the Far East. He wishes to see England dominated by Germany, with Canada falling naturally to the United States." Dodd "repeated in confidence the Senator's statements at Mr. Tugwell's" to President Roosevelt. The President guessed his name right.

In a recent press conference, Mr. Roosevelt stated that the name he guessed was Senator Wheeler's. The Senator's reply was interesting—that he had never been at Mr. Tugwell's house when Senator Glass was there. But the diary entry does not mention Senator Glass —only some Representatives and Senator Bailey. Is it a fair conclusion that Senator Wheeler was less than candid in his statement? The editors of this volume were also careless. While sedulously writing "Senator X——" on page 213, they let the cat out of the bag on page 342. I quote the passage: "Wheeler was among those at a dinner in Washington where Germany's right to be dictator of all Europe was approved."

I think Senator Wheeler owes the country either an explanation or else proof that Dodd was lying. So far he has furnished us neither.

1941

Hitler as Medicine Man [2]

OUR generation will probably live through a spate of books by men who saw Hitler plain and with whom he stopped and talked. This is one of the first; [3] and because Rauschning is literate as few of Hitler's inner circle are, and has philosophical interests of a sort, the book is not without importance in helping to form the historical picture of the man of Berchtesgaden. But I suspect that Rauschning's purpose is more immediate than historical. In the last war, we had a series of "out of their own mouths" books about the enemy—about the German doctrine of force and egotism, about German military philosophy as expressed

---

[2] Since this and the following two essays deal with aspects of Hitler's mind, the reader may wish to consult my earlier "Hitler as Thinker" in *Ideas Are Weapons* (1939), pp. 356–74.

[3] *The Voice of Destruction* by Hermann Rauschning. New York, G. P. Putnam's Sons, 1940.

through Clausewitz and Bernhardi. This is doubtless a necessary and legitimate war activity, only we had better recognize that Rauschning is at war and this is in a real sense a war book.

Which leads to the moot question of Rauschning's credibility. These are presumably conversations he had with Hitler, either alone or in the small Nazi inner circle. Suppose we set aside the doubts that may arise from Rauschning's lack of scruples about joining the Nazi Party and his six-year silence since the last of the talks (they cover the years 1932–1934): his own explanation, that the book would not have been believed until his first book and Hitler's own acts had cleared the path for belief, seems a bit lame; more likely that the book was saved for the strategic moment. But beyond that it is in the very nature of this kind of confession that there can be no canons of historical evidence to apply, since the other witnesses are unavailable. The time may come soon when other books of the same sort can be used to check on this one. Meanwhile a reviewer can only express his opinion as a hunch; and my hunch is that the talks are substantially, if not in every detail, authentic. Reservations must be made of course for the lapse of time, for wisdom after the event, for Rauschning's own bias. But even after all that has been considered, the metal of Hitler's conversation rings true enough.

True enough to be a bit terrifying and true enough to jolt us out of the usual simplistic picture of Hitler. For there are at least two Hitlers: one who shows to the world the aspect of himself that happens at the moment to be convenient, and the other who reveals something of himself (surely not all) to his inner circle of accomplices and disciples. This duality is true of all public figures, but it is peculiarly true of Hitler because the essence of his genius is deliberate manipulation of men and events. And the manipulator, even when he does not start as a schizophrenic, cannot help becoming one at least to a degree.

Rauschning is principally concerned with the private Hitler— the Hitler who is carefully hidden away from the pages of *Mein Kampf* and from the public harangues. And there are three interlinked phases of this Hitler that are most clearly brought to view: his cynicism, his nihilism, his revolutionism. It is scarcely news that Hitler, as the great modern exploiter of violence and manipulator of myths, has a complete contempt for treaties, honor, faith. But no one has underlined with such persuasive detail as Rauschning the extent of Hitler's frank avowal of deliberate political immorality and brutality, not as necessary evils but as positive principles. Jews must be tortured, not so that they will be destroyed (in fact, if they were destroyed it would be necessary to invent them again), but because the exercise of the brutal in him welds a man to a movement; in the same way party functionaries must be encouraged to corruption and loot so that they will be caught in an inescapable web of guilt. Even for the doctrine of nationalism Hitler has a cynical contempt, regarding it only as a prejudice of the masses to be exploited, transcended, and replaced by a mystical Order of the Elite of all nations.

As for Hitler's nihilism, it is a theme familiar from Rauschning's first book. I was skeptical of that when I met it there and I am even more skeptical now. For all of Hitler's denial of our traditional Western values, he does seem to be reaching out in a blundering way for new values. Only he thinks of himself as doing it all alone—by a sheer creative act of will shattering and reconstructing a world. Hitler as revolutionary is thus the final product of the individualist dream: his "revolution without end" is an inversion of Trotsky's "permanent revolution," imposed on the masses by single heroes and lawgivers rather than coming from the creative energies of the people.

It is hard to tell from Rauschning how much of this Hitler himself takes seriously, and how much is shrewdly gauged for the manipulation of his Gauleiter and other lieutenants. The portraits Rauschning gives us of the frenetic Röhm, the massive peasant intelligence of Gregor Strasser, the sycophant Goebbels, make me wish he had given even more attention to the gallery of disciples. For I am convinced that part of Hitler's success is due to his seeing the pivotal need of holding the allegiance of his immediate subordinates. Hence the heroics, hence the emotionalism, hence the elaborate posing as a mystic figure of destiny. Hitler to his lieutenants is like a lover to a mistress he must hold at any cost. It is important that Hitler does not see himself as an absolute dictator but as a sort of broker between the conflicting wills in his party and the other dominant groups in Germany. And I suspect that much of the torrent of talk in Rauschning's book must be seen not as what Hitler believes but as what he would like his disciples to believe of him.

The book does not resolve the puzzle of Hitler's personality; if anything, it increases it. Here is Hitler roaring with his comrades over the sadistic treatment of the Jews while they are gathered German-bourgeois fashion over coffee and cakes; Hitler reducing, with complete assurance, all complexities of program and tactic to a single question of belief in him and flexible adjustment to the party will; Hitler, the mystic, believing in a "human solstice," in his power over white magic and black magic, preparing a new god-like order of youth who will transcend the mortal coil; Hitler with his eerie lack of sexuality, Hitler pawing the arms of blond girls, Hitler surrounded by blowzy ladies and responding to their mystical flattery; Hitler indecisive in all the great crises of his life and having to lash himself into a fury to make decisions; Hitler dreaming Nietzsche-like of his godlike loneliness, self-pitying, with a conviction of impending martyrdom, hoping against hope that he will be granted time to conquer the world and as a great lawgiver remake it in his own image.

This is not, whatever we may wishfully think, a puny and unimportant person. Even Rauschning, for all his over-accented efforts to minimize Hitler's stature, is obviously fascinated by him. Here is one of the extraordinary men of modern times. Rauschning comes close to the truth when he says, "He is simply a sort of great medicine man." I should add, not so simply. The kind of medicine he uses is the darkly primitive in all men, such as Freud and Jung have sought to reveal to us. Hitler has had the morbid daring to see that in a chaotic and indecisive world a medicine man who exploits the most primitive instincts with complete assurance will carry the day. How much of this insight is his own, how much he borrowed, it is hard to say. Rauschning asked him about Sorel and Pareto and met only evasions. Hitler spoke mainly of his debt to Wagner and to Machiavelli's *Prince*. He must have picked up much of the tattered romantic talk around him, including much of Nietzsche, and turned it to his purposes. Yet neither Nietzsche nor any of the others will go far to explain this lonely ugly little man with the dead eyes sitting in his mountain retreat dreaming of godhead and scheming all the time how to exploit the bestial in man in order to attain that godhead.

One may perhaps add a note about Rauschning himself. His first book [4] received the overwhelming praise of our liberals and intellectuals. Was it because here was finally an anti-fascist who was also anti-socialist and anti-democratic, and who had even been a Nazi himself? The present book is a chaotic one, not only because of its loose structure and obviously careless writing, but even more because Rauschning provides us with no real framework of counter-values through which we can examine Hitler's values. It is dangerous business to present Hitler's brand of iconoclasm and radicalism to the world without sifting it through a mind that is prepared in its own way to reach as deeply to the roots of the modern chaos as Hitler claims to do. Rauschning's reactionary beliefs in the Junkers, the army, the church, and the agrarian tradition are of no use as a critical approach to Hitlerism. Always one feels in him, not that he has rejected Hitler, but that Hitler has let him down. And one senses the curious delusion that there is a half-way house of terrorism and destruction; that a polite fascism might be possible; that you can unloose forces as demonic as the barbarism of Hitler's world view and arrest those forces when they have done your work and before they have done their own.[5]

1940

Hitler's American Dream

AMERICA's minister to Belgium when there was a Belgium, Mr. Cudahy, was recently granted an interview by Goebbels. The Nazi propaganda lord assured our greatly impressed statesman-reporter that Americans need not fear German intentions. The Nazi General Staff, it seems, had canvassed all possibilities and concluded that an invasion of America was not feasible.

It was a curious statement and a curious interview. You need

---

[4] *The Revolution of Nihilism*, New York, Alliance, 1939.

[5] Since the above was first printed, Rauschning has published *The Conservative Revolution* (New York, Putnam, 1940), which contains an account of his own political beliefs at the time he joined the Nazis. Nothing in his new book causes me to change my estimate of him.

not fear my intentions, I say to you. I have seriously canvassed the possibilities of assault with intent to kill, but it will not succeed.

Why did Goebbels take the trouble to exercise his charm and exert his intellect on our former meat king? He was not chatting out of ennui. He knew that in the battle of opinion in America the legions whose views on the war he favors expose their most vulnerable flank here: if Britain goes down, America will have to face the Nazi power, whatever its intent, alone. Hence his anxiety to reassure us.

But we must not be content merely with seeing Goebbels as manipulator and Cudahy as dupe.[6] The argument itself must be confronted. And I have grown ever less satisfied recently with the form which this sort of discussion has taken. I have been reading Lindbergh and John T. Flynn, who say that America cannot be invaded. And I have also read the letters by divers military authorities[7] saying that an invasion of America is possible. I find myself more convinced than ever that it is, and yet curiously unsatisfied about the question itself. Obviously the clearest answer is that if the Nazis smash British sea power and annex its residues to existing German, Italian, French, and Japanese sea power, our naval position becomes impossible. Even should we eventually get a two-ocean navy we would no longer, as Samuel Grafton suggests, have any oceans to float it on. When Hitler wins, the Atlantic becomes a Nazi lake, the Monroe Doctrine becomes untenable, Latin America is opened to Nazi power and falls away from us, and through Latin America there begins an economic, political, ideological, and military penetration of America by Nazi power. In the shadow of that power we should have to live until either we confronted it directly through war or it overcame us through civil war.

Make no mistake about it. If the Nazis intend to attack us after they have disposed of Britain, they will find a means, direct or indirect—probably the latter. Their armory of means has proved inexhaustibly various and resourceful. That is why the more important question is, What is their intent? Does Hitler mean to move against us? The political intuition of most Americans says that he

---

[6] A little later Hitler himself used Cudahy for the same purposes, to assure the American people that he had no intentions against them.

[7] In the *New Republic*, May 12, 1941.

does, that his designs for empire do not stop at the boundaries of Europe. But how much basis has this intuition?

To start with the obvious, the recent protestations of Hitler and his propaganda lords have no reliability. In fact, they have a negative reliability: the fact that they are made should put us on our guard. Most of Hitler's invasions have been preceded by a promise not to invade. He is a master of the political lie. That is a matter of record. I wish someone would send Mr. Cudahy that record, as contained for example in Frederick L. Schuman's documented *Europe on the Eve* and *Night over Europe*.

Yet the argument persists: Hitler wanted *Lebensraum* for Germany, hence his broken promises; with the defeat of Britain he will have it, hence he will stop. Let us examine this. In the Nazi drive for expansion there have been other logical stopping-points. Hitler might have stopped after regaining the European territory Germany lost at Versailles. He did not. He might have stopped later, after supposedly reuniting the German minorities on the Continent in a Pan-Germanic racial entity. He did not. He might stop now, as Lindbergh suggests, after a successful bid for European hegemony, and live side by side with the remaining imperialisms elsewhere. But why should we assume he will stop here, when in the past he has gone on despite an equal logic for stopping?

The fact is that even if he had an inclination to call a halt at the full tide of victory, there are forces within the Nazi system itself that would prevent him. We should be blind to the workings of that system if we did not see in it a compulsive expansionism.

And first, the Nazi economy requires war if it is not to shift to some other kind of economy, perhaps a more purely socialist variety. I am not one of those who lump the Nazi with other controlled economies as indifferently "managerial" structures. The technicians are, to be sure, in control in Germany, but the economic system is still potentially explosive unless the business groups, the army groups, and the government bureaucrats are all at least marginally satisfied. Ever since he came into power Hitler has used war and preparation for war as a way of driving a wedge between business and the army, to keep them from uniting against him. He has offered the army a world to win, and he has offered business full capacity today in war orders plus pie tomorrow in the new regions opened for industrial exploitation. Once he stopped he would have on his hands a restless army and a business group that called on him to fulfill his promises. And here he would be caught between the danger on the one hand of a business economy with its restrictionism, and on the other hand of a socialist economy with its equalitarianism. Either would set up internal tensions within the regime—tensions that Hitler has ridiculed in other social systems and that would be dangerous to his own power.

One might argue here that this ultimate reckoning might be long postponed by the tasks and the opportunities of organizing a European Nazi economy. And recently revealed facts indicate that such an economy is already on its way. But it would be a mistake to regard it as merely a form of economic regionalism. If it is true that Hitler can avoid internal social problems only by maintaining his national economy as a war economy, it is also true that he can maintain his type of power over a Nazified Europe only by projecting his European economy into a world economy. We must remember that for Hitler, as for Spengler, economics is only a branch of politics—the economics of force. Hitler must use his European economy as a weapon, not for peaceful competition with other imperialist systems but for domination of them. The present Nazi economy requires war to prevent economic democracy; the Greater Nazi economy will require war because it must operate on a world scale.

Moving up in the Nazi hierarchy, I turn to the nature of the political system and its ideology. Both have ceased to be nationalist. Both envisage a racial and administrative elite in every country which cuts across national lines, all of them tied to a central elite in Berlin. Such a conception is, as has been often pointed out, a world-revolutionary one. Hitlerism is the bastard successor of Trotsky's dream of a "permanent revolution." From Spengler, from Haushofer, from a whole variety of mystico-realists, there sprang Hitler's now famous sentence in *Mein Kampf:* "Germany will be either a world power or will not be at all." In that belief the Nazi ruling group has been brought up. Upon it they have pinned their lust for earth and their hope of heaven.

Why should America be exempt from this drive toward world power? Anyone with even the most elementary knowledge of Nazi writings on America (there is a convenient compendium of them in Robert Strausz-Hupé's useful book, *Axis America*) knows that we have always hung before Nazi eyes as a succulent prize. To Colin Ross *"unser Amerika"* is an unredeemed German country; to Spengler, in his *Hour of Decision,* America is ripe for a revolutionary thrust. Within the confines of those two perspectives lies Hitler's American dream.

I have left to the last Hitler himself. Even if the Nazi system were not inherently expansionist, Hitler would supply its drive. There have been in our literature many underestimates and overestimates of him. But about his megalomania there can be no doubt. And it is Hitler who runs the Nazi show, not the lieutenants. His is the will, the conception, the driving zeal. That is why Hitler, for all our more impersonal analyses, must matter in our reckoning. And his megalomania has caused him to think of himself as a world conqueror and to reserve a special hatred and avidity for America. His own sense of stature will drive him either toward his world goal or to suicide. He has already come as close as Napoleon. Without America his dream cannot be fulfilled.

1941

Russia and the War of Ideas

HOWEVER the military fortunes of war go, Hitler's invasion of Russia has changed the nature of the entire struggle. The war now enters its second phase. For the first time two major fronts can be created; there is recognition that a *Blitz* will not succeed against England and America; and there is a chance, if Hitler is not successful, for the Allies to get a continental foothold against Germany. I know we must keep our eyes on these military realities. But we must keep in mind also the ideological realities. For this has from the start been a war of ideas as well as of men and machines. And in terms of ideas the war has now been given a new and, from most viewpoints, better orientation.

To start with, the Russian campaign marks the end of several illusions. One is the illusion of appeasement, which held on toughly in Russian soil long after it had withered elsewhere: it is ironic that the original masters of modern propaganda should have been duped by the pupil who has now become the greatest master of all. Another illusion is the one held by writers like Lawrence Dennis, who for all their "realism" are wishful, that the new

world order will be built on co-ordinate "socialist" imperialisms—
Germany, Russia, America, Japan. That Hitler will stop at nothing
short of world power is now clear—otherwise the campaign against
Russia would be the sheerest adventurism.

But the greatest illusion was that which saw Hitler through the
blinded eyes and felt for him through the dulled heart of a mechanical Marxism, as a social revolutionary by deputy. It needs
saying again and again that the malady of leftism was not just that
communists turned, as by a tropism, toward the party line. It was
rather the fatal habit of seeing history as a set of impersonal forces
wrenched loose from the by-whom and the for-what. When the
communists thought at all, and did not act as robots, they had a
curious sub-belief that Hitler's legions were, by their chores of
destruction, doing the work of communism—corroding the
strength of capitalism, removing the huge obstacle of the British
Empire, plunging the world into a chaos out of which anything
might emerge. And Hitler talked just enough of the have-nots and
of the pluto-democracies to fill in the lineaments of a common revolutionary mission. But today he has changed his propaganda role.
He is once more the enemy only of "international Bolshevists" and
the defender of the faith against the godless Reds. And Stalin and
his satellites have their hearts laden with rue and their minds, let
us hope, cleared of fog.

It is a tragic irony that it should have required an act of Hitler,
the success of which would spell the end of the Soviet Union, to
bring the forces of the left together. Yet some can learn only after
the juggernaut of events has passed on. Now in the wake of it they
will make major readjustments in their thinking. The wounded
communists will crawl back into the stockade of the Popular Front.
The talked-of rift in the CIO will be healed, and without his communist support John L. Lewis will be not only isolationist but
isolated. Wildcat strikes like the North American will subside.
New virtues will be discovered in Roosevelt and Churchill, although it is unlikely that the revaluation will reach as far as
La Guardia.[8] The energy that was channeled into "peace mobiliza-
tion" will now be channeled into making lease-lend a reality for

[8] From present appearances, as I prepare this for the press (September 1941), I
seem to have been wrong about La Guardia. The prospects are that the communists
will throw their support to him in the coming mayoralty campaign.

Russia. Thus once more, as in 1939, we see both with Hitler and with the communists how flexible ideologies may be if they are viewed only as things to manipulate.

But Hitler must know that he runs the risk of unifying the left against him. What then is his compensatory tactic in the war of ideas? It is to unify the right in his favor. Will he succeed? The answer must be a qualified one. For the Christian Front and America First the invasion is a propaganda natural. They can now demand to know whether we shall spill blood to make the world safe for communism and godlessness. But the crucial question comes not with these groups but with the conservatives, who are genuinely anti-Nazi but who also fear communism. The one thing Hitler hopes is that enough of these people will say: "Let the two bloody dictators fight it out while we stay on the sidelines and cheer." If he hoped for a peace move from England on this account, Churchill's speech and the RAF raids are a sufficient answer. But in America there is a chance that we shall turn a cold stare on Russia and "wait and see" at the very moment when we should be hurling everything into the conflict.

If the conservatives reason thus, or if they content themselves with organized lukewarmness, it will be the "end of conservative man" (to adopt a phrase of Guenter Reimann's) in America and the world as a whole. In terms of poetic justice, of course, the Russians deserve the bitter medicine they are drinking, as England deserves her medicine for Munich. But poetic justice is a luxury reserved for the survivors. For the present we must understand that if Hitler gets Russia's rich food and oil stores he will either succeed in a peace offensive tantamount to total victory, or enter a long-drawn-out war against England and America with renewed strength. But if Russia resists even until winter, Hitler's war will be stalled, Britain and America saved, and a foothold gained for the liberation of the European continent. Even the conservatives who have been fearing a long war of attrition between the democracies and Hitler, on the ground that Stalin would be the residual legatee, can now forget their fears. For now that Russia has been drawn into the war on England's side, even if she survives she will be a responsible partner in a common peace.

Ours will be a witless course if we do not see all this clearly, and if we allow ourselves to be deflected from our path by the dead

horse of communist fear. A reporter asked Mr. Roosevelt whether
the defense of Russia was also the defense of America, and the
President ridiculed the question. Politically he may have been
shrewd. And yet the answer is yes. Here is one case where Churchill
has proved himself the bolder and more decisive leader.

If we are hesitant in our moves, much of the blame will be with
the very liberals who are today the spearhead of the anti-Nazi effort,
but who have said repeatedly that there was nothing to choose between the Nazis and the Soviets. And again we see that ideas have
consequences. The invasion of Russia is in itself of course no proof
of the difference. Yet historic events are not pulled out of a hat.
From the very start there was a desperate opportunism about the
Nazi-Soviet pact that gave it a febrile quality. Hitler's policy could
be summed up in the line from Racine: "I embrace my enemy in
order the better to strangle him." And Stalin's was born of appeasement and sired by resentment of England. Despite the pact, the
hostility reaches beyond personalities and beyond power politics.
It is true that Russia and Germany are both totalitarian and both
despotisms. But the deeper truth is that social systems remain somehow moored to their ideological origins. The Nazi origins were in
the anti-humanist and life-denying doctrines of war as an end, of
racial exclusiveness, of contempt for the common man. The origins
of the Soviet system, for all the perversions that Stalinism has been
guilty of, were in the humanist and life-affirming doctrines of mass
progress and human worth, the Marxian conviction that men can
build a world through rational effort, that by transforming their
social universe they can transform themselves.

The calculable future we face is bleak and arduous no matter
how this war turns out. But if something can be done by this war
to bring Russia back once more into the stream of direction from
which she has been so drastically diverted—back toward a humanist socialism and a planned democracy—it might be a major
turning-point in history. I do not have much hope for Stalin and
his yes-men. Lenin would have done by deliberate policy and deep
humanity what Stalin has had forced on him by Hitler's will. Yet
the long run in Russia goes beyond leaders. The Russian people
are now learning what an unbridgeable gulf separates them from
the Nazi outlook. That lesson is being burned into them by Stukas
and flame-throwing tanks. We would do ill if by our half-hearted-

ness we were kept from helping them freely and generously, and thus from bridging the gulf that has separated us from them.

These considerations go beyond the war. The future of the West and the chances of a viable international order depend largely upon our finding common ground on which the American, British, Chinese, and Russian peoples can act. When we have that we shall have a base strong enough and broad enough to bear the weight of a democratic regeneration of the European continent, and decisive enough to furnish a directive for the still uncertain energies of Latin America.

If that happens, Hitler's labyrinthine mind will for once have overreached itself by its own resourcefulness. He will meet his defeat not only, as Napoleon did, from the scorched earth of Russia, but from a misreckoning of the power of unity still left in our world. That puts the burden where it belongs—on us.

1941

3

◆

Propaganda in Our Time

THE excellencies of the new Institute for Propaganda book [1] belong to its authors; its weaknesses belong to the intellectual climate of our time. Both are considerable.

To begin with, Mr. Lavine and Mr. Wechsler have done a first-rate job of craftsmanship—large masses of material well handled, a lively and intimate sense of the channels through which opinion is formed, details fitted into a colorful mosaic. They have written as complete a record as we have thus far of the attempts by Britain, France, Germany, and Russia (in a descending order of emphasis and importance) to influence American opinion and policy on the war. They have treated censorship as well as propaganda; dealt with the radio, the movies, the newspaper columns, the drama, the pulp magazines; examined the official hand-outs and the unofficial "plants" for correspondents; looked "inside the lie factories." In one sense they are a step ahead of the standard American works on the propaganda of the first World War. While Lasswell and Millis and Peterson had to wait until their war was over before they studied it, the present authors have photographed the bird on the wing.

But that has its dangers. Like almost everyone else, the authors seem to have been unprepared for the change in the character of the war. One gathers that most of the book was written before the invasion of Norway, and the final chapter added within a week after the invasion. The book is thus on the propaganda of the *Sitzkrieg* rather than of the *Blitzkrieg*. More serious (the greatest single weakness of the book) is its failure to deal adequately with German propaganda while dealing more than adequately with Allied propaganda. Only one brief chapter out of ten is directly de-

---

[1] Harold Lavine and James Wechsler, *War Propaganda and the United States,* New Haven, Yale University Press, 1940.

voted to Germany. This has nothing to do, of course, with the personal animus of the authors, which, for all the paraphernalia of detachment in the book, is anti-Nazi. It flows rather from two other sources. One is that German propaganda, operating secretly as part of the whole German social and administrative organism and in the face of American hostility, is more tortuous and less accessible for the American writers than is, let us say, Lord Lothian's appearance at a Newport charity fete or a speech by Alfred Duff Cooper. The second source is the authors' failure to grasp the relation of propaganda to the Nazi scheme of total warfare.

In a sense the propaganda of war has undergone recently a revolution as profound as the techniques of war. I am not speaking of a change in the basic strategy of either. German war strategy is still (if our experts are to be believed) the strategy of Clausewitz and Schlieffen; and similarly German propaganda may have made no great discoveries that can be labeled as such in their outward shape and smell. Dr. H. C. Peterson, who knows the propaganda of the first World War, has remarked that there is nothing particularly original about the devices Goebbels now uses, and that many of them still smell of the shelves from which they have been taken. That may be true. Where then does the revolution in propaganda come in? Just as the German war machine is a mechanized, planned, co-ordinated, and ruthless economic and administrative system, so the novelty of German propaganda lies less in new devices than in its integration with the rest of the activity of the Nazi war lords. It lies in the whole framework of the creation of terror and passivity, and the uses to which they are put.

I fear that the reader will get far more insight into German war propaganda and the United States from Rauschning's *Voice of Destruction* and Taylor's *Strategy of Terror* than from this book. And the reason is that, while Rauschning and Taylor have little to say about America, they have understood the shift of axis in Nazi war propaganda which wrought the appeasement havoc in Europe and is now producing its impact on America. One phase of the German propaganda effort is aimed at us only indirectly: it is the propaganda of completed terrorism in Europe, with meaningful implications for us. The other is directed squarely toward us: the links with Coughlinite, Christian Front, Ku Klux Klan activities here (the authors do a good job on these); the activities of the German and Italian ambassadorial and consular staffs; the activities of the *Auslandsorganisation* of the Nazi Party, under the Gauleiter for America, E. W. Bohle, who is not even mentioned in the book; the decorations given to key American figures like Henry Ford, Colonel Lindbergh, Thomas J. Watson, James D. Mooney; the stream of anti-Semitic and anti-alien literature; the organized calumny of President Roosevelt and his whole administration; the aid given to isolationist and pacifist rallies and movements; the intimate talks of men like Westrick with American business leaders to win them over to appeasement. This is the real German war propaganda in the United States—meant to cripple, confuse, demoralize, terrify us until the time when Hitler can turn his main attention to us.

Why have the authors failed here? Largely, I think, because they start with a false notion about what propaganda is. And that in turn has less to do with them than with the widespread disease of sloppy thinking about propaganda in our time.

Let me quote from the introduction to the book, signed by two directors of the Institute for Propaganda Analysis, Clyde Miller and E. C. Lindeman. It defines propaganda as "a method utilized for influencing the conduct of others on behalf of predetermined ends." From this it follows unerringly that "every articulate person with a purpose is a propagandist." But this is to regard as propaganda the whole range of intellectual activity, and to reduce the effort at propaganda analysis to an absurdity. In these terms a book on war propaganda and the United States would have logically to be a book surveying the words and activities of every articulate person who has sought to influence American policy according to his ends. And if this is true, then the truism with which the introduction opens, "we live in a propaganda age," would be no truer of our age than of any other.

I have no particular animus against this conception of propaganda, other than its uselessness. If we interpret all efforts to shape our foreign policy as propaganda, how shall we distinguish between a Presidential message, an editorial in the *New Republic*, a Coughlin broadcast, a classroom discussion, a speech by Joe McWilliams, a Congressional debate, a column by Westbrook Pegler, a communiqué from the German army staff, a manifesto by the Harvard Defense Group, a broadcast by Elmer Davis, an appeal for relief funds, a photograph of mangled children, and a sermon by Father

Curran? Anything that holds them all together must be a clumsy receptacle indeed.

It is little wonder that in such a mental climate we have become a nation of amateur detectives looking for concealed propaganda in every effort to awaken America to the real nature of Nazi world strategy. It may be because we have felt cheated and disenchanted by our role in the last war, and are determined never again to be tricked. The result is reminiscent of the rural visitor to the World's Fair who had heard so much of the pickpockets, the sirens, and the false enchantments of the big city that he spent all his time eluding their snares and at the end found that he had failed to see anything. For America today the important thing has become to *see* the dimensions and conditions of our world. And we shall never do that if we reject as propaganda every fact in it which may lead to action. To view, as this book tends to, the whole realm of opinion as one of "competing propagandas" and every effort at persuasion as an effort at propaganda is to see the world through the word instead of through the thought and deed, in monstrously inflated terms. The consequence is a collective indecision which makes us powerless against the single-minded intelligence and the ruthless will of Hitlerism. And, curiously, this same bland envelopment in a universal skepticism, which paralyzes our action and strips us of all sense of values, leaves us in the end a prey to the real propaganda and the real fifth columnism of Hitler's agents. A mind without beliefs is incapable of criticism, heroism, or tragedy. If you suspect everything indiscriminately you end by suspecting nothing very strongly.

What conception of propaganda then would be a usable one? I suggest toward a working definition, first: that not all efforts at persuasion for predetermined ends are propaganda, but that the beginning of wisdom here lies in making distinctions. I do not mean distinctions between "good" and "bad" propaganda, which seem to me worse than useless, since those terms have meaning only in a subjective estimate made by the observer. I suggest, second: that the propagandist is primarily a manipulator of beliefs, emotions, symbols. When I call him a manipulator I say that his primary concern is to find the symbol or argument that will work, that he concentrates only on the relation of his device to his end. I suggest, therefore, third: that for the propagandist the validity of his material or the sincerity of his own belief in what he is saying is irrelevant. He may be stating what is factually so, or he may not: even Goebbels has been known to say truthful things or, for all his cynicism, things he believed. But if what the propagandist says is valid or sincere it is in the deepest sense an accident—i.e., beside the point. I suggest, fourth (and most important): that there is always in the propagandist some crucial concealment, some relevant duplicity. He sees all the cards, you do not. And the card he is not showing you is the very card which, if you saw it, would deflect you from the belief the propagandist intends you to have or the action he wills you to take. From this viewpoint the talk about "a propaganda of reason" simply makes no sense.

Any such attempt at definition must be judged by whether it enables us to salvage out of the wreck of beliefs some materials for a critical credo. I disagree strongly with the impassioned isolationism of Charles Beard, but that does not make him a propagandist, since however predetermined his ends may be, his passion is spent in analyzing and urging rather than in manipulating. William Allen White's committee to aid Britain may echo Lord Lothian's appeal for the sale of American destroyers, but that does not make the committee a propagandist group unless it deliberately conceals some crucial item such as (if it were true) the fact that America cannot spare the destroyers, or (again if it were true) that the committee has hidden connections with the British government. Hitler may well believe his own anti-Semitism as Goebbels may disbelieve his, yet both are propagandists, just as Coughlin is, since they never reveal that anti-Semitism is for them primarily a device for power through spreading confusion and hatred. The Nazi talk of the American threat to the sovereignties of the Latin American countries is propaganda: partly because the aim is not to help Latin America but to entangle it, and partly because on the record the Nazi solicitude about the sovereignty of nations is hypocritical. Whether Lindbergh is a propagandist or only a naïve and confused young man depends upon what relations he may have with the Bundist and native fifth column groups who staged his mass meetings, since the concealment of such a relation would indicate that his attempt was not to persuade for American ends but to manipulate opinion for Nazi ends. Always there are as the basic tests the intent to manipulate, the irrelevance of validity or sincerity, the concealment of some crucial ingredients of belief.

All this is difficult. But the lumping of all degrees of propaganda and persuasion is worse than difficult—it is destructive. If we could get along without propaganda as a concept, I should be the first to rejoice over its embers. But since we must have it, let us restrict it, make it wieldy and sharp, and turn its sharpness against the possibility of a propaganda-dominated world. And we shall do that only if we use propaganda analysis to create, and not to avoid, a body of belief.[2]

---

[2] The following exchange of letters which appeared in the pages of the *New Republic* may be of some interest.

Sir: Max Lerner's review of *War Propaganda and the United States* by Lavine and Wechsler in your August 26 issue seems to me a just and adequate appraisal save in one respect: that is Mr. Lerner's quarrel with the Institute for Propaganda Analysis over the definition of the term "propaganda."

Mr. Lerner, like many, appears to believe that propaganda is always something sneaking and deceptive, if not sinister. The Institute holds otherwise.

If Mr. Lerner's definition is accepted generally, it then becomes more easily possible for a person who is stacking the cards to put something over to assure his audience that he is not a propagandist, but rather an educator spreading truth and enlightenment. Neither the dictionary definition of the term "propaganda" nor the activities of innumerable propagandists make Mr. Lerner's definition valid. He says:

"I have no particular animus against this conception of propaganda, other than its uselessness. If we interpret all efforts to shape our foreign policy as propaganda, how shall we distinguish between a Presidential message, an editorial in the *New Republic,* a Coughlin broadcast, a classroom discussion, a speech by Joe McWilliams, a Congressional debate, a column by Westbrook Pegler, a communiqué from the German army staff?"

Precisely because all of these and uncounted other expressions of opinion, fact, alleged fact, and actions intended to influence human beings are propaganda, the Institute for Propaganda Analysis was organized to devise methods for recognizing and analyzing propaganda.

Mr. Lerner seems to say that if a man is sincere, he is not a propagandist however much he urges his case; whereas if a man is insincere, he is a propagandist. Indubitably many of the Nazis, for example, are sincere, however much they may be deluded. By Mr. Lerner's definition, therefore, such Nazis because they are sincere, though deluded, are not propagandists. Anyone who has studied the rise of the Nazi movement knows that some of its most effective propaganda has been spread by very sincere people. Mr. Lerner writes:

"Hitler may well believe his own anti-Semitism as Goebbels may disbelieve his, yet both are propagandists, just as Coughlin is, since they never reveal that anti-Semitism is for them primarily a device for power through spreading confusion and hatred."

As a matter of fact, Hitler has revealed with utmost clarity that his anti-Semitism is primarily a device for power through spreading confusion and hatred. See *Mein Kampf* and his conversations with Herr Rauschning in *The Voice of Destruction* for proof of this.

Clyde R. Miller,
Secretary, the Institute for Propaganda Analysis
New York City

Sir: I am grateful for Clyde Miller's letter, but surely he is too generous: if my definition of propaganda is wrong, my appraisal of the book could not possibly be "just and adequate." Our differences are, I fear, fundamental rather than verbal. Mr. Miller has misunderstood me when he says that I "seem to say" that my conception of propaganda turns on the question of sincerity. Actually I said no such thing, and the very passage about Hitler and Goebbels which he quotes from me in his letter shows that I said the exact opposite—that the question of sincerity and belief has nothing to do with the matter. I spoke explicitly of "the irrelevance of validity or sincerity." The distinguishing mark of propaganda is, I have said, the intent to manipulate the minds and beliefs of others, rather than merely to persuade. But since intent, as a subjective matter, is hard to get at, I added that one can infer it from the objective existence of some crucial concealment, some relevant distortion. Mr. Miller cites against me the practice of propagandists throughout history and the dictionary definition. As for the first, it begs the question: how can we know who were the propagandists in history until we have a clear notion of what propaganda is? As for the second, I have not consulted the dictionary and I don't care. The dictionary-maker follows rather than instructs the social thinker; and if he finds confusion in social thought, he mirrors that confusion.

I have no intent to do injury to any group with whose social outlook I am in as great agreement as with the Institute for Propaganda Analysis. But when the work of such a group is founded on a basically false conception of propaganda, it has already impaired its own value; and the book under review seemed to me to illustrate the results of that false conception. Mr. Miller says that "opinion, fact, alleged fact, and actions intended to influence human beings" are all "propaganda." This, I repeat, embraces the whole area of human expression. To call it all propaganda makes the job of "analyzing" it hopelessly difficult and, what is worse, misleading.

Max Lerner

1940

4

Democracy for a War Generation[1]

Now that the struggle over aid to England has been settled, Americans must look about to measure the implications of their position and the course their next acts must take. As we look back at the battle of opinion over our foreign policy, two things stand out strikingly. One is that while our political methods have worked tolerably in enabling us to fashion decisions with less hysteria and more freedom of debate than might have been expected, they have been unconscionably dilatory at a time when delay might spell death. The other is that, for all the urgency of the issues and the stakes that various interest groups had in them, the divisions of opinion have not been along class lines.

Interventionist opinion has united for common ends from diverse motives. There have been the Anglophiles who loved England so well that the white cliffs of Dover became a symbol blended of nostalgia and mysticism. There have been the professional militarists for whom the whir of airplane motors has replaced the rattling of sabers. There have been the capitalists who feared for the Bank of England not because it was English but because it was a bank, and the chauvinists of big money for whom the quest for capitalist power smelled sweeter under the name of the "American century." There have been the Wilsonian liberals who saw a chance to redeem a memory and retrieve a cause once thought lost. But above all there have been the quietly convinced anti-fascists, who never sought involvement in war for its own sake but also never flinched from it when it remained the only way to save men's dignity from the ungentle embrace of the total state; and who, with-

---

[1] This essay in its present form appeared in the April 1941 issue of *Decision*. An expanded version of it was also presented as a speech at the meetings of the American Academy of Political Science, in Philadelphia, and was published in the *Annals* of that society under the title "American Leadership in a Harsh Age."

out any hankering to rebuild the world, were willing to have America assume world leadership if that would help lead to a degree of world order.

On the other side, the distances between the groups thrown together by the iron logic of events have been even greater. On the extreme right have been the big industry appeasers and the only slightly concealed fascists—both groups feeling that the hour had struck, yet both uneasy as to whether the role it held for them was that of proconsuls under a Nazi Caesarism or that of leadership in an American Caesarism. In the center were the traditional isolationists, honest but provincial, whose provincialism not even the march of Nazi tanks had shattered; the pacifists who kept their eyes on the Prince of Peace but had no eyes for the Christ who was being daily mutilated from Poland to Spain; and the continentalists who thought that if they played Candide and cultivated their own and the Latin American economic garden, Hitler would turn ascetic and be content with the hegemony of Europe. And on the left there have been the dogmatists of socialism and liberalism, who found the world moving so fast that their only security seemed to lie in holding tight and shouting the old slogans while the landscape whirled by; the perfectionists, both in the universities and in the labor movement, who wanted to be sure we had solved all our economic and moral problems before we faced the forces loose in the world; and the adventurists, both among the communists and some of the populist politicians, who felt that an anti-war record would be a badge of political advantage in the post-war reaction.

It will be clear that these attitudes cut across class lines. Particularly important for the social observer are the splits within the capitalist and worker classes, since the middle class has been traditionally divided in its opinions. There are big industry and finance groups on both sides of the fence; the same applies to the trade unions, although with a notable tendency to stay shy of the whole issue. This has, I think, two sets of implications.

One is that the dominant stakes in the war and the world struggle as a whole are not economic—that they are matters of ideology, political methods, and national power and survival. The crisscrossing of these new elements with the traditional attitudes will serve to account for the gridiron pattern of opinion I have described. The second is that the very lack of sharpness of the eco-

nomic interests has been a factor of safety for us, because it has
denied success to Hitler's hope of winning America through the
"inside job" of fomenting a civil war. To be sure, the appeasement
and "negotiated peace" camp contains the most formidable gathering of potential fascists we have ever witnessed; yet they can begin
to operate only in the event that we are too late to save the British
from the Nazis or too weak to save ourselves. But the obverse of
this is also true: that even in the event of a Nazi defeat we shall
still have to resolve the problems of class conflict and still have to
face the internal obstacles in the path of a humanist and democratic socialism.

But we have never had a right to expect more or to ask for more.
Those of us who look forward to a functional society understand
that the struggle with Nazism is not in itself a solution. It is only the
fearful necessity of destroying a power-group and an outlook which
seek to destroy us. Once we have fulfilled that necessity we shall
have only the grim satisfaction of knowing that we can then turn
to the unending but affirmative job of finishing the unfinished
business of democracy. And yet that does not exclude from the war
all affirmative importance as a means. Even the unsought struggles
in our life often reveal to us depths and resources within ourselves
that had gone unnoted. That has happened to democratic man,
who has found out not only his weaknesses and indecisions but his
basic strength as well, and even a touch of heroism. And, as the
English have learned, the fight against Nazi reaction, even on the
part of the conservative middle class, may become a way of releasing in them their latent liberal energies.

The principles that can guide liberal thought with some clarity
in the uncertain tangle of events are, however, neither very sweeping nor very glorious. Wilsonian liberalism in the last war made
the mistake of thumping too hard the drum of national and world
salvation. We must deflate our claims to the span of real choices
in a real world.

One principle is that first things come first; and the first things
in our world are the imperatives of survival against fascism. We
understand the nature of British imperialism in the past, British
treachery in the pre-Munich world, and the elements of British
appeasement still surviving. But our choice is still for first things.

Machiavelli, who was clear-eyed and unsentimental before he was anything else, never tired of repeating that in politics men must choose between varying degrees of what they dislike.

Another principle: in choosing partnership with Britain, China, and Greece, even to the extent of actual belligerency if that should prove necessary and possible, we must remember that our fight cannot be carried on along one front. I have said that the act of fighting Nazi reaction may be a liberating act; but it is also true that a war state brings the economic and political systems closer together, and puts reaction at least partially in the saddle. There is today not only an enemy to be fought abroad but also an enemy at home: an unholy combination of corporate potentates, dollar-a-year men in the administration, generals and admirals in social blinkers, anti-labor Congressmen, the barons of opinion, the self-appointed vigilantes in local communities. This should be no surprise. Politics is an organic affair—what you do in your foreign policy becomes an inseparable part of your domestic policy; and your domestic strength or weakness is revealed only when you put it to the test in power politics. There are those who say we must choose between fighting for democracy abroad or making it work at home. That is an unreal choice. We must fight on both fronts—not because we want to take on a double battle, but because each battle today involves the other, and neither can be fought without the other. For democracy's enemies at home will take power if fascism wins abroad; and fascism can never be beaten abroad unless we organize our industries and strengthen our morale by drastic democratic measures here.

That is our dilemma. And that is also our opportunity.

What this leads to may turn out to be the greatest lesson of our generation: that you have no right to view democracy as a desirable end unless you view it also as an effective means. Democracy can be not only the product of winning the war but also the means for it.

Here belong the most important phases of the American governmental effort today. We have an armament economy which must be geared to the one objective of producing the maximum of war materials. Today the generals in that war effort are industrialists operating not as parts of an army but as *condottieri*—mercenaries who hire their men and seek to get the greatest profit out of it for themselves. Some of them have no real anti-fascist convictions; but even worse than that, they have a tenacious sense of "business as usual" which makes them archaic in a modern war of factories. Some of them, like the officials of the Ford Company and of Bethlehem Steel, carry their primitivism into the field of labor as well. Democracy as a means requires a planned organization of the war of factories. It requires an approach such as is contained in Walter Reuther's plan for turning idle capacity in the auto industry toward the mass production of planes, or such as is contained in the steel union's plan for expanding steel capacity, or in Philip Murray's plan for the establishment of industrial councils which will increase production, keep prices down, and avoid labor trouble. If I mention the labor proposals, it is because labor rather than management has shown an awareness of what is required to make the American armament economy click.

Democracy as a method will also, on the premise that a revolutionary situation exists today in the world, seek to convert the military war into a civil war and thus energize the anti-fascist forces everywhere. It will energize the morale of the plain men and women in England and America by showing, through its speed and decisiveness and effectiveness of action, that a dynamic exists in democracy fully as much as in the most single-willed dictatorship. It will thus not only evoke the productive energies of labor and the technicians and administrators among the peoples still fighting the Nazis, it will also sustain and increase the rebellious energies of the peoples enslaved by the Nazis. One does not need to be a military expert to know that while Hitler's armor must be cracked in direct military and economic warfare, the final defeat of Hitlerism must come from the widespread uprising against his rule over the enslaved democracies of Europe. But the sparks for this fire must be furnished by us—by democracy's demonstrated capacity to fight a hard war of factories and morale, and to fight it in the service of ends which cut across our national boundaries and our economic empires, and reach the economic and social needs of plain men everywhere.

To do this we must have an expression of war aims, in word and in deed. These aims must come from England—despite the obvious realistic difficulties which only a dreamer or a liberal would fail to recognize; but they must come from America as well. They must encompass the kind of war this is, the enemies in every country against whom it is fought, the kind of men and the kind of ideas that can best fight it, and finally the kind of world that can arise out of it. This is not too much to ask of those to whom we have entrusted leadership. In fact, it is a minimum earnest of their capacity for leadership.

This is not the place for a discussion of the outlines of the peace after the war.[2] Certain things, however, are clear enough not to need much detail. What a Hitler peace would mean is today already written over the face of the European continent which is dominated by the Nazi "master race." A "negotiated peace" would not be very different: it would mean only that we sought to bridge the chasm in two jumps rather than one. But what would a peace following a drastic defeat of Hitler and his war lords and his propaganda lords mean? First, it would have to avoid the Carthaginian pattern and forgo vindictiveness against the German people as a whole. Second, it would have to make economic settlements as well as political, and arrange for going regional economic units. Third, it would have to provide the beginnings of an international federal structure.

These are broad vistas, and yet, considering the travail through which our world will have gone, they are modest enough. We are not avid for perfection or hot for certainties, and for that reason we will not be content with dusty answers. We want only the answers we can ourselves forge, out of the human materials we have— which, however imperfect, will have to do. We want a fighting chance to make of democracy a dream and instrument together.

1941

---

[2] For such a discussion see the chapter "If We Own the Future," above, p. 58. The reader will find there also a later and more qualified view of the utility of a statement of war aims.

PART FOUR

The Unfinished Business of Democracy

1

Case Studies in Democracy:
Some Archaeological Notes[1]

The Case of the Corporate Surplus Tax (1936)[2]

PUT it down to Mr. Roosevelt's eternal credit that he has managed somehow to make a good show even of taxes. Here is a subject that has been handled in more or less routine fashion year after year, with the Treasury experts and the financial big shots dominating the scene and effecting a compromise between what was administratively necessary and what would least injure the delicate pecuniary nerves of the big owners. And, presto, this subject is whirled into the news in dramatic fashion, evoking the most emotional philippics and the most heroic defenses—the sort of thing that is generally reserved for boondoggling and Liberty League dinners and Supreme Court justices and the impounding of telegrams. In this dramatization Mr. Roosevelt has been impresario rather than actor. In making a big show out of the tax on corporate surpluses, he has of course had the help of the Republicans, the corporation heads, the Presidential campaign, the Supreme Court; possibly also the taut nerves of the Senators, Treasury officials, witnesses, frayed by the incessant hammering of recent events in the New Deal.

---

[1] I should like to warn the reader that the four essays that follow are journalistic pieces and should be read in the context of the years in which they first appeared. So far as possible I have avoided making changes in them. I reprint them as a not unuseful record of the travail of a democracy in its internal and foreign policies even before Nazism had come to dominate our perspective.

[2] This appeared as an article in the *Nation* in May 1936, with some sections omitted for reasons of space. Those sections I have now restored. The reader should not take it as a description of the present American tax policy, since I have made no attempt to bring the subject of corporate taxation up to date.

But all these aids, even under Mr. Roosevelt's talented guidance, would have been unavailing if the stage had not been set for them by the pressure of enormous expenditure on government finances and the danger of weakening the structure further by imposing taxes on the underlying population. In this sense some sort of tax on corporate surpluses is an inevitable part of a program of reform capitalism. If the Republicans and the conservative wing of the Democrats succeed in defeating it, as they seem to have done at the present writing, it will come back to plague them in the not far distant future. Only it may require another, stronger Roosevelt to bring it back.

But all that is in the realm of ultimates. As far as the immediate battle over the tax is concerned, it is hard to grasp the forces at work behind the scenes until you have seen them in dynamic form in the welter of a Senate committee room. Away from Washington, no matter how much you read and ponder over the bill and the testimony and the newspaper accounts, the thing somehow fails to come to life. You say to yourself: this pother over a six-hundred-million dollar budget item—big as it is—is out of proportion to its budgetary importance. The struggle must have some other meanings, some other roots. What are they?

It was the desire to discover what they are that sent me to Washington. I had been informed that on Tuesday, May 12, Treasury Counsel Herman Oliphant would be given a chance to answer the barrage of objections to which his bill had been exposed. He would undoubtedly confront some of the enemies of the bill and bring into the open forces which I felt to be silently operative but whose pattern I had not been able to grasp. I believe I must be the only mortal who ever traveled to Washington to get closer to a tax hearing out of sheer intellectual passion. I wanted a ringside seat at the tax fight. Others might pick Joe Louis or Tony Canzoneri, mauling a hapless victim in the glare of the arc lights while thousands cheer. I picked Mr. Oliphant and Senator Byrd, both stripped (intellectually) to the waist in a hot committee room, fighting over the corporate surplus tax with no one cheering, and with only a tableful of yawning newspapermen and a scattering of others there to see the carnage.

You come into a room already half filled with smoke. At one end

a raised platform of horseshoe formation, and behind it the members of the Senate Finance Committee, posing a little—as the Roman Senate did—as an "assembly of gods" and a little as a group
of American "regular fellers." Somehow this particular collection
of Senators is not one to make you despair of representative government. As the discussion proceeds you find that many of them are
men of ability, and that there is even passion and sincerity among
some of them. Many of the faces are fine. The full committee is
twenty-one—fifteen Democrats, five Republicans, and a Progressive.

Pat Harrison, of Mississippi, in the chair. He turned out what I
thought was a consummate bit of chairmanship. He had the respect,
mingled somewhat with fear, of most of the men there. At the bar,
facing Harrison and with his back to the newspapermen and spectators, stood Herman Oliphant, Treasury Counsel—more responsible
for the fate and merits of the bill than any other man in Washington. He spoke slowly but with a bitter intensity. For months he has
been the target of attack, not only from the Republicans but from
within the Administration itself. He is a little man, with a bullet
head, eyes sunken but flashing, finely chiseled features. Most of the
time he speaks straight at the Senators, but when he has something
to say that he regards as of particular importance he swings his body
slowly around and faces the newspapermen and spectators. It is
hard to meet the glance of those eyes, but easy to read almost anything into them—certainly zeal, tenacity, conviction. He is a former
law professor at Columbia and Johns Hopkins who, as law professors
must, knows the corporate structure. I have a suspicion that he takes
the New Deal seriously. He has a very poor memory for figures,
which is unfortunate, because his prestige as a Treasury official
seems to have suffered from the conviction of some of these Senators
that practical business is the only school Treasury officials should
ever attend. Like other professors in Washington he tends to doff the
academic too easily—probably as a defense gesture. In two and a
half hours of speaking the only academic remark he made was a reference to the difference between "the law in books and the law in
action."

One thing that is omitted amid all the sword-play of Administration and anti-Administration forces on the committee is the
framework of the measure. Oliphant touches on it somewhat, but
most of it has to be supplied. The whole episode started, of course,

when a soviet of judges and soldiers combined to take over the budgetary reins from the hands of the constituted authorities. The Supreme Court had declared the processing taxes invalid in the Hoosac decision, and then the veterans had marched in and mopped up after the court by getting their bonus. Since the Republicans had openly rejoiced over the foray of the judges, and aided the foray of the veterans, they were in no position to raise an outcry when the President and his financial advisers looked about for ways of restoring the raided revenue. Actually they were a bit happy about it; taxes are never popular, and raising money is a poor way of enhancing your political prestige. They felt that they had the President in something of a hole. If he did not succeed in balancing the budget, they could raise the cry of extravagance; if he did, it would necessarily involve "nuisance taxes," and cost him votes. There was dark talk of having to make a choice between a sales tax and an increase of the income tax in the lower and middle brackets. At his press conference on February 28, 1936, the President gave no indication of how he would resolve his dilemma. There was a rumor that a new corporate surplus tax was being considered, but it was never strongly bruited. When, therefore, Mr. Roosevelt sent his special tax message to Congress on March 2, his novel tax proposal found the country dazed. The only people who knew what to say were the Republicans, but they said it more out of principle than understanding: it was enough for them that the source was satanic. The Democrats, on the whole, tended to stand behind the proposed measure—for the same reason reversed. The reaction of the stock market was decidedly favorable, on the theory that corporate dividends would be distributed instead of being piled up as reserves.

That was ten weeks ago. After the first few weeks it became clear that we were in for a long siege of tax discussion. Two things had happened. One was that while the President's message had outlined the general principle of the tax, the drafting of the act itself was entrusted to the mercies of the House Ways and Means Committee, which proceeded to wrangle about it for a while and then threw the measure open for public hearings. The second was that what the New York *Times* so magnificently calls "public opinion" —that is, the opinion of the *Times* editors and owners, and their friends in the business and banking worlds—recovered from its daze and began to assert itself. When it became apparent what the tax meant to do and how it meant to do it, a storm broke.

What sort of tax universe was the proposal born into?

Whether the combatants knew it or not, it was the concept and nature and structure of the corporation as a business unit which dominated the committee hearings throughout. The rapid growth of the corporation in the past few decades has cut under the entire tax structure of the country. What had formerly been more or less tangible income now became intangible claims to income. A mechanism which has in its construction engaged the best legal resources of the country was bound to create problems both for Treasury officials and for the state as a whole—problems of the concentration of financial power, the wresting of control from the investors, its capture by a small group of insiders who often used it in the manipulation of securities and in a ruthless march toward monopoly. One of the central features in this picture of corporate control has been the accumulation of a huge corporate reserve. Complaints had for years been pouring into Washington pointing to the abuses of such a surplus. It was a happy coincidence, therefore, when Mr. Oliphant's analysis of the possible sources of new revenue fixed upon business profits as having advanced furthest in the movement toward recovery. His proposal to place a heavy graduated tax on the corporate surplus seemed to offer a chance to combine a sound revenue objective with a long-needed social objective.

The present (1936) corporation tax is not very fruitful of revenue. It is an attempt to tax at the source only, and not a very successful one. A tax twelve and a half to fifteen per cent is levied on the net income of all corporations—net income being computed after deducting all sorts of items including a reasonable reserve for expansion and other purposes. What constitutes a reasonable reserve is, of course, so subjective as to elude even the most competent tax administration we have had thus far. Everyone knows that this elastic section nullifies any purpose the act might have had of taxing surpluses as well as the distributed dividends. Actually it is doubtful whether the purpose was ever there. A Washington official remarked to me with some cynicism, "There has never been an income-tax bill framed yet that really had the interests of the country in mind and that wasn't a series of weak compromises and crudely concealed surrenders." The effect of the present corporate tax is generally that corporate income pays a far lower rate than it would pay if it were counted as part of the income of the individual stockholder, since as an individual the stockholder is exempted from paying taxes on his dividends from corporation stock. Another effect is that corporations are enabled to pile up huge reserves on the ground that they consider them reasonable. A common device among the big corporations is to place these reserves in the hands of holding companies created for that purpose, and whenever the pile reaches dangerous proportions a reorganization is quietly effected and the entire process begins again.

It is true that an attempt is made under Section 102 of the present law to remedy this defect. Any corporation which is *prima facie* a holding company created for the purpose of tax evasion, or any corporation accumulating capital beyond the reasonable needs of its business expansion, is held subject to a tax penalty. But administrative difficulties have prevented the enforcement of this well-intentioned section. The Aluminum Company, owned by Mr. Mellon, can for example make out a very good case for large reserves as necessary for expansion, and it would take an extremely persistent and clever revenue agent, as an outsider to the affairs of the company, to break through the company position. The Treasury once selected for study what seemed the fifty best cases of this sort—the fifty in which, if anywhere, the government might expect to press for surtax revenue—and after considerable scrutiny it was clear that none of them would stand up under a cold denial and a clever exposition on the part of the corporation officials. This is not to say that, because this section has never been enforced, it never could be enforced. It does mean that it poses an enormous administrative problem. I am convinced, however, that in their zeal to find another method for getting at the revenue, the Treasury officials have disposed too summarily of the possibility of revising Section 102 and putting teeth into it.

The President's tax proposal was aimed at getting some revenue out of this undistributed surplus. To this end it first cleared the ground of the existing corporate taxes. This may seem strange, since the avowed purpose of the act was increased revenue yield, but the Treasury mind evidently had its own grooves along which it moved. The Treasury officials were determined to set up a "simplified" corporate tax system, stripped of subjective elements, easy of administration, and operating on a formula that would make sure of yielding the required revenue. To some extent, also, the repeal of the existing corporate taxes might have recommended itself as making the drastic features of the measure more palatable to the large corporations, but the bill did not remain in its original state. In its passage through the House committee and its thus far very eventful career in the Senate committee it has gone through three or four major mutations and any number of minor ones. When the House committee got through with the bill, any pretense it may once have had to simplicity was ridiculous, and the opposition made a good deal of capital out of its involved schedules and its 280 pages of text. Some editor in a happy inspiration dubbed it "the bill nobody knows," and the name has stuck.

The most fatal blow struck at the proposed measure was the impressive array of witnesses who appeared to testify against it. The political astuteness of the plan from the very start had rested on the fact that while every tax measure had to cause pain somewhere, the pain in this case would be visited on those who were already anti-Administration. Opposition from the business interests was of course expected. What was not expected was its volume and unanimity and the form it took. The initial mistake the Treasury made was that it did not come prepared with a bill but left the House committee to frame it. The witnesses who appeared at the hearing were thus emboldened in dealing with what seemed a hastily assembled measure. Their attack, moreover, was not just the tory attack of big corporations. It became apparent that the attempt to get at the corporations that evaded a surtax on their undistributed profits would in the process sideswipe the smaller corporations which were in genuine need of building up surpluses. The case was stated most clearly and cogently in the climactic testimony of George O. May, whose prestige in the financial and accounting world is unsurpassed.[3] He not only spoke caustically of the "slaughter of the innocents" that would follow on the attempt to get at the malefactors, but also challenged the Treasury estimates of the probable yield of the tax. The result, of course, was such as to dampen the enthusiasm of even the most zealous Administration

---

[3] Since this article appeared Mr. May's prestige has suffered because of the connection of his accounting firm, Price, Waterhouse and Company, with the McKesson-Robbins episode.

Congressman. The government forces, facing the enemy fire, could not hold their lines intact. In the House committee only one Democrat, Representative Lamneck, deserted, but in the Senate committee the revolt took on serious proportions. The conservative wing of the Democrats broke away from the Administration wing and joined the Republicans. Byrd of Virginia, Bailey of North Carolina, and Clark of Missouri, a trio of able Democrats, led the defection. In fact they attacked the bill more vigorously than did the most vocal of the Republicans—Hastings of Delaware, who acts as Senate warder for his feudal masters, the du Ponts.

What I was witnessing in the Senate committee room was the last attempt of Senators Harrison and Barkley, the Administration stalwarts, to salvage the principle of the bill. Mr. Oliphant came with a prepared statement which was as closely and powerfully reasoned a document as I have yet seen on the subject, and which under any other circumstances should have proved effective. He came flanked by Treasury experts and by statisticians armed with charts. If this last stand of the Administration was unsuccessful in persuading some of the Democratic rebels, nothing would remain but the desperate remedy of carrying the fight to the Senate floor. The most distressing element in the whole situation was the persistent rumor that Mr. Roosevelt was himself uncertain about the measure as it stood. He had, it seems, been half persuaded by some of the objections that had been raised, especially those dealing with the effect of the tax upon the smaller corporations.

Every important issue that had been raised by the experts and witnesses appearing before the committees cropped up again in the course of Mr. Oliphant's plea and the responses it evoked. Certain of these issues, while of great emotional and tactical importance, may be dismissed as not of the essence of the matter. Among these are the problem of the complexity of the measure and the tilt between Mr. May and Mr. Oliphant on the probable yield of the taxes. These are matters of draftsmanship and administration, and while they are important as such they can be remedied by a little hard thinking and hard work.

Much more important were the far-reaching issues of policy and tax structure which the hearings raised. They may be roughly grouped under four headings: the philosophy of a tax on corporate surpluses; the relation of such a tax to the corporate structure and the principle of corporate democracy; the question of the relative effects of the tax upon large and small corporations, and in general upon big ownership and the little fellow; the effect of the tax upon the economic structure as a whole and upon the business cycle.

As regards the philosophy of the tax, the Administration finds itself in a ticklish position, much as it did in the case of the TVA. Actually the tax would not be worth writing about if it did not reach much further than a new technique for raising some six hundred million dollars of needed revenue. The corporate surplus tax fits integrally into the logic of the entire Roosevelt Administration. In addition to the raising of revenue, it has four non-revenue objectives—reforming the corporate structure, protecting investors, putting individuals and partnerships on an equality with corporations, forcing the distribution of corporate income and therefore the more rapid circulation of purchasing power. These are not accidental consequences of a tax of this sort. They are an integral part of an administrative policy which has created a Securities and Exchange Commission, sought to regulate the more flagrant malpractices of corporate finance, pushed through the Public Utility Holding Companies Act, and emphasized the purchasing-power theory of prosperity and depression. Mr. Roosevelt has been praised and attacked for his political astuteness in proposing such a tax, since it got him out of a serious budgetary difficulty. But this measure is not merely a Roosevelt trick. Mr. Roosevelt has generally been found to play the politician in what he fails to do rather than in what he does, in his retreats rather than in his attacks. The real political astuteness of the measure is that it was intended to jibe with the concern that the Administration has always had for the small investor and small business man and to carry that concern into the field of taxation.

Given a philosophy of this sort in the tax measure, why has Mr. Oliphant been so concerned to keep it in the background? The answer seems clear. There are one or two points in the measure which are, even as they stand, of doubtful constitutionality. For Mr. Oliphant to say very much now about social objectives rather than about revenue would be to invite disaster when the tax bill comes up before the final tribunal of the Supreme Court.

The basic weakness of the plan, however, lies in the fact that these two objectives do not quite coincide. This was most clearly brought out in the verbal tilts between Senators Byrd and Bailey, on the one hand, and Mr. Oliphant and Senator La Follette, on the other. With impressive tenacity Senator Byrd clung to his contention that the plan would injure the small corporation and favor the larger one. The large corporation is obviously in a much better position to distribute its entire income and thus avoid the payment of a tax completely. Mr. Oliphant's reply that government would get its revenue from the individual income taxes of the stockholders was satisfactory from a revenue point of view, but inconclusive from a social viewpoint. What had evidently happened was that in order to meet his revenue objectives, Mr. Oliphant proposed removing the existing tax on corporate income; but in the very process of removing it he was defeating his social objective.

This was a fatal error in strategy, for it gave the conservative forces exactly the handle they were seeking. I do not mean that all the opposition to the bill came from conservative quarters. Among liberals, many were genuinely solicitous lest in trying to achieve a much-needed tax and social reform the government was adopting techniques which defeated that very purpose. But within the Senate committee itself the opposition was from the conservative rather than from the liberal angle. Senator Byrd, who has been anti-New Deal from the very beginning and who has played closely with the big interests, now stepped forward in a surprising role as the champion of the rights of the little fellow. Senator Bailey of North Carolina, who stands for the big tobacco interests of his state, if he stands for anything, vied with his Virginia colleague in the unction he showed in defense of their new cause. Senator King of Utah, who throughout the afternoon ranted in spread-eagle fashion and made no point that he did not botch and befuddle, found himself surprisingly swelling the chorus of so-called "liberal" protest. Even Senator Couzens, who stands head and shoulders above all these men, was forced into opposition to the measure, for Senator Couzens uses as the symbol of his financial thinking the Ford corporation with which he has been so closely identified, and as he became increasingly convinced that this bill would hit the small corporation even harder than the large he gave more weight to the argument that under a measure which compelled the distribution of a corporate surplus the rapid expansion of the Ford concern would have been impossible.

This leads us to the final issue of the effect of the tax measure on the structure of business prosperity. This issue cropped up time and again in the argument about the desirability of encouraging savings and the need for reserves as cushions against depression. Anyone who followed Mr. Oliphant's answers to these contentions with any sort of detachment must have remained satisfied with their cogency. He pointed out that the argument about savings would apply equally to a reduction of the individual income tax; that if savings were needed for reinvestment it would be a simple device for a corporation to declare a dividend and for the stockholder—especially in the case of the small corporations whose stock is closely held—to plow the dividend back into more stock; that the effect of large corporate surpluses upon booms and depressions was not at all what was contended but more likely to be the reverse. Ultimately the argument came back again to a question of corporate democracy. The opponents of the bill insisted that once a dividend was declared it was doubtful whether it would ever find its way back into investment, since the flotation of new stock might be difficult or the tendency to spend the income prove overwhelming. Here Senator La Follette invariably took his stand on the ground that such a decision was for the stockholder himself to make, and that he was a better judge of his own interests than some member of an inner corporate directing group. Even more important than these arguments is the growing conviction among our economists that we suffer from too much saving rather than too little.

At the present time the outlook for a corporate surplus tax is dark indeed. The primary objective of corporate reform which gave importance to the original tax proposal, whatever its shortcomings, has now vanished. All the talk now is, what will raise the revenue? The committee cerebrations seem to point to (1) a slight increase of the corporate income tax to eighteen per cent; (2) a six or seven per cent surtax on undivided profits; (3) an increase of the individual income tax from four per cent to five per cent. This confirms the remark I have quoted that there has never been an income-tax bill framed yet that was not a series of weak compromises and crudely concealed surrenders. The Republican members of the committee know that an increase in the individual normal tax is likely to weaken Roosevelt's support in the election. If that happens, it will be a fitting climax to the series of blunders which has marked the handling of the proposal thus far. It would be indeed an irony if the heralded Democratic reform in the tax structure and the corporate structure should turn out to be in the end nothing but a preliminary approach to a raising of the income tax.

If the Administration keeps clearly in mind what it is driving at, the framing of a tax measure does not present insuperable difficulties. The primary objectives are three: to produce the needed revenue; as far as possible, to force dividend distribution along to the stockholders, without affecting the smaller corporations adversely; to prevent the accumulation of huge reserves on the part of the large corporations, with the resulting tax evasion, oversaving, and corporate manipulation. One essential in any tax proposal is that the present corporate income tax should not be eliminated or decreased. To it should be added a tax on all corporate surplus, large enough to be persuasive but not such as to embarrass the small corporation. A second is the removal of the exemption of the individual taxpayer from the income tax on dividends: thus the dividends whose distribution is forced along will finally yield tax revenue. A third is the enforcement of Section 102 of the present revenue law with a heavy penalty surtax on the unreasonable surplus. For example, the exemption of corporations with a relatively low income from the operation of the penalty surtax on undistributed profits will ease the administrative problem considerably; a rule that any corporation distributing a very high proportion of its profits (to be set by the Treasury) will be deemed to have a reasonable surplus will ease it further. What remains is a problem for administrative ingenuity. If this section can be rigorously enforced, it should serve to penalize the improper accumulation of surpluses, which is after all the principal reform aim of the House bill.

Regardless of what the Senate committee does, the corporate-tax battle is not over. There remains the conference committee of the two houses, and there remains also the President. An abandonment of the principle of penalizing large surplus accumulations may mean an early adjournment of Congress, but it will also mean a betrayal by Mr. Roosevelt of his own reformist philosophy. He is strong enough to apply pressure, if he is willing to exert his strength. If he yields, it will be a proof that only a genuine labor Administration will ever have the courage to place the tax burden where it belongs, and to use the taxing mechanism for making sense of the economic structure.

1936

The Case of "Black Tuesday" (1937)[4]

WALL STREET combines somehow the characteristic features of all the places where men have to chart their chances against fate: it has the atmosphere at once of the sickroom, the gambling-house, the battlefield. And so when the fever chart of Wall Street, usually a matter of only intramural concern, showed a panicky drop last week, the rest of us felt a concern far beyond our own stake in it. It was not only that some twenty-five billions in paper equities were destroyed and thousands of small accounts completely wiped out. What happened on Wall Street was more than a collapse of paper values. It was another of the periodic crises in the history of our capitalism. The dip was so sharp, the charts proved so frightening, that for two days at least Wall Street ran amuck.

I speak of the market break in the past tense, not to propitiate the future, but because—whatever fluctuations may still be in store— the market's record from early August to late October is a significant bit of history. It may be because hard-headed business men are not interested in history that the causes they advance for the market break sound thin and strained. One gets from them an impression of bewilderment seeking refuge in aggressive assertion. I have heard blame laid variously on organized bear raiders, the President, the SEC, the Federal Reserve Board, anti-New Deal feeling, margin requirements, the capital-gains tax, the corporate-surplus tax, John L. Lewis, and the trade unions. I have listened while one man proved that the state of the market was an index of general business conditions, and another argued as cogently that the market was an entity in itself unrelated to the real world of business.

---

[4] "Black Tuesday" was October 19, 1937, when the stock market dropped sharply.

One man states that because of government policies the sources of saving and therefore of capital investment have been dried up, and another man complains that because of the same policies there has been a lot of idle money lying about. I have heard the element of fear minimized and maximized. I have heard that a big factor was Japanese selling by order of the Japanese government, and that the same applied to Italy. Many of the people I talked to were so close to the market that they needed perspective; for them the lights of the world went out when stock prices zoomed down. But there was one, a nationally known economist, whose comment had a startlingly Olympian ring. "To us, of course," he said, and he seemed thousands of light-years away, "such things are merely secondary epiphenomena."

On the whole, you can range the explanations in four groups. There are the theories of deliberate conspiracy. There are the theories that run primarily in economic terms. There are the theories that look to government and politics for the real causes. And finally, there are the psychological theories, which stress fear and hysteria. You may be a one-theory man; if so, you may have your pick. I happen not to be, and I find it interesting to look back at this bit of history and construct out of it something of a mosaic.

It is hard to have much faith in the conspiracy theories, whether the sinister figures in them are the manipulators or government functionaries. I cannot believe that Mr. Morgenthau, Mr. Douglas, and Mr. Eccles are conspiring to destroy the exchanges; I don't hold bears like Ben Smith or Matt Brush responsible; nor can I believe that Mr. Gay and Mr. Aldrich, the head of the Stock Exchange and the chairman of Chase National, are suicidal wreckers, bent on going to their own doom if thereby they can prove Mr. Roosevelt wrong.

One may salvage from this whole approach a single item, which relates to the perversely different attitude of the business community toward this stock break, as compared with the 1929 break. Take the case of Charles R. Gay. Here is a mediocre man, blundering but well intentioned, placed at the head of an immense gambling establishment that happens to be integral to American business. His August 17 statement took the form of sharp criticism of government regulation of the market, yet actually it made Wall Street examine itself critically. Evidently the figure in the mirror was not reassuring, for the speech was followed by a stock drop; and though James Landis answered it vigorously in his farewell statement as chairman of the SEC—a statement, incidentally, that cost him the editorial plaudits that he would otherwise have received on retirement—the damage was done. Or take the case of Winthrop W. Aldrich. President of our biggest bank, brother-in-law of John D. Rockefeller, formerly a New Deal supporter, such a man obviously speaks with deliberation. His speech, too, was an attack on government regulation, and contained, in addition, a demoralizing analysis of the weakness and thinness of the market. Again, on October 14 as on August 4, there was a drop, but this time sharper and more panicky. The interesting thing is that in the Coolidge and Hoover administrations men like Mr. Gay and Mr. Aldrich were talking not defeatism but optimism. These two men were not conspirators, but, given slight market disturbances, they used them consciously or unconsciously to frighten the Administration and extract concessions from Mr. Roosevelt, who was already showing signs of weakening on the budget issue, along the lines of tax alleviation and changes in the SEC.

It is best not to emphasize the personal element. It is only a phase of the larger perspective. And that perspective must be viewed in terms of the basic business conditions. Nothing that the business leaders said and very little that the government did would have much effect if it were not for the framework of business discouragement. It should be seen, I think, in terms of a failure of hopes and not of a definite business recession. There were few signs of actual recession, and even now the combined business indices show a sharp drop after rather than before the stock decline. What was wrong, briefly, was that Wall Street had been experiencing a stock boom in anticipation of an industrial boom that failed to come off. When it became abundantly clear that the industrial boom would not materialize and that the future looked dreary, the stock boom collapsed, and in its collapse—pushed on by anti-Administration sentiment, blundering strategy, and general hysteria—it turned into a panic.

The curious thing is that, however much Wall Street and the Administration differ on other matters, they join forces in insisting that there is not much connection between the stock collapse and industrial conditions. Yet the evidence would indicate, as the English *New Statesman* pointed out recently, that the wheels of capitalism are again slowing down, not only in America but in England and France as well. As far as America is concerned, judged by previous depressions, the process of recovery has been curiously long and slow. The stock crash came in 1929; the low point industrially was reached in March 1933. There was a sensational spurt of business recovery in the summer of 1933, due largely to the stocking up of inventories in an attempt to beat the NRA, followed by a sharp recession. Another spurt was made in 1935, which in turn slowed down. Economists and business men had been looking for a third spurt in the fall of 1937. There were ample supplies of cheap money; in fact, one of the remarkable things about this depression has been the continuance of low interest rates into a far later stage of the recovery than usual. There was also a good consumer demand, stimulated by re-employment, by wage increases following a successful labor-organizing campaign, and by government outlays for relief and public works. The stage was set for a boom in the durable (or capital) goods industries, including construction, railways, and the utilities. New housing especially was hoped for, and there were good prospects of a demand from business and industry for replacement of equipment that had been long deferred.

None of these expectations has been realized. The housing boom, for complex reasons, has not come through. New equipment and replacements have not been ordered. The reason is that easy money available at low interest rates is not being taken advantage of. How much this is due, again, to fear and hatred of the Administration, how much of it is due to the hostility of business to the corporate-surplus tax and the capital-gains tax, how much responsibility must be assigned to rising prices and labor costs are questions beyond the scope of this article. A drive will undoubtedly be made to fix the blame on taxes and labor costs. But I find the best economic opinion convinced that these factors are by no means primary. The important fact is that investments in the stock market have been booming, and stock prices rising fantastically to a point where they have been twenty-five or thirty or even forty times the net earnings. That has meant an inflated market, and the wind had somehow to be taken out.

The question of the government's role in the market break is a vexed one. I am convinced it is by no means as clear as either side makes it out to be. The Administration feels itself blameless, and attributes the whole thing to Wall Street's hostility and its case of jitters. The Street on the other hand accuses the Administration of meddling and persecution. Its indictment may, I think, be put under two heads. One relates to the regulatory agencies. The second relates to general Administration policies.

It may be said quite confidently that the case against the regulatory agencies is almost wholly baseless. The agencies principally involved are the Federal Reserve Board and the SEC. The Reserve Board is attacked from the left for not lowering the reserve requirements when it spotted danger, and thus moving back toward inflation; but the argument seems to ignore the fact that there was no lack of money for investment, but rather a lack of desire to use it. The SEC is attacked from the right for tying the market up with petty regulations, reducing its volume of operations and making it "thin" by unreasonable restrictions, and in general entangling it in a bureaucratic net. As far as bureaucracy is concerned, there can be no doubt that it takes a huge staff operating under detailed rules to regulate a crowd as slippery and intransigent as the stock-market crowd. That drastic regulation was needed is no longer arguable. The interesting thing about the recent stock break is that it was not primarily the result of a speculative frenzy, as was the case in 1929. The market was to a great extent an investors' market, thanks largely to the SEC regulations. It is true that the thinness of the market made it more vulnerable to the impact of bearish factors and forced liquidations. But if it had been a larger and more speculative market, and if the margin requirements had been lower, many feel that the crash would have been even more severe.

What Wall Street will not recognize in all its criticism of the SEC is that the stock market as we know it is a relic left over from a past Golden Age. The Exchange still lives in the memory of its vanished splendor of the 1920's and it maintains in million-share days the proportions it had in the five- and seven-million-share days. There is literally not enough business to go around among the 1500 members. The brokers, many of them rich men's sons for whom there was no other career, have fallen on lean days. They cannot make enough on stock commissions, they are hemmed about in their attempts to speculate on the side, and there seems to be no way by which they can reduce their numbers and shrink the business to profitable proportions. They have become fretful and embittered, and spend their energy making a butt of the nearest object —the SEC.

Far more serious is the indictment that may be made of general Administration policy. I am not referring to the tax policies, which, compared with the English, are anything but excessive. What is more in point is the indecision of the Administration as to where it is going and what methods it will employ in getting there. I sympathized with one banker when he said that he could understand a capitalist regime and he could understand a collectivist regime, but he was baffled by this mixture of the two. He was, of course, regarding it from the right and I from the left, but we both recognized the same fact. Compromises in scope and aim must always be made in a real world, but it seems part of the Roosevelt policy to achieve its compromises through vacillations between groups of advisers whose aims and premises are wholly different and cancel each other out. I refer in this connection to the recent deflationary moves of the President in seeking to balance the budget by cutting down relief and construction funds rather than by seeking new tax sources. Business had, to be sure, been calling for budget balancing and reduction of expenses; yet Roosevelt's moves in this direction came at a time when the anticipated business pick-up was not materializing, when it was becoming clear that stock prices were too high. Thus even for business the result of such moves was disastrous. The President chose exactly the wrong time to return to a more primitive capitalism.[5]

If these are roughly the factors that brought about the stock break, there still remains the question of how it gained enough acceleration on the way down to produce for two days a frenzied panic. Empirical conditions, either in industry or in government policy, will not explain the swiftness and extent of the decline. For that we must turn to the psychological—to fear, and how it has battened on the tensions of the eight years that have elapsed since 1929.

It must be remembered that what we are pleased to call the busi-

[5] In the perspective afforded by the lapse of time since this essay was first published, this contraction of government expenditures stands out as the most important factor in the economic "recession" of 1937. For a fuller discussion see John Strachey, *A Programme for Progress* (1940), ch. XVI, "The 1937 Slump." See also my essay "Keynes Meets Marx," below, p. 337.

ness community can become under extreme pressure a chaotic and irresponsible mob. A man who witnessed the trading on the morning of "Black Tuesday" told me that it gave him the feeling of a trampling mob in a theater fire. There were stretches of time when blocks of "blue chip" securities, offered at almost nothing, could not get a bid. The truth is that Wall Street men, like other organisms highly specialized for predatory pursuits, have not been able to accommodate themselves to the conditions of change. They have been battered for years by forces they cannot understand, and they are ridden by the most irrational fears. The Wall Street jungle of today is filled with Emperor Joneses. What we have regarded as the toughest and most viable of all capitalisms is at the same time as subject to panic as a frightened savage caught in a jungle at night—a jungle of his own fears, superstitions, and racial memories.

1937

The Case of Governor La Follette (1938)[6]

I CAME out to Madison to talk with Governor La Follette because overnight he had vaulted into the national picture as a potential progressive leader, yet no one was clear where he was going or how he proposed to get there. And of the two La Follettes, it is Phil rather than Bob [7] who is the prime mover in the new National Progressives of America. Phil received me cordially. We had a two-hour talk in the morning at the State House and another two-hour talk in the afternoon at the Executive Mansion. I came primed with many questions. I cannot quote the answers, but I have his permission to set down my interpretation of the gist of our discussion and my deductions about his thinking. If some of these deductions are not sympathetic, it is because they have been filtered through my own hopes and fears about the future of our country.

---

[6] At the end of April 1938, something of a sensation was caused by the announcement that Governor Philip La Follette, of Wisconsin, would lead a new national party, the National Progressives of America; the movement was launched at a mass meeting at Madison, the capital of Wisconsin. The essay that follows is the result of talks with Governor La Follette early in May. The new party was still-born, but the issues raised by it and by Mr. La Follette's ideas are of continuing interest.

[7] Senator Robert M. La Follette, Jr.

No one in Wisconsin thinks of calling the Governor anything except Phil. His people either love him or hate him, quarrel and make up with him as they might do with members of their family. And Phil cultivates that feeling. He received me at his home in shirt-sleeves, as if I were a neighbor who had dropped in for a friendly call. Madison, far away from the fierce antagonisms of urban centers such as New York or Chicago, is folksy and middle-class in tone.

But Phil is not just small-town stuff. At forty-one he is already the stuff that legends are made of, and I heard many of them. He is a man of enormous ambition and personal mastery, grooming himself for a great destiny and believing utterly in that destiny. There are some who think that the new party grows out of the local Wisconsin situation, that Phil faces a fight for his fourth term as governor, and that he knows he cannot be governor unless he finds a place in the national political sun. I doubt that. Phil's prestige in Wisconsin has never stood so high as today,[8] and it has grown especially with the more liberal business men. Besides, he does not talk like a man who wants only to be governor. He is playing for high stakes.

The first impression one gets of him is of a frank, warm, alert, but unassuming person. Despite his gray hair, he looks at times and from a certain angle, infinitely young, like an eager schoolboy —small, lithe, round-faced. Watch him further and he is the administrator galvanized into action, with an air of curt and sharp command. There is economy in every gesture—the economy of a big executive or of a general in the midst of a campaign. Leadership is very much on his mind. I have been told that while he was at college his room was hung with pictures of great historical figures, including Napoleon. Today his sitting-room is cluttered with photographs of the great ones of the earth. There is one of Justice Brandeis and one of Mussolini. That in parvo is Phil.

He stands with one foot in the old La Follette tradition and the other in a strange world just coming into being. He is proud of what his father and mother did in public life, proud of his pioneer stock, steeped in the tradition of the frontier, deeply influenced by F. J. Turner's frontier theory. He would like to project the Wisconsin achievement onto a national plane.

---

[8] I was wrong. He was later defeated for the governorship.

Phil's strategy today has two premises. One is that Roosevelt's political prestige is bankrupt; the other is that the New Deal is, from an economic viewpoint, basically wrong. There is no doubt that he has broken with both the President and his program. He has never been more than a fellow-traveler of the New Deal, critical of its policy ever since his speech in 1933 attacking the AAA program. He has consistently refused offers of administrative posts in Washington. Latterly the distance has widened, as he has become convinced that the President is succumbing to the Democratic Old Guard and not making a state-by-state fight against the party machine. There are those in Washington who believe that Phil was not averse to seeing the process of the President's defeat hastened, and that the five Wisconsin members of the House, whose votes against the reorganization bill [9] proved the decisive factor, would not have done so without at least Phil's tacit consent. Phil knows that the common people of the country still have a loyalty to the President; that when Bill Evjue, editor of the Madison *Capital Times,* wrote an editorial on the day of Phil's big Madison speech, saying that whatever happens the new party must not be anti-Roosevelt, his phone rang all day with congratulations; and that when Phil mentioned the President that night and again at Cedar Rapids, there were great bursts of applause. Yet he also feels that the common people are bewildered and have lost their sense of direction; and that, when their personal warmth about Roosevelt has worn off, nothing but disenchantment will remain. He wants to prepare for that time.

About the danger of dividing the progressive forces through his new party, he is skeptical. If the New Deal shows increased strength in the 1938 elections, I am convinced that the new party will be used mainly to put heat on the tories and insure the nomination in 1940 of a fairly liberal candidate. If the New Deal's prestige continues to fall, the party will strike out for itself. This does not mean nominating a candidate for the Presidency. Phil knows that a party is not created by fiat or by a single speech, no matter how histrionic, but it has to be built from the ground up. He plans to work assiduously in every state and every county. If he has any guess about 1940 it is that the Democrats will win, but only by nominating a

---

[9] The proposal for administrative reorganization of the federal government. At first defeated, it was later enacted in revised form.

more conservative candidate than Roosevelt.[10] He has no illusions, as La Guardia seems still to have, about the Republicans' nominating a liberal.[11] But whoever is elected, he is convinced that the program after 1940 will be pretty much the same as the program today—one of borrowing and spending. And being thus convinced, he has no worries about his timing. If the progressives are temporarily split, that is a risk that has to be taken whenever a new party is started. Meanwhile my guess is that Phil feels he can wait until 1944, when he will be only forty-seven and still in the prime of life.

What sort of economic program has he? Phil is thus far much clearer in his criticisms of the New Deal than in substitutes for it. He argues that we shall get nowhere by the restrictionism of the farm program, that borrowing and spending do not solve a depression, and that expenditures for relief do not constitute a way of ordering the economic system. He believes that the Administration has erred in doing both too little and too much: too little in that, if it had to spend, it did not spend soon enough or heavily enough; too much in that it set itself the enormous and impossible task of regulating the entire economy instead of concentrating on the crucial phase of it.

What is that crucial phase? The mechanism of investment and credit. After the 1936 elections the President might have concentrated on getting the bugs out of our machinery. He did not, and now there is idle capital lying about. How put it to work? Phil's analysis up to this point would grace the pages of the *Wall Street Journal*.[12] But his remedy, as far as I can make it out, is a cross between socialism, technocracy, and what used to be called in the 1920's "the new capitalism."

I mention socialism despite the fact that Phil has almost no socialist consciousness in him, and mentions the word only to deride it. Yet his general outlook is away from laissez faire and toward increased governmental power. His is the socialism involved in any project for a huge and collective national effort to master the economic problem. But it is not socialism in the sense of envisaging

---

10 He was wrong. The Democrats nominated Roosevelt again in 1940. See the essay "Roosevelt as Symbol," below, p. 400.

11 The Republicans nominated Wendell Willkie in 1940.

12 I did him an injustice here. His analysis was more Keynesian than orthodox.

any broad program of socialization. At least for the present, Phil has in mind less heroic remedies. And among them his attitude toward credit and his attitude toward the price structure loom most important.

I could not help being struck, as he talked, by the degree of similarity between his emphasis on nationalized credit and Dr. Schacht's method of rationalizing the German economy by leaving private ownership and profit undisturbed but using publicly controlled credit as the principal means of leverage. And since Phil has autarchic ideas as well, I assume this control would be extended to foreign exchange. The savings banks would continue their deposit functions; but investment banking, which has already become practically inactive, would be turned over formally to the government. Private enterprise would move from a credit to a cash basis. That is to say, all credit would be governmental. Mortgages and bonds, instead of being fixed claims upon income, would be transformed into participating interests in the fortunes of an enterprise. Thus the credit system, which Walter W. Stewart has defined as "suspicion asleep," would be socialized, along with the monetary system. And with it one of the most rigid elements of our economic system would be removed.

Another element that would have to be made amenable to control is that of cost and thus of price. Phil's approach to the railroad problem is well known; it involves a moratorium on the present bond structure and the calling in of new investment. His approach to agricultural and labor prices is similar. He believes not in sharing more equitably what wealth we have, but in producing more wealth for everyone to be satisfied with. The farmer today, he argues, is geared to selling a decreasing number of units—whether of milk or hogs or cotton—for the highest possible unit price. Actually the farmer would be better off if he sold more units, even though he got less for each. Labor is in the same situation. There are times when wages should go up, but times also when wage rigidity is catastrophic to the whole economic structure and wages should go down. If labor were interested, he argues, not in price per unit of work but in its share of a larger number of units, costs could be reduced and volume increased.

This is not a program but a philosophy. With Phil it is a basic philosophy and furnishes the clue to his program—increased national production, using nationalized credit, monetary control, and a guaranteed annual wage or farm income to effect it. It is, in a way, the core of the National Expansion bill, originally drawn with the help of Mordecai Ezekiel, introduced into the House by Amlie, Voorhis, and other progressives, and now languishing there.[13] But Phil would not go so far as that bill in his program of regulation of industry. The power of the state, he feels, must be used not to administer the business units but to give direction to them. Once that direction is achieved business can be left to its own devices and its own pioneering inventiveness. This does not mean, despite the applause from Walter Lippmann and Dorothy Thompson,[14] a return to the ancient simplicities of laissez faire. Actually, in what Phil has said thus far, there are holes broad enough to drive through an entire program of government control. But I am convinced that he would resort to that only if his socialized-credit and price-control methods were to fail.

For the present, he is beautifully vague and evasive about ways and means. Why should he not be? He knows that third parties have in the past foundered on the rocks of over-concreteness at the start. Moreover, he does not want Mr. Roosevelt to steal his thunder, as he has done with others. Finally he is convinced that the only people who want blueprints are the intellectuals, with whom it is an occupational disease, and his enemies, who want them to distort them.

He has a contempt for the intellectual, especially the radical intellectual, with his *isms* and his dogmas. He believes in action. Act first, show that something can be done, and people will follow you. To get such action, democratic government must be mobile and efficient. Hence Phil's reorganization of Wisconsin's executive departments, which he carried through with far more astuteness than the President showed in his own plan. He gave either house of the state legislature the power, by a simple majority, to undo any reorganizing act of his after it was done. Phil knows the value of the *fait accompli*. "Give me power," he says in effect, "then you may hedge that power about with checks and balances."

---

13 Nothing came of this bill.
14 Both these columnists greeted the announcement of the formation of the new party with a considerable measure of approval.

Despite his roots in the La Follette tradition, Phil is a new plant, growing in a changed soil of economic circumstance and a new climate of opinion. He still points with pride to the Wisconsin social legislation; relief, despite his rash remark about "spoonfeeding and coddling the American people," is still a problem to him, but it is subordinate to the larger problem of mastering the economic drift; and on that, some of his perspectives come from present-day Germany. He went to Germany in 1933. He brought back a deep sense of the economic roots of fascism in the degraded living conditions of the people. Yet he thinks that it is easy to underestimate Hitler's positive achievement, and admires the energy he has shown in reorganizing an anarchic economy. Even more is he impressed by what Mustapha Kemal has done in Turkey in evoking a new economic energy and a new nationalism.

Phil's own nationalism goes deep, and it is no accident that he calls his party the National Progressives of America. To do a creative job, people must have belief in themselves. In America that belief has been corroded, since the turn of the century, by economic collapse. His paean about the sanctity of the North American continent is not a literary figure of speech but a mystical conviction. And that conviction is fed by his isolationism in foreign policy. He made a public statement in 1933 against the Jewish boycott of German goods. The Jews, he feels, have—because of their economic success in a declining capitalism—become easy marks for vindictiveness. They must not dissipate their energies in foreign boycotts, but concentrate them on the opportunity for reform within their own country. They must be Americans first and Jews afterward.[15] Phil insists that the nationalist pattern is a deep and slumbering force in American life, with enormous power for evoking middle-class and mass support. He sees what the Marxian parties have hitherto overlooked, that the middle-class mentality and nationalist feeling are still our ruling divinities.

Phil's eyes glow when he talks of mass movements. Intellectuals may fear to contemplate the mass unleashed, but he has no such fears. We must reach the masses if we are to survive as a nation.

---

[15] La Follette is now (1941) closely associated with the isolationist group and the America First Committee. It will be apparent from the above that he shares also the views that some of them, like Charles Lindbergh and Senator Nye, have expressed on the matter of Jewish attitudes.

They want to know where we are going and why, but they do not want to be burdened with blueprints. Men think in terms of symbols. Hence the adoption of the new symbol of the cross by the new party. "Why fear it?" asks Phil. Communism has its symbol in the hammer and sickle, Nazism has a symbol in the swastika; democracy alone lacks a symbol. Phil proposes to equip democracy with a symbol through which the common man—since he cannot write laws or articles or make speeches—will get a sense of participation, the mystical sense of unity. All this may sound dangerous to many. It sounds very dangerous to me. And Phil knows that he will be called a fascist. But he is willing to venture it.

Phil insists that this is no "third party" he is forming: it is *the* party (does he mean *the* progressive party or the only party of the future?). He also insists that it is no popular-front party and no labor party in its usual sense. He wants no more to be tied to trade unionism, as the British progressives are, than he wants to be tied to popular frontism, as the French progressives are. What remains for him is to build on a middle-class base, counting on the probability that the trade unions will soon attach themselves to it.

Yet it is strange that Phil should have held himself so completely aloof from labor. I have it on good authority that none of the top leaders of the CIO was brought directly into the picture. It is a sensational fact that a few days before the new party was formed Phil had a long talk with John L. Lewis on another matter during which he never so much as mentioned his coming political venture. Labor, he feels, should know the La Follettes' labor record in the Senate and in Wisconsin, and should count them among its friends. Labor will remember the La Follettes' record, but it will also remember that a party that starts out to keep clear of the labor stigma may end by fighting labor.

1938

The Case of the Spanish Embargo (1938) [16]

IT HAS been customary to regard Cordell Hull as a prisoner in his own house. Among the State Department career men and the cynical checkerboard diplomats, the Secretary has stood out for his rugged purity of purpose; but he has seemed helpless in the clutch of department routine and the vested habits of the foreign-office mentality. For like all foreign offices the State Department has drunk the heady wine of being at once a political elite and a corps of experts. Like all foreign offices it has therefore claimed diplomatic immunity to the democratic demands to which the more prosy government departments are subject.

Mr. Hull has had his alternations of quiescence and energy. In the beginning there was Moley; and there was a point during the London economic conference at which a witty Britisher, impressed with the ascendancy of Moley over Hull, sang: "Moley, Moley, Moley, Lord God almighty." But Hull roused himself—and Hull can be stubborn when aroused—and Moley vanished. But once the domain had been reconquered, the deputies became king. For the shy charm of Mr. Hull is the charm of a man who is uneasy in the world in which he moves. Passionately absorbed in his trade treaties, he allowed other decisions to be made by his skilled subordinates. Rumors began to grow of major blunders, of crucial decisions reached without the Secretary's adequate knowledge or in his absence, of a pro-fascist trend in the department. It was the Pearson and Allen "Washington Merry-Go-Round" series with its brilliant behind-the-scenes disclosures that particularly got under his skin.

The Secretary comes from Tennessee, and for all his retiring ways a mountaineer's rages slumber in him. Once more, as in the Moley days, Mr. Hull was aroused. He took command of the de-

---

16 The whole history, public and secret, of the embargo on American munitions and other war supplies during the Spanish Civil War has yet to be written. The present essay is reprinted as a minor contribution toward that history. It was written as a dispatch from Washington to the *Nation* in May 1938. By that time the cause of the Spanish government was critical in the extreme, and only the resumption by America of its traditional policy of free shipping and freedom of the seas could have saved Spain from a fascist triumph. America did nothing to repeal the embargo, Spain was destroyed, and the Nazis gained a victory that was a prelude to their conquest of the European continent.

partment again. He held a press conference in which he had a
historic tilt with Drew Pearson, distinguished more by the Secretary's zeal in defending his subordinates than by his knowledge or
his logic. He took the entire responsibility for department policy
on himself. Finally he wrote the letter to Senator Pittman embodying his views on the embargo, and refusing to recommend that
it be lifted. Mr. Hull is once more master in his own house.

But in what sort of house? To answer that, one must examine in
detail the case of the Spanish embargo.

Congress passed a neutrality law in February 1936. It was a bad
law because it was either too rigid or not rigid enough. But the
nation was neutrality-mad and ridden by what Mr. Hull calls the
"storm-cellar psychology." When American policy toward Spain
had to be shaped, late in 1936, Hull and Under Secretary Sumner
Welles were away in South America. Judge Robert W. Moore,
counselor to the department, was in charge. Moore, a close friend
of Hull's, is seventy-eight now, stiff and formal but with years of
political experience and a sensitiveness to political opinion. He
bet on the isolationist drive, and applied the existing neutrality
law so rigidly to Spain that he authorized Joseph C. Green, head
of the munitions control board, to announce the names, makes,
and engine numbers of all equipment being sent to Spain. Green,
an able career man and far from a liberal, was happy to fall in with
this policy. When word came that the *Mar Cantabrico* was sailing
with a Loyalist shipment, Moore and Green trained all their publicity guns on it. The result was the farce of the race between Congress and a freighter. The freighter won, clearing the three-mile
limit just before the embargo resolution was rushed through Congress early in January 1937. For a time under the embargo the
State Department sought to bar even the passage of doctors, nurses,
and medical supplies.

The State Department has recently tried to wash its hands of
responsibility for the embargo resolution. True, Congress passed
it in a moment of hysteria. But that hysteria was created largely by
State Department publicity; and the resolution itself was undoubtedly the work of its officials. It is needless to underline that the embargo has played into Franco's hands and those of Germany and
Italy, that it has penalized a legally constituted government com-
bating a rebellion, that it has acted as a sanction for intervention

by "non-intervention" countries, that it has run counter to our whole traditional foreign policy. As this became clearer, the movement for repeal began.

I have been told in the State Department that this is a left-wing movement, and thus the Catholic press and certain dispatches in the New York *Herald Tribune* depict it. This does too exclusive honor to the left. The support for repeal in the Senate has come from men like Borah, Nye, Pope, Thomas, and—so long as the Administration smiled—Pittman. The *Herald Tribune's* own Walter Lippmann and Dorothy Thompson, citizens like Henry L. Stimson, Raymond L. Buell, and Carrie Chapman Catt, papers like the Chicago *News*, the Washington *Post*, the Portland *Oregonian*, even the New York *Sun*—these are among the left-wingers in the movement. The other charge I heard in the State Department was that there was a munitions lobby in the background, organized by Miles Sherover, the fiscal agent for the Loyalist government. This struck me as curious, since nothing that we know about American munitions men would indicate Loyalist sympathies, and since the arms manufacturers already have a market in Europe for everything they can make.

When Senator Borah, anxious to discuss repeal with the President, received a White House invitation in April (he would not go without one), he was preceded at the White House by Sumner Welles. Welles is the President's man far more than Mr. Hull is. His mind is sharp while his manner is smooth and his purpose firm —always a powerful combination. Personally sympathetic to the Loyalist cause, he is a career man who knows his talents will carry him far, and he has learned to distinguish personal sympathy from political exigency and to conceal both behind a perfect mask of a face. His training has been mainly with Latin American problems, and he struck me as having carried over to his larger task the assurance with which a diplomat of wealth and social standing customarily deals with backward governments. What he may have told Mr. Roosevelt on that visit is not known. But it may be inferred from the fact that the President, in talking with Borah, raised difficulties about repeal: it was too late; the munitions would fall into Franco's hands; a third of the American ships would be sunk. There is a persistent report in Washington that some time during the past month Nazi Ambassador Dieckhoff warned our government about ships that might be sunk. Mr. Welles denies it. Yet the warning need not have been anything more than a discreet report of the number of ships already sunk by Franco's submarines (although Franco has no submarines of his own).

But the door was not closed tight. All through April the Administration dawdled with the idea of repeal, torn Hamlet-like between conscience and cowardice. When Senator Nye introduced his resolution, on May 2, rumors began popping that Roosevelt and Hull had swung over to it. Senator Pittman, an Administration wheelhorse, grew more interested. Sumner Welles and Judge Moore were reported as working actively for it. James C. Dunn alone, among the powers in the department, was holding out. Dunn has always been the chief target of the attacks on State Department "fascists." He is a favorite of Hull, who found him arranging place-cards as chief of protocol, and stepped him up until he became political adviser. His wife, a member of the Armour family and a converted Catholic, had been reported in the press as being openly anti-Loyalist, and Dunn was suspected of sharing her persuasion. But aside from him, the impression spread that the path of repeal was smooth.

Excitement ran high. On May 5 the New York *Times* printed its sensational story that repeal was assured, and that the State Department had given its *nihil obstat*. There can be no doubt the story was true. But when it appeared, the Catholics got busy and reached the President, who was fishing in Southern waters. High church dignitaries came to Washington and talked cold politics. Administration sources of whom I have inquired have denied the report that Cardinal Mundelein of Chicago interceded with the President through Mr. Farley. Yet the report will not down; and Mundelein, as the prize New Deal cardinal, would be the strategic link between Catholic reaction and New Deal realism. Along with the Catholics, the British Foreign Office and its satellites among the major American ambassadors in Western Europe got busy. Mr. Roosevelt came back, his leaning toward repeal vanished. So also was Mr. Hull's and that of the minor Hulls. A new spirit of Chamberlain "realism" pervaded the halls of the archaic building that houses the department. When one found even a guaranteed liberal like Assistant Secretary Berle, a former brain truster and a crony of La Guardia's, enthusiastic about "facing facts" and irritated with the "propaganda" for repeal, it was clear that the game was pretty much up.

The final blow was Secretary Hull's letter to Senator Pittman. I am told that the individual sentences of this deliberately worded and coldly chiseled document were worked over by many hands; but it is clear that the final product and the final responsibility were Mr. Hull's. The Administration put all its force behind the letter. Only a band of heroes could have withstood the combined effect of Catholic votes, State Department learning and authority, Administration pressure, and mental sluggishness—and the Senate committee was not heroic.

I do not believe in personal devils. I hold the President and Mr. Hull responsible for what happened, but there is no sense in railing at them. They did what they did in response to effective forces. What were they?

Let us talk first of the British lion. I know that oversimplifies it, but it will at least serve as a symbol for a complex of forces. It is silly to call any group in the State Department "fascist," unless you are going to find fascists throughout the government. But as far as I can learn, there is a wing of the department that has not yet discovered the New Deal, and even those who know about it have no conception of how to embody it in our foreign policy. The career men have never got over their feeling of awe for the predatory gentility of the British ruling class. It is not necessary to be fascist in the State Department; the Chamberlain line is enough and has the same consequences as far as foreign policy is concerned.

The passage of the Nye resolution would have been a staggering blow to Mr. Chamberlain's plans, to which a speedy Franco victory is central. The Chamberlain game has been to convince the Administration that the Loyalist cause is hopeless, convince Daladier that America would never lift the embargo and that keeping the Spanish frontier open would be futile, and convince the British people that Mr. Roosevelt approved of the Chamberlain policy. This policy worked as far as we were concerned because foreign offices are prone to act wishfully on inadequate information.

All the "realistic" reasons which the President and the officials of the State Department have given for their decision have been vitiated by being based on British premises and official information. Why should we believe that Loyalist resistance is over? It is not over unless British tactics are successful. Why should we believe that American supplies would not get to the Loyalists? Actually, non-war material has been getting to them, as have Soviet munitions. I understand the State Department is in possession of a complete report that shows the amount of shipping that has entered Mediterranean ports. Why should we believe that Daladier will close the frontier, when he would risk serious riots throughout France and his Soviet alliance in the bargain? What actual weight have we given to the reports to the State Department from our own ambassador in Spain, Claude Bowers, an able observer and a passionate believer in democracy, whose version of the facts differs in essence from the British?

In addition to the British lion, there is the Catholic vote. The biggest factor within the State Department was British pressure, but the biggest factor in the mind of the President was the Catholic vote. Mr. Hull has said some indignant things about organized pressure from the left. Will he deny that the greater part of the congratulations he has received on his stand come from Catholics? If this is a fact, he can scarcely feel elated over it. The Washington *Times* had the courage to write, "It is a cold political fact that the Catholic Church has taken a determined stand in favor of General Franco." There are more than twenty million Catholics in this country. On the issue of the Spanish struggle, as on other issues, their hierarchy is now presuming to speak for them and is using their potential political power in such a way as to create a state within a state. And so far they have succeeded. For it is another "cold political fact" that Mr. Roosevelt, who has braved concentrated wealth, has not braved the risk of losing the votes around Boston, New York, Chicago, Detroit, Baltimore.

I have just seen a letter by Guy Emery Shipler, editor of the *Churchman,* to leaders of Christian thought throughout the country. It is a good letter, because it speaks plainly when the time has come to speak plainly; yet it handles the delicate issue without rancor or intolerance. It challenges the hierarchy to prove that its rank and file stands with it on the issue of Franco. And it calls on the Christian conscience to redouble its efforts to lift the embargo. Meanwhile the real historical irony in this politicizing of the Catholic Church is that the most effective blow in defense of British foreign policy has been struck by the American Irish.

The Secretary of State is a sincere man. He is primarily an international liberal, believing in low tariffs, economic freedom, and international good will. But that is only one aspect of the man. The other side is only now emerging from the alembic of the embargo crisis. One phase of it is the sheer and amazing political cynicism of the letter to Senator Pittman. I am informed that the composition of the letter caused agonies of mind and heart. I can well believe it, knowing the Secretary's past record. The contradiction in Mr. Hull is that while the Secretary is a liberal, he has not proved himself a democrat. If he were, he could not have allowed his irritation at the pressures and criticisms directed at him to develop into a hostility toward the movement for lifting the embargo. To be sure, the delegations that visited the Secretary and Judge Moore allowed their sense of urgency to interfere with the best State Department manner. They were teachers, ministers, workers. What right had Mr. Hull to resent them? This was no synthetic lobby. This was a movement that came closer than any other in recent times to being the authentic voice of the American conscience.

And for that reason the struggle is not over. The State Department and the President have spoken; the people have yet to be heard from. The tragedy is that victory, when it comes, may come too late to be more than a gesture to the ghost of Spain. Or the result may be not even a phantom victory but a vast disenchantment of Americans with all our fumblings toward "neutrality"— a disenchantment sharp enough to increase isolationist sentiment to the point of tying the President and the State Department hand and foot in their foreign policy. And the Administration game is dangerous for another reason as well. The victory of Spanish landlordism and feudal tyranny is the victory also of the mother of all South American tyrannies. No one should know better than Cordell Hull and Sumner Welles how perilous the Latin American situation is, and how responsive to what happens in Europe. And no one should know better than they that you cannot be Old Deal abroad and remain New Deal at home. For every triumph of the totalitarian states creates a climate of opinion at home in which American democracy must in the end stifle.

1938

Constitution and Court as Symbols[1]

We live by symbols.

—MR. JUSTICE HOLMES [2]

I. SYMBOLS IN POLITICS

LIKE children and neurotics, man as a political animal lives in a world riddled with bugbears and taboos—a dream world of symbols in which the shadows loom far larger than the realities they represent. Political thinkers as diverse as the English idealists and the classical Marxians [3] have incurred a common fallacy: they have taken their own sense of the logical relation of things and read it into the way men behave. Actually men behave in their political lives with a disheartening illogicality.[4] They live in a jungle of fear, filled with phantoms of what they have heard and imagined and been told. Their world is the world of a child's nightmares—dark and brooding, crowded with dreads and anxie-

---

[1] It will be readily apparent in this essay how much I owe to other writers: to Corwin, "The Constitution as Instrument and as Symbol" (1936) 30 *American Political Science Review* (Harvard Tercentenary address); to Schechter, "The Early History of the Tradition of the Constitution" (1915) 9 *American Political Science Review* 707; to Hamilton, "Constitutionalism" (1931) 4 *Encyclopaedia of the Social Sciences* 255; to Arnold, *The Symbols of Government* (1935); to Frank, *Law and the Modern Mind* (1930). I have, incidentally, used rather freely sentences from my series of articles, "The Riddle of the Supreme Court" (1936) 142 *Nation* 121, 213, 273, 379.

[2] *Collected Legal Papers* (1920) 270.

[3] For the English idealists, see Laski, *The State in Theory and Practice* (1935) c. 1 ("The Philosophic Conception of the State"). The rationalism of the classical Marxians seems to me their greatest weakness; nor have the contemporary Marxians yet succeeded in effecting a fusion between their profoundly valid theory of history and a usable psychology.

[4] Sigmund Freud's profound although erratic insights into the human mind have not yet been measurably appropriated by social theory. His own attempts to apply his method to the problems of culture, including his *Civilization and Its Discontents* (Riviere trans. 1930), are readable but rudimentary. Modern readers will still find Bagehot, *Physics and Politics* (1873) and Wallas, *Human Nature in Politics* (3d ed. 1914) suggestive; while the first writer was a conservative and the second a Fabian,

ties, with the distortions of real objects, with the cruelest non sequiturs and anti-climaxes.

That is why men always find themselves forced to seek some symbol of divine right. Talk to the men on the street, the men in the mines and factories and steel-mills and real-estate offices and filling-stations, dig into their minds and even below the threshold of their consciousness, and you will in the main find that Constitution and Supreme Court are symbols of an ancient sureness and a comforting stability. If you watch the black-robed justices as they come filing in, if you listen to them read their opinions, you will be strong not to succumb to a sense of the Court's timelessness. Americans have been told that they are a people without a tradition, without a culture.[5] And it does in truth seem surprising that the restless, unstable energies of the American people should have created anything that seems as deep-rooted and as timeless as the Supreme Court. Even today, in its new and imposing building, the Court still wears the ancient garments of divine right. The building has changed since the days of John Jay and John Marshall; the fashionables, the men of power, the plain men and women who come to visit the Court have changed; there is even that strange and modern creature, a "press contact man," to explain to correspondents the mysteries of a writ of *certiorari* and a dissenting opinion. But despite these concessions to the spirit of the times, the Court maintains its tough historical fiber. It has, to be sure, walked along the evolutionary path, but only as Orpheus once walked along the pathway out of Hell—with head turned backward.

What accounts for the extraordinary toughness and viability of the Court? Why has it emerged relatively unscathed from its mor-

---

both were radical in the sense that they refused to believe in the fiction that man is a rational animal. Illogical behavior and logical rationalization of that behavior go hand in hand. This is the core of truth in Pareto, *Mind and Society* (Livingston and Bongiorno trans. 1935). For the American reader Thurman Arnold's book, *The Symbols of Government* (1935), is much more to the point than Pareto. One of the most suggestive and readable explorations of irrationality and rationalization in the Western world is still Robinson, *The Mind in the Making* (1921).

[5] Especially by the English commentators. This has been the principal element in what James Russell Lowell called "a certain condescension" in them. It is notable that no Englishman, with the recent exceptions of Harold Laski and D. W. Brogan, has concerned himself much with American judicial review. Bryce was not particularly acute about it. And even Dicey made the mistake of seeing judicial review as an inherent part of the federal structure.

tal combats with Presidents, Presidential candidates, and political reformers from Jefferson to Roosevelt II? The defenders of the Court answer that its survival indicates the hollowness of the attacks on it. The assumption seems to be that what is involved is a medieval ordeal by fire, proving innocence. But the successive crises of the judicial power can no more be exorcised by this sort of mumbo-jumbo than can the crises of the economic system. They cannot be explained away merely as "the same old story." The attacks on the Court's power have been real enough and dangerous enough. Its survival thus far shows that it has deep historical and psychological roots in American life: it has a clear relation to the development of the power of business enterprise; it has a strong symbolic hold over the American mind.

Most clearly and simply I should put it as follows: the nature and extent of the Supreme Court's power are best understood by seeing it as our basic instrument of sovereignty—an integral part of the American capitalist economic order. But the support of the judicial power lies largely in the psychological realm; its roots are in the minds of the people. Historically the judicial power must be seen as the instrument of the few; psychologically it is the symbol of the many. "We live by symbols," wrote Mr. Justice Holmes. It is to the Supreme Court and the Constitution as symbols that we must first turn.

Men have always used symbols in the struggle for power, but only latterly have we grown aware generally of their importance. For realistic students of government today know that the state is not ruled, as the unwary reader of Plutarch might suppose, by copy-book maxims and civic virtues.[6] They know that one of the essential techniques of power-groups is to manipulate the most effective

---

[6] The power of ideas, symbols, and myths, regardless of their validity, to rule men's minds in politics goes back, of course, to the Platonic myths; it reaches through Machiavelli to its modern fruition in Sorel, *Reflections on Violence* (Hulme trans. 1914), from which writer it was presumably derived by Mussolini. It is noteworthy that Sorel, as well as Pareto, was an assiduous student of Greek culture; and Mussolini's fealty to Machiavelli is made explicit in the dictator's introduction to a French translation of *The Prince*. The most systematic treatment of the role of symbols in the making of the civic mind will be found in the series of volumes edited by C. E. Merriam, notably in Merriam's own summary volume, *The Making of Citizens* (1931), and in Kosok, *Modern Germany* (1933). See also Harold Lasswell's works, especially *World Politics and Personal Insecurity* (1935) and *Politics: Who Gets What, When, How* (1936).

symbols in such a way that they become instruments of mass persuasion. The World War with its use of propaganda brought that lesson home,[7] and if it was not clear at the end of the war, it has become clear enough through European experience with fascist and communist governments. Men are notably more sensitive to images than to ideas, more responsive to stereotypes than to logic, to the concrete symbol than to the abstraction. Today we all recognize the power of the newest devices such as the radio, the movies, the press, to act as instruments of social cohesion, and to line up an entire nation behind a single set of interests. The established weapon of dictators has become the microphone. But these *techniques* depend for their effectiveness upon the *symbols* that they manipulate, and the symbols depend in turn upon the entire range of association that they evoke.

Actually the whole of a culture is shot through with symbolism. Man is under the constant necessity, writes Thurman Arnold, of putting on ceremonial robes, and watching himself go by.[8] There are symbols like the flag and the national anthem that are clearly recognized as such—well-defined abbreviations of the national culture, sometimes called "referential symbols" because they refer directly to the things they symbolize. But the more important symbols, because their working is more obscure, are the "condensation symbols," which Edward Sapir defines as "a condensed form of substitute behavior for direct expression." [9] This is the symbolism to be found in neurotic behavior, in the life of savages, in the heavily charged symbolic atmosphere of religion and politics.

The Supreme Court as symbol goes hand in hand with the Constitution as symbol. Since the Supreme Court is popularly considered as exercising a guardianship over the Constitution, the result has been to invest the judges of the Court with all the panoply of sanctity with which the Constitution has itself been invested. This has had for American history an importance that can scarcely be overestimated. Constitutions, like all creations of the human

---

[7] Two of the important American books derive from the war experience: Lasswell, *Propaganda Technique in the World War* (1927), and Lippmann, *Public Opinion* (1922); it is from Lippmann that I have got the concept of the stereotype. It is not surprising that it is especially in periods of social unrest that the attention of social theory should turn to the irrational elements in mass psychology.

[8] Arnold, *The Symbols of Government* (1935) iii.

[9] In his suggestive article on "Symbolism" (1934) 14 *Encyclopaedia of the Social Sciences* 492, 493.

mind and the human will, have an existence in men's imagination and men's emotions quite apart from their actual use in ordering men's affairs. This function has been called "constitutionalism," which Walton Hamilton has defined as "the name given to the trust which men repose in the power of words engrossed on parchment to keep a government in order."[10] Edward S. Corwin, in his Harvard Tercentenary paper,[11] has pointed out that the Constitution has two aspects: it is an *instrument* and a *symbol*. As an instrument it must be viewed hard-headedly and used flexibly to promote the people's welfare in the present and future. As a symbol it is part of the mass mind, capable of arousing intense popular hysteria, loaded with a terrible inertia, its face turned toward the past.

II. Constitution into Fetish

To understand the fetishism of the Constitution one would require the detachment of an anthropologist. Every tribe needs its totem and its fetish, and the Constitution is ours. Every tribe clings to something which it believes to possess supernatural powers, as an instrument for controlling unknown forces in a hostile universe. This is true of civilized nations as well. Men need always something on which to fix their emotions, whether positively in the form of adoration or deification, or negatively in the form of a taboo. Like every people, the American people have wanted some anchorage, some link with the invariant.

> Change and decay in all around I see,
> Oh, Thou who changest not, abide with me.

---

[10] Hamilton, "Constitutionalism" (1931) 4 *Encyclopaedia of the Social Sciences* 255. See also Friedrich, *Constitutional Government and Politics* (1937), especially c. 8–10, for a view of constitutionalism that differs from Hamilton's.

[11] Corwin, "The Constitution as Instrument and as Symbol" (1936) 30 *American Political Science Review* 1071. Corwin's contrast between the Constitution as symbol and as instrument will, like so many of his analyses, prove fruitful for constitutional theory. I have only one warning. "Instrument" may be used in two senses: in one it means, as with Corwin, a frame of government adequate to the weight placed upon it; in another sense it may mean a technique for defeating the democratic will. In this second sense the principal *instrument* has been the power of judicial review. The true antithesis would place on the one side a pragmatic use of the Constitution, whether through liberal interpretation or through constitutional change; on the other side the symbolism of Constitution and Court going hand in hand with the instrument of judicial review. Since the original publication of the present essay B. H. Levy, *Our Constitution: Tool or Testament?* (1941), has elaborated a somewhat similar theme.

And the Rock of Ages has been as essential in the politics of America as in its religion. In fact the very habits of mind begotten by an authoritarian Bible and a religion of submission to a higher power have been carried over to an authoritarian Constitution and a philosophy of submission to a "higher law"; and a country like America, in which its early tradition had prohibited a state church, ends by getting a state church after all, although in a secular form.

Some day there will be a historian with insight and imagination enough to write the real religious history of America. It will not be the history of formal churchgoing religion, nor even that of the sects and the hellfire revivalists. It will be on the one hand the worship of the dynamo and the gods of business enterprise; it will be on the other hand the worship of the Constitution and the Supreme Court. For in the first pair Americans have made concrete the deepest strivings of their nature and era—the quest of what William James called "the bitch-goddess Success." In the second pair they have made concrete their own hopes and fears for their social order.

If we wish to understand with some sense of immediacy the early American hopes and fears we have only to look at the Soviets today. Travelers returning from Russia agree that the Russian people are filled with a sense of the revolutionary role they have played and the greatness of their destiny. We get from contemporary records a similar sense of America in its days of early statehood. Even as late as the 1830's, young Alexis de Tocqueville, traveling through the new America and contrasting it with the Europe he had just left, was impressed by one thing: the feeling that Americans had of being the carriers of a new philosophy of democracy and equality, the sense they had of their peculiar mission in world history.

Actually, of course, all peoples have one time had this sense of uniqueness and mission, although in the older cultures it tends to wear off and a revolution of some sort or other is needed to renew it. Robert Michels has spoken of the two basic myths of patriotism —the myth of unique national origin (*der Mythus der Woher*) and the myth of unique national destiny (*der Mythus der Wohin*).[12] In America the two converged in the myth of a democratic revolu-

12 Michels, *Der Patriotismus* (1929).

tion and a revolutionary democracy. Americans took great pride in their revolution, although it must be noted that the pride increased in retrospect as the revolution receded, the revolutionary energy ebbed, and the democratic élan grew too dangerous for the men of substance.

The rhetoric of national unity marked the beginning of Constitution-worship.[13] The people rejoiced that the disunity of the Confederation had been turned into the unity of the Constitution. To be sure, only about five per cent of the country voted on ratification. But there seems little doubt that most of the rest, for all their suspicions that their liberties might be taken away from them, were not averse to the change. A correspondent wrote to Rufus King in 1787:

Our people expect so much happiness from the doings of the Convention that they stand ready to adopt anything which may be offered.[14]

Partly the spontaneous result of this expectancy, partly planned and prompted by the Federalist supporters of ratification, processions were held in 1788 in Philadelphia, Boston, New York, Baltimore, Charleston, and New Haven to celebrate the ratification. In them mechanics marched side by side with noteholders and merchants. An opponent called the Boston procession "a great fulsome parade"; it "may serve to please children, but freemen will not be so easily gulled out of their liberties." That the children were pleased was more important than the gentleman knew. The procession, wrote a Philadelphian to a friend in another city,

has made such an impression on the minds of our young people that "federal" and "union" have now become part of the household words of every family in the city.[15]

It was on these "young people" that the success of the new govern-

---

13 For much of the material in this section dealing with the first decade of the Constitution I am deeply indebted to Schechter's pathbreaking article, "The Early History of the Tradition of the Constitution" (1915) 9 *American Political Science Review* 707. I have borrowed from him not only several of the quotations, but much of the perspective. I fear he errs, however, in attributing too happy a set of consequences to the tradition of the Constitution; if it exercised a cohesive force, it lent itself also to the uses of ruling minority groups.

14 1 King, *Life and Correspondence of Rufus King* (1894) 259; this and the quotations that follow are cited in Schechter.

15 Hopkinson, *An Account of the Grand Federal Procession* (2d ed. 1788) appendix.

ment depended; and when "union" became a household word half the task was done.

What with real enthusiasm and drummed-up eloquence, the myth of a perfect Constitution got off to a fine start. William Maclay, whose acid words in his journal ate away many of the contemporary pretensions but none the less recorded them, wrote in 1791:

It has been usual with declamatory gentlemen, in their praises of the present Government . . . to paint the state of the country under the old Congress as if neither wood grew nor water ran in America before the happy adoption of the new Constitution.[16]

What eased the path of Constitution-worship further was the fact that the new government was ratified on the ascending arc of a period of prosperity. It was thus possible to attribute to the government not only those effects which genuinely flowed from the stopping of the trade wars and the increased sense of confidence among the mercantile groups, but those also which, because of a war-locked Europe, were for a quarter-century to play economically into the hands of America. On the crest of this wave of prosperity the exultation over the new America was converted into the tradition of a perfect Constitution. Undoubtedly the sponsors of the new government were happy to have the decision about their work transferred from the plane of debate over principles to the plane of emotion and faith.

There were some, like James Madison in his famous tenth essay of the *Federalist,* who saw that faction founded upon disparate property interests lay at the core of all government; but that meant merely that they and others were grateful for the emergence of a rhetoric of the national interest to push class interests into the background.[17] How Constitution-worship could be used thus was illustrated in the early jockeyings of the Federalists and anti-Federalists

---

16 *Journal of William Maclay* (1929 ed.).

17 The students of today have accepted too uncritically the epithet "faction" which was always hurled at attempts to build up a party-system. The reason that Federalist theorists were so bitter at the idea of faction was that they feared the party-system would show where the majority stood: the rise of parties has been thus the principal instrument for making democratic government effective. Parrington [1 Parrington, *Main Currents in American Thought* (1927)] sees this clearly, in his discussion of political theory at the Constitutional convention; so also does Beard, *Economic Origins of Jeffersonian Democracy* (1915) especially c. 1 and 8. On Madison in this connection see Beard, *The Idea of National Interest* (1934) c. 1.

for positions of advantage. At first the anti-Federalists opposed ratification. But when it became clear that the new government was popular, the Jeffersonian party accepted its defeat and sought even to train the enemies' guns back on them. In doing this the Jeffersonians had the precedent of a skillful maneuver by which, in 1787 and 1788, the nationalists under the leadership of Hamilton had appropriated the name "Federalists" with all the emotional associations of decentralization and states' rights that went with it. It was a daring stroke, "this clearly conscious philological ambuscade into which the American masses fell." [18] But Jefferson was no less daring and in the long run more effective when he and his party abandoned their opposition to the Constitution and became the eager rivals of the Federalists in worshiping it. Both parties showed an amazing unanimity in pointing out the perfections of the Constitution; they delighted in honoring it, and they measured their distance from each other by reciprocal charges of violating it and departing from its spirit. Their divergences were those of interpretation.

Thus the Constitution was serving its purpose as an anchorage of government against the storms of party strife. W. H. Crawford of Georgia had ample reason to complain when he said in 1811 in the House of Representatives:

It has become so extremely fashionable to eulogize the Constitution, whether the object of the eulogy is the extension or contraction of the powers of the government, that whenever its eulogium is pronounced, I feel an involuntary apprehension of mischief.[19]

His barb was delightful; but it was this very fact that all parties had become rival worshipers in the cult of the Constitution which proved the greatest stabilizing force in the new government. Always the task of a state has been to find some object of common allegiance which would allow internal quarrels to rage *within* the fabric of government without destroying it.[20] A generation like

18 Schechter, *supra* note 13, at 714.
19 Quoted in Corwin, *supra* note 11, at 1077.
20 Von Holst, in his chapter on Constitution-worship in America [1 Von Holst, *Constitutional and Political History of the United States* (Lalor and Mason trans. 1881) c. 2], quotes Governor Hamilton of South Carolina on "the beauty of our Constitution" at the very moment when Hamilton was nominated as president of the nullification convention in 1832, and Alexander Stephens to the same effect only a month before he became Vice-President of the Confederate States. This "contradiction"

ours, living in a "time of troubles," can understand the value of the symbol of national unity and the fetishism of the Constitution in cementing internal order.

But when we have allowed for the rhetoric of national unity, the persuasion of prosperity, the advantages of having a safety valve to let off the steam of party conflict; when we have added the propaganda of clergymen, lawyers, editors, teachers, we have not completed our analysis. Deeper than any of these were forces operating on the less conscious levels of the popular mind. One was the belief that ordinary people, as well as lawyers, have in word-magic. The American was the first written national Constitution. What matter that it was a broad pathway of government rather than a fixed and narrow code of law? The very definiteness with which the design for a government was set down in words on parchment was enough to command admiration and then reverence.[21] What was wanted was a visible symbol of the things men hold dear. The American people had conquered a domain from its natives, wrested the sovereignty over it from the greatest power in Europe, fought their way to liberty. They wanted a visible mark of their accomplishment: *ecce signum*. And they wanted it all the more strongly as they began to suspect that in the process of consolidating their regime they had lost sight of their original impulses and the goals they had dreamt of. What they did, to still their doubts, was what every man does when troubled about his failure to realize his youthful dreams: they sought a way by which their revolutionary ideals could be worshiped without being followed. They found their peace in the safe haven of the Constitution. Here was the document into which the Founding Fathers had poured their wis-

---

fascinated von Holst and even made him angry, which is not surprising when we remember that von Holst was passionately influenced by the German constitutional movement, and wished earnestly to believe in the integrity of constitutionalism. But the serious count in the rhetoric above is not that it was out of line with the behavior of the two Southerners. It is rather that while in 1832 the rhetoric served its purpose, in 1861 it did not. That purpose was to settle internal clashes without resort to bloodshed.

21 On word-magic, see Kenneth Burke's suggestive, if somewhat chaotic book, *Permanence and Change* (1935). There is an item in the article, "The Constitution of the United States" (July 1936) 14 *Fortune* 56, where it is reported that of the thousands who stream through the Library of Congress to gaze at the document in its glass case, many fall to their knees before the magic of the word that holds their national destiny. There are some, of course, who ask to see the signatures of Christopher Columbus and Colonel Lindbergh; but when was ignorance ever held a bar to the appreciation of magic?

dom as into a vessel; the Fathers themselves grew ever larger in stature as they receded from view; the era in which they lived and fought became a Golden Age; in that age there had been a fresh dawn for the world, and its men were giants against the sky; what they had fought for was abstracted from its living context and became a set of "principles," eternally true and universally applicable.[22] When the Americans began seeing the revolutionary heroes in the hazy light of semi-divinity and began getting them associated or confused with the framers of the Constitution, the work of consolidating the new government was assured. The Golden Age had become a political instrument.

The amazing function that the Constitution as symbol performed was to serve as a link between the revolutionary ferment of the 1770's and the new nationalist government of the propertied minority.[23] On the one hand the prosperity and the sense of order that accompanied the new regime were attributed to the Constitution; by a process of abbreviation, one said "Constitution" when one meant the new government, thereby assigning to the instrument what was intended for the whole organism. On the other hand, by a process of association, one also said "Constitution" when one meant the ideals for which the revolution had been fought, thereby investing a conservative document with the halo of a revolutionary movement. That the Constitution could serve thus as a link between the Boston Tea Party and Hamilton's Report on Manufac-

---

22 The process described here is obviously not restricted to American history. It forms the theme also of Carl Becker's brilliant *Heavenly City of the Eighteenth Century Philosophers* (1932). The appeal to a Golden Age is a common thing in the history of national emotions and political tactics. In fact, Americans were only carrying on what the English had done in their struggle for parliamentary liberties when they had appealed to a Golden Age of primitive Saxonism, with its reliance on the sturdy and deep-rooted habit of meeting in assemblies, as against the Golden Age of the Briton kings, which the Tudor and Stuart apologists sought to emphasize. See Brinkley, *Arthurian Legend in the Seventeenth Century* (1932).

23 The Constitution as it was framed and ratified was, of course, far from a revolutionary document; the new government was a republic rigged up with contrivances for safeguarding the interests of the propertied minority. But the symbolic power of a Constitution was recognized very early by those who had the sharpness to pierce history. Tom Paine, revolutionist as he was, saw from the beginning the power that lay in a "charter" for lashing down the allegiance of the masses to the new regime: "Let a day be solemnly set apart for proclaiming the charter; let it be brought forth placed on the divine law, the word of God; let a crown be placed thereon, by which the world may know that so far we approve monarchy that in America the law is King." Paine, *Common Sense* (1776); quoted in Corwin. This was in 1776, but as a good propagandist Paine was already drawing the blueprints of Constitution-worship.

tures, between the Declaration of Independence and Dr. Timothy Dwight's speeches as President of Yale University, is a tribute not so much to the document itself or to the wisdom of its framers; it is a tribute ultimately to the ironic sequence of events in history, and to men's capacity for fashioning myths that will allow them to adjust themselves to that sequence.[24] One could, if a dash of cynicism were allowable, lay it down as a political axiom that at least in the early stages of a revolutionary regime a constitution is worshiped in inverse proportion as it embodies the principles for which the revolution was fought, and in direct proportion as it succeeds in creating a framework for order and prosperity.

But the Constitution was no static symbol. Its fortunes were entrusted to the perilous voyages of the union experiment. There were two powerful thrusts at work in the period before the Civil War—one toward nationalism, the other toward particularism; one emphasizing the needs of survival for the whole, the other clinging to the assertions of freedom for the parts. The quarrel was not one carried on in the void; it mounted in passion and intensity because with it were involved the fortunes of slave-holding and of industrialism. But it is important to note that the fight over these issues of economic interest and state policy had to be waged with constitutional brickbats. That is why the principal figures in the struggle were constitutional lawyers. They were the heroes in a war of words. On the nationalist and industrialist side the great figures were John Marshall on the bench, Daniel Webster and Henry Clay off it, and Joseph Story whether on or off. On the localist-slavocracy side were Roger Taney on the bench and John C. Calhoun and Thomas Benton off it. And in the wake of these judges and legal scholars came their camp-followers—the nation of amateur constitutional lawyers. It was in this period, it must be remembered, in the early 1830's, that de Tocqueville came to America and put down his observation that every issue of policy with us was first translated into constitutional terms and debated as a legal issue.[25]

But in the thickest of the battle, the Constitution itself went un-

---

[24] Americans of the 1790's were able the better to adjust themselves to the contradiction of their position through the figure of George Washington, who spanned the transition from the old fervor to the new order, and who was utilized to the hilt as a symbol.

[25] De Tocqueville, *Democracy in America*, vol. 1, 284.

questioned. In fact, the more hotly the diverse interpretations of it were contested, the more unwaveringly did both sides pay homage to it. The climax of the war of words came in 1830, in the debate in the Senate between Webster and Hayne.[26] There is a sultry magnificence in Webster's "Reply to Hayne," which quickens the blood even of the skeptical reader today. But more important is the fact that this debate was the climax of the attempt to solve national problems through constitutional symbols; and the attempt was a failure.

Webster's speeches represent the high point of the establishment of the constitutional tradition. Never before had men been so aware of the full emotional meaning of national unity. He urged the Constitution as a completed contract between the people themselves—immediate, fundamental, irrevocable, sacred. But it was not so much his legalistic arguments as the finality and fervor of his statement of them that counted. The notion of a united people superior to the will of the states now emerged, and became identified with the Constitution. This notion reached its full consciousness on the rising arc of our national life, when the emerging industrialism was creating in economic terms the organic sense of unity that Webster was trying to use for the purposes of his class and outlook. Webster's speech was therefore a resounding success. It sold as a pamphlet more widely than any other pamphlet since Tom Paine's. It gave balm and reassurance to a people already troubled by the impending sectional conflict. The enormous impression that Webster's oration made was, however, not due wholly to the "godlike Daniel's" divine eloquence. It must be remembered that this speech, and also the one he made three years later which with the help of the *Commentaries* of Justice Story was more closely reasoned as a piece of constitutional theory,[27] were both filled with a sort of

---

26 This debate has been insufficiently studied in terms both of its symbolic and of its economic context. I have found the comments of Warren [1 Warren, *The Supreme Court in United States History* (2d ed. 1926) c. 18] and Fuess [1 *Daniel Webster* (1930) c. 15] valuable despite—perhaps because of—my disagreement with their interpretation. Parrington's sketch of Webster [2 Parrington, *op. cit. supra* note 17, at 304–16] is brilliant. So also is Charles Beard's discussion in *The Economic Basis of Politics* (1934 ed.) 33–40.

27 The 1833 speech on "The Constitution Not a Compact between the Sovereign States" [6 *Works* (Natl. ed. 1903) 181] is the speech which best expresses Webster's constitutional theory. There is fairly clear evidence that Webster got much of his theory from Story. See 2 Parrington, *op. cit. supra* note 17, at 311. The "Reply to

inspired Constitution-worship. It was this which stirred the country. That it did so was evidence of the hunger of the people, in the midst of the incertitudes of the slavery debate, to be reassured by some comforting symbol. That symbol was an indivisible union resting upon a sacred charter which was, in Webster's words, a "Constitution," not a "Confederacy."

But the hunger for a national symbolism was not enough to solve the problems of sectional and class interests. Von Holst, writing of this period from his vantage-ground after the Civil War, states quite clearly the dual result that attended the use of constitutional debate as an instrument of national policy:

The Constitution afforded such a field for a war of words . . . that . . . the erroneous view began to obtain currency in the third decade of this century that all difficulty would end in a war of tongues . . . the extraordinary dilatability of the boundaries postponed the moment of the breach.[28]

Von Holst was right in both respects. The common clinging to the Constitution while disputes raged over its interpretation—the limitation of the struggle to the arena of constitutional argument—*did* postpone the moment of the breach. But it was a dangerous method, for it tended to lull men to an oblivion of the bitter realities involved in the struggle. When they placed their complete reliance upon this "war of words," the Civil War became not the irrepressible conflict but the incredible conflict. Hence the necessary economic and political adjustments were not made.[29] The politicians

---

Hayne" [6 *Works* (Natl. ed. 1903) 3] is not his best constitutional argument, but it is the best rhetorical statement, which is much more to our purpose.

28 1 Von Holst, *op. cit. supra* note 20, at 78. It was in this period that the fiftieth anniversary of the Constitution was celebrated. For a typical discussion, using the occasion for a bitter indictment of the states'-rights doctrine, see John Quincy Adams, *The Jubilee of the Constitution* (1839).

29 The immediate context of the Webster-Hayne debate was the struggle over the land question as related to the slavery question. The Beards [*The Rise of American Civilization* (1927)] point out that Webster sought to split the West from the South in their common struggle against Northern industrialism, by yielding to the West on the land issue, and by setting up a nationalist ideal to the appeal of which the West was not wholly immune But by relying too much on the latter, constitutional rhetoric, the Easterners did not push their practical concessions far enough. If they had gone beyond Webster's gesture to the West, "if they had then and there effected a union with the West by yielding on the land question . . . they would have made the forces of the Union a combination of power so formidable that secession would have scarcely dared to face it." 1 *id.* at 565–66.

of the 1830's, like all politicians, finally fell under the sway of their own rhetoric. They actually believed in the efficacy of their legalistic arguments. They trusted in the sanctity of the Union within the symbolism of the Constitution to preserve the Union. The tragedy of Webster's "Reply to Hayne" was that symbolism did not prove enough.

While the war itself was a tragic defeat for the efficacy of the constitutional symbolism, the Northern victory only served to confirm that symbolism. As we shall see in the next section, however, the Constitution itself was no longer asked to bear unaided the burden of solving the problems which threatened the national unity. To the rhetoric of the Constitution was added the divine right of judges and the yeoman's work that the judicial power had to do. The heyday of constitutional symbolism was over with the Civil War. I do not say there was a slackening of constitutional fetishism. By no means. If anything, that fetishism grew in passion and intensity. But it no longer had to bear the heavy freightage of keeping party disputes in bounds and hemming economic conflicts within the ambit of peaceful political brawls. It is not too much to say that after the Civil War the *function* of constitutional symbolism became auxiliary to the cult of the judicial power.

Within these limits the Constitution has functioned as a symbol with great effectiveness since the Civil War, and its very removal from the area of direct conflict has made it more rigid and unyielding as a symbol. As the continent was opened, and a new immigration poured in from Europe, and the population moved toward the Pacific, new sectional, racial, and class cleavages emerged. The Constitution was more than ever needed to tie together the loose bundle of fagots, the collocation of races and peoples, the sprawling geographical expanse we call our country. Henry Adams, musing on the Virgin and the dynamo, rifling European capitals for the wisdom stored in their cathedrals and chancelleries, took the Constitution for granted, and had perforce to fall back upon inexorable cycles of history in order to find some anchorage in a shifting and turbulent cosmos. Not so the immigrant, first landed on these shores, who found in the Constitution the certain guarantee of stability that Adams had hunted for throughout Europe.[30] The

---

[30] The part that the immigrants have played in building the effective symbolism of American life has never been adequately explored. It seems clear, however, that their

Constitution has thus become since the Civil War principally an *assimilative* and fagot-binding agency, betokening the encompassing tradition into which all sorts of diverse traditions could pour themselves. And thus for the children of the new industrial age, native and immigrant alike, the Constitution became once more what it had been for the generations that succeeded the Revolution —the symbol of a Golden Age. Only the Golden Age, instead of lying in the past, lay in the future. It was located no longer in the lost Atlantis of the Revolution; it was a gateway opening on bright and illimitable vistas of the golden dollar.[31] As the pecuniary values of a capitalist society supplanted all others, the Constitution was used more and more as a symbol to place a sanction upon those values. It became merged in men's minds with the capitalist myth of the career open to talent in the land of opportunity; the capitalist legend and the constitutional legend blurred into one another until finally their outlines could no longer be distinguished, and they themselves became interchangeable. Which was as it should be in a capitalist democracy.

All this took place by no means spontaneously. The dynamics of building the constitutional symbol are lost for us among the myriad daily activities of the past. What we do know is that the process of building the constitutional legend was equal to the task imposed. It became the staple of after-dinner speeches at Bar Association meetings, of occasional addresses by judges, of conventions of patriotic societies, of classroom recitations and nation-wide contests sponsored by newspapers, of talks before immigrant groups, of newspaper editorials in the great urban centers and cross-road towns, of radio commentators and movie newsreels. All the media through which popular opinion is created and entrenched were enlisted in its service. Those who are curious will find a revealing cross-section of the constitutional legend in the records that have remained of the centenary celebration of the ratification of the Con-

---

role has been central and at the same time curiously dual. On the one hand, the immigrants have with a naïve eagerness tended to swallow whole both the myth of a perfect Constitution and the myth of capitalist success; on the other hand, the "Americanism" which represents the fusion of the two myths has fed largely on native hatred of immigrants.

31 The classic works on the capitalist myth in America are, of course, Thorstein Veblen's, especially *Absentee Ownership* (1923). Of value also is Josephson, *The Robber Barons* (1934), especially the chapter "What the Young Men Dream."

stitution, held in Philadelphia in 1889.[32] But if several of the exhibits in that record seem to some a bit archaic and baldly naïve, let them reflect that in the half-century that has elapsed the process has gone on apace. That our constitutional commentaries have something of the timbre of what the band plays at Fourth of July parades should not disconcert us. It is of the essence of such works that they should celebrate their fear of change under the guise of a passion for the moral foundations of the Republic.[33]

Latterly constitutionalism has tended to lose its original richness and, as it has more and more hardened into a fetish, to be turned with increasing naïveté to the purposes of reactionary groups. It has, of course, always been true that not all who have made a fetish of the Constitution have believed in it. Samuel Johnson said of patriotism that it was often the last refuge of the scoundrel. This is true of constitutionalism as well. Many is the newspaper and political group in this country which appeals to the sanctity of the Constitution with its eyes fixed on the immensities and its hands reaching out for its own special interests. They are the professional patrioteers, and they use the Constitution in a coldly instrumental way for their own purposes. The professional patrioteers may, if we have luck, go the way of other excrescences on the body politic, and be sloughed off in time. But for the present the fetishism of the Constitution on the part of the common man, which has become so deeply part of our tribal ways that it must be taken as a datum in our politics, plays into the hands of all sorts of constitutional "leagues" and Americanism-mongers. It may perhaps be considered evidence of the disintegration of the constitutional symbol that what once served to weld the discordant groups of a nation together has now become the easy label of a whole host of "patriotic" organi-

---

[32] Carson, ed., *History of the Celebration of the 100th Anniversary of the Promulgation of the Constitution of the United States* (1889). It is worth noting that J. Franklin Jameson, writing in 1886, observed that increasing interest in the Constitution over the last few years had caused the State Department to take it out of the "little tin box" and place it on exhibition. Jameson, *An Introduction to the Study of the Constitutional and Political History of the United States* (1886) 5.

[33] Take, for example, the amazing book by Beck [*The Constitution of the United States* (1922)]—amazing not in that it differs so much from what ninety-five per cent of the "constitutional lawyers" of today would write if they wrote books, but in that it was written and published at all as a scholarly commentary. In his review of the book, under the title "Constitutional Metaphors" (1925) 41 *New Republic* 314, Thomas Reed Powell has set down as pitiless a dissection of the anatomy of constitutionalism as exists anywhere.

zations whose purpose is to stamp out any protest against the existing economic set-up and whose function is to build a popular apologia for the present distribution of power.

III. DIVINE RIGHT: AMERICAN PLAN [34]

In a democracy in the twentieth century it may seem irreverent or whimsical or even merely literary to talk of divine right. Yet very little is clearer in the American scheme than the fact that the cult of the Supreme Court is the characteristic emotional cement by which American capitalism and American democracy are held together. The celebration of the Supreme Court in the capitalist America of the nineteenth and twentieth centuries performs the same social function as the celebration of kingship in the mercantilist Europe of the sixteenth to eighteenth centuries. On the main highways of the development of the Western world, what used to be the divine right of kings has been replaced by the divine right of judges.

I mean this of course, as a rough analogy, and yet I mean something beyond that too. The feudal economic system wore the panoply of idea and allegiance furnished by the universal church. The mercantilist economic system that emerged in early modern times clothed itself in the vestments of a kingship that would have the strength to break down and override the princelings and local potentates who stood in the way of the expanding economic unit; but it had to contend with the spiritual authority of the church, and it did not shrink finally from claiming for its kings the same divine right with which the church had invested itself. In fact, as Figgis has pointed out, the great ideological struggles of the sixteenth century were waged over the claims of the kingship to divine right; and the crux of this struggle is reached when the absolute monarchs in England evolved their *dispensing* power to set over against the power of the church to grant *indulgences*. It seems to be a rule of

---

[34] The reader is warned that throughout this section there is an emphasis on the judicial power which may appear extreme as of 1941. When this and the following essays were first published (1936 and 1937) America was in the midst of a severe constitutional crisis caused by the extension of the judicial power. That crisis has now been resolved. But it must still be reckoned with in the future. See the chapter "Constitutional Crisis and the Crisis State," below, p. 305, for the best perspective of this problem that I can now muster.

the struggle for power that one species of appeal to divinity can be displaced only by another. The divine right of the church had to yield to the divine right of kings which invested the absolute monarchy. That, in turn, in the course of the parliamentary struggles of the seventeenth century in England and of the eighteenth- and nineteenth-century struggles that followed in their wake on the Continent, had to give way to the divine right of Parliaments; for representative institutions were able to displace absolute monarchy only by grace of appealing to a "higher law"; the "divinity [that] doth hedge a king" was transformed into the divine sanctions of some unchanging body of principles in terms of which the king's acts had to be measured and weighed.

But the logic of development did not stop there. America, which has carried capitalism to its highest peak of perfection, needed also a divine sanction of unusual potency with which to invest it. Because our parliamentary institutions—our Congresses and Presidents—are potentially too responsive to democratic impulses, the "higher law" was extended to hem in the acts of the people's representatives themselves. That "higher law" was located in the Constitution, but being divine it could not be contained even in that. So it overflowed and became a "brooding omnipresence in the sky" [35] which could be brought to earth only when it was finally located in the minds of the men who took over the exclusive function of interpreting the Constitution. As Brooks Adams wrote in 1913, in his masterly *Theory of Social Revolutions,* by the "rule of reason" in the Standard Oil case of 1910 which exempted the Oil Trust from the operation of the Sherman Anti-Trust Act,[36] the Court was taking over the authority of the church to "grant indulgences for reasonable causes." [37] From the medieval church to American finance capitalism the wheel has come a full turn.

There are three principal elements in the pattern of divine right as it may be found in the popular mind. One is the fetishism of the Constitution, the second is the claim of the Court to the exclusive guardianship of the Constitution, and the third is the tradition of

---

[35] The phrase is, of course, Holmes's, who was more canny in seeing through the judicial symbols than any other incumbent on the Court. It comes from his opinion in *Northern Pacific Co. v. Jensen,* 244 U.S. 205 (1917), and refers to the mystical conception of the common law.

[36] *Standard Oil Co. v. United States,* 221 U.S. 1 (1910).

[37] Adams, *The Theory of Social Revolutions* (1913) 119–31.

judicial neutrality. I have already dealt with the first in the previous section of this article. To no small extent in the past century the fortunes of the Constitution as symbol and the Supreme Court as symbol have been linked. What enabled the propertied groups, in the last analysis, to make use of the judicial power was the strength and evocative force of the constitutional tradition.

But this tradition, seen as a cohesive force for the nation, had one great weakness, which I have already sought to suggest. It left the gates wide open for divergent interpretations that, as shown by the quarter-century that furnished a swift runway to civil war, might grow in passion and intensity until they led to open conflict. The Civil War burned deep into the people the consciousness of the value of the constitutional symbol; it burned even deeper the danger of the conflicting interpretations of the fundamental law. As long as the polity had to cope only with the oppositions of the party-system, the constitutional symbol was broad enough to contain those oppositions and give them scope and play. But when the oppositions took on the fierceness of class and sectional conflicts, and when two well-knit economies, each with its emotional loyalties and intellectual rationalizations, met in a head-on collision, it was clear that something more was required than the constitutional symbol. That something more was judicial review. Since an open area for endless debate and conflict had been left in a federal framework, based on the separation of powers and subject to a fundamental law, that open area had to be closed. Someone had to be empowered to decide finally how that fundamental law should be interpreted. The decision might, of course, have been left to Congress, but that would have been unthinkable before the Civil War to the slavery interest and localist sentiment; it was unthinkable after the Civil War to the capitalist interest, which above all else feared democracy. Something else had to be found. The fetishism of the Constitution, as a flexible instrument open to various construction, was in itself inadequate. In short, a *faith* was not enough. It had to be a faith deposited in a *power*. That power was the judicial power. The function of interpreting the Constitution had to be specialized in a single tribunal.

Thus arose the second element in the pattern of divine right: the exclusive claim of the Supreme Court to a guardianship of the Constitution. John Marshall and Joseph Story urged it very early in our history, primarily from the viewpoint of safeguarding the Federalist interests. Webster's "Reply to Hayne" is principally important as a defense, not so much of the Constitution, as of the judicial power. It is significant, as Charles Warren has pointed out, that it came at the end of the first fierce attack on the judicial power since Jefferson's. Webster saw the judicial power as adding a new bulwark for the propertied interests to the bulwark of the Constitution [38]—which could be used quite as much by Calhoun and Benton to their purposes as by Clay and himself to their own. What Webster did not foresee was that even the judicial power could be used by the enemy—if they captured the Court. It was one of the ironic twists of history that the arrow which Webster aimed at Hayne and the slavocracy he stood for was picked up by Taney, another champion of the slavocracy, and aimed back at Webster and the capitalism of the North. The Dred Scott decision was the logical fulfillment of the "Reply to Hayne."

From Marshall through Taney, and increasingly after the Civil War, the Supreme Court offered to guard exclusively the charter of fundamental liberties. They offered to play the role of the Platonic guardians that watched over the mythical Greek republic; they were ready to furnish at once wisdom and militancy. Part of John Marshall's genius lay in his skill in pushing into the background the power that the Court was gaining over economic policy, and thrusting into the foreground its role of guardianship. This the later judges have encouraged by their continued utterances, and it has become the official theory of the Court's power. To be sure, the fact that the *role of guarding* the Constitution involved also the *power of deciding* what the Constitution was did not by a whit diminish the ardor of the Court in offering its services. Like a jealous Cylops, it was willing to rule the domain that it guarded.

By the stress laid on this guardianship, the judges have been associated in our minds with the function of protection rather than with the struggle for power. This has been of enormous importance. It has conscripted to the service of the judicial symbol all the ac-

---

[38] In the long Congressional debate that followed Webster's speech, the issue of the judicial power was thrashed out at greater length than at any time since the Great Judiciary Debate of 1802. In it one may find a full exposition of the claim of the Court to the exclusive guardianship of the Constitution.

cumulated Anglo-Saxon tradition of the "rule of law." [39] America carried it over from England. But this tradition was in a vague way and under the form of "natural law" itself a carry-over from the Middle Ages. It had become domesticated in England—first, in the subjection of King John to the Magna Charta of the barons at Runnymede; later, by the rising English middle class, acting through Edward Coke, the tough and sturdy Lord Chief Justice stubbornly fighting royal prerogative in the cause of parliamentary liberties, and writing a magnificent commentary on Magna Charta which was more influential than was the instrument itself in building up the conception of the rule of law. This idea—of the subjection of all public officials to a higher law that is "common" not only in the sense that it is available to all men but also in the sense that it exempts none—was carried over into the American colonies, and took the form here of the conception of the Constitution as a "fundamental law." It cropped up timorously in some of the early cases that are now cited as forerunners of *Marbury v. Madison*,[40] and in that case took its first long step toward being converted into the doctrine of judicial review. It has been the principal ideological force bolstering judicial review, as a necessary doctrine in "a government of laws and not of men." It is an influence that lingers today in the minds of those who have never heard of Coke, and who do not know the meaning—much less the "spirit"—of the common law.

From Coke to Marshall, Story, and Chancellor Kent, to Cooley on "Constitutional Limitations," to the New Deal cases, is a series of legal steps, but the continuity in them is the appeal to a higher law in the interests of the mercantile and industrial class. There is one paradox worth noting: in England, Coke's doctrine has been main-

---

[39] I have not spoken in the text of one of our links to English legal development—the fact that there is a basic character which the possession of a "common law" gives to a people. The emphasis on this by such writers as Pollock and Pound is expressed in phrases like "the spirit of the common law," "the genius of the common law." The latest commentator to stress this is, significantly enough, a student whose thinking was formed under the influence of continental juristic thought—Max Ascoli. See his *Intelligence in Politics* (1936), especially the suggestive section on American legal institutions and the national character, at 120–42. I am willing enough to accept such an approach, provided one is aware of the danger of slipping into the *Geist*-mongering of the Savigny school; provided also one adds that a common law not only helps create the national character, but is itself hammered out along with other institutions by the driving set of forces in the history of the culture.

[40] 1 Cranch 137 (1803).

tained only so far as it called for a legal check upon the monarch, but not so far as it applied to a legal check upon the Parliament; in America the check was placed on both the executive and the legislature. From having such a check it was only a step to identify it with the Constitution, and from that point only another step to identify it with the guardians and interpreters of the Constitution, and thus to establish judicial supremacy. The paradox, however, resolves itself when ideas are referred back to the interests they serve. It was no accident that the idea of the rule of law was among the reigning forces at our nativity as a nation. It is historically, as well as psychologically, linked with the development and power of the middle class in the Western world. It is part of the body of liberal doctrine that the middle class forged in the centuries during which it was clearing its way to power, and that the same class used as a rationalization and as an instrument for achieving power.[41] Just as it was useful originally to the rising capitalist class in removing the obstruction of monarchical and aristocratic interference, so it is useful now to the entrenched capitalist class in fighting off the threat of democratic and labor groups.

Its emphasis has changed, but it has kept its function and its psychological appeal. It has found favorable soil in America, where there has always been a dominant legalistic strain and an elaborate respect for the legal fabric of things. And it has been cherished most by the liberal tradition in American life, which has done little to orient itself to the new demands made upon it by changing industrialism, and which is still fighting all over again the battles of the Stuart period.[42]

This brings us to the third element in the pattern of divine right: the tradition of judicial neutrality. The judges could not be proper

---

[41] I borrow here, of course, from Laski, *The Rise of European Liberalism* (1936), which seems to me enormously valuable as an attempt to apply the Marxian methodology to the history of Western social thought; see my review, "Liberalism's Family Tree" (1936) 143 *Nation* 396 (reprinted in my *Ideas Are Weapons* (1939) pp. 343–47); see also, for a different view, Coker, Book Review (1937) 46 *Yale Law Journal* 1096. I have developed this at greater length in *It Is Later Than You Think* (1938), pp. 6–13.

[42] "Against an unplanned and undirected industrialism, and its imminent hazards to life, liberty, and property, we have no constitutional rights. But thanks to John Locke—or to the thinkers, statesmen, warriors, business men, and jurists who put the punch in his words—we have adequate safeguards against the resort by any state to the kind of stuff the Stuart kings used to pull." Hamilton, "Property—According to Locke" (1932) 41 *Yale Law Journal* 864, 880.

guardians of the Constitution unless they approached it with detachment. We have somehow managed in our minds to place the judges above the battle. Despite every proof to the contrary, we have persisted in attributing to them the objectivity and infallibility that are ultimately attributes only of godhead. The tradition persists that they belong to no economic group or class; that they are not touched by economic interests; that their decisions proceed through some inspired way of arriving at the truth; that they sit in their robes like the haughty gods of Lucretius, high above the plains on which human beings swarm, unaffected by the preferences and prejudices that move common men.

There is a curious cult of judges that has grown up in America. President Taft, in the 1912 campaign, said with a trace of seriousness that he believed that Heaven got its quality from the judicial character.[43] No German bourgeois ever surrendered himself more completely to the commanding dignity of a *Geheimrat,* no pre-Soviet peasant ever bowed lower to the Czar's tax-collector, than we bow before the judicial symbol. Office-holding is, in a democratic state, at best a paradox: we seek after election day to invest with authority a man whom we have the day before impaled upon our invective as the blackest sort of scoundrel. In this sense, democratic government is a perpetual phoenix-renewal of the vigor and dignity of office that have only just now been consumed in the flames of party passion. Our experience with elected judges—with the state courts and with the whole army of lesser judicial stalwarts and mercenaries—has certainly not been such as to add to the stature of the judicial office they hold. For that reason the cult of judges and the belief in their neutrality are all the greater paradox.

It is partly explained by our association of judges with the "rule of law." But even more it springs from a deep need in us for some final authority. We are, in a sense, a barbaric people, only several generations removed from the wilderness psychology. The whole development of American life has been riddled with violence, from the first extermination of the Indians, through the ruthless rifling of a continent, to the use of spies and thugs against labor unions and the mowing down of gangster "mobs" under the fire of sub-machine guns. We live in fear of such violence, and our exag-

---

[43] "I love judges, and I love courts. They are my ideals, that typify on earth what we shall meet hereafter in heaven under a just God." Speech at Pocatello, Idaho.

gerated lip service to "law and order" and our cult of judges are functions of that fear. Most of us feel economically helpless in the midst of a ruthless exploitative capitalism; we feel alone in a vast impersonal urban civilization. We turn to "the law" as our final protection, and we read into the judges our hopes for someone who will be above the battle.

Most of us associate judges with the settlement of ordinary litigation, where political bias seems to us irrelevant; or with criminal trials, where the judge seems to sit as an avenging and impersonal deity, expressing through his function the sense and conscience of the community. What easier than to transfer this conception to the Supreme Court? Especially since there are four elements that seem to magnify the objectivity of the Supreme Court judges as compared with those of lower courts.

One is that they are in a "supreme" court, and presumably of some higher stature than ordinary mortals. The second is that they are appointed and not elected, and escape thus the grueling experience of a political campaign. The third is the greatness of the judicial tradition of the Supreme Court: some of our judges have actually been men of enormous ability; the fact that their ability has not been conspicuously in the direction of detachment is not generally known; what comes down to us is the almost Periclean devotion to their public trust shown by men like Marshall, Taney, and Holmes.[44] The fourth factor, and perhaps the most important, is that we transfer our sense of the definitive and timeless character of the Constitution to the judges who expound it. From our image of the Constitution as the ultimate wisdom in government, it follows that the men versed in its lore must reach their conclusions not by the paths of ordinary men, but by some mysterious and inspired processes. The judges become, thus, not ordinary men, subject to ordinary passions, but "discoverers" of final truth, priests in the service of a godhead.

---

[44] For a good analysis of this devotion, see Frankfurter, *The Commerce Clause under Marshall, Taney and Waite* (1937), which, although a small book, is crowded with insights into the psychological and historical character of the judicial process on the Supreme Court. There seems to be something about the judicial robes that not only hypnotizes the beholder but transforms the wearer; Marshall and Taney are the principal, but not the only, instances of men whose capacities for greatness no one suspected until they faced the crucial tasks of the Court.

IV. New Symbols for Old

The men who fashion America's symbols have, on the whole, wrought well with the Supreme Court symbol. They have used every material at the command of minorities of privilege when such minorities seek to protect their threatened dominance. They have controlled the newspapers, dictated the editorials, contrived the slogans, selected the textbooks, approved the lectures, filled the pulpits, guarded the microphones, spoken with learning and authority through their proper oracles, the lawyers. They have, perhaps, benefited most from the ministrations of the lawyers. For the lawyer, by the air of mystery in which he wraps himself, and by the impenetrable jargon he uses, is adept at the creation of symbols. The lawyer, moreover, as the expert technician in the refinements of corporate strategy, becomes the lieutenant of Big Enterprise, its closest adjunct in the whole range of professional groups. Most important of all, the lawyer—even more than the preacher and the professor—being specialized in persuasion and hypnosis, manages finally to persuade himself and induce a sort of self-hypnosis that makes him forever after a servitor of the propertied groups. And he is aided in this functioning by his special type of mentality which, as Jerome Frank has pointed out,[45] has its essence in the clinging to the symbols of authority.

The symbol-makers have, I repeat, wrought well. But recently two sets of forces have been at work undermining the fabric they have been at pains to build. One set has operated through our economic institutions themselves and through the cross-purposes inherent in them. The other has operated through the nature of the judicial process itself.

One consequence of industrialism is that it creates a climate in which a symbol has to be hardy to survive. There is an erosive power in the machine process which makes men think increasingly in matter-of-fact terms and before which legends tend to crumble away. Thorstein Veblen has pointed out that the technicians and operatives of machines, who spend their days in making, weigh-

---

[45] Frank, *loc. cit. supra* note 1. A good analysis will also be found in Robinson, *Law and the Lawyers* (1935), and in Berle, "The Modern Legal Profession" (1933) 9 *Encyclopaedia of the Social Sciences* 340.

ing, counting, measuring tangible things, are apt finally to be skeptical of intangible—or what he called "honorific"—values. But even more important is the instability of capitalism as a system of economic order. The successive crises of American capitalism have left their mark on the judicial power. And the history of the Supreme Court is a sequence of crises of the judicial power which have been related to the crises of the economic system. It is no accident that the gravest constitutional crisis should have coincided with the gravest economic crisis in our history, and that the key-figure in both should be the same President. And each crisis of the judicial power, each conflict with the democratic elements, weakens the judicial power and leaves its deposit for the next crisis to build upon.

This brings us to the second set of forces—those operating through the judicial power itself. Historians of the future will probably count it not the least important result of the Great Depression that it made Americans judge-conscious to a degree they had never been before. The setting of this new consciousness is to be sought in the sharp contradiction between economic collapse and the "trained incapacity" to deal with it of a political system hampered by judicial review. The judges were faced by a fateful choice between the freezing of the vested interests and the survival of the capitalist system—and when they chose the latter and turned "liberal," they revealed all too glaringly a very human changeableness. Moreover, although they had to think in legalistic terms, they had also to respond to social pressures, to the political threat of President Roosevelt's Court reorganization proposal, to such faits accomplis of the economic process as the success of the steel and automobile organization drives, which left little choice in the Wagner Act decisions. And for judges who were accustomed to talk in absolutes to act like any deliberative assembly through pressures and majorities was to forfeit their godhead.

These were the forces at work; the precipitation of these forces was accomplished by the judicial debate of 1937, which turned the eyes of the nation upon the judicial power. Men began to translate what they learned from watching the decisions into terms that had meaning in the debate over the reform of the judicial power. The most lasting result of the conflict between the New Deal and the Supreme Court was educational. There was a vast area in which

Americans had been politically untaught—the area of the judicial power.[46] A set of forces converging on the New Deal decisions accustomed them to regard the judges as interested in social policy and capable of changing their minds. The Supreme Court became its own bitterest enemy, and Mr. Justice Roberts an excellent schoolmaster whether he turned his face stonily toward the past, as in his decision in *United States v. Butler*,[47] or reluctantly toward the future, as in his vote in the Jones and Laughlin case.[48] Either way, Americans learned how the judicial power works.

They were no longer in complete innocence about the functioning of the judicial process. They began to see that judicial decisions are not babies brought by constitutional storks, but are born out of the travail of economic circumstance. They learned that judges are human, and that the judicial power need be no more sacred in our scheme than any other power. They learned, in their own way, that in America the real political sovereignty resides in the odd man on the Court.[49] But they learned also that the odd man cannot remain an isolated globule of individual desires and convictions, but must respond finally in moments of intense economic and constitutional crisis to the desires and convictions of the people and the facts of the national life. Whatever happens, it is not likely that they will easily forget that experience. If only for a moment, they peered beyond the symbol of the divine right of judges to the realities of the judicial power. They dared look upon the judicial Medusa-head, and lo! they were not turned to stone.

---

[46] Just as there was a vast area—that of federal regulation—in which they had been economically untaught. It was Mr. Roosevelt's historic function to serve, more or less consciously, as the instrument for both these tasks of national education. Just as under him Americans went a long way to unlearn their myth of individualist capitalism, and to accustom themselves both to federal regulatory action and to trade-union bargaining, so under him they took the biggest step they had ever taken in unlearning their allegiance to the judicial power.

[47] 297 U.S. 1 (1936).

[48] *National Labor Relations Board v. Jones & Laughlin Steel Corp.*, 57 Sup. Ct. 615 (1937).

[49] The theory of judicial decision as resting on the "odd man" owes more, I think, to Thomas Reed Powell than to anyone else in American legal thought. See, e.g., his remarkable articles, "Commerce, Pensions and Codes" (1935) 49 *Harvard Law Review* 1, 193. The theory holds validly enough for a period of extreme constitutional tension such as that of 1935–1937; it is less valid over longer periods; and it is always subject to the criticism that it splits up reality unduly into atoms. I have attempted a criticism of this and other atomistic explanations of the judicial process in "The Supreme Court and American Capitalism" (1933) 42 *Yale Law Journal* 668, especially at 696–701 (reprinted in my *Ideas Are Weapons* (1939) pp. 425–60).

Education such as this comes hard and is hard paid for. It comes with crises, economic and constitutional. Men are not moved to question their most deeply rooted and most skillfully publicized symbols except under enormous pressure and great need. Only then does the erosive power of their reason begin to function, and their myth-making processes turn to the future instead of the past. In the great need of economic crisis, the measures which were taken to relieve and temper that crisis met and were blocked by the judicial power. It was then that the symbol of divine right began to crumble.

> Thou wast not born for death, immortal Bird!
> No hungry generations tread thee down.

Thus wrote John Keats, addressing himself to the deathless symbol of the nightingale. But the Supreme Court is no deathless and unwavering symbol. If its evocative power declined during this period, as I believe it did, it was because it had done what no institution can do and remain unimpaired—stood between the hungry generations and the appeasement of their hunger, between Bill Jones and a minimal standard of decency in living.

I have spoken of hunger. There is fear also to consider.[50] And because of that, the fate of the judicial symbol, for all the erosive processes I have described, is far from clear. The ultimate power of the Supreme Court and the Constitution does not come wholly from the driving force of the vested interests, with all their external control over the molding of opinion. It comes from what is, in the last analysis, the strongest support any institution or tradition can have—namely, fear. I do not mean fear of the Court, fear of the judicial power, the fear one has of the whip-lash of tyrants. I mean the fear of not having Court and Constitution to fall back upon. I mean the terrible fear of change and the unknown, which is to so many people more powerful even than the felt needs and pressures

---

[50] The classic philosopher to make fear the psychological basis of state power was Thomas Hobbes. The best modern statement I know is Woolf, *Fear and Politics* (1925), probably the only instance in the literature in which a debate on political theory has its setting in a zoo. There is also a discussion in Wallas, *The Great Society* (1914) c. 6. I agree with Laski, however, that the motive to obedience in the state is by no means solely fear. "It may be doubted whether, save in times of passionate crisis, the vast majority of people ever think of fear in the contest of obedience to the law." Laski, *The State in Theory and Practice* (1935) 17. I have in mind not the (conscious) fear of state power, but the (largely unconscious) fear of the absence of state power.

of the day. For it is fear and not will that underlies a good part of our politics—the creeping fear of people who do not want to make decisions, and prefer to surrender their decisions to others.

This sort of womb-retreat is no unknown thing to social psychology. It is a phenomenon common in every period of reaction, and familiar enough in fascism.[51] It riddles the middle-class mind especially—the minds of those who have lost their secure economic roots in capitalism and have not yet found roots in the emerging collectivisms. We in America are just beginning now really to explore and understand the length and breadth and depth of the middle-class mentality in our politics—fear-ridden, standardized, negativist in its outlook, tenacious of symbols. For that mentality the Court's ancient sureness seems something not to be abandoned, lest we confront an uncharted future.

The propertied groups are not immune to fear, either. Their attitude toward constitutional law has in the past been on the whole coldly instrumental. "Every dominant class, as it has arisen," says Brooks Adams, "has done its best to use the machinery of justice for its own benefit." [52] The capitalists, as a dominant but minority group operating under democratic procedures, have used the Su-

---

[51] See, e.g., Schuman, *The Nazi Dictatorship* (1935); Lasswell, *World Politics and Personal Insecurity* (1935).

[52] Adams, *The Theory of Social Revolutions* (1913), quoted in 3 Parrington, *op. cit. supra* note 17, at 232. It is interesting that Mr. Justice Holmes, who came from much the same aristocratic social environment as Brooks Adams, should have arrived at results not very different from his, although by a different route. "This tacit assumption of the solidarity of the interests of society is very common, but seems to us false. . . . But in the last resort a man rightly prefers his own interest to that of his neighbors. . . . The more powerful interests must be more or less reflected in legislation; which, like every other device of man or beast, must tend in the long run to aid the survival of the fittest. The objection to class legislation is not that it favors a class, but either that it fails to benefit the legislators, or that it is dangerous to them because a competing class has gained in power, or that it transcends the limits of self-preference which are imposed by sympathy." "The Gas Stokers' Strike" (1873) 7 *American Law Review* 582, 583; reprinted in Shriver, *Justice Oliver Wendell Holmes: His Book Notices and Uncollected Letters and Papers* (1936) 104, 107–08. Holmes's view at that time was thus a curious approach to the Marxian concept, but arrived at through social Darwinism. Where Adams was far more realistic was in seeing that the dominant class ruled not by capturing the *legislative* machinery, as Holmes thought, but the entire *machinery of justice*—that is, the judicial system. Actually the legislative machinery, in a democracy like America, is more likely to be captured not by the dominant economic minority but by the non-propertied majority. But Holmes wrote the above in 1873, before judicial review as we know it had begun to be fully developed. Adams wrote forty years later, when it had reached its climax. A revaluation of the approach to law and legal history through economic interests is badly needed in American jurisprudence.

preme Court so long and so blindly for their own purposes that they have finally succeeded in undermining its strength and prestige. The spectacle of a presumably national symbol being twisted and turned to class interest has finally broken through even the barrage of rationalization. The capitalists find themselves thus faced with the prospect of losing their principal protection against the tyranny of the majority. And this they can ill afford to do. It is, says Nietzsche in one of his scorching passages,[53] a sign of the weakening of our ruling aristocracies that they hide behind constitutions, higher laws, humanitarian and judicial symbols; and much the same thought will be found in Pareto and his picture of the elites which do not have the stamina to defend themselves by force and so give way to new elites. The American capitalist elite is caught in a cruel dilemma. As a non-military ruling class it must depend for its protection upon the courts and the fabric of legality which it can control; as a group specialized to pecuniary values and bent upon maximizing profits and minimizing costs, it must twist the courts to its own purposes, defy laws openly when they are aimed at wresting a share of the national income from them, and thus break the very fabric of legality upon which they depend. Small wonder, then, that they are of a divided mind today; that the crumbling of the judicial symbol fills them with fear; that they do not contemplate with equanimity the prospects either of the gradual surrender of their economic power or of the adventure of fascism.[54]

Their fears, and the fears of the lower middle class, have as usual been communicated to the intellectuals—even to those liberated "liberals" who pride themselves on seeing through symbols. They, too, fear the breaking of the fabric of legality—a break which might result either in a revolutionary thrust from below or in a fascism imposed from above. We live, they feel, in a complicated and fragile civilization, where it is conceivable that a violent wrench

---

[53] Nietzsche speaks in *Beyond Good and Evil* (4th ed. Zimmern trans. 1923) 109–10, of "the moral hypocrisy of the commanding class" which "knows no other way of protecting themselves from their bad conscience than by playing the role of executors of older and higher orders, of predecessors, of the constitution, of justice, of the law, of God himself."

[54] Brooks Adams's comment in 1895 seems relevant today: "The only question which preoccupies the ruling class is whether it is cheaper to coerce or bribe." Adams, *The Law of Civilization and Decay* (1st ed. 1895) 292.

might send the whole structure toppling. What separates us from anarchy is principally the accumulated crust of convention, otherwise known as "law." Like the Britisher in the jungle who clings desperately to the amenities of London life, they are jealous of any infraction of law, especially of property law and constitutional law, which form the fabric of the capitalist order. If they yield an inch, they surrender all. They too are caught in a cruel dilemma. For intellectual groups have learned that revolutions and coups take place when a deadlock in the capitalist system makes democracy incapable of dealing with the continuing crisis of the capitalist system; that democracies remain paralyzed so long as they will the ends but do not will the means; and that the further Constitution and Court move from the realities of the common welfare, the more barren they become as symbols and fetishes—fetishes that could easily become in the end the rallying-points of movements to suppress liberal democracy, impose fascism, and stamp out the intellectual groups. Thus they too are divided: at once fearful of the crumbling of the American pattern of divine right, and yet disturbed at the way it functions.

With the lower-income groups the case is somewhat different. Their role—the role of the common man in every culture—has always been at once symbol-breaking and symbol-making. For the common man in the past the Constitution has been a symbol of hope and authority, and the judicial symbol one of protection. He has become the carrier of those symbols; to appease him and to lash down his allegiance to the existing order have been their functions. With insecurity and hunger, he has turned increasingly to the symbols of his more direct representatives—to legislative remedies, to executive action—above all, to trade-union organization. From the California lettuce-picker to the Pennsylvania steel-worker, from the Minnesota truck-driver to the Arkansas tenant-farmer, he has begun to scrutinize afresh the myths that stand between him and the satisfaction of his needs. Like the middle-class clerk, store-keeper, white-collar worker, farmer, intellectual, he is insecure and fearful, and insecurity is a breeding-ground for myths and symbols. But he differs from them in one important respect: the path he is treading in his quest for security in the economic system is the path that leads necessarily through new forms of social construction and therefore through the creation of new myths.

Thus the common man is again assuming his historic function of symbol-breaker and symbol-maker. Trade-union action, mass political action based upon common mass interests—these represent new collectivities. They are capable of building new myths and are on the way to doing so. But like the constitutional myth in our early years, they promise to be myths emotionally rooted not in fear but in hope, not in negation but in affirmation, not in clinging to the old but in a collective will to build the new; and economically rooted not in the class power of a minority group but in an expanding economy for the majority groups. If these groups succeed in their efforts to make out of the Constitution once more, in Corwin's phrase, an "instrument" for the common interest, the constitutional symbol will get renewed strength; but the path toward such a reshaping of the constitutional symbol lies necessarily through the decline and fall of the symbol of the divine right of judges.

These are the forces at work. What pattern they will fall into one cannot prophesy. One can, however, see in what is going on now in the American mind the ultimate struggle that is at the core of every human society—the thrust of hunger against the thrust of fear: fear, clinging to the old symbols, and looking toward the past; hunger, looking toward new economic constructions, reshaping old symbols, shaping new.[55]

1937

---

[55] Since the first publication of this essay, Kenneth Burke has included in his *Philosophy of Literary Form* (1941), pp. 104-5, a highly suggestive discussion of the extent to which a "ritual drama" pattern underlies the structure of my analysis. According to Burke, the central theme of my essay is "the symbolic slaying of the sacrificial king" of the judicial power. I am almost convinced. But Burke says that in "Act [section] 4," I move from the "dramatic" to the "naturalistic," in my discussion of hunger and fear as motives, and thus from social to biological co-ordinates. That too may be so, but a fusion of the dramatic with the naturalistic, the social with the biological, would seem desirable from the viewpoint of analysis, even if it disturbs the ritual drama.

3

Notes on the Supreme Court Crisis[1]

The Divine Right of Judges

A LONG view of the power of the Supreme Court is difficult to
achieve in the midst of immediate issues and angry passions.
But it would start with the fact that what the Court is doing
now, in smashing the best legislative efforts of the community, is no
novelty, just as the attacks on the Court are no novelty. It would try
to get at the nature, the psychological roots, and the economic consequences of the power of judicial review—presumably America's
most beautiful and original gift to the art of government.

Judicial review is a political device by which the Court passes on
the constitutional validity of legislative and executive acts. It
enables the judges to apportion powers between the states and the
national government, and between the legislative, executive, and
judicial branches. This is a power nowhere to be found expressly
granted in the Constitution itself. But it has by this time written
itself into the Constitution by Court interpretation, and although
only a custom it has become as commonly accepted as if it were
clearly granted in the document.

There are two opposing theories as to how the power grew up.
One is the usurpation theory. It goes back to Jefferson and is repeated afresh in every period of constitutional crisis. It holds that

---

[1] I have put together in this section several essays relating directly to the Supreme
Court crisis of 1933–1938. Some of these essays were written during this crisis and
some after it. There will be, accordingly, as the reader proceeds, a temporal shift
from present to past tense. I have made only very slight revisions, and have pre-
ferred to let the essays stand as published. For related material on the Supreme
Court, see my *Ideas Are Weapons* (1939), pp. 27–41, 54–116, 190–3, 228–34, 254–66,
425–83.

judicial review is sheer usurpation and that the Supreme Court has deliberately filched powers belonging to other departments. This point of view is generally highlighted with charges of tyranny that transport us back into the pages of Plutarch. The other is the Federalist view that the judicial power flows from the inherent nature of our federal system, and that without it our government would be unworkable and our democracy unthinkable.

I shall confess I cannot subscribe to either of these theories, although they both offer fragments of the final answer. It is true that there have been some men on our Court with a will to power. And it is true, on the other side, that given our federal-state governmental system, when both the states and the nation try to ride the same horse someone must finally decide who shall ride in front. But a clearer answer than either would be that the Court's power is a natural outcome of the necessity for maintaining capitalist dominance under democratic forms; that judicial review has proved to be a very convenient channel through which the driving forces of American economic life have found expression and achieved victory. Such a view could be documented by reference to the history of the judicial power since Marshall first established it in 1803 by his decision in *Marbury v. Madison*. The high points in the story would be Marshall's use of the judicial power to give enlarged scope to the expansion of business enterprise, the development of the doctrine of due process of law after the Civil War, and the reading of a laissez faire social philosophy into the Constitution in the decades around the turn of the century.

Today the Court is re-enacting the role it has always played whenever a resurgence of popular feeling has threatened to sweep away some of the established power of business enterprise. Nor has there been in all this any consistency of judicial doctrine or of political theory. When the people have gained control of the state legislatures, as happened in Marshall's day and in the decades of agrarian revolt, the Court has denied power to the states and concentrated it in the federal government. But when, as is true now, the people have captured the federal offices, then the Court denies power to the federal government and reserves it where it must be ineffective in the task of business regulation—with the state governments. The Republicans now find themselves amazingly the devoted adherents of states' rights, and the Democrats (shades of the Jeffersonian tradition!) are earnestly seeking to increase the national power.

There are several rather striking misconceptions today about the Court's power and function. One is that judges decide as they do because they can do no other—that they follow an inflexible path of constitutional doctrine. Only a little less remote from the truth is the second and opposite misconception—that the judges are un-trammeled in the expression of their own social attitudes and that they can play ducks and drakes with judicial precedent. What are actually the limits within which the Supreme Court has to work? It can decide only specific cases and not abstract questions—the case of the Schechter brothers,[2] for example, and how they sell their chickens—and out of those specific judgments the body of constitutional law grows up. Once a case is settled, however, a rule of law is established for future decisions, and every judge must abide by it (*stare decisis*) regardless of his previous views. The Court works, moreover, within a difficult technical tradition, under a limited jurisdiction, and with severe procedural regula-tions. Finally, its role with respect to legislation is negative and passive. It can initiate nothing of itself. But after you have said all that, the fact remains that the judge retains a great latitude of decision. On the same set of facts in the Hoosac case,[3] after hearing the same arguments and reading the same briefs, with the same body of precedent to draw on, possessed of the same degree of integrity and patriotism, Mr. Justice Roberts comes to one con-stitutional conclusion and Mr. Justice Stone to exactly the oppo-site one. What can explain this? Only the hypothesis that the judge works within limits and with material flexible enough to allow for personal choice. The *determining* factor becomes not some rigorous rule but the judge's own social philosophy. This in turn is shaped by his class roots, his education, his experience, and the elements in the contemporary climate of opinion to which he is responsive.

There is another misconception. We tend to believe that the Court shows its power only when it declares an act of Congress unconstitutional. Actually the Court has exercised this judicial veto only on some sixty occasions, many of them of slight moment.

---

[2] *Schechter v. U.S.*, 295 U.S. 495 (1935).
[3] *U.S. v. Butler*, 297 U.S. 1 (1936).

The judicial veto represents the outer limits of the Court's power. It shows how far that power can go. But usually the Court influences the shaping of an act even before it is passed, for the knowledge that the act will have to run the gantlet of judicial review is a sovereign acid for eating away features that the Court will predictably disallow. Once the act is passed it may be whittled into ineffectiveness (as happened with the anti-trust legislation) without any actual declaration of unconstitutionality, or the agency set up (like the Federal Trade Commission) may be crippled by Court interpretation without being destroyed outright. Thus the Court's power is broader and more continuous than the exercise of its veto. Even when it upholds legislation it is directing our economic life. The entire landscape of life as it is lived today by the common man is ultimately at the mercy of the Court's action or sufferance.

The essence of the Court's position in our system is that it takes problems that are primarily economic and clashes of interest that are economic, and translates them into terms of legal doctrine. It thus becomes the bottleneck of economic policy. I believe that is the one overwhelming fact that we must face today. As long as economic issues are fought out frankly as such, their solution lies with the people and with their representatives in the legislature. But when economic issues are translated into legalistic terms, when the question of the fate of the farmers and workers and housewives and working children becomes a matter of hosts of none-too-angelic lawyers dancing on the needle of due process of law, then the big electoral battalions are left helpless. If we face it clearly, looking beyond the tangle of our traditional usages, the question of what we shall do with our farms and our factories is not ultimately a question for lawyers or judges to settle. It is a question of economic and social policy. To allow our economic policy to be shaped by the judges is wrong whichever way you look at it. If they decide, as is often asserted, on purely legal grounds, then those are the *wrong grounds* on which to decide questions of economic policy. If they decide, as is sometimes admitted, on economic and social grounds, then they are the *wrong people* to be entrusted with decisions on these grounds, for they are judicial and not economic technicians.

In passing thus on economic policy the Supreme Court has

throughout our history functioned as the last bulwark of the possessing classes. It has always been a final line of defense for them, a sort of Hindenburg line that would stand fast when all else crumbled. Beaten at the polls, in danger of having the economic institutions of a plutocracy leveled by the political forces of a democracy, the defeated group has always turned to the Court for shelter and has found it in the safe haven of constitutional law. Jefferson discovered this fact when he and his party of small farmers and mechanics turned the Federalist propertied interests out of Congress and the Presidency in 1800, only to find them dug in again behind the earthworks of the Court. Jackson discovered it in the 1830's, Lincoln in the 1850's, the agrarian leaders in the eighties and nineties, the Progressives such as La Follette and Theodore Roosevelt as the century ended. And now Mr. Roosevelt is discovering it afresh. It seems to be the fate of American reformers to conduct their education in public.

Each of these men sought to attack the Court. In no case has the Court's power been successfully limited. What accounts for this extraordinary toughness and viability of the Court? Each attack on the judicial power in America has been not merely an unaccountable bit of behavior of the democratic mass. It has been the expression, in constitutional terms, of the inability of our state to adjust its own power relations and resolve its own contradictions. And for that reason each successive crisis of the judicial power has taken its color, its substance, its tension from the contemporary stage of the struggle of economic groups and classes. That is happening today too. And today, as in the past, the Court will survive the attack on it, not because of any inherent rightness in the judicial power, but because the larger number of our people still have a sense of the sanctity of the Court.

There are several elements in this pattern of divine right as it exists in the popular mind.[4] One is the fact that we have been encouraged for more than a century to make a fetish of the Constitution. The second is the belief that the Supreme Court is the special guardian of the Constitution—and a better guardian than Congress or the President. This the judges, from John Marshall on, have encouraged by their continued utterances, and it has become

---

[4] The paragraph that follows is a brief summary of section 3, "Divine Right: American Plan," of my essay "Constitution and Court as Symbols," above, p. 249.

the official theory of the Court's power. The judges have thus been associated in our minds with the function of protection rather than with the struggle for power. The third element has been the tradition of judicial neutrality. We have somehow placed the judges above the battle. Despite every proof to the contrary the common man attributes to them the objectivity and infallibility that are ultimately attributes only of godhead. The tradition persists that they belong to no economic group or class; that they are not touched by economic interests; that their decisions proceed through some inspired way of arriving at the truth; that they sit in their robes like haughty gods, unaffected by the prejudices that move common men.

How long a myth built of such baseless fabric can continue is another matter. It is undoubtedly weakening and may be expected in the end to crumble. Meanwhile, however, its force and its hold on the popular mind are enough to daunt Mr. Roosevelt and keep him from making an open attack on the Court's power. In the end it will not be the Roosevelts who will restore to the popular will the power of deciding on economic issues. The Supreme Court may be expected to be its own bitterest enemy. Even the myth of the divine right of judges will not survive many more decisions like Mr. Justice Roberts's masterly essay in obfuscation in the Hoosac case.

1936

The Lawless Majority

NOTHING is clearer in Washington today [5] than that the Supreme Court justices are at sixes and threes. The personal tension among them is no mere accident of individual temperament or will. One of the marks of constitutional crisis is the sharpening of differences on the Court.

During the preliminary skirmishes on the New Deal legislation the Court seemed to fall into three loose groups. The most cohesive was that of the four "diehard" conservatives—Justice Van Devanter, Justice McReynolds, Justice Sutherland, Justice Butler. At the opposite extreme were the three "liberals"—Justice Brandeis, Justice

---

[5] 1936.

Stone, and Justice Cardozo. That left a "balance-of-power" group
of two—Chief Justice Hughes and Justice Roberts. It was these two
who by their vacillations sent the judicial fever chart of the New
Deal careening from high to low. As the sense of economic panic
decreased and the political tension increased, the three groups became two. The bitterness of the diehard judges reached such a
pitch that they became completely indistinguishable from Liberty
Leaguers. The liberals suspended whatever differences of economic
philosophy they had, and even grew critical of the inherent abuses
of the judicial power itself. The balance-of-power pair, after a somewhat indecent flirtation with the liberals in the Minnesota moratorium case and the Nebbia milk-control case, were finally forced
to make a definite choice. They could not continue to commute between two worlds. Nor could they, when the heavens were falling,
merely stand aloof and murmur, "A plague on both your houses."
Whatever may have been their previous constitutional waverings,
they threw in their lot with the diehards and chose the side of the
intrenched order. The Supreme Court is now two armed camps
confronting each other.

To the believers in the judicial power, this is of course distressing. It is not so much that the Court fails to present the serried ranks
of a united front. Since the days when John Marshall held the Court
under his hypnotic sway, no united front has been possible except
sporadically. What is distressing is that a persistent series of six-
to-three decisions will weaken the prestige of the Court. When justices divide with a monotonous uniformity, even the hardened
believer in divine right may feel that the Constitution is curiously
unclear for so compelling a document.

When the crisis was most desperate it seemed for a time that
the Court might join the colors in the war against the depression.
Among the brilliant young lawyers who flocked to Washington
there was an amazingly sanguine view that the New Deal would
prove constitutional. It seems surprising now that anyone should
ever have thought we could have a drastic dislocation of our economic life, with all the desperate efforts at economic control that
it entailed, without having a constitutional dislocation as well. With
the advantage of hindsight we glimpse today what the relation of

the Supreme Court is to capitalist crisis. At the period of greatest panic and despair the Court is likely to sanction heroic remedies. Enough liberals and balance-of-power judges can be mustered who have the wisdom to see that capitalist survival would be impossible without a summary use of the federal power. But it is only when the economic crisis itself has eased, and business enterprise has recovered from its mortal anguish, that the real constitutional crisis comes. The old taboos against government control are reasserted. The Court seeks to prevent the country from making the new measures of control permanent, and so from paying too high a price for survival. The liberals on the Court find themselves isolated. The balance-of-power judges find it is no longer necessary to be liberal. The conservatives give every indication that in them is the grace confessed, if not the mercies multiplied.

To trace the career of the New Deal in the Court is to describe the rise and fall of a felt need. In 1933, before the New Deal legislation was passed, Chief Justice Hughes speaking for the Court took judicial notice of the depression. That was in the Appalachian coal case.[6] In the Minnesota mortgage-moratorium case, in January 1934, Justice Hughes read a five-to-four decision upholding the government.[7] In March the same Court majority, speaking now through Justice Roberts in the Nebbia case, upheld price-fixing by the New York State milk-control board.[8] The Panama (hot-oil) case [9] represented the first break. But the case turned on delegation of powers and administrative carelessness rather than on the substance of the legislation; and the next cases—the gold-clause cases [10]—reassured those who had grown anxious. There Chief Justice Hughes seemed to go out of his way in unusually tortuous reasoning to save the financial stability of the government and uphold its contentions. This augured well, and Justice McReynolds's dramatic outburst in the courtroom, when he warned that the Constitution had been scrapped, seemed merely to be an elegy over an order that was dead. It was then that the really ominous decision came—the five-to-four opinion against the government, read by Roberts in

---

[6] *Appalachian Coal, Inc. v. U.S.*, 288 U.S. 344 (1933).

[7] *Home Building and Loan Assn. v. Blaisdell*, 290 U.S. 398 (1934).

[8] *Nebbia v. N.Y.*, 291 U.S. 502 (1934).

[9] *Panama Refining Co. v. Ryan; Amazon Petroleum Corp. v. Ryan*, 293 U.S. 389 (1935).

[10] *Norman v. Baltimore and Ohio R.R. Co.*, 294 U.S. 240 (1935), and related cases.

the railroad-retirement case.[11] This opinion, when compared with Justice Roberts's earlier Nebbia opinion, measured the judicial crack-up of the New Deal. After that, of course, came the Schechter brothers, the Hoosac mills, the rice processors' case, and a brood that threatens to lengthen out into the future.

There is a measure of truth in the contention that if the crucial New Deal measures—NRA and AAA—had come before the Court sooner, they would have fared differently. The timing was undoubtedly bad, and time was the heart of the matter. And yet the President had able lawyers among his advisers, some of whom may have felt, along with General Johnson, that the NRA should be given time to become an effectively functioning mechanism before it ran the gantlet. Meanwhile, however, the crisis tension was passing. If the cases had been pushed earlier they might have been validated. If they had been declared unconstitutional early enough President Roosevelt would have had behind him a vast force of opinion for any attack he might make on the judicial power.

Such reasoning, however, does not go far enough. When the economic tension was finally eased, the Court would have found little difficulty in retracing its steps. The crux of the constitutional impasse today is that any permanent extension of the federal power would be regarded by concentrated wealth as a decisive threat to its dominance. The constitutional crisis might have been delayed; it could scarcely have been eliminated.

The overwhelming issue today is whether we shall have a power in the federal government that can meet and cope with the concentration of economic power in our society.

This question really involves something like a three-ring circus. It involves first what we may call *the area of economic activity,* which has moved from independent farming and petty trade to the scale of the giant corporation. It involves, secondly, *the area of government control* of that economic activity. It involves, finally, *the area of judicial tolerance*—the extent to which the Supreme Court will allow government control. While the first is part of the inevitable sweep of the machine process, and the second has responded to waves of democratic feeling, the last is unlimited except as it may limit itself. In the now famous words of

---

[11] *Retirement Board v. Alton R.R. Co.,* 295 U.S. 330 (1935).

Justice Hughes, spoken while he was still Governor of New York and therefore relatively irresponsible, "We are under a Constitution, but the Constitution is what the judges say it is." [12]

What has happened since the eighties is that government control on the plane of state units has grown increasingly irrelevant. While the Court has through most of its history been intolerant of state control, and fought it especially through the doctrine of due process of law, Justices Holmes and Brandeis succeeded in developing a persuasive philosophy of judicial toleration. Holmes was for allowing experiments in "the insulated chambers afforded by the several states." Brandeis was for giving the decisive weight to the legislative history of an act and the social context in which it was placed. But such philosophies are now less applicable. We have an economic system that can be run successfully or curbed effectively only on a national plane.

We must face the fact that the area of government control today must coincide with the area of economic activity. Since one is on a national scale, so must the other be. Industry is not contained within state lines. Mining, manufacturing, transportation, communication, labor, finance—all constitute an unbroken industrial chain flung out over a national market. Moreover, industry not only operates on a national scale, but its power is national in its magnitude and concentration. And when our economic system breaks down, it can be restored only by governmental action on a national scale. In fact, whether the economic system is functioning or threatening or in collapse, the states as the principal regulatory agencies are now anachronisms.

Can we achieve genuine control on the plane of the federal power? The answer that the Court is spelling out, in one grim decision after another, increasingly dooms the federal power. But there is something even more important than to grasp the answer—and that is to grasp the fact that it is not the only possible answer the Court could give. "That is not law," said a trial judge to Daniel Webster. "It *was* until you spoke, Your Honor," answered Webster. Each time that the Supreme Court has spoken since Justice Roberts's fatal decision in the railroad-retirement case, something that had been law ceased to be law. Each time some path that might

---

[12] *Addresses and Papers of Charles Evans Hughes* (1908), p. 139.

have led toward an adequate federal power was blocked or hopelessly rutted. When Justice Holmes once stated that "hard cases
make bad law" [13] he was looking ahead into 1935 and 1936 with
amazing clairvoyance. The general run of cases that come before
the Court are fairly clear. They involve usually the extension of an
old rule to a new instance. They do not involve lengthy opinions,
bitter dissents, personal tension among the justices, counsel on the
point of collapse, and an agitated country. The New Deal cases
have been "hard cases"—where novel issues are raised, or where
the familiar issues are pushed so far that they seem to change their
character.

The New Dealers relied on three Congressional grants of power
in order to have the courts decide the "hard cases" in their favor.
One is the power of Congress to regulate commerce, the second is
its taxing power, the third (closely related to the second) is its spending power.

The commerce power was the most relied on for vaulting into
the heaven of federal control. There was a strong tradition of liberal interpretation of the commerce power, and it did not need
much stretching to make it adequate for industrial control. The
tendency toward a broad construction, as Professor Corwin has
shown, became marked under the influence of Holmes and Taft,
starting with the Swift case in 1905.[14] The Court had accepted the
regulation of the meat-packing industry and of the grain-futures
exchanges as coming within the scope of the commerce clause. The
only real stumbling-block was *Hammer v. Dagenhart* (1918), the
first child-labor case, which held invalid a federal act forbidding
the shipment of the products of child labor in interstate commerce.
The Court has, in interpreting the term "commerce," fluctuated
between restricting it severely to physical transportation and expanding it to mean anything essential to the functioning of the
economic mechanism. In interpreting the term "regulate" it has
at times restricted it to the Hamiltonian sense of fostering and aiding commerce, and at times ventured into the more militant sense
of subjecting it to government restraint. Accordingly, when the
Court in the railroad-retirement case and again in the Schechter

---

[13] "Great cases, like hard cases, make bad law." Justice Holmes, dissenting, in
U.S. v. Northern Securities Co., 193 U.S. 197 (1904).
[14] *Swift and Co. v. U.S.,* 196 U.S. 375 (1905).

NRA case adopted the narrow view of the commerce power, it was a deliberate choice of the less liberal among alternative lines of precedent.

When the commerce power had been blocked, the new white hopes became the taxing power (under the general-welfare clause) and the power of making appropriations. Both were clearly and deeply intrenched in American constitutional history—in the history of legislative practice and in that of judicial interpretation. To have overturned these powers directly would have meant a judicial revolution. The only real precedent that the government had reason to fear was the child-labor tax case (or the second child-labor case) [15] in which, after the Court in *Hammer v. Dagenhart* had held an attempt to regulate child labor invalid under the commerce power, Congress sought to accomplish the same regulation by imposing a tax on the products of child labor. As is well known, the Court, when confronted by the problem of the taxing and spending powers in the Hoosac case,[16] tried the flank attack. It studiously avoided passing directly upon the scope of the general-welfare clause or of the spending power. It insisted that the purpose of the act was the federal regulation of agriculture, that under the Tenth Amendment this was reserved to the states, and that Congress could not assume such a regulatory function under the guise of taxing the processors or making appropriations for the farmers. While legally a loophole was left open for the use of the taxing and spending powers (if such a use refrains from being coercive), the practical effect of reasoning from the Tenth Amendment would seem to be a flat, clear, and positive judicial prohibition of attempts to use these powers for regulatory purposes.

I know that it is a paradox and also lèse majesté to speak of the Supreme Court as lawless. And yet, if the meaning of the word be properly understood, the conviction is overwhelming that the Supreme Court majority as at present (1936) constituted represents the most lawless force in American life.

I can only list the counts in the most summary fashion. First, in economic terms, the present course of decision can only lead us to economic chaos. By denying the federal government the power to

---

15 *Bailey v. Drexel Furniture Co.*, 259 U.S. 20 (1922).
16 See note 3, above.

deal on a national plane with the problems of economic control, the Court is doing more to weaken the American economic structure than all the allegedly subversive radical parties in the country. But it is accomplishing more than a blocking of the federal power in the name of states' rights. By a process familiar in our judicial history, which we may without loss of dignity call the "two-way stretch," it is also blocking the state power of economic control. The same session which saw the Hoosac decision saw the decision in the Vermont income-tax case and the North Dakota tax-commission case. The result is to cripple both state and federal control, leave the public interest in a dark no man's land, and leave business enterprise itself at the mercy of the forces of collapse.

To economic chaos must be added administrative anarchy. It is not only that the Supreme Court's animus against legislative control is encouraging the lower federal courts to grant injunctions generously and give free rein to their inherent conservatism. Something even more serious is presented in the Court's ruling in the rice millers' case.[17] With a reckless disregard of administrative consequences, the Court in effect placed a premium on refusal to pay taxes. Those who do not pay but seek injunctive relief may have their taxes impounded in court and eventually returned to them. This would effectively sabotage any administrative set-up, no matter how good.[18]

More strictly within the judicial realm are two other matters. One relates to the Court's cavalier treatment of established and fairly clear precedent, as pointed out earlier in the article. The other relates to the departure from the tradition of constitutional law which holds that if a case can be disposed of on narrow or procedural grounds, the larger issues ought not to be raised. If this tradition had been followed, much havoc might have been avoided in the interpretation of the commerce power. For some reason the Court seems anxious to look ahead and pass on the large and impending constitutional issues. The result is a needlessly rapid and savage rate of legislative destruction.

Finally, there is a lawlessness involved in the Court's being a law

17 *Rickert Rice Mills v. Fontenot,* 297 U.S. 110 (1936).

18 Eventually Congress provided that taxes be refunded only to the extent that the processors could show they had not passed the tax on. This was upheld in *Anniston Mfg. Co. v. Davis,* 301 U.S. 337 (1937). And later still the second AAA was upheld in *Mulford v. Smith,* 307 U.S. 38 (1939), turning on the commerce power.

to itself. Justice Stone, in his brilliant Hoosac dissent, charged the majority with assuming an arbitrary and irresponsible power, subject to no restraint except their own self-restraint. In a supposedly democratic state, based on the separation of powers, this is the height of lawlessness.

1936

The Fate of the Supreme Court

IN THE halcyon days before the Schechter decision Professor Corwin of Princeton had the courage to write a book under the title *The Twilight of the Supreme Court*. He said that the Court was on its way to a dignified but ineffectual old age, and that its sun was setting. The book was a good book and a learned book. It was well reasoned, and its conclusion should have been a sound one. But scarcely was the ink dry on its pages when the Court handed down the first of its series of hostile decisions on the Roosevelt legislation. Instead of subsiding into twilight, it shone forth with the blaze of noonday strength.

The moral is, I suppose, that it is always bad policy to compose a man's obituary before he is for certain dead. Yet Professor Corwin was less wrong than would appear. During the next decade or more the power of the Supreme Court will undoubtedly be challenged as never before. But if there is a decline in the Court's power it will not come about by any gentle slipping into euthanasia. It will come about only after a stiff fight. There are any number of evidences that the fight has already begun. The Court is now entering its iron age.[19]

Proposals for dealing with the Court have been thick as blackberries. They have come from professional and amateur constitutionalists of every kind. They fall into three general groups: the remedial proposals, those looking toward a Congressional curb on the Court's power, and those looking toward a constitutional amendment.

The first group, the remedial, implies the existence and desira-

---

[19] In his *Constitutional Revolution, Ltd.* (1941) Corwin notes dryly that, when his earlier book appeared, "some impatient critics were disposed to scoff at the prophecy implied when it was not realized overnight" (p. 108).

bility of the Court's power. They are more concerned with lopping off the excrescences of that power than with challenging it. Perhaps the simplest proposal is that of a eugenic program for the Court. Just as the vitality of the race is held by some to depend on selective breeding and thus getting the right babies, so the proper functioning of the judicial power is held to depend on getting the right judges. And that of course goes back to getting the right Presidents, who will appoint the right judges, who will in turn render the right decisions. This view, of course, sees judicial decisions as almost entirely a matter of the personnel of the Court. Everything depends on the individual judge. In this sense, such a view is too optimistic. Individual judges are themselves products: their minds and their direction have been shaped by the dominant institutional forces of our life. Another difficulty is that getting the right President does not seem to insure getting the right judge. Examine the present composition of the Court and you will find that Justice Brandeis, leader of the liberals, and Justice McReynolds, the most inveterate tory of them all, were appointees of President Wilson. Justices Roberts and Cardozo, confronting each other in opposite judicial trenches, were appointees of President Hoover.[20]

More drastic than the pious hope that better justices will be appointed is the movement for advisory opinions. At present a law is enacted, administrative machinery is set up to enforce it, taxes are levied, government and business expenditures are made on the strength of it, men are set to work—only to have the Court, in passing finally on a specific case, declare the whole thing unconstitutional. The proposal for advisory opinions would have Congress get from the judges their opinion on the constitutionality of a projected law before it has come into force and economic interests have become entangled with it. The great merit of this proposal is that it would do away with our present uncertainties. And one of the refreshing things about it is that, like the child in the Hans Christian Andersen tale, it innocently announces the nakedness of the king. It recognizes frankly that the Court is a third legislative chamber, and insists that since this is so we ought to know the fate of our legislation as quickly as possible.

---

20 I should nevertheless add that President Roosevelt's appointments, from Justice Black through Justice Jackson, have all been in the liberal direction. Justice Byrnes is still an unknown quantity.

But for that very reason the proposal runs counter to the entire tradition of the Court. That tradition is the tough, concrete tradition of Anglo-Saxon case law, in which the individual case has to bear the freightage of weighty issues. An issue of constitutional law does not arise until a specific case has arisen that involves it. Until then the heavens may fall, but the Court knows no generalizations and will give no advice. Its wisdom is a pragmatic one. There is a good deal to be said in support of this approach. The true meaning of a law is not to be found in the bare statute. The statute must take root, like a tree, in the soil of actual circumstance, it must bear a leafage of functioning and consequence before it can be seen as a reality. "How do we know what we think," the judges may ask, "until we see how things work out?"

The proposal from the liberal members of the Court is the exact opposite of advisory opinions—namely, judicial self-limitation. This tries to carry the implications of case law all the way. It denies that the Court has anything to do with legislation directly, and insists that the judges must restrict themselves to the narrowest issues in the cases that arise. Judicial self-limitation of this sort was an integral part of Justice Holmes's entire philosophy of judicial tolerance. It is part also of Justice Brandeis's philosophy that a case cannot be torn out of its context—and that context includes the impulsions to the legislation, its consequences, and the entire economic and procedural history of the case itself. Judicial self-limitation has always been given some lip service by the Court, as in the rule that the judges will consider no "moot" cases, nor any cases raising only "political questions" (blessedly vague phrase). The deliberately adopted strategy of Justices Brandeis, Stone, and Cardozo at present is to push this form of judicial hara-kiri much further. It has found its best expression in Justice Stone's dissent in the Hoosac case, Justice Cardozo's dissent in the Mayflower Farms case, and Justice Brandeis's concurring opinion in the TVA case. These opinions not only made the general plea of judicial restraint (in Justice Stone's words, "The only check upon our own exercise of power is our own sense of self-restraint") but pointed out the two directions in which it is to be exercised: always passing on as few issues as the Court can get away with, and always giving the legislation the benefit of any reasonable doubt.

It may well be asked how dependable such a method is in solving the problem of the Court's power. It involves not only the selection of extraordinary judges who will be willing to limit their own power. It involves the shaping of a new method, a new mood and temper, a new conception of the scope of the Court's power. And to achieve changes in the midst of the present social tensions is a heroic task. The Court has never operated in a social vacuum. It has always been an integral part of the social struggles of every period in our history. It has taken its temper from the prevailing ideology of an aggressive individualist capitalism. It has been part of the fiber of a culture dominated by business enterprise. It is too much to expect the Court to generate a new humility now. The whole idea of judicial humility is strikingly like the plight of the gigantic Ferrovius in Shaw's *Androcles and the Lion,* whose powerful frame shakes with all the passions of a healthy beast, yet whose Christian principles bid him stay his hand whenever it is raised to strike. How can a Court cultivate this sort of humility when issues are at stake throughout our national life that touch the justices as much as they touch anyone else? That may account for the fact that, despite the perilous health of several of the justices—in both the liberal and conservative camps—there is no sign of any intention of resigning. They are holding on for dear life, lest someone take their place who views liberty and property differently.[21]

I have mentioned the remedial proposals at some length partly because it is unlikely that we shall get anything more than that in the immediate future, partly because they go to the heart of the problem of the judicial power. But the most discussed proposals are the group that seek directly to curb the Court's power. These are the proposals that rouse Liberty Leaguers to the highest pitch of fury. But they are not new. Although they have never been advanced in such profusion until this year, they have cropped up periodically when the Court was under attack.

The simplest way to curb the Court would seem to be to "pack" it. Congress has undisputed power to determine the size of the Court. In Jackson's Administration the number of judges was increased from seven to nine in order to counterbalance the influence of the Marshall tradition. Under Lincoln, during the Civil War,

---

21 It is worth noting that the present Court (1941) is following the principle of judicial self-limitation; but it is a new Court, with a new majority and a new spirit.

the Court was conveniently increased to ten, to make it safe for the war powers of the President. There seems to be ample proof that Grant packed the Court in order to get a favorable decision on the Legal Tender cases.[22] This is a technique that Mr. Roosevelt might have used if an unfavorable NRA decision had come down earlier than it did, while the country was still under the spell of the New Deal; and especially if the Court had been closely divided on the issue. Now such a procedure would be fruitless—and what is more, impossible with a campaign pending.[23] Eventually of course an Administration with enough temerity may do what the liberals did in England to the House of Lords—threaten the creation of so many new justices that under the threat the Court would yield up some of its power.

The most frequent suggestion for a judicial curb is to regulate not the number on the Court but the manner of their voting. It would provide that a majority of the justices is not enough to invalidate an act of Congress. Some number such as seven or eight or more than two-thirds of the Court is usually suggested. The obvious answer is of course that, granted the existence of the judicial power, this would leave the decision on constitutionality in the hands of one or two justices. The answer to that answer is that just such an event is intended: that since you can usually count on one or two justices who will vote on the side of Congress, this leaves the decision on economic issues where it belongs—with Congress and the President. Another device, intended to have somewhat the same effect, would be to provide that unfavorable Court decisions could be overruled by a two-thirds vote of Congress. Still another would be to abolish entirely, by Congressional action, the Court's right to invalidate acts of Congress; or to take certain types of cases or certain issues of legislation out of the jurisdiction of the Court.

About all these the same three questions arise. Are they constitutional? Would they be effective? Could they be accomplished? A strong case could be made out, on the basis of precedent, that Congress has the power to set the conditions under which the Su-

---

[22] See Sidney Ratner, "Was the Supreme Court Packed by President Grant?" in the *Political Science Quarterly*, 1935, vol. 50, pp. 343–58. But see also Charles Fairman's more recent article, "Mr. Justice Bradley's Appointment to the Supreme Court and the Legal Tender Cases" (54 *Harvard Law Review* 977, 1128), which reaches a different conclusion.

[23] This was written before the Presidential campaign of 1936. Mr. Roosevelt's reorganization proposal followed his re-election.

preme Court shall function, and that such a power would include the regulation of its number, voting, jurisdiction. The supreme irony of the whole situation is of course that whether Congress has such a power would have to be finally decided by the Court itself. And it is very unlikely that, given the present temper of the Court and the present tension of the country, the Court would be willing to sign its own death warrant. If it did, some such proposal would seem an eminently desirable one.

One proposal for dealing with the Court's power that has the amazing distinction of being favored by both sides is the amending process. The liberals and radicals want it because it seems to them a fundamental attack on the whole problem. The conservatives do not object to it because they do not really think an amendment has any chance of being adopted. The idea is therefore one calculated to assuage them in their present constitutional agony, and postpone a reckoning to the dateless future.

The questions that have been most often raised as to what form a constitutional amendment would take seem to me comparatively unimportant. We are not lacking in the political inventiveness and legislative draftsmanship adequate to solve the problem. More serious is the question whether the Court will not interpret away any amendment, no matter how skillfully and shrewdly drawn, just as it has interpreted away many a statute in the past. But most serious of all are the issues of power. An amendment giving Congress the right to legislate on all issues affecting agriculture, industry, labor, and finance on a national scale would be so direct a path to the control of business enterprise by the state that it would meet the massed force of opposition from business enterprise. What lengths that opposition would go to it is now difficult to say. But it is clear that such an amendment could be carried through only as part of a larger movement not only to curb the Court's power but to establish a controlled economy. Such a movement involves a greater degree of organization of the productive groups in our society than has yet been achieved, and a new political alignment. Into it the best democratic energies of the country will be poured. The Court and the country are both entering on an iron age. The struggles of that age will determine whether the promise of American life can be made constitutional.

1936

The Supreme Court Revolution

HISTORIANS will describe the Supreme Court term which has just ended [24] as crucial in the history of both Court and country. With the quickening pace and tension of social change, "periods" in the Court's history are now shorter than they have ever been. In the six years since 1932 we have witnessed the following periods: the tendency to construe governmental power broadly in the midst of depression, the sharp swing against the New Deal, the reorganization battle, and the present liberal trend.

This is no place for a detailed discussion of the past term's achievements. Briefly they fall under four heads. The first and most important, despite the efforts of the tory press to play down their significance, are the labor decisions. From its sensational reversal of itself in the Washington minimum-wage case [25] over a year ago up to the most recent order in the Republic Steel case, the Court has given judicial sanction to a new legal framework in which labor can carry on. The decisions have completely upheld the NLRB, cut the ground from under the attack on the board's personnel and methods, and placed the designers of the Girdler-Ford resistance to the Wagner Act in a humiliating position. The second important series of cases was the tax decisions. While less sharp than the labor decisions both in their formulation and in their consequences, these showed the Court moving toward a firmer assertion of the federal taxing power and toward a whittling away of unsocial tax immunities. Thirdly, the Court upheld the New Deal on a scattering of fronts—in allowing PWA loans for the construction of municipal power plants; [26] in upholding, in the Electric Bond and Share case, the registration of public-utility holding companies with the SEC; [27] in affirming the municipal bankruptcy act; [28] in fighting off attacks on government monetary policy in three new gold-clause cases; and in strengthening the anti-trust drive, the Federal Power Commission, and the Home Owners' Loan Corporation. Finally, in a series of rate-valuation cases, the Court, while still in

---

[24] 1938.
[25] *West Coast Hotel Co. v. Parrish,* 300 U.S. 379 (1937).
[26] *Alabama Power Co. v. Ickes,* 302 U.S. 464 (1938).
[27] *Electric Bond and Share v. SEC.,* 303 U.S. 419 (1938).
[28] *U.S. v. Bekins,* 304 U.S. 27 (1938).

considerable confusion, has shown a movement toward the liberal doctrine of prudent-investment cost.

Much of this has been given in newspaper and Sunday-section summaries, which do not weary of relating to their readers their discovery of the new Supreme Court liberalism. Other aspects of the past term of the Court have also received publicity—the dispute over Justice Black's competence, for example, and the tilt between Secretary Wallace and Chief Justice Hughes over the powers of administrative boards.

What has been less noticed is the meaning of the doctrinal struggle now going on within the Court's own ranks. A "new left" has emerged in the decisions of Justice Black, reaching further in its implications even than the "new left" of Justice Brandeis in 1916. Justices Brandeis, Stone, Cardozo, and Reed represent a social liberalism sharply defined against the reactionary background of the Court's tradition or the grudging "liberalism" of Justices Hughes and Roberts, but primarily they have aimed at a decent amount of judicial restraint and self-limitation. This is an excellent principle when contrasted with the history of the Court's previous thirst for power. So, also, is the present majority's courage in over-ruling past decisions, which was revealed most dramatically in *Erie Railroad Company v. Tompkins,*[29] where the Court declared it had been wrong for nearly a century on the question of recognizing the construction of common law by state courts.

But the weakness of this attitude is that it is negative and belated. It lacks the clear-cut and affirmative outlines of a fighting faith which can keep pace with changes in governmental power. Such a faith has emerged in Justice Black's opinions. The real doctrinal struggle within the Court is no longer one between a "broad" and a "strict" construction of federal power. The Supreme Court revolution has, at least for the present, decided that struggle in favor of the broad construction. What we have now is a struggle between a negative and an affirmative attitude toward the process of governmental activity, between two views as to the pace of social change. This struggle is best illustrated in Justice Black's dissent from the *per curiam* opinion in the Indianapolis Water Company case, in which he sought to get for once a sharp definition of the Court's attitude on rate valuation in public-utility cases in

---

[29] 304 U.S. 64 (1938).

place of its traditional floundering in a bog of metaphysics.[30] It is illustrated also by the contrast between Justice Stone's opinion and Justice Black's dissent in the New York Port Authority tax case, in which Stone sought to narrow the base of the Court's opinion as far as was consistent with his liberalism, while Black called boldly for a declaration that the Sixteenth Amendment meant what it said.

It is here that the real meaning of Justice's Black's much-discussed dissents lies. Leafing through the Court records for the term, one is impressed by the courage, integrity, and consistency of his position. He has proved himself potentially the most significant figure for the future of the Court. His position corresponds, in terms of constitutional doctrine, to the emergence of a militant left-democratic and labor movement and its bid for continued national power.

But another revolutionary cycle in the Court's history is beginning. What we have at present is a breathing spell in constitutional politics. Constitutional crises are not made by judges alone. They emerge out of a battle fought on two fronts—a doctrinal clash within the Court and a political and economic struggle outside it, to which the Court responds. The past Supreme Court term testifies that the New Deal has won the Court war up to now, although it lost the reorganization fight. But the next phase of the constitutional struggle will be over the question of the government's power to enter upon the decisive program of economic planning which is necessary to meet the problems of collapse. And the progressive group on the Court will be the group that considers the Court's function to lie in administering justice to individuals within the framework of what the President and Congress decide rather than in setting limits, however enlightened, to their power.

1938

Labor and Civil Liberties

THE recent series of Supreme Court opinions bearing on labor and civil liberties are far-reaching in their implications and shed considerable light on the character of the present Court.[31] Within the space of several weeks the Court has handed

---

[30] For a discussion of this case, and of Justice Black's role, see "Mr. Justice Black, Dissenting," in my *Ideas Are Weapons* (1939), pp. 261–6.
[31] February 1941.

down important decisions in five related areas within this field.

In the first place, the federal wages-and-hours law has been upheld by the Court. This was no surprise, and (with Mr. Justice McReynolds gone) it was a decision handed down by a unanimous court of eight judges. They held that Congress had the power under the interstate-commerce clause to regulate interstate traffic in goods produced under substandard labor conditions, whether too low wages or too long hours. Thereby two things were accomplished. First, the final step was taken in the validation by the Supreme Court of the essentials of the New Deal social program. Second, the old 1918 decision of *Hammer v. Dagenhart,* in which the Court had held that the federal government was powerless to deal with the products of child labor in interstate commerce, was overruled.

In another important area, the Court ruled that the Sherman anti-trust laws do not apply to labor disputes. A few words are worth saying on the wider implications of the decision in the Hutcheson case.[32] What the Court majority said, through a clear and forthright opinion of Mr. Justice Frankfurter, was that the case must be decided in the light of the repeated attempts which Congress had made in the Clayton and Norris-La Guardia Acts to exclude labor disputes from the provisions of the anti-trust laws. Those attempts have finally, after more than a quarter-century, borne fruit in a Supreme Court decision. The result is a blow to Assistant Attorney General Thurman Arnold, whom I regard as one of the most valuable of our public officials, and who is in general performing a great service in his campaign to enforce the anti-trust laws. Yet the course of the Court was clear, and only the Chief Justice and Mr. Justice Roberts voted against the ruling. It is now decided that a jurisdictional dispute, such as the Carpenters' Union was carrying on against the Machinists' Union, is not a conspiracy in restraint of trade, and cannot be prevented by criminal action any more than (under the Norris-La Guardia Act) it can be prevented by injunction. This still gives Mr. Arnold leeway in the cases where he can prove collusion between labor unions and employers to affect prices. That is the area where his approach has the greatest validity. He has recently announced that he intends to carry on his fight in the hope of getting the Court to reconsider its divided anti-trust

---

[32] *U.S. v. Hutcheson,* 61 *Supreme Court Reporter* 463 (Feb. 3, 1941).

decisions of the past. That is all to the good: and if the Court sees the problems as realistically and reasons as clearly as in the Hutcheson case, I shall be content.

With the Court's ruling in the fight between Henry Ford and the National Labor Relations Board there can also be no quarrel, even on the part of conservatives. The Court refused to consider Ford's appeal from an NLRB order charging him with violations of the labor law. The real importance of this opinion is that it removes the last prop from those who argued that there was no sense in denying the Ford Company defense contracts, so long as the Supreme Court had not finally adjudged him a violator of the labor law. I never went along with this reasoning, because it puts a premium on litigative delay. Yet now even the Supreme Court has spoken. The problem of Mr. Ford is now out of the area of legal rights, and squarely in the area of the power and integrity of the government.

But perhaps the most important recent labor cases that the Court has decided have to do with the relation of labor action to freedom of speech. This issue came up in two recent cases of the first importance. One is the case of the Milk Wagon Drivers' Union v. Meadowmoor Dairies.[33] The question was whether the Illinois state courts could issue an injunction to restrain all picketing, peaceful and other, where there was a "context of violence." Mr. Justice Frankfurter, speaking for a majority of five, wrote the decision that the Court could not interfere with such an injunction. There were two dissents, one by Mr. Justice Black, speaking for himself and Mr. Justice Douglas; and one by Mr. Justice Reed. Both dissents stressed the position that to enjoin peaceful picketing as well as violence was to deprive labor of the right of free speech guaranteed it under the Bill of Rights.

There can be little doubt that the Court decision in this case will be the subject of discussion in liberal circles almost as intense as that which followed the difference of view between Justices Frankfurter and Stone in the Jehovah's Witnesses flag-salute case last year.[34] Here again the problem is one of seeking to adjust the delicate balance of states' rights and civil liberties. And here again the Court majority takes the view that, where the issue of civil liberties

---

[33] 61 *Supreme Court Reporter* 552 (Feb. 10, 1941).
[34] *Minersville School District v. Gobitis,* 310 U.S. 586 (1940).

is not so clear as to be "a palpable violation of the constitutional guarantee" of freedom of speech, the power to determine social policy lies with the state rather than with the Supreme Court. The majority agrees that if only peaceful picketing were involved, the injunction would be unconstitutional. What in their mind changes the situation is the fact that the picketing is here "blended with violence": that fact neutralizes the constitutional immunity that labor would otherwise have.

I believe with Justices Black, Reed, and Douglas that this is a dangerous view, both for the labor movement and its fate, and for the cause of civil liberties as a whole. What the Court is doing, by making the question of the blending of violence with picketing the central problem, is to bring into the adjudication of the question of civil liberties in labor disputes a factor which it cannot in any way control. It thus opens the door to reactionary assaults upon labor by state and local authorities. There are few picketing cases in hotly contested labor disputes in which the charges of violence are not part of the record. We can trust the present Supreme Court to discriminate, but can we trust the lower federal courts and the whole galaxy of state courts? It is not hard to envisage in the future the operation of *agents provocateurs* who by inciting to violence and creating a context of violence will succeed in prejudicing the entire picketing drive of the union.

Even in the present case Mr. Justice Black presents a persuasive argument which casts some doubt on how integrally the initial violence in the milk-wagon drivers' strike was related to the picketing which the court injunction sought to stop. And while the Supreme Court decision leaves room for unions whose interests are prejudiced by injunctions too loosely and broadly drawn to make a final appeal to the Court, it is in the actual practice of labor disputes something that belongs in the Cold-Comfort Department. We know that the whole history both of the use of the injunction in labor disputes and of the interpretation of violence by the courts is one that has run consistently against labor. Without making an absolute fetish of an abstract doctrine of free speech, dissociated from the living context of social relations, we believe that the Court has not made out an adequate case for qualifying the doctrine here.

There remain two considerations. One is the contention that Mr. Justice Frankfurter, by putting the burden for liberal action on the legislature and courts of Illinois rather than on the Supreme Court, is actually performing a strategic service for the liberal cause. That is a doubtful argument, and could be applied to any case in which states' rights are involved. What we know is that the threats to civil liberties come generally from reactionary state legislatures and local vigilantism. In such a context the emphasis should be not on state sovereignty but on fundamental civil liberties as protected by a Supreme Court. The other consideration is the argument, suggested by Mr. Justice Frankfurter, that labor must be treated as the employers are treated: just as Ford's freedom of speech in a Labor Board case is judged in the context of company violence, so must trade-union picketing be. The analogy is attractive but ultimately breaks down. For there is a basic distinction between regulation by court injunction and regulation by administrative agency. The National Labor Relations Board has built up an *expertise* on the problem of labor disputes which no Illinois court can approach; its realistic knowledge of the technical and social context of the struggle for union organization and its ultimate responsibility to the people furnish warrant against abuse which the court process as a way of determining social policy does not furnish.

It is to the credit of the Supreme Court that it has not followed blindly the logic of the Milk Drivers' case. In another case, *A.F. of L. v. Swing*,[35] involving the question whether secondary picketing qualifies the guarantee of free speech to workers, the Court majority decided that it does not. Mr. Chief Justice Hughes and Mr. Justice Roberts held out for applying the Milk Drivers' decision to this situation as well. But the Court, again speaking through Mr. Justice Frankfurter, held, in a decision which is likely to have very far-reaching consequences, that workers have the right of peaceful picketing even where the pickets are not directly in the employ of the firm being picketed.

1941

---

[35] 61 *Supreme Court Reporter* 568 (Feb. 10, 1941).

The Personnel of the Supreme Court

1

IT IS curious that the blood and flame of the Supreme Court reorganization struggle of 1937 has not left any appreciable effect on the literature of the judicial process. Jefferson's bout with the judiciary stirred up some grand talk in Congress in the Great Judiciary Debate of 1802, provoked the writings of John Taylor, and gave vitality to the polemical literature of the Court for a long time. Theodore Roosevelt's proposal for the recall of judicial decisions formed the center of a judicial controversy that led to a whole body of commentary by Beard, Boudin, Corwin, Goodnow, Haines, and others. But to date, Franklin Roosevelt's "court-packing" scheme has from a literary viewpoint been almost barren.

To be sure, the earlier struggle between the New Deal and the Court raised problems of constitutional interpretation, and American scholarship has addressed itself to them: as witness Corwin's, Frankfurter's, Hamilton's, and Powell's writings, and the essays in the American Historical Association volume, *The Constitution Reconsidered*. But these dealt with doctrinal matters. Mr. Roosevelt's Court plan sought to politicize the judicial process by concentrating on the strategic questions of the number and the retirement age of judges. It dealt, therefore, with matters of personnel. On these matters the general level of the writing has been that of the *Debaters' Manual* or *Vital Speeches* type, or of the Columbia Broadcasting System's pamphlet containing some of the most turgid oratory that ever clogged the air waves.

The two books under review [36] are worth some attention because they represent an old and a new method of approaching the problem of Supreme Court personnel and the relation of the judicial process to politics. The old way is the apologia or attack. The new way is severely factual. One deals with pieties and demonologies. The other deals with description and statistics. We have had re-

---

[36] *Our Eleven Chief Justices: A History of the Supreme Court in Terms of Their Personalities*, by Kenneth Bernard Umbreit, New York, Harper & Brothers, 1938. *Judges of the Supreme Court, 1789-1937: A Study of Their Qualifications*, by Cortez A. M. Ewing, Minneapolis, University of Minnesota Press, 1938.

cent instances of the first in Burton J. Hendrick's *Bulwark of the Republic* and Pearson and Allen's *Nine Old Men*. The instances of the second are distressingly few.

Both Mr. Umbreit's book and Professor Ewing's are concerned with the technical competence of the Supreme Court personnel and its relation to politics. Both authors have used the Roosevelt Court plan as the starting-point of their intellectual voyage. In Professor Ewing's case there is a frank statement that the controversy over the President's plan crystallized an earlier interest in the geographic distribution of appointments to the Supreme Court, and broadened it to include other influential factors in the selection and qualifications of judges. In Mr. Umbreit's case the relation of the book to the Court plan is tangential and implicit rather than avowed. The book was undoubtedly in process before the President's plan, but it seems to have been written in its shadow.

2

Mr. Umbreit's book is a venture in the art at once of biography and of judicial history. I have little to say about the former, except that the author has used what may be called the *mélange* method in biography, mingling chatty bits and revealing anecdotes with rather stiff expositions of judicial opinions. The result is diffuse rather than Stracheyan. Yet we must be grateful that the author has even attempted the task. While we have had encyclopedic biographies of judges we have in no sense had the good biographical essay. Mr. Umbreit's book is a great advance upon such compilations as Flanders's *Lives and Times of the Chief Justices* both in biographical art and in the critical use of the material. He has, moreover, performed the very useful function of gathering together the material on the Chief Justices that has remained uncollected for the last half-century—since Flanders in 1875 and the 1882 edition of Van Santvoord. But he has not made a meaningful pattern of his material. One of the reasons lies, I think, in his bias against theories of the judicial process. The other lies in his anti-New Deal bias and his over-filial attitude toward the Chief Justices.

I am not certain from the book whether Mr. Umbreit regards all theory as gray, with Goethe, or whether he reserves this judgment only for the newer and more radical theories of the judicial process. He seems to lump together the Marxians, the new realist school, the psychoanalysts, and the environmentalists, and to condemn them all under the contemptuous caption of "the breakfast theory of jurisprudence." Obviously this is an easy straw man. "The breakfast theory of jurisprudence" is, strictly speaking, naïve. Its force lies in the insistence of the realists that the old mechanical and hieratic conception of the judicial process must be dissolved by studying the personal and psychological factors in each case. Thus the breakfast theory is a gesture. Going beyond gestures, however, one must see that the judge is a part of his time and a product not only of his own biography but of the biography of his class and era as well. By rejecting this view Mr. Umbreit is in the curious position of denying the relevance of the material from which he must make his selection. He is writing biography in contempt of biographical factors and history in despite of historical forces. To be sure, he introduces into each sketch elements of both individual biography and national history. But since he admits of no reasoned theory of the relation of the factors in the judicial process, it is difficult to decide whether he has introduced enough of a man's life to explain his decisions, or enough of his decisions to illumine his life. Theoretically he is writing in a social vacuum.

But only theoretically. Actually his social theory is implicit in the whole book. It serves to rationalize judicial supremacy as it has been built up and to defend it from attack. "His work," he says of John Marshall, "was to prove to the world that limitations on power can be made effective." Limitations, one may ask, on whose power? On the power of the democratic Jeffersonian and Jacksonian majorities, yes. On the power of the ruling economic and judicial elite, no. The book shows every mark of having been written under the negative influence of Mr. Roosevelt's New Deal, when the economic minority and its apologists among scholars and journalists began once more to talk desperately of "limitations on power."

The author's treatment of John Marshall illustrates both the strength and weakness of the book. To an extent Marshall does come alive in the sketch—Marshall with his long gangling frame, his frontier ways, his casual reading, his impatience with legal erudition, his daringly incomplete syllogisms, his outward carelessness, his inward convictions, his adoration of his wife, his hatred of Jefferson and the Jeffersonians. Yet the sketch is in no sense an advance on the picture contained in Beveridge's *Marshall* and Warren's *Supreme Court in United States History*. Its emphasis is Federalist and it accepts all the unexamined preconceptions of the Federalists about the sanctity of the propertied minority and the tyranny of the mass. It accepts Marshall's nationalism on his own terms. It omits his flirtations with New England secession. It omits the extent to which nationalism was good strategy, and the extent to which the Marshall appointment itself was part of a larger Federalist strategy. It omits the material recently uncovered by Professor Adams in Marshall's autobiographical letter to Story indicating that the appointment to the Chief Justiceship was not a surprise to him and had been a matter of discussion between him and the President. It mentions, but glosses over, the details of Marshall's speculation in land and its effect on his land decisions. The contract decisions, in which Marshall may be seen in his most reactionary colors, are given in a bare recital stripped of significance because they are not set in the context of the land capitalism and rising merchant capitalism of the period. The same applies to Marshall's great nationalist decisions, which, except in a legalistic sense, have no meaning outside of the economic context of the need for giving security to the new corporate enterprise and for supplying it with a stable national banking and transportation system.[37]

There is a similar lack of tough-mindedness in the author's treatment of the other Chief Justices. With the exception of Fuller (it would be a strain on almost any writer to regard him as great), Rutledge (who suffered from a "mental affliction, the precise nature of which is unknown"), and Chase (whom the author depicts as vaguely ambitious and too engrossed in his political career to make a good Chief Justice), the portraits are definitely on the sympathetic side. Taney is treated with sanity and sense, and the notion that he was a radical Chief Justice who set himself in a direction diametrically opposite to that of Marshall is given the summary negation it deserves. Yet the author has not sought to resolve the problem of Taney's intricate personality and curious outlook, the enigma of reconciling his early Whiggism with his attack on the Bank, or the latter with the Charles River Bridge case, or either with the Dred

---

[37] For a further discussion, see my "John Marshall's Long Shadow" in *Ideas Are Weapons* (1939), pp. 27–37, and "John Marshall and the Campaign of History" (March 1939), 39 *Columbia Law Review* 396–431.

Scott case.[38] For Taft and Hughes the author has great enthusiasm. His lead on Taft—that he was a man who tended to show his judicial side as an administrator and his administrative side as a judge —is a good one. But he has brushed aside the anti-labor cases which made Taft acceptable to the higher powers before he came to the Court, and his ingenuity on the Court in finding sophisticated ways of destroying social legislation. Incidentally, Mr. Justice Hughes is today following in Taft's footsteps in his recent opinions on the finality of administrative findings in the National Labor Relations Act. Perhaps the least satisfactory sketch in the book is that of Hughes. Mr. Umbreit's approach to his "liberalism" is one of the most fantastic I have seen in the literature of the judicial process. He begins with the fact that Mr. Hughes is a Baptist, expatiates on the lack of a ritual and formal organization in the Baptist Church, and ends up by proving that therefore Mr. Hughes's appointment to the Supreme Court was "the triumph of a new way of democracy." Could any breakfast theory be more far-fetched than this Baptist theory?

Despite his interest in the political careers of his subjects, Mr. Umbreit misses the relationship between politics and the judicial process. He admits that politicians have become judges and insists that many of them have made good judges. This is true, and an important truth. Yet here in this book, as elsewhere in the literature, this is regarded as a marginal fact and something to be in each case explained. The fact is not that individual judges have in their earlier careers been politicians, but that the whole process of constitutional interpretation is in its deepest sense political: in the sense that every judge necessarily has a view of the limits outside of which there can be no proper polity, and with more or less articulateness and honesty translates this view into his decisions. The failure of both our judges and our commentators to admit this has resulted on the one hand in our tendency to regard as usurpation what is the very essence of judicial supremacy and on the other hand in furtive and underground political activity on the part of judges. There is some immensely illuminating material in William Allen White's recent biography of Coolidge, *A Puritan in Babylon*, that indicates how far a presumably upright judge will go in under-

---

[38] For a further discussion of Taney, see my "Taney Redivivus" in *Ideas Are Weapons* (1939), pp. 38–41.

ground political activity. While Chief Justice, Taft went as emissary from Coolidge to Harry L. Daugherty to get him to resign from the Attorney-Generalship. He was also ring-leader of a group, along with Hilles of New York and Butler of Massachusetts, that sought to persuade Coolidge to run for a third term in 1928, and fought against the early Hoover boom. Also while Chief Justice, Taft pulled wires to sabotage Senator Walsh's investigation of the Aluminum Trust. It is arguable that even if these items had been available to Mr. Umbreit, they could scarcely with any consistency have found room in his uncritical sketch of Taft.

3

There is a good deal that is realistic in Professor Ewing's little book. He got fed up, during the controversy over the Court plan, with "the mere drivel that passes for weighty argument in the political arena about the excellence or derelictions of our Supreme Court members." Hence his "determination to shun mere uninformed opinion and moralization." Hence also his use of statistical techniques in an attempt to get at an *inconcussum quid* beyond the reach either of partisanship or of conjecture.

And so he makes a series of statistical studies, segmenting American judicial history in time (four periods: 1789–1829, 1829–1861, 1861–1897, 1897–1929) and space (four sections: east, south, middle west, west). He asks a whole set of questions. How long has it taken on the average for nominees to the Court to be confirmed? Where do they come from? What have their ages been? What have been their previous legal and judicial training, their educational attainments, their previous public service? The result is a little book to which one can only apply the adjective that the author applies to the graphs and tables he has constructed—"interesting." We feel somehow that there ought to be a relevance for our problems in this absorbing collection of facts and figures, but we are at a loss to determine what it is.

Thus we learn that seventy-seven per cent of the judges whom the Presidents have nominated have been confirmed by the Senate, and that in the most recent period (since 1897) this tendency has been most striking. The period of delay in confirmation has also tended to decrease. In the most recent period there has been a sixteen-day average wait before confirmation, while only in four of the twenty nominations since 1897 has there been a delay of more than twenty days. Yet while this seems to give us a certitude, in terms of mathematical probabilities, that the next appointment will be confirmed with a delay of only about sixteen days, it tells us nothing of the operative dynamic forces in the relationship between the President and the Senate over judicial appointments. In fact the author is compelled to conclude that "if a fundamental difference of opinion arises between the Senate and the President there is no reason to believe that we might not, in the future, enter into another period in which the Senate will take its power of confirmation seriously."

So also with the question of geographical representation. Professor Ewing says his original approach was heavily influenced by Turner. "With reliable technique this line of attack might ultimately prove valuable," he says, "if there were any distinctly sectional convictions upon political problems." But he goes on to say that, "unhappily, each general geographical section embraces men of almost every shade of political conviction." Which means that the geographical approach becomes meaningless as an index to the mentality of the judges. Turner's thesis had validity so long as Turner was using the term "section" not only in a geographical but also in an economic sense. An attempt to make a correlation between the economic views of Supreme Court judges and the section they come from might have proved an interesting statistical venture. Failing this, the author is reduced to a statistical treatment of the rather obvious truism that in making appointments to the Court the President must consider geography, and the less obvious truism that he will respond to geography in proportion to the importance of the particular section in party councils and political struggles and ultimately in national economic life. Thus the South was heavily represented in the period before the Civil War, reduced almost to a nullity in the period immediately afterward, and has been making a slow recovery recently; while the Middle West, which gained at the expense of the South in the post-Civil War period, lost that dominance afterwards. It is significant that as soon as Professor Ewing comes to the interpretation of his figures he is in the more or less speculative realm of analysis.

It is when he comes to consider age qualifications that Professor

Ewing tends to think in feelings rather than in figures. His figures reveal that there has been a constant trend toward an increasing appointment age in the past hundred and fifty years of Court history. The average appointment age in the first period (1789–1829) was forty-seven and one-half. The average appointment age in the last period (1897–1937) was slightly over fifty-seven (this does not include Black, Reed, Frankfurter, and Douglas). Here is definitely a fact to hold on to and to make something of. But what does Professor Ewing make of it? "The increased appointment age average derives, I believe, from the fact of national maturity." This is a strangely unscientific conclusion. Actually it might derive from one or a combination of a dozen other factors. The one that comes most readily to mind is that, given the desire to appoint conservative lawyers who will protect business from governmental interference, our Presidents have turned to men who were at an age at which their own financial success has been completely established and the desire of the human organism for security and the status quo had had time to set in. Professor Ewing's hunch is as good as mine —but no better.

He addresses himself with some heat to the charge that there is a relation between age and conservatism. Obviously the charge has often been made in an extreme and mechanical form, and stated baldly—in such a form as to say that all old judges are conservative and all conservative judges old—it is entirely untenable. Yet that does not dismiss the problem of whether a judge tends to grow more conservative as he grows older. At this point Professor Ewing moves away from statistics to argument about individual instances. Of the names he mentions—Holmes, Taney, Duval, Field, Marshall, Nelson, and Brandeis—Duval and Field, like Grier, should by general consent have resigned long before they did: they were instances of intellectual obsolescence at a heavy national cost. Marshall, Taney, Holmes, and Brandeis remained intellectually vigorous. Yet Marshall, never a radical to start with, grew more conservative as the years went on, as witness *Ogden v. Saunders* (1827), which was too much even for his faithful colleagues. And who will deny that the Taney of the Dred Scott case and the Taney who in his last years sat up in his invalid bed falteringly writing a hypothetical opinion declaring the Emancipation Proclamation unconstitutional were different Taneys from the one who as Attorney-General carried on his shoulders Jackson's war against the Second United States Bank. As for Holmes, the author does not mention that it was Holmes who first said, "You cannot govern a country with a document and nine old men." Holmes was never anything except a conservative in his economic views: it was his intellectual vigor which made him a constitutional radical, and amazingly he never lost that. Neither did Brandeis. But Professor Ewing's appeal to the particular instances of Holmes and Brandeis, even assuming that both of them prove his case, is unstatistical. For Holmes and Brandeis are mutations all too rare in judicial history to count from a statistical viewpoint.

On education and prior public office experience the record is clearer. It shows that more and more judges have tended to hold degrees from educational institutions. Whether this has added to their wisdom or their liberalism the author does not say. In fact he is careful to point out that these figures "are not intended to reflect any trends as to judicial ability." The percentage of judges with previous judicial experience turns out to be relatively high, ranging from seventy-five per cent in the first period to fifty-seven per cent in the second, the other two periods falling in between. Yet here, too, one must not be hasty to draw conclusions. There can be little doubt that there has thus far been almost no correlation observable between—what would be really significant—the Great Tradition on the Court and prior judicial experience. Where Professor Ewing's figures speak most convincingly is in the proof they exhibit that an overwhelming proportion of Supreme Court judges, great and small, had held some kind of elective office previously. They were, says Professor Ewing, "politicians of extraordinary ability," as is proved "by their ability to secure election to political office." Here is some genuine realism about the Court which will not be welcomed by those who hold to the myth of judicial neutrality.

What is best in Professor Ewing's book is, first, his frank recognition of the role that political experience has played in the making of Supreme Court justices; second, his suspicion of all forms of bunk (even though, in the case of age, he tends to fall for some himself) and his resort therefore to hard-headed statistical devices; third, his determination to look at the office of Supreme Court justice not in terms of a divine afflatus but as a job to be filled and there-fore one requiring certain mortal qualifications. Such a point of view, if carried out successfully, will transform the discussion of the Supreme Court in relation to the political process.

4

Thus our two books: one in the old tradition, for the most part a biographical compilation but with fitful flashes of polemical in-sight and acerbity; the other striking out on new paths but not get-ting very far. The books lead to some reflections on the possibility of developing an approach that will not be as barren as the polemi-cal apologia or attack must be, or as truncated as the statistical tech-nique by itself must be. What is obviously needed is a method in which the analysis is kept from shooting off into the void by being moored to a statistical and factual base, and in which fact-gathering is kept from becoming meaningless by being related to significant analysis.

But what is also needed is a recognition that these men on the Supreme Court are public officials who ought to have the best pos-sible training and qualifications for their jobs. They should be studied, therefore, as one might study the personnel of any branch of the government. The recent renaissance in the biographical study of the Court will contribute rich material to such an approach. But what we want to know about the judges is pretty much what we want to know about any of our public officials: their education, their political and social outlook, their class roots, their training in legal discipline, their political ties, their experience in responsible public office, their sensitiveness to those currents of informed popu-lar opinion upon which ultimately the democratic fate depends.

I have said that the Supreme Court personnel should be studied as any other personnel would be studied. There is, of course, one qualification to be made here. The Supreme Court judges are not part of a bureaucracy where the problem is one of more or less measurable competence. Their qualifications cannot be reduced to a civil service code. The approach to a person like Marshall or Taney or Miller or Holmes or Black must deal even more with the imponderables of social outlook and national statesmanship than with the ponderables of schooling, sectional provenance, legal training, age, and public office. We shall never dispense with the need for delicate and skillful analysis of the factors that have made the Great Tradition on the Court.

1939

Landscape with Judges

A S JOHN ERSKINE did with Galahad, the Attorney-General of the United States has given us enough of the Supreme Court's history to explain its reputation. His book [39] is less than a history of the Court and more than the story of the reorganization fight. It is a survey of the judicial power, foreshortened so as to concentrate for half its length on the New Deal judicial crisis. It presents a broad constitutional landscape, with the judges of the 1933–1938 Court in the foreground.

But for all that, it is a military landscape, and he paints it from the peculiar vantage-point of one who has himself been in the thick of the battle. He knows what "government by lawsuit" is because he has had to prepare the briefs and argue the cases. If consequently some bitterness and impatience has crept into the book (it is amazing how little), a good deal also of the clarity and orderliness of Mr. Jackson's mind has found its way in.

The echoes of the Court fight seem muted now. But those who followed the constitutional wars know that they were not sham and bloodless battles of the categories. They were struggles for power and struggles over order. Mr. Jackson sees this clearly. That is why he has chosen to write not of judicial review but of judicial supremacy. I take it that he is willing to accept the one as part of a working scheme of government, but not the other.

Where does the distinction lie? Perhaps no sharp distinction can be drawn. Judicial review means the power of the courts to review acts of the other branches of the government. Judicial supremacy is nothing more nor less than the position of overlordship which results from that power. The power of judicial review is nothing if it is not supreme. But here is Mr. Jackson's dilemma. He feels that judicial review may, if kept within bounds, be a perfectly good instrument of government. He is sure this is so in the protection

---

[39] Robert H. Jackson, *The Struggle for Judicial Supremacy*, New York, Alfred A. Knopf, 1941.

of civil liberties and in keeping the states from acts of petty economic tyranny and anarchy that would pulverize the federal structure. What then remains? The courts, says Mr. Jackson, must be kept from judicial supremacy, that is, from "unwarranted interference in the economic affairs of the country."

But who decides what is warranted and unwarranted? "As the decisions now stand," Mr. Justice Holmes once admonished his colleagues, "I see hardly any limit but the sky" to the judges' own conception of their power. And Mr. Justice Stone put the same thought in different words when he said that while the executive and legislative branches were checked by the judges, "The only check upon our own exercise of power is our own sense of self-restraint." It is that which Mr. Jackson ultimately falls back upon —the Holmes-Brandeis-Stone-Frankfurter doctrine of judicial self-restraint as the line of distinction between judicial review and judicial supremacy.

Perhaps it is as good a formulation as you can get—and the rest has to be spelled out not in doctrinal terms but in the history of the Court-in-action. This Mr. Jackson does admirably. He reviews the part that John Marshall (and also Taney's Dred Scott decision) played in establishing judicial supremacy. He sketches in the high points of the crucial period of the development of judicial supremacy, from the Civil War until the New Deal. He adds little that is new, but he reduces much that is well known to order and proportion.

It is when he reaches the New Deal crisis that he breaks fresh ground. Mr. Jackson divides the New Deal judicial war into four phases. The first was the period of uncertainty, in which the Court hesitated between two worlds, with four justices definitely living in the old, three in the new, and Mr. Chief Justice Hughes and Mr. Justice Roberts commuting between both. That was in 1933 and 1934, when state reform legislation was being upheld by the Court by a 5-to-4 vote, and everyone was on tenterhooks. The second phase was in 1935 and 1936, when the commuters decided to settle down and the Court, in Mr. Jackson's words, "nullified the New Deal." With dramatic power Mr. Jackson describes the succession of blows the Court inflicted on the majority will—the "storm signals" in the Hot Oil and Railroad Retirement Pension cases; then "Black Monday," May 27, 1935, when the Court handed down in a single day adverse opinions on farm debtors' relief,[40] the President's removal power over appointees,[41] and the NRA; then the locust swarm that was set loose of injunctions in the lower federal courts whereby a single judge might sabotage the results of years of national effort; then in succession the AAA decision, the Jones stock-fraud decision that almost turned over the SEC applecart,[42] the Carter Coal decision,[43] the municipal bankruptcy decision, and, as a climax, *Morehead v. Tipaldo*,[44] outlawing the New York minimum-wage law, and saying in effect that neither the national government nor the state governments had power to deal with sweat-shop wages.

The third phase of crisis was what Mr. Jackson calls "the challenge" of the President to judicial supremacy—the reorganization plan. Clearly it was a counter-attack against the justices. Mr. Jackson made the best defense of the plan that it had before the Senate Judiciary Committee, but he is chary of any real defense in this book except one: that there was plenty of provocation for it. I think also he is right in saying that the alternative to the plan, once it became the center of a battle, was not some other sort of Court reform but none at all. For the rest, he plays down the plan itself, contenting himself with emphasizing that while the President lost the battle, he won the war.

This victory marked the fourth phase of the crisis—the retreat of the Court to a restrained exercise of judicial review. In another long and dramatic line of cases, the Court in 1937 sought to undo all the damage it had done in 1935 and 1936. Mr. Justice Roberts switched back again, and the minimum-wage law of the state of Washington was called constitutional,[45] whereas exactly the same one in New York had formerly been unconstitutional. The same temper was shown in the Labor Board cases.[46] Moreover, and this is important, the change from judicial supremacy to judicial restraint had been accomplished without a single new appointment by the

---

[40] *Louisville Bank v. Radford,* 295 U.S. 555 (1935).

[41] *Humphrey's Executor v. U.S.,* 295 U.S. 602 (1935).

[42] *Jones v. SEC,* 298 U.S. 1 (1936).

[43] *Carter v. Carter Coal Co.,* 298 U.S. 238 (1936). For an extended discussion, see Hamilton and Adair, *The Power to Govern* (1937).

[44] 298 U.S. 587 (1936).

[45] *West Coast Hotel Co. v. Parrish,* 300 U.S. 379 (1937).

[46] *NLRB v. Jones and Laughlin,* 301 U.S. 1 (1937); *NLRB v. Fruehauf Trailer Co.,* 301 U.S. 49 (1937); *NLRB v. Friedman-Harry Marks Clothing Co.,* 301 U.S. 58 (1937); *Associated Press v. NLRB,* 301 U.S. 103 (1937).

President. It was not until the change was made that Mr. Justice Van Devanter retired. It was the old Court that had reformed itself. With that reform, the New Deal constitutional crisis was at an end.

There will be others who will rework the ground Mr. Jackson has staked out. I should like to see some time an attempt to construct a theory of the nature and dynamics of constitutional crisis. Mr. Jackson, as narrator, gives a history of a particular one; but there were others—in Jefferson's time, in Taney's, during the Civil War, at the time of the income-tax decisions. What do they have in common? I suspect the answer lies in whatever it is that makes our system of constitutional interpretation too rigid for the imperatives of social change.

For the rest, Mr. Jackson sees all the implications of the story he tells. He sees that litigation has become an organic part of our political system, a way of shaping social policy, and he does not like it. He proposes that we deny judicial review to the lower federal courts, restrict it to a single court, and provide some means for a prompt settlement of the constitutionality of social policy, so that there will be no doubt and no long delays. If he still relies for his remedies mainly on the restraint of the judges, he is in no different position from that of other spokesmen of liberal judicial thought today. My own feeling is that we shall still have to tackle the power of judicial supremacy in a constitutional crisis that may crop up once more in our generation. Mr. Jackson must think so too. In a striking parable manner at the end of the book, he tells the story of how the arrogance of the Taney of the Dred Scott decision prepared the way for the Civil War and therefore the humiliation of the Taney of the Merryman case. For it is not too far-fetched to say that the cost of judicial supremacy when it goes too far is revolution and civil war.

1941

4

✦◆✦

Constitutional Crisis and the Crisis State[1]

1

BECAUSE American constitutional history has been crisis history, the absence in the political and legal literature of any theory of constitutional crisis appears as striking as would the absence of a condemned man at his execution. One might speculate about what economics would be like without a crisis theory, or psychology without a body of material seeking to explain the growth and resolution of psychic tensions. To build such a theory in constitutional study is a perilous task; and where the Warrens, Corwins, Powells, and Boudins have feared to tread I do not propose to rush in. Yet I should like to set down in a tentative fashion some notes on the relation of constitutional crisis to the democratic state of today.

There have been three major types of constitutional crisis in our history. You get one type when there is a sharp discrepancy between the needs of effective government on the one hand and on the other the limits of tolerance imposed by the Supreme Court on the policy (generally economic policy) of the government. You can, if you wish, put it into somewhat Freudian terms: the *id*, or driving part of the governmental psyche, wants desperately to follow certain lines of action; the *superego*, or the censor in the shape of the Supreme Court, says No. If the cleavage between the two is acute enough, you get breakdown.

The second type of crisis, generally linked to the first, comes when there is a frontal attack (or counter-attack) on the judicial

---

1 This was first delivered as the James Goold Cutler Lecture at William and Mary College, in the spring of 1941, and was published in the William and Mary *Bulletin*.

power, whether on the part of Congress or the President, generally (although not necessarily) in order to make it more responsive to the popular consciousness of the time. In this sort of crisis the desire for a realignment of Supreme Court policy clashes with the sense of the need for retaining judicial independence of political change, and with the related sense of the Constitution as a basic protection of our liberties and of the Supreme Court as having a guardian-role toward the Constitution.

The third type comes when the Constitution, in emergencies, is actually stretched beyond its usual bounds, and where the unwonted stretching, necessary though it may be, raises questions of the breakdown of the whole constitutional fabric. This generally occurs in periods of military emergency, as during the Civil War, the World War, and the present one, and relates generally to the expansion of Presidential power.

In oversimplified terms, the first may be called an *economic* constitutional crisis, because its origin and occasion are economic change and economic policy. The second may be called a *judicial* constitutional crisis, because its origin and occasion are the expansion of judicial power and the threat to it. The third may be called a *war* constitutional crisis, because its origin and occasion are the demands that a war makes upon executive leadership, with all the dangers that it involves for civil liberties and political responsibility. All three are facets of the democratic crisis state.

I do not know whether it is subversive to use the term "crisis state" to apply to our democracy. I included it one summer in a catalogue description of a course I was to give at a university, and I received a polite little note saying that one of the university authorities questioned the wisdom of using that phrase. Wisdom or no wisdom, the reality of our crisis is a fact. It is not something that can be exorcised by verbal magic. We have on our hands a crisis democracy—one that must navigate through the shoals and scudding drifts dangerous to a democratic bark, one which seeks to use every aid on its voyage but must cling to the difficult course of state power without state monopoly of thought or action, one which must contrive ever-new strategies of economic control and create ever-new administrative mechanisms, one which must somehow survive as a constitutional system while fighting its enemies without and within, one which must become a planned economy without destroying democratic responsibility and a military state without suppressing civil liberties. You can, if you will, refuse to use the term "crisis state." But our ancestors found they could not wipe out the fact of sex by calling a leg a limb.

2

We must start with the need for effective government. The greatness of the *Federalist* lies not so much, as has been thought, in the exposition of valid principles of political philosophy. It lies rather in the theme of a government effective enough to meet the problems it confronts. Many of the political attitudes of Hamilton, Madison, and Jay have been whittled down by time, and have been converted to the uses of minority rights rather than majority rule. But the *Federalist* remains one of the world's great books because, as in all great literature, its core theme is ever new. And that core theme is the need for adequate government.

Today a new *Federalist* could be written, recounting the changes and chances of our national life, and the new requirements of effective government. It has been remarked that the Supreme Court is an adjourned session of the Constitutional Convention. There is a sense in which this carries an ironic freightage. But the irony is not, as we have tended to suppose, merely in the reference to judicial law-making. There have been ample instances of a proper place for interpretive creativeness by the Court. "We must never forget," John Marshall said, "that it is a *Constitution* we are expounding." The irony lies in the fact that the Court has more often used its great power for sterilizing than for fertilizing the materials of American growth. And the irony lies also in the fact that the Court has claimed for itself alone the creative potential. The fact is that in every crisis we must govern with the freshness of eye and the largeness of spirit of a Constitutional Convention. There are times when we must act like the Founding Fathers or commit national suicide.

> If we really want to live, we'd better start at once to try;
> If we don't, it doesn't matter, but we'd better start to die.[2]

---

[2] W. H. Auden, *Poems*, New York, Random House, 1934.

Part of the problem of democratic survival is constitutional, much of it is political and economic. We cannot continue to draw the sharp boundaries between the two realms that we have drawn in the past. The fact is that in a constitutional democracy, whatever the reality of the forces involved in the struggle over direction, the rhetoric that the minority groups will use in opposing changes is always the rhetoric of constitutionalism. There is an interesting comparison to be drawn here between the situation a half-century ago, in the days of the triumph of Mr. Justice Field, and the situation today. The conservative Court majority at that time formed an idea of a rigid economic system that was best left alone and that could not be violated; it alone was identified with constitutionalism. The enemy they were fighting was "socialism," and anything was socialism that did not fit into their accustomed economic scheme. The constitutional crisis of 1935–1938 was the final term in the propositional sequence of their reasoning. Today a similar group in the country has fetishized a rigid political system. To our amateur constitutional lawyers in Congress and out that alone is constitutional. The enemy they are fighting is "dictatorship," and anything is dictatorship that does not come within their accustomed view of administrative function, Presidential power, and the shaping of foreign policy. Fifty years ago this group stood for inaction in the sphere of the government of industry. Today it adds inaction in the fashioning of foreign policy.

The issue is still the adaptability of our constitutional framework, its adequacy to meet the demands laid upon it. There are, however, differences between the two situations. Except in an indirect sense, the struggle today is not one over economic organization, although it is likely to become so when the question of the organization of a war economy reaches—as it may reach soon—a constitutional phase. Thus far the struggle is mainly over the limits of political action and the lines of the distribution of power. Another difference is that the force obstructing effective government is no longer the Supreme Court, which with its present personnel and in its current doctrinal phase is reasonably ready to give the green light to expansive programs for domestic and foreign policy. The obstructive force has come to be located mainly in Congress, and in areas of the press and particular interest groups.

But if the accidental factors have changed, the essential problem of effective government remains. And the aspects of constitutional crisis in which this problem has at various times been clothed are worth reviewing.

3

Some day the full and rounded story of the New Deal constitutional crisis may be written. To say that may, of course, be only a pious hope. For the full and rounded story even of the Jefferson-Marshall constitutional crisis has not been written, despite the zeal of many of our historians. We have had accounts of Jefferson's attack on the Court, and accounts of the Court's attack on Jefferson and states' rights. But we have had no detailed account of each attack in relation to the other, of both in relation to the economic factors of a developing industrialism, the political factors of a new federal structure, and the psychological factors of the clash between old and new symbols; and finally of all these factors in the context of an international climate of opinion that had been created by the world revolutions of the eighteenth century.

So too with the New Deal constitutional crisis. We have had, in Alsop and Catledge's *The 168 Days,* an account of the legislative battle in a popular vein written from the bias of critics of President Roosevelt's Court proposal. And former Attorney-General (now Mr. Justice) Jackson has given us, in his *Struggle for Judicial Supremacy,* a survey of the Court's behavior before and after the legislative fight. Justice Jackson's book reads a little like the testimonial of a man who is sure that the medicine made all the difference in the world between the feeling before and the feeling after, but is a little ashamed—being a doctor himself—of being beholden to what may have been, after all, a somewhat slickly concocted patent remedy. But we have not yet had, and it may be a long time before we get, a history of the crisis which sees it steadily and sees it whole—which relates it to economic changes, to the class structure of our society, to the struggle for political power, to the world crisis, to the psychological roots of fear and insecurity.

What I set down here is no history: merely a sequence of reflections on the course and the meaning of a particular constitutional crisis. Before we can understand the New Deal crisis, we must understand that it followed on two developments. One was

a revolutionary situation in the world at large, which produced
and was produced by economic dislocation, and which put an enormous strain on our economic and political invention and our national will. The second was a felt need for decisive action in the
economic realm, for a sort of legislative *Blitzkrieg,* and the development of administrative strategies so considerable that the past decade may well go down in American history as most significantly
that of our administrative revolution.

It was some dim knowledge of the revolutionary situation in the
world at large, and of its bearing on American history, which im-
pelled the Administration to make its relatively vigorous attempt
to seek a solution of the problem of production and employment
by new economic strategies and administrative controls. It was the
unwillingness of the Supreme Court majority to recognize the nature of world economics that led to their following the one tradition of seeing the Constitution as an inflexible verbal testament,
rather than the other tradition of seeing it as a tool for effective
government.[3] Out of this clash between the action of the Administration and the opposition of the Court, an irresistible force and
an immovable object, came the constitutional crisis.

Or perhaps I should put it somewhat differently. We start with
economic breakdown. The Administration makes a decisive attack on the problem in terms somewhat novel for America, economically and administratively. The Court answers not by an attack on the problem—insists, in fact, that it is quite unconcerned
with that—but by an attack on the attackers. This course was
taken, as is fairly clear now, not because of the inherent inelas-
ticity of the Constitution, or the inevitability of the particular tradition of constitutional interpretation that was chosen, but primarily because of the inflexibility of the majority's social philosophy. The struggle was joined between effective government and
judicial supremacy.

And yet again, in stating it thus, the truth is likely to prove
elusive. It would be a mistake to view the Supreme Court's role
wholly in terms of inertia. While the social philosophy of the
majority was a quietist one, their judicial philosophy was decidedly
activist. Their attack on the New Deal program of social legislation

---

[3] For the terms used here I am indebted to B. H. Levy, *Our Constitution: Tool or
Testament?* New York, Alfred A. Knopf, 1941.

was vigorous in the extreme. (It is worth nothing, in contrast, that while the economic and social philosophy of the current Court majority [4] is a dynamic one, its judicial philosophy is quietist—that of judicial tolerance of legislative action.) If we premise some sort of equilibrium in the attitude of the people, between their attraction to the idea of necessary legislative change and their clinging to the traditions of necessary judicial guardianship of individual rights, we may say that the violence of the Court's attack threw it off its keel, so far as the delicate balance of public opinion was concerned. The President, reinforced in public opinion by his election for a second term, sensed this and counter-attacked the Court with his proposal for reorganization. But the President too attacked more violently than he could afford to. He too was thrown off his keel. And he left himself vulnerable to an onslaught that, using the Court plan as the immediate target, went far beyond that target. The varied forces that had been generating opposition, for one reason or another, to the social philosophy or the political tactic of the Administration were polarized around this issue. Especially was this true of many of the liberals, who, while supporting the New Deal, had unquiet doubts about its seemingly erratic course and the crudity of its energies: they now had a chance to release those doubts of a general character under the guise of opposition to a specific break with tradition. And in the course of the turmoil over the President's plan, his opponents—liberals, conservatives, and reactionaries alike—were able to reach deep to the basic fears of the people. For what finally defeated the President's plan was the sense of fear that we were breaking loose from our moorings in the Constitution and setting sail for shores unknown. The result is history.

The course that the constitutional crisis ran is now fairly clear, and has been given some precision in Mr. Jackson's narrative. There were four phases.[5] The first, in 1933 and 1934, was when the Court "hesitated between two worlds," upholding some of the state reform legislation but giving no clear indication of what it would do with the national program. The second was the "nullification" period in 1935 and 1936, in which the Court used its ax freely on

---

[4] 1941.
[5] The paragraph that follows is a rapid summary of Jackson. For a somewhat lengthier discussion, see "Landscape with Judges," above, p. 301.

national legislation. The third was the President's reorganization plan, the struggle over it, and its legislative defeat. And the fourth was the new line of decisions by the Court, indicating a changed orientation, and eventually the formation of a new majority.

Certain questions arise. Could the crisis have been avoided? The answer must be clearly in the affirmative, unless we premise an inevitable and determinist relationship between capitalist economic crisis and a quietist social philosophy on the part of the Court majority which the later history of the Court does not bear out. Need the crisis have been as acute as it was? This is more difficult of answer. One thing is clear: once the Court acted with the extremism it did, and once the President's dramatic plan was announced, compromise became exceedingly difficult. Many who had been disquieted by the Court's decisions found it necessary now to suppress their doubts about the Court in their zeal for the defense of judicial independence. And many who were disquieted about the particular plan of the President found it necessary to suppress their doubts in their zeal for some sort of judicial reform. Once the battle was joined, the alternatives for both groups became absolute. For one group it became a question of either complete judicial supremacy or judicial subordination. For the other it became a question of either the President's plan or no judicial reform at all. In the clash of power politics the desirable direction was transformed into an ideological absolute which had either to be defeated as a whole or accepted as a whole. Everything intermediate was squeezed out.

I turn now to a crucial question. How was the constitutional crisis resolved? In answering it we must seek a different solution from what it would be were our question, How was the political struggle over the Court reorganization bill resolved, and who was the victor in the legislative battle? For the resolution of a constitutional crisis involves not the determination of victor and vanquished, but the clearing of the obstacles that stand in the way of effective government. Thus there was a shift in judicial philosophy on the Court from one militantly opposed to the Administration to one tolerant of its efforts to resume its attack on the basic economic problems. And that change, as Mr. Jackson tells us, took place even before the active changes in the personnel of the Court through resignation and replacement. The change was made partly as a tactical matter, to help persuade Congress to vote against the Court bill.

Yet, it would be wrong to say, as Jackson does, that therefore the ultimate change in the Court's attitude was not due to a change in personnel. For without the actual changes in personnel that followed, the balance of power would have remained in the hands of Justices Hughes and Roberts, and the victory for the New Deal, represented by the Court's shift in orientation, could not have been consolidated. The first period of uncertainty and hesitation that opened the constitutional crisis might have been repeated. And it is significant that the recent Supreme Court policy indicates that what change there has been in the judicial philosophy of Justices Hughes and Roberts has not been so essential as to take them out of the category of frequent dissenters from the current Court majority on economic cases.

Thus the crisis was resolved in two stages: first, when the threat of Court reorganization resulted temporarily in a shift of judicial attitude in the balance-of-power group; and later, when the way was cleared for changes in the personnel of the Court. As a result of both there was a return to the more flexible of the Supreme Court traditions of constitutional interpretation.

There are several other observations that may be worth making, and I am the less disinclined to make them because I have not seen adequate emphasis on them in the literature. They have to do with the resolution of the crisis. But their emphasis is not with the legislative struggle or the Court personnel or the doctrine or philosophy of the judges: rather with popular consciousness and class tensions in our society.

If the Court bill had been passed and we had in that way (through the forced substitution or addition of judges) achieved our present Court liberalism, it would have been difficult for the country to accept that liberalism with the lack of social tension that now characterizes our attitude toward the Court. The Big Industry groups would have felt it to be an unparalleled exercise of arbitrary power. Even the large majority mass would have found it difficult to accept the results, however these results might have comported with the effective government they wanted. For even the majority fears to get the right things in the wrong way. And enough of it had by that time become convinced that the Court plan was the wrong way.

As it happened, the Big Industry groups were estopped from the sort of vociferous and active resistance which they would have offered to the decisions of the new Court if, in their minds, judicial independence had been destroyed through the "packing" of the Court. So, in a deep sense, it was well that while the Administration got the brunt of popular attention in 1933–1935, and the Court's decisions got it in 1935, it was what happened between Congress and the President that got the brunt of attention in the 168 days. The (at least outward) victory of Congress deflected attention from the actual resolution of the constitutional crisis through the play of power politics upon doctrine. The popular mind, which had been stirred to the depths by the events of the Court fight, and in which allegiance to effective government had been aligned against allegiance to judicial independence, was now allowed to go back to its traditional channels. The people could have their cake and eat it too. As for Big Industry, it could not eat its cake, but it also could scarcely protest; for it was *its* cake, was it not? It had won the fight against the Court plan. Even Mr. Willkie, in the campaign for his nomination, was not able, through his well-known *Saturday Evening Post* article on the new Court orientation, to stir up resentment against a too liberal Court that had after all *not* been "packed."

Thus what might have meant a more or less serious impairment of the prestige of the Constitution and Court has been averted. And this has happened largely because the settlement was accomplished within the Constitution rather than outside it. What a theme here for a Thurman Arnold on the way in which everything turns on the decorous observance of symbols—were not Mr. Arnold himself far too busily engaged these days in the decorous observance of symbols to write about them.

But perhaps because of the very fact of the observance of symbols, the central problem of judicial supremacy has been left unaffected. For if we again get a Court which believes that social policy must be shaped by a process of litigation we shall run into another major judicial constitutional crisis.

4

I have spoken thus far of an episode in recent American history which presented an example of an interlocked constitutional crisis, which was in its first great phase economic and its second judicial. It is, moreover, an instance of a completed crisis cycle—one that has run its course, although it has left a residue of effects.

I turn now to a different type of crisis—what I have termed the war constitutional crisis. The democratic crisis state, after weathering pretty well its first (domestic) storm, is now facing its second (international) storm. It was inevitable, as we entered into the phase of severe international strain, that constitutional difficulties should arise. The need for extraordinary pace and decisiveness in action necessarily placed strains on the constitutional limits of the state. But it was also to be expected that those strains would apply not to the relations between the Administration and the Court, but to those between the Presidency and Congress, and that they would be fought out not in Court decisions but in Congressional debates and the channels of opinion formation.

That is happening now. I do not consider that we are at present in a state of serious constitutional crisis. I do think that we are in a state of constitutional expansion which has crisis elements and potentials. I shall speak later of the broadening by the present Court of the limits of tolerance for social legislation both of the federal government and of the states. Yet while some of our constitutional troops are thus employed in consolidating their victory, the real spearhead of constitutional expansion must be sought elsewhere—in the Presidency in wartime.

You will undoubtedly have noted the important new Presidency books that have been published this year by Laski, Corwin, Herring.[6] This concentration on the Presidency represents a sound instinct, born of a dual outlook: first, a sense of the need for great leadership in America's hour of decision; and second, a sense of the difficulties that will be (and have already been) encountered in the reaching out for Presidential effectiveness.

---

[6] Harold J. Laski, *The American Presidency*, New York, Harper, 1940; E. S. Corwin, *The President: Office and Powers*, New York University Press, 1940; E. P. Herring, *Presidential Leadership*, New York, Farrar & Rinehart, 1940.

I shall not present an analysis of the constitutional aspects of the Presidency. That has already been done with considerable sharpness and in great detail by Corwin. Again I want only to set down some reflections on aspects of our constitutional system in wartime.

One of the difficult but exciting things about the democratic crisis state is that it must carry on under democratic forms in a world that is abandoning them. And this paradox becomes particularly acute in wartime. Although I shall not discuss our foreign policy from the angle of its merits, it is important to note that we are today committed to full aid to the anti-Nazi nations. What does that mean in governmental terms? It means we must fulfill the conditions of modern warfare to survive, just as in the domestic crisis we had to fulfill the conditions of modern economic and administrative strategy to survive. War today is of a dual nature: it is a war of factories and a war of morale. To organize our armament power to aid Britain requires the delegation of vast powers to the Presidency. To mobilize our factory power will raise further questions of war-industries control. To deal with morale will raise problems of civil liberties. But the exacting thing about our situation is that everything we do in our defense effort is geared to the pace and scope of the efforts of the fascist powers. In effect—and here is the paradox—although not yet at war, we are having to operate as if we were fighting a war. Yet, since we have not declared it, our officials do not have either the legal or the psychological powers they would otherwise have.

The problem here, as in the crisis of 1935–1938, is again one of the dominant need of governmental effectiveness if we are to survive, as against an inflexibility of governmental doctrine and machinery. But the differences are important. The struggle is not primarily in the economic but in the political realm. The difficulties do not center in the Supreme Court but in the relation of the President to Congress and sections of public opinion. The ideological minus-symbols that are in use are not those of (economic) socialism but of (political) dictatorship; and the opposite plus-symbols are not judicial authority but civil liberties and political survival.

The institution of the American Presidency is confronting the severest test of its whole history. For no matter what happens in world affairs, the path ahead of us is likely for some time to be as difficult and stumbling as any we have taken. And the Presidency will have to bear the brunt of the burden. For while Congress will have its path cut out to subject the acts of the President and the administrative and military arms of the government to the pitiless test of discussion, and the Court will have to draw a perilous line between public need and private wrong, the great shaping and formative work must be the President's. That has always been true in times of crisis in America, but it will be particularly true in a war crisis of the world era of totalitarianism.

Have we a conception of the Presidency adequate to this need? Here too, as in the case of the scope of the judicial power, there are several alternative traditions we can draw upon. One starts with Jefferson but has generally been associated with the weaker Presidents and the laissez faire executive doctrines: that the President dots the i's and crosses the t's for Congress, and acts as a sort of *tabula rasa* on which "the laws of economics" are written. The other starts with Jackson and Lincoln and includes Cleveland, Theodore Roosevelt, Wilson, and Franklin Roosevelt. I should like to submit that a conception of Presidential leadership adequate to our needs would have to be based on a conception of a militant and affirmative democracy. It would draw upon the second list of names and examples I have mentioned, but it would set them in the international context of today.

What is that international context? It may seem a far cry from a discussion of world forces to the American Constitution, but the latter will not be either workable or intelligible from now on except in that context. It is a context of changing technologies of diplomacy and war. It is a context in which national isolation or neutrality is no longer possible. It is a context of the break-up of the international order we have known. It is a context in which only the strong and affirmative state can survive.

In the light of this the Presidency in the democratic crisis state is likely to extend its power in four areas—first, the military forces, over which the President is already commander-in-chief. Second, the organization of the war industrial structure. Third, the further extension and co-ordination of the administrative agencies. Fourth, the shaping of foreign policy.

Of these, the President's control of the military forces is the least likely to be called in question. Yet this is exactly the point where Lincoln exceeded his powers by taking upon himself in the early stages, without Congress, the responsibility of getting the country ready to fight a civil war. That contingency will probably not arise again unless a Nazi victory over England should align against each other the groups that want to bring our institutions into the orbit of Hitler and the groups that would fight such an eventuality to the bitter end. And yet the President, because of the anomaly of our being at war yet not at war, is today having friction with Congress in regard to the disposition of the armed forces. The difference is that what the President as commander-in-chief could have done under a state of war now has to be done more laboriously as part of the shaping of foreign policy. Yet even here recent events have shown the President has broad enough range in negotiation to commit the nation step by step to a definite foreign policy.

In two of the other three areas there will probably be a good deal less friction before a declaration of war and more after it. In the area of industrial organization, while the crucial problems will not immediately be constitutional, we have learned that questions of property have a way of converting themselves into questions of constitutional power. In the area of administrative control enough has been done in an experimental way during the New Deal (for example, the recent Acheson report [7]) to mitigate the potential difficulties during the war years. But it is in the area of the shaping of foreign policy that the great difficulties have already cropped up and will continue to do so.

There are already many who fear this expansion of power as dictatorship, and others who welcome it as a departure from the cumbersomeness of a leaderless democracy. But surely we need not accept either position. Our task is neither to whittle away the necessary power nor to submit blindly to arbitrary power. Rather is it to give the President the powers he needs, but encircle them with institutional safeguards, and build into them, in the fashioning and execution of policy, those who represent various groups with a real stake in the fight against totalitarianism.

This will still leave knotty problems—of civil liberties, of labor's claims, of the competition of political ideas and political policies. Once more the Supreme Court will have to wrestle with the

---

[7] *Report of the Attorney-General's Committee on Administrative Procedure,* 77th Congress, 1st Session, Senate Doc. 8 (1941).

"clear and present danger" doctrine, in its application to untried situations.

5

I say there will be knotty problems, for several basic reasons. For first, a war or defense emergency brings closer to each other the political and economic structures of a nation. The imperatives of production become political imperatives. The scope of labor choice and bargaining and organization becomes a question fraught with immense political importance. At what point labor is being asked, like any other group, to serve the nation's interest and at what point it is being victimized, under the guise of the national interest, by dollar-a-year men in the government and by army men who sometimes have no sympathy for labor—those too may be tough and intricate questions. The safest general course is again to apply the rule of participation—to ask whether labor has had a hand in administering the machinery to which it is being subjected. Second, a war or defense emergency whittles away the line between utterance and action, between private right and public responsibility, between conscience and constraint. And third, a war or defense emergency brings various local communities together in common and more or less standardized sentiments; and while it infects them with a central tension, it has rarely the machinery for keeping their potential vigilantism in check. It is in these local areas, I think, rather than in the action of the national government, that most of the civil liberties cases will arise. And here too the only possible defense against them is the persistent attempt to spread a sense of the rule of law and the fabric of equality.

I have said above that these will be knotty problems for the Supreme Court to solve. I have relatively few fears about the quality of their solution. It is not only that I consider our present Court a great and technically proficient one. It is also that through all the crises of the past decade—economic, political, constitutional, international—our democracy has retained the essential fabric of legality, the patient education of opinion by the government, and the responsiveness of the government to opinion.

This deserves a word. For we have allowed our thinking about democracy and dictatorship to become thin, smug, and superficial.

We judge them in quantitative terms, as if we were grocers weighing out potatoes. Dictatorship means great power, we say; democracy, little power. Dictatorship means concentrated power; democracy, safely dispersed and divided power. But to say and think that is to fall victim to the great tragic fallacy of our age. For it is not true that to survive a democracy must be weak. In any form of government, power must be adequate to the tasks placed on it. And in any form of government, power must be concentrated as far as may be necessary for survival.

The crux of the problem must be sought in legal, political, and economic responsiveness. The Nazi war lords must by their very nature be lawless, because if they once admitted a system of law to which their power would be subject, by which it would be measured and its arbitrariness checked, their whole house of cards might fall. The only law they recognize is the law they declare, just as the only international order they recognize is the order they can enclose within their iron ring of coercion and terror. And what goes for legal responsiveness goes also for political and economic. So long as we can keep our leaders in office or turn them out at will, so long as jobs are not dependent on state or party, so long as we can keep open the channels for the competition of ideas, the democratic crisis state can be at once decisive and constitutional, strong without sacrificing the liberties of its people.

1941

5

Legalism and Legality

1

FRED RODELL has written a book to end all books on the law and the lawyers.[1] It is not an easy book to write about, and its impact thus far on the reading public has been difficult to determine. It has grieved the judicious, yet left them uneasy; it has delighted the lawyer-haters while leaving them with some doubts about their champion. It is not so much a book as it is a one-man manifesto for the overthrow of the Dictatorship of the Law. Its chief merits are indignation, courage, and a vernacular clarity. Its faults are a shrill insistence, a vaudeville grin while the performer is doing his sleight-of-hand, a lack of body and depth in the development of the theme, and a tendency to be satisfied with brashness when the real intellectual difficulties call for insight and judgment.

Yet whatever its merits and faults, the book must be reckoned with. I am sorry the *Harvard Law Review* (are there no rules of comity in law schools?) saw fit to dismiss it magisterially as evidence of how far someone will go to sell a book. I know enough about publishing to know there is more money to be had in glorifying the fat boys than in attacking them. It is one thing to answer Rodell's blast—which I have thus far seen no one do: it is quite another thing to sneer at it. May I add that it is still a third thing to analyze it. And I refuse to be put off by Rodell's own whimsical manner. For all the bad-boy attitudinizing the book is seriously meant.

"No lawyer will like this book," Rodell begins. Watch out for the logical trick: that does not mean, though it sounds as if it did, that if you do not like the book you must be a lawyer, or at least as thin-skinned as one. I wish Rodell had been less his own kind of lawyer

---

[1] *Woe unto You, Lawyers!* New York, Reynal & Hitchcock, 1939.

and more an intellectual craftsman. He has discarded the high-priest's robes of legal abstraction, but he has retained the lawyer's arts of extreme advocacy. The law is in the dock, and the prosecution is bending every effort to show him up as a cross between Cagliostro and Simon Legree. The book is striking as an indictment. It would have had real force and stature had it been an analysis as well. Nor are the two incompatible, as witness Arnold's *Folklore of Capitalism*.

What is the indictment? Very simply stated: the law is a fraud. Legal words, legal language, legal rules and principles, legal machinery, lawyers and judges and law teachers and law students, criminal law and civil law, common law and constitutional law, substantive law and procedural law—the whole thing is a clear, deliberate, sustained, and unmitigated fraud—carried off for profit, for power, and for the perpetuation of a priestly caste. If I have omitted anything, Rodell has not. All of which will suggest that there is more than a hint of absolutism in Rodell's judgments. And most absolutisms are likely to strike very wide of the mark, for the world tends to go by halves and quarters instead of by wholes. Had we been living for generations in ignorance of the sort of strictures Rodell brings to bear against the law, we might accept him as sort of muckraker-prophet. But most of the criticisms we have heard before. Rodell synthesizes them with a sweeping absolutism. Actually it is not the attack on law itself that is ever novel in any generation. "Let's kill all the lawyers," Shakespeare makes a mobster say, and there has never been a lack of someone to say it since.

What distinguishes one thinking generation from another in this regard may be set down in four categories: the intellectual resources that each generation draws on for its analysis of what is at fault with the law; where it chooses to make the attack and what ground it selects for the battle; how it proposes to rally the effective battalions in the fight; and what it proposes to substitute for the phases of law that it destroys. It is in terms of these four questions that I want to evaluate Rodell's book. The book may seem to many, and perhaps to the author himself, a bit light to bear the burden of so elaborate an analysis. Nevertheless, the problems it poses are problems that must be faced seriously, whether they appear in the utilitarian polemics of Jeremy Bentham or in a jazzed-up Peglerized attack on the law by a Yale Law School professor.

2

Rodell is a product of the strong intellectual currents of our time. He has borrowed from cultural anthropology the idea that every legal system is an organization of group power, that all legal lore is magic, and that every legal class is a priesthood; from contemporary psychology the idea that our thinking is a screen or rationalization for our deeper impulses; from semantics the idea that words may be used to conceal as well as to reveal meanings; even from Marxism the idea that law is a glove that covers the naked fist of class power. And he has borrowed from the popular consciousness the idea that of all the easy rackets in a society thriving on rackets, law is the easiest. I welcome these borrowings, and I welcome the insights he has himself added and the energy with which he has fused the whole. The fact is that we are in a better position today than ever before to write a profound book on law and the legal profession.

But Rodell has not written it. And I think the reason he has not written it is that he has explored only the surface of the various intellectual areas I have mentioned. Take, for example, the realist school in legal thought, to which Rodell patently belongs. The whole burden of this school has been the attack on conceptualism in law. In the hand of some of the earlier realists this was a good attack; with several of the latter group it grew crotchety; but now the attack on concepts seems to be reaching the ultimate denial that any concepts are possible, or any particulars either for that matter: the single case ceases in Rodell's book to have any existence, along with the general rule. The whole legal element of society is wiped out, and we wander about in a law-shorn universe, consoled only by the hope that we may be able some day to decide particular quarrels in a common-sense way through practical technicians who are economists and engineers. Rodell's book illustrates what happens when an idea with considerable validity in it is pushed to the extreme of a crotchet, when the crotchet becomes a popularization, and when the popularization is linked with a crusade.

I confess I am troubled by the anti-intellectual and anti-rational strain in Rodell as I have been troubled by its appearance elsewhere in the realist school. Rodell's gesture is that of a desperate man who, because he dislikes the pedant, is willing to wipe out education.

There can be no question that legal formalism has been historically one of the vicious forces in every culture, and that it has waged a ceaseless war against the best in the human spirit. Yet a closer exploration of anthropology should have taught Rodell that every culture needs a principle of cohesion, and that whether you call that principle The Law or not, that is what it is. And a closer exploration of contemporary history should teach us all that once we give rein to the forces of anti-intellectualism and anti-rationalism we are likely to end up not in a freer and more fluid society, but in a society of more frozen status. Once Rodell has discarded both legalism and legality, the only thing he can fall back on is what he calls "common sense." What a mirage common sense has been for reformers who have not met the radical evils of their time with philosophy equally radical! Surely both Veblen and Thurman Arnold should by now have taught us that what is called common sense is usually only the more reactionary distillation of ruling-class moralisms.

3

My basic quarrel with Rodell, then, on the first score, is that he has not made use of the full intellectual resources of our time. In terms of what we know today from anthropology, psychology, and political theory, we ought to know that what is at fault with the law is not legality but legalism. And this furnishes a clue on the second score. Rodell has selected the wrong ground for his attack on law and the lawyers. To lump together good lawyers with bad, good judges with bad, good legal systems with bad, is to use comprehensiveness when what is most needed is discrimination. Rodell professes not to care whether the lawyers and judges he is considering are liberal or conservative, whether or not the decisions he is talking about are decisions which advance democratic purposes. I know there is something sweepingly attractive about such a general condemnation. It was attractive to the anarchists, who rejected the state as such, and included good states with bad. It was attractive also to the mechanical Marxism of the past quarter-century, which refused to discriminate between reform governments and reactionary governments, and which lumped them together as equally the executive committee of the capitalists. And there is un-doubtedly an element of truth in these absolutisms, in the sense that even a Justice Holmes or Brandeis or Frankfurter operating within the limits of the doctrine and judicial supremacy cannot transcend those limits. Similarly a Cardozo on a state court must be seen as adding to the prestige of a judicial system which, for every Cardozo, includes nine hundred and ninety-nine mediocre or even vicious judges. Nevertheless, after we have recognized this element of validity, it will not do us much good to press it fiercely to its conclusion and sweep out (even if we could) the whole judicial personnel and legal profession. In fact, the reactionary corporation lawyers and judges will have reason to welcome a general attack so sweeping that it obliterates the distinctions between them and the liberal judges and lawyers.

I do not think it was necessary for Rodell to accept the ascetic Catonian doctrine that the whole of the legal Carthage must be destroyed. Nor was it necessary for him to get himself into the posi-tion of having to reject a Holmes or a Frankfurter along with the rest. What he has done has been to keep his attention fixed so com-pletely upon the sins of the legal structure as such that he has made a faulty analysis of what those sins proceed from. Rodell feels that their source is the inherent mumbo-jumbo of legal technicians and the inherent tendency of lawyers and judges to form a caste—that there is something in law as such which converts it inevitably into a tyranny over men's minds and lives. I shall consider later what the implications of this position are in terms of what will have to be substituted for law. But immediately it must be pointed out that this view is very much the sort of absolutism which sees the inherent evil of tyranny in all political power, the inherent evil of material-ism in all economic activity, the inherent evil of egotism in all in-dividual life, the inherent evil of sin in mankind. It is essentially an original-sin view, and for one who professes not to be a moralist it is a strangely moralistic approach.

We are having to learn slowly and painfully that social institu-tions are what you make them, that their evil is not inherently resi-dent in them, and that when they cease to be creative forces and become oppressive forces it is because of the uses to which they are put and because of their relation to other institutions. There is a place within an economic democracy for a legal system, for a legal profession, for a group of judicial technicians. Even the Marxian thinkers of the Soviet revolution, who wanted to sweep away the whole legal and judicial profession, found themselves eventually bringing it back. What is at fault today with our legal institutions is that they are in the service of a small economic oligarchy and are being used by that oligarchy. Rodell is quite right to be impatient of legal reform which operates only within the interstices of the prevailing legal system. Nevertheless, it is almost as futile to expect a revolution that touches the law alone as it is to expect a reform which operates only within the legal system. And what Rodell is calling for is a revolution within the legal system that will not touch any of the other social institutions of our culture.

4

This leads to the third question of how Rodell proposes to rally the effective battalions in his fight against legal evils. I can understand that he has tired of attempts to reform the bar and bench from within by unctuous lawyers and half-liberal judges, and from without by politicians. What he seems to want is a sort of *jacquerie* or syndicalist direct action against the law. Rodell writes with the tough-boy manner of one who in his own field is a Westbrook Pegler *manqué*. He is tired of indirections, tired of quibbling, tired of abstractions, tired of big words. He steams into the harbor of his subject with all flags flying and every gun booming. His anti-intellectualism makes him want to brush aside the mountainous tomes of literature of legal reform and the hypocrisies of after-dinner bar association speakers. He is writing for the laymen. But he is not restricting himself to writing for them: he is also issuing a call to action by laymen.

Yet, curiously and ironically, the *Zeitgeist* does not seem to be on his side in this effort. The great irony is that though the book was written to shock lawyers it will be bought and read mainly by lawyers, and that although it was written to be read by laymen it will be neglected by them. My guess is that the layman's hostility to the law is less pronounced today as compared to the hostility to other institutions than it was, for example, in Bentham's period and in Romilly's. I shall not consider the question of how the sort of revolt Rodell envisages could be organized and built into a movement. It is enough to question the basic premise that you can get laymen today to rise up against the lawyers, or that if they did their action would lead to anything.

And because Rodell's analysis is faulty on these scores, his solution is one of the weakest parts of his book. He proposes an *ad hoc* treatment of every item of litigation by technicians, engineers, economists. That anyone as tough-minded as Rodell should be guilty of so tender-minded a simplicity as to believe that engineers, technicians, and economists differ essentially from lawyers is difficult to see. I tremble to think of what someone like Rodell could do in an analysis of the wisdom and "sound principles" of the economists: in fact, Thurman Arnold has done it. After Thorstein Veblen's excursion into an engineer's Utopia, I should have thought that the narrowness and the lack of social vision of the engineers would also be apparent. Lawyers are not alone in fetishizing their own craft. Nor are they alone in building abstractions and generalizations. Rodell at one point inveighs against "the wilderness of single instances" which the law has become. Undoubtedly an attempt would at first be made to keep every instance single; nevertheless, the experience of our own administrative commissions today shows how cases group themselves into general categories and abstractions arise. The experience even of technicians on legal arbitration boards indicates the same thing. One is reminded of James Thurber's *The Last Flower,* and of what Nietzsche called "the eternal recurrence" that one finds throughout history and society. What Rodell has done by emphasizing the *kind* of people who ought to take care of legal disputes means that he has deflected attention from the more serious problem of the *way* in which those disputes should be handled. I agree completely that when a legal question goes beyond the boundaries of individual litigation and becomes a basic problem of social policy, lawyers and judges are not equipped to handle it, and we need social technicians, democratically responsible to the people. But as long as we are in the realm of litigation it will not do much good to kill the lawyer and set the engineer or the economist up in his place. This is a sort of homicide of the instrument, and in its own way a thoroughly mechanistic approach.

5

By concentrating on the weaknesses and inadequacy of the book I have done less than justice to its freshness, its vitality, and its courage. I have far more admiration for Rodell's book than I have for most of the reviews of it. Rodell at least has shown a radical approach and solution, although I feel that his radicalism is the wrong sort and is misdirected. But those who have railed at the book have for the most part done so on grounds that condemn them more than Rodell. Emerson once in a description of Daniel Webster said that he was a man "the beads of whose blood have eyes that turn to the past." We shall never solve the problem of our legal profession or of our other social institutions, in that spirit. Only those have the right to criticize Rodell who are willing to meet him on grounds as radical as his own.

1940

6

Aspects of Economic Strategy

TNEC: a New Technique

THE monopoly inquiry has finally swung into motion. The first full meeting of the joint Congressional and administrative committee has been held, and to each of the government agencies represented has been assigned the task of collecting and digesting the material in its files bearing on some potential phase of the inquiry. The hearings themselves are likely to begin in September and run until 1940; but it is almost certain that a preliminary report will be made containing recommendations for legislation and suggestions for anti-trust revision. After that the inquiry should settle down to a comprehensive probing of how our industrial system works and how to make it work better.

I consider the launching of this inquiry one of the most important events of our recent history. For a half-century the anti-trust problem has been agitated in this country. Thus far it has produced no results except a moral fervor against monopolies that has gone hand in hand with a complete paralysis of action, and which has permitted the giant corporations to grow until today they dominate our entire economic life. We have entrusted our destiny as producers and consumers to the frail procedures of common-law litigation, and our economic welfare has been bogged down in the metaphysical swamps of legalistic concepts. What is new about the new trustbusters is that they no longer view the problem of monopoly through the blinkers of the anti-trust laws. True, under the vigorous energies of Robert H. Jackson and now of Thurman W. Arnold, even the existing anti-trust laws have been given some meaning and sting. Nothing comparable to the speeches and reports of these two men is to be found in the records of the Department of Justice. What happened in the oil-company trial and what is happening now in the aluminum- and milk-company trials are proof that good public officials do not allow inadequate laws to stand as an excuse for inaction and collusion. But more important than this is the effort to extend the boundaries of the whole monopoly problem.

The time has come to remove the scales that have been on the people's eyes for decades. When the Sherman law was passed in 1890 the anxieties of the nation were directed toward the open and shameless "trusts" that had departed from the ideal competitive norm in which we still believed, and that had cornered control of some market. In the intervening half-century American economic life has moved in seven-league strides toward a condition of vassalage to the huge corporations. No one of these corporations may be in complete control of an industry; yet the reality is that competition no longer exists, and price, wage, and production policies are decided by agreements among a few dominant operating and holding corporations. The avenues by which these results are attained are often so complex, so elusive, so indirect, that they ramify into every area of our industrial, financial, legal, taxation, and investment structure.

That is why it would be impossible, for all the fears and jeremiads of the editorial writers, to make a "witch-hunt" out of the present inquiry. Witch-hunting had its place when there were a few "malefactors of great wealth." But the problems we must get at are too involved in our business structure to be solved by hunting out any single malefactor. The prices of aluminum utensils, automobiles, tires, gasoline, milk, meat—almost everything that we use—are determined by large corporate concentrations of power. Whether they shall be rigid or flexible depends not on the social welfare but on the calculations for maximizing net profits. It is more than merely a matter of price, for production and employment policies as well are subject to these decisions. Investment trusts, government contracts, the investment policies of insurance companies, the structure of holding companies, labor legislation—all are an integral part of what we have been accustomed to call the "monopoly" situation.

Not since the Pujo investigation, a quarter-century ago, have we had the chance we have now of attacking the problem as a whole. We muffed it then, and we may muff it now; but if we do, it must be for failure to will the means of carrying out our objectives. The personnel of the inquiry is not a bad one. The Congressional group leans toward the right. But in the administrative group there are men of the stature of Leon Henderson, Thurman Arnold, William O. Douglas, Isador Lubin, Jerome Frank, and Herman Oliphant.[1] They have a chance to make a chart of the workings of our economic system. They have a chance to see the picture as a whole and to make a co-ordinated attack on the entire problem.

We are not suggesting that we can enter a Promised Land where a single blueprint will solve all our problems. If there is one thing that recent studies have taught us, such as those in the book just published by Walton Hamilton and his associates,[2] it is that every major industry has its own problems of price determination, and that the politics of industry is as complex as the economics of industry. But there are also levers that control the mechanisms of industry as a whole. To make those studies and get at those mechanisms is to accomplish the prelude to economic planning.

The men who rule our industry know this. They have their eyes fixed on this inquiry. They will smash it if they can. They will seek to control it if they cannot smash it. Or, if they cannot control it, they will seek to keep it all in the realm of research and abstractions, and let it peter out there.[3] It is our job to make the inquiry the first step toward a real grappling with the problem of socializing industry.

1938

Trustbuster's White Paper

ADMINISTRATIVE history, like any other form, has its paradoxes. And one of them is that the Thurman Arnold who wrote the savage chapter in *The Folklore of Capitalism* deriding the anti-trust laws should have turned out to be, in his tenure as Assistant Attorney-General, the most militant enforcer the Sherman

---

[1] Mr. Oliphant has since died. Some of the other members of the committee transferred their energies to crucial administrative posts even before the work of the committee was ended.

[2] *Price and Price Policies*, New York, McGraw-Hill, 1938.

[3] Since this was written the TNEC has issued both its individual reports and its general Report. The reports themselves represent a great achievement in economic research and scholarship. But the general Report fails to draw fully the implications of the specific analyses and is largely in the nature of a non sequitur.

Act has had in the half-century of its history. The "theorist," as theorists have in our time increasingly a way of doing, has shown himself fully a match for the "practical men": he has been resourceful, hard-hitting, decisive, knowing when to put on pressure and when to compromise. As the newspaper accounts testify day after day, he is doing a thoroughgoing job of policing the whole range of price policy in American industry. And he does it with an eye so closely fixed upon the American tradition, both in law and in economics, as to make his position hard for the big business men to assail.

Arnold as traditionalist may seem a new Arnold to the many readers of his two earlier books, *The Symbols of Government* and *The Folklore of Capitalism*.[4] And in some ways it is a new Arnold who speaks in this third book,[5] which presents the philosophy, the purposes, the procedures, and the tactics of his job as anti-trust enforcer. In *The Bottlenecks of Business* you will not find the witty, suggestive, and irresponsible play of thought which had by turns shocked and delighted his readers. The present Arnold is first and foremost a hard-working government official—one of the best of the group of legal and economic technicians in Washington who are making administrative history. His new book is clear, direct, and forceful, with an earthy tang to it. In a real sense it is a government document of great importance—an explanation of what a crucial part of our apparatus for economic control has been doing, and why. It is the White Paper of the 1940 version of American trustbusters. But it is an amazing White Paper, with warmth and simplicity, and hard horse-sense.

Let me say first of all that the 1940 version of the trustbuster is very different from the 1900 version of T.R., or the 1912 version of Wilson's New Freedom, or the 1933 version of the NRA days. The men of 1900 assumed, as we can no longer assume, a normal competitive economy that is disturbed by monopolists and can be restored by judicial policing. T.R. made a great show of trustbusting, but—as Arnold points out—there was very little enforcement activity under him, and his staff during his whole anti-trust

---

4 For a discussion of these, see my "The Shadow World of Thurman Arnold" in *Ideas Are Weapons* (1939), pp. 198–217.
5 *The Bottlenecks of Business*, New York, Reynal & Hitchcock, 1940.

crusade consisted of five lawyers and four stenographers. Wilson put his faith in the searchlight of public exposure plus the Federal Trade Commission to regulate unfair competitive practices. And the Roosevelt of the NRA days felt that he had to relax the anti-trust laws by necessity, as his predecessors Harding and Coolidge had relaxed them by inattention. What changed the direction of New Deal anti-trust policy was not only the collapse of the NRA, but even more the recognition that monopoly was a far-flung problem of price and production policy in the whole economic structure. This recognition was the occasion for the work of the TNEC (Temporary National Economic Committee) and has in turn been strengthened by its investigations.

Arnold's thesis about our economic system is that it is intended to be, and can be, a free-market economy; and that what prevents it from being one is "the private seizure of industrial power" through price-fixing and agreements to limit production. It is thus that he redefines the Sherman Act's phrase "restraints of trade" to fit the facts of what economists have called "oligopoly." He cites instance after instance—glass bottles, tobacco, meat-packing, milk, flour, cheese, spectacles, gasoline, medical services—in which the agreement of a few powerful corporations as producers or processors gives them control over price and production policy and stifles any competition from the many small units in the industry. Arnold describes them as the "log jams," "toll gates," "bottlenecks" of our economic process. To use an illustration contained in the Department of Justice charges against the Big Four in tobacco, there are at one end three and a half million persons dependent on leaf tobacco for their livelihood, and at the other end three-quarters of a million retail distributors of tobacco products; in between these two there are a few big corporations that occupy a strategic place in this industrial territory and are able to levy their toll on grower, jobber, retailer, worker, and consumer.

But such a realistic economics is only one of three weapons in the new approach to anti-trust enforcement. The other two are a new strategy of procedure and an enlarged staff. The strategy of procedure consists partly of a new use of the device of grand-jury indictment as a way of forcing restrainers of trade to mend their ways, plus a consent decree when they have submitted a plan of economic organization acceptable to the Anti-Trust Division and the courts. It consists also of a shift of emphasis from private to public suits. In a striking chapter Arnold points out that in the past the Sherman Act has been used mainly when invoked by corporations that had the money and the legal talent to push the suit through. This has meant that instead of being used *against* the controlling corporations, the Sherman Act has been used *by* the controlling corporations against labor, farmers' co-operatives, and organizations of small producers. But to do a good job of public prosecution means to make a systematic survey of the industrial system in order to locate the bottlenecks, and then to learn enough about each case in both economic and legal terms to make the charge stick. That means a large staff. Arnold aims at something like the 1200 people that the SEC has. "You cannot keep order in a nation with a corporal's guard," he says. If I were a Congressman I should vote for increased appropriations to provide him with his army.

I know I have not been able to do justice to Arnold's whole case, but I have said enough to indicate my admiration for the vigor and the realism of his approach. Yet I must express a set of doubts and caveats some of which may go to the roots of his position.

Let me put them down quite summarily. First, there is Arnold's recurring praise of traditionalism. He has always poured out his scorn on moralists and reformers. He speaks here as a government official who accepts the limits within which he has to do his work. Those limits are free-market capitalism, the main lines of the governmental tradition, and the accepted ideas of the American people. I do not know how much of this may be tongue-in-cheek irony. But if Arnold be taken seriously, he is in effect saying that there can be no radical innovation in government and no fundamental changes through education. I should not in any way object if he were to say, "My job as government official limits me to working within the accustomed limits of American opinion"; although even on that score I might point out that his chief, President Roosevelt, has done a first-rate job of economic and administrative education. But his book goes further and says, in effect, that any except a traditionalist realism is unworthy of comment.

Let me, second, and by way of illustration of the above, refer to Arnold's simple and yet suggestive discussion of the use of court procedures as against administrative tribunals in government. If you have a broad job to do, he says, involving the use of a general formula, such as "restraint of trade" or "due process" in its application to specific cases, use the courts. If you have a specific job to do such as regulating the bituminous coal industry, use an administrative commission. The reason is mainly that the courts are a great positive symbol in the popular mind, and administrative bodies are still a negative symbol. This seems to make sense. Yet I should like to differ with Arnold. The Anti-Trust Division used legal tribunals for almost fifty years with hardly any results: it was only Arnold's vision in seeing the need for a large administrative staff of experts and a new administrative strategy of which court processes form a part which has led to its renascence. And on the NLRB, which tries to apply a general formula of collective bargaining to specific cases, a new commissioner, William Leiserson, is now urging that there has been too much emphasis on lawyers and legal procedures and not enough on expert administrative processes. Whoever is right, Arnold must understand that, regardless of symbolism, the path of government advance leads away from the omniscience of judges to the *expertise* of administrators —like himself.

There is, third, the question of his attitude toward trade unions. I am not one of those who regard Arnold as a labor-baiter. If the bottleneck conception is once admitted and collusive price-and-production practices limiting the freedom of the market are viewed as the essence of monopoly, then trade unions cannot be left out of the picture. It is well known that there are American trade unions that have adopted the philosophy and tactics of American big business, just as there are some trade unions that are the instruments of racketeers. It would be strange if this were not so. Arnold's case against the building-trades unions, for example, is a persuasive one. Yet I should have welcomed in his book a clearer statement that the building trades are marginal to trade unionism rather than characteristic of it, and a recognition of the dangers that in other hands than his own may attend such an anti-trust conception.

This leads to my fourth doubt about Arnold's position: his basic middle-class outlook. There is a sort of "plague on both your houses" attitude on Arnold's part toward business and labor. He regards both as threats to a free market, and in a chapter on "The Rise of the Consumer Movement" he tries to find some base for his efforts in consumers' interests and consumers' organization. I do not think he succeeds. It is a truism that we are all consumers, but each of us is primarily something else. I should myself be more sympathetic to a functional nationalism which made the national welfare itself the basic objective. And such a nationalism would emphasize a strong and productive labor movement as one of its essential parts. Arnold comes closest to evolving a broad national (not just consumer or middle-class) view in his brilliant treatment of restraint-of-trade prosecutions as related to national defense. Here he seems to me to be dead right, and the Knudsen-Stettinius group dead wrong.

I end with a comment on Arnold's general economic conceptions. There are, he says, only two methods of distributing goods—the free market and the military or authoritarian system. If he means what he says here, I must dissent strongly. Between the free-market conceptions of the economists from 1890 to 1940 and the authoritarian economies of either Germany or Russia there are a whole variety of intermediate and new forms which it is our function to explore. America today is no longer a free-market economy: it is a form of democratic state capitalism, trying to minimize the area of state control but moving steadily toward an ever-wider area. In this movement Arnold's ideas and procedures in enforcing the Sherman Act are part of a broad strategy of government control of industry. For him to say that he wants only to restore the free market may be good rhetoric and may strengthen his position. But it does not alter the fact that through him the American people are today taking a major hand in determining price and production policies. This is all to the good. But when Arnold condemns other elements in the government's economic strategy, and particularly when he rules out further movement toward economic planning, he is allowing his sense of the importance of his own job to obscure its place in the general campaign.

1940

Keynes Meets Marx

IT IS a new John Strachey who emerges from the covers of this book.[6] Remember the young aristocrat-Marxist who frightened English and American conservatives half out of their wits in his *Coming Struggle for Power,* with its cocky assurance of the approaching triumph of the proletarians? Well, he is no longer so sure of himself. Ironically, his first book, which doomed capitalism in any form, appeared almost simultaneously with the election of Mr. Roosevelt and the triumph of Hitler. The seven years since then have been disillusioning years for Mr. Strachey. He gave us a brilliant economic analysis to support his views in *The Nature of Capitalist Crisis,* but in his present book he retracts much of what he said there. His *Theory and Practice of Socialism* was a study of contracting economic systems in action and a paean to socialist planning. There is little mention of it here. In *What Are We to Do?* there was a paean on a strong united-front labor party, but there is little in the present book on political tactics either. And after the writing of this book, Mr. Strachey definitely broke with the communists over their attitude toward the war.[7] The crack in Mr. Strachey's earlier convictions came with his little book *Hope in America,* which although acceptable to the communists in the united-front period, was not really part of the traditional Marxist thinking. Already in that book Mr. Strachey thought that capitalism might be temporarily saved by an extensive governmental spending program. Ever since his writing of *The Nature of Capitalist Crisis,* Mr. Strachey has become increasingly an economist, has come to know the views of the Keynesian economic school in England, and has swapped ideas as well as blows with the younger group around Mr. Keynes. This combination of external disillusionment and internal education has produced the present book.

It presents the most striking blend of Marxism and Keynesism in our literature—of the basic internal contradictions of capitalism on the one hand, and on the other hand of the possibility of keeping capitalism going through the governmental control of savings and investment. Actually, as Mr. S. Alexander points out in the

---

[6] *A Programme for Progress,* New York, Random House, 1940.

[7] The break has since become complete, as is indicated by Strachey's two most recent books, *A Faith to Fight For* (1941) and *Digging for Mrs. Miller* (1941).

February 1940 issue of the *Review of Economic Studies,* there has never been any reason, except the self-imposed insulations of both schools, why the Keynesian and Marxian doctrines should not fit together. Each in its own way represents a powerful attack on the laissez faire doctrine and the school of classical economics. It is interesting that Mrs. Joan Robinson, a follower of Keynes, speaks of him as having "breached the citadel of classical economics from within." Keynes has had an amazing influence in the past decade upon the economic policy both of the capitalist democracies and of the fascist governments.

Strachey's concern is with the problem of unemployment and with the task of full employment. The first of the three parts into which the book is divided is a masterful analysis, for the layman, of the economics of investment control. He starts with the basic contradictions of capitalism—the falling rate of profit due to surplus value, which makes it impossible either to cut wages (leading to underconsumption) or to raise them drastically (leading to the drying up of production). He avoids the dilemma by saying that the problem is neither with profits nor with wages, but primarily with investment. Progressive governments under democracies can put idle money back into investment channels through a program of governmental spending and tax programs which eat primarily into savings. But their attention would be directed primarily to interest and rent, rather than to wages and profits. His program for progressives is an expansionist program, involving increased public works, further expenditures on the social services, governmental lending at low interest rates approaching zero, and taxation to redistribute income and to cut into savings. In this respect there is a striking similarity between his program and that of Stuart Chase, embodied in the "Six Modest Proposals" to the President, which is a chapter in his *Idle Money, Idle Men.*

Mr. Strachey is at his best in the second part of his book, involving an analysis of the New Deal. The distinction that he draws here between the program of the Blum government and that of the Roosevelt government is especially interesting at a time when so many special pleaders in our own country are trying to equate them. His distinction runs in terms of Blum's attempt to tackle the problem of unemployment by raising wages and lowering hours, as contrasted with President Roosevelt's at least partial understanding of the need for confronting the realities of the investment process. Roosevelt, of course, lost his great opportunity in 1933 for a national policy of credit socialization and investment control, but after the depression of 1937, which Mr. Strachey interprets primarily as having been due to Roosevelt's return to orthodox budgetary ideas, he redeemed himself by a forthright lending-spending program.

Even more interesting, though far more fragmentary, is the third part of Mr. Strachey's book, an analysis of expansionism and investment control in the Nazi German economy. Strachey answers the question as to whether the Nazi regime is capitalist or socialist by pointing out that Hitler has achieved a full re-employment of German labor and all that this involves in terms of increased national income, while keeping the average wage of the German laborer at roughly six dollars a week. This means that there is an enormous surplus going to German capitalists in the form of profits, interest, and rent. Hitler's solution of the problem of this surplus has been to borrow or take in the form of taxes the whole surplus which could not otherwise be reinvested and put it into the production of armaments. This keeps the money moving (although it forces it into socially unproductive channels) and therefore maintains full employment. If fascism were content to remain a peaceful regime, Hitler might have hit upon a solution—however ridiculous —to the unemployment problem. He might build and scrap armaments, build and scrap them. But this would not satisfy the capitalists, who want new and profitable fields for investment. Hence fascism is by necessity an imperialist economy, and the capitalists accept its regime not only because of its coercive power and its terrorism and the prestige which they associate with it, but also because its imperialism promises them new investment opportunities outside of Germany for their idle surplus.

In the light of events since this book was written, two striking conclusions can be drawn from this analysis. One is that if Hitler can consolidate his recently acquired territorial gains and offer the capitalists expanding investment opportunities in the industries of Holland, Belgium, Norway, and France, he can ward off— perhaps for a generation—the inexorable problem of accumulating surpluses. The second is that he cannot ward it off forever. Ultimately, Nazism, for all its features of economic planning, is an unstable economy. Sooner or later, even assuming a period of relative peace under the *pax Hitlerica,* the Nazis would face the alternatives of further imperialism and further war on the one hand and of socialism on the other.[8]

I regard this as Mr. Strachey's best book since *The Coming Struggle for Power.* It is not surprising that it has been severely criticized by the English communists. For it shifts the basis of discussion not only of Marxian economics but of progressive political action. I have two essential criticisms of this. One is that while Mr. Strachey has developed as an economist, he has not equally developed as a political realist. An expansionist program such as he envisages would lead to bitter opposition not only of the rentiers and the finance capitalists against whom it is directed, but of the industrialists as well, and of the middle class whose attitudes are controlled by the stereotypes of the press. When one considers the resistance that Mr. Roosevelt's program has already met, one can begin to calculate the increased resistance that the expansion of that program would entail. My second criticism is that in his analysis of Nazism, as also in his analysis of progressive democracy, Mr. Strachey is not enough of a psychologist; he omits therefore the factors of social allegiances and hierarchical authority which have come recently to cut across economic life. In both these respects perhaps the position of America in a new and dangerous framework of international crisis may be of some help. In the face of extreme national danger, resistance to necessary economic reforms may be weakened; and a democracy such as ours may learn to build up that sense of the individual's organic relation to the group on which ultimately our power of survival depends.

1940

---

[8] For a fuller discussion of this problem, see "Economic Empire and Monopoly State," above, p. 46.

7

The Administrative Revolution in America

1

SINCE Hobbes, we have spoken of the modern state as "Leviathan"; and only a year ago there appeared a book by Robert MacIver [1] using the same phrase in its title and raising the old and ever-new question whether democracy can survive in so cumbrous a form and when the demands made upon it are so great. Today's technologies have played havoc with yesterday's ideas and are shaping the outlines of tomorrow's governments. Perhaps a third of the world has had to turn the burden of running its economic systems almost completely over to its governments, and the portion that has not done so is imposing scarcely less a burden in the complex and delicate tasks of regulation.

So much is clear to the point of common assent. Less clear is the effect this has had on the discussion and operation of government. When John Stuart Mill wrote his famous chapter "On the Grounds and Limits of the Laissez-Faire or Non-Interference Principle" [2] he was concerned with "the limits of the province of government" mainly from the viewpoint of individual liberty and property rights. He could afford to be. Whether and how far the hand of government was to reach into the economic province was (or at least seemed) still a matter of choice. True, it has not yet become a matter of inevitability. But it is significant that the focus of debate has shifted. We have come (except in the intellectual hinterlands of newspaper columns and radio speeches and academic textbooks) to accept the proposition that in the immediate future govern-

---

[1] *Leviathan and the People*, Baton Rouge, Louisiana State University Press, 1939.
[2] *Principles of Political Economy*, Bk. V, Chap. XI, 1848.

ments will have to assume a major rather than a marginal share of economic control. We now ask: Given such a trend, how and by whom shall the government be organized so as best to transact this business? And how can such a government itself be democratically controlled? We have moved, I think, from the voluntaristic to the functional, from the whether to the how.

In that transition are contained at once the tasks, the dangers, and the opportunities of administration.

2

In terms of sheer volume, of course, even if in no other, the functions of government have increased. The increase in volume is partly due to the new importance of the "social services" of the national government—and we must remember that in addition to the "service state" we now have the "service city." The increase is due also to the new governmental functions which Lyon, Watkins, and Abramson, in their recent Brookings study,[3] discuss as the "implementation" of economic activity. It is clear that, regardless of the inner tensions and conflicts of the economic mechanism, the burden on government in terms of sheer administrative routine was bound to grow much heavier. It is equally clear that this alone would not have added up to our present administrative crisis. The evolution meant a greater strain on the technological resources of government and its regular services—patent registration, old-age insurance, labor statistics, crop information, foreign commerce services. But it would not have created what I have called elsewhere the "crisis state." [4]

For it is not alone economic growth and "complexity" (how overburdened a word!) that have posed the tasks of contemporary government. It is the conflicts of interest within the economy, and the breakdown of the economic machinery on which we had hitherto relied. To supply farmers with crop information and run agricultural experiment stations represents one kind of governmental task; to administer a system of agricultural crop and price control represents a very different kind. To run a Bureau of Labor

---

[3] *Government and Economic Life,* Vol. 1, 1939.
[4] *It Is Later Than You Think,* New York, Viking, 1939.

Statistics or even a Labor Arbitration Service is one thing; to administer a National Labor Relations Act is quite another.

The outstanding fact about the administrative structure of the crisis state is that it has had to be built up to meet the conditions of economic conflict and breakdown. That the free-market economy which formed the basis of laissez faire theory no longer exists is a fact now scarcely questionable.[5] Its passing has led to new forms of economic insecurity—hence the recent social-insurance programs of the government; to a stoppage of function in various economic areas—hence the role of the government as entrepreneur and investor; to clashes between economic-interest groups—hence the government as umpire and equalizer of bargaining power; to new industrial practices—hence the government as regulator; to a concentration of income and economic power—hence the government as controller. Nor are these new functions a matter of passing emergencies. They obtain even in what we have learned to call "normal" periods.

In the face of all this, it is notable that much of our reasoning about public administration still rests on the premise of a separation between problems of governmental operation and problems of governmental and economic power. This is true both of the writers who leave the power aspects wholly out of the picture and of those who concentrate on the menace of bureaucracy and the dangers of power inherent in government business. It takes a wrench in our thinking to recognize that power is today an integral part of the problem of administration; that the new governmental agencies, by the very analysis of their origin and function, must operate within a framework of economic breakdown, economic conflict, economic control.

3

I have spoken thus far of the widened scope of government. But it must not be concluded that the change and stir have been entirely in the economic area. While technology has been moving onward relentlessly in industry, it has not been standing still in

---

[5] For recent treatment, see A. R. Burns, *The Decline of Competition*, New York, McGraw-Hill, 1936; and Walton Hamilton and Associates, *Price and Price Policies*, New York, McGraw-Hill, 1938.

government. Innovations have been introduced into the administrative process—borrowed largely, to be sure, from other disciplines, yet none the less far-reaching for that. We have transferred to the government sphere the results of scientific management so as to create a new phase in the history of Taylorism; the techniques of business administration, especially of corporate planning and fiscal control; the techniques of military organization, of propaganda, of research. If we had publicists to glorify these innovations as there have been publicists to glorify the march of the machines, one might perhaps speak of an administrative revolution comparable in its own realm to the industrial.

If we are witnessing such an administrative revolution it has, in America at least, a triple axis. One is the creation of new administrative forms to meet new governmental objectives. I am convinced that we are only on the threshold of almost limitless possibilities in this field. The independent administrative commission and the government corporation are important mainly because they show our capacity for political and legal invention. They have by no means exhausted that capacity. What is most important about the independent commission, as Dean Landis has pointed out,[6] is its flexibility for its task. It must meet problems that concern the whole of an industrial complex, as for example the communications industries; or some entire phase of economic activity, such as the investment process or labor relations. To do so it was forced to cut across the separation of powers, and fuse whatever powers might be necessary in performing its task. It enables us to confront an economic power entity with a governmental power entity.

The second axis is the idea of planning. It has been taken out of the area of the dream. It is already in force, in a piecemeal way and in unrecognized forms, yet none the less significantly as representing a start. However we may disapprove of the principle of crop limitation, agriculture is today planned in America. Regional use of electric power is planned. Old-age and unemployment insurance are planned, even if badly. So too is our whole military and naval machine. And it is important that out of the bitter debate on relief, the one idea of significance to emerge is that the problem must be shifted from the plane of erratic Congressional hand-outs to the plane of a planned program in which probable needs are

[6] *The Administrative Process*, New Haven, Yale University Press, 1938.

scientifically calculated and anticipated, and the cost distributed between co-operating federal and local governmental units.

Finally there is the axis of a new attitude toward the government service and the new morale in it. For all the cries of bureaucracy we are not frightened at the idea of a trained elite of administrators and technicians to carry the burden of government business. Real ability is being conscripted—organizational, legal, economic, engineering, publicity. The brain trust was a phenomenon so long as these special skills had not yet been built into the whole administrative structure. We can see now that the important thing about the brain trust was not that it was a group around the President. The important thing was its character as improvisation. What was improvised can, however, also be institutionalized. It may lose some of its dramatic character, but it gains in effectiveness and responsibility.

4

If we are able to push further this administrative revolution, we need have few fears that our governmental techniques will lag seriously behind the tasks with which we must cope. The controlling problems of government in the calculable future are likely to be not problems of management but problems of power relations. Consider, for example, some of the spheres of acute social conflict today. In the case of the Tennessee Valley Authority there can be no question of the administrative efficiency with which it has performed its business; its troubles have come mainly from obstruction in the courts and from hostile publicity directed at it by the private utility groups. Even in the case of the National Labor Relations Board, which had to assume governmental functions without an adequately equipped staff, and which had to build its organization in the thick of political and economic struggles, there can be little doubt of a steadily increasing efficiency; here also judicial resistance and press campaigns have furnished the principal difficulties. In the area where economic breakdown has had its main impact, that of relief, we are gradually moving toward more scientific methods of administration; again, the uncertainties of the future are uncertainties that flow from the area of struggles over power.

The great fact about the crisis state is that it had to carry on its efforts toward administrative efficiency in the midst of tense battles.

This is true in agriculture, in relief, in labor relations, in electrification, in investment control. And the fighting has left its scar tissue that disfigures the administrative organism. Every one of the new agencies has been compelled to dissipate much of its energy by having to defend its existence at the same time that it has been trying to do its work. Every one of them has had to work in the context of a hostile organization of opinion industries, and against the grain of what Thurman Arnold has called the "folklore of capitalism"— that is, the pecuniary fabric of our institutions and our thinking. Moreover, every agency has been more or less isolated, projected for a specific purpose, and rarely if ever made part of an articulated plan. Finally, it is a serious count against our administrative structure that it tends toward overcentralization and does not use adequately (as the Tennessee Valley Authority is doing increasingly) the administrative resources of local units and the support of local opinion. The top-heavy structure is to no small extent due to the very fact that the backers of the various measures had to fight so hard for centralization that they were unable to do justice to the claims of decentralization. To all of this we must add the absence of a reservoir of adequately trained personnel to draw from.

It will be difficult but not impossible to overcome the present deficiencies. To be sure, the lack of plan is not simply a matter of ineffectual and anarchic governmental organization. Those who have diagnosed it in this fashion have urged the need of governmental reorganization. The Report of the President's Committee on Administrative Management is a powerful plea for a rational governmental structure. There can be no doubt that the recently enacted reorganization bills will go a long way toward fitting together the loose joints of administration. But it would be an error to regard the defects as primarily within the governmental structure and remediable by the blueprints of a new management technology. What is needed is the type of planning which fits the administrative structure on the one hand to the economic structure and on the other to the federal and regional structure. In that sense the current researches of the Temporary National Economic Committee are more crucial toward the attainment of administrative efficiency than most of us may recognize. For if we can achieve a realistic picture of how the economic system actually operates, and where its strategic leverages are located, we shall be able more easily to fit the various parts of our governmental program into an operative whole.

5

If we can accomplish this even to an extent, we shall to that extent have reclaimed some of the waste lands of social confusion and disorganization. We have heard in the past few years a chorus of praise for the merits of enterprise management as a science and an art and along with it a chorus of abuse of public management. It is time that we grew aware of the affirmative functions of management in a democracy such as ours.

One such function has been the setting by federal agencies of minimum standards of social decency and security. The device of federal grants to states and local governments conditioned upon their acceptance of such standards is the obvious way of getting around the difficulties of our obsolescent federal structure. But it is more than that—two things more. It is a method of introducing into our economic system at least a measure of respect for the aged and the unemployed, and of extending this conception on a nation-wide scale. And it is a form of administrative pioneering, the setting of an example for backward regions to follow. For our federal system, Justice Holmes once spoke of experiments carried on in the "insulated chambers afforded by the several states," and as long as the problem of control was one for which isolated state action still seemed effective his was the course of administrative as well as constitutional wisdom. But the reach of economic ills has far outdistanced the grasp of state action. As a result, the burden of administrative innovation has fallen on the federal agencies. They have had to become leaders in experiment as well as co-ordinators of state action.

Another function has been the assumption by public management of social tasks that would otherwise have been left unperformed. The public-health work of the federal government with its informational campaign against venereal diseases is a case in point. More important still is the educational work of such federal agencies as the Works Progress Administration and the Resettlement Administration which have extended the scope of education for the masses, brought literacy to new hundreds of thousands, and burst the bonds of the traditional district- and county-school system. Still another instance is the work of the Tennessee Valley Authority, which has brought cheap light and the amenities of a mechanized civilization to the low-income groups of an entire region.

Beyond any of these functions, the real role of public control must be sought in its relation to a society which is in a process of dissolution and which has not yet found the conditions for reorganization. It is a truism by now that the ordinary person in our culture has been torn from the earlier anchorages of family, neighborhood, and church, and has found no new ones. We have tended in the past to talk as if economic reconstruction would in itself contrive substitutes for these older bonds. Yet this is to ask too much of purely economic action, which can at best furnish a means of living without furnishing the conditions of a life. It is not too much to ask of those who are thinking in terms of new administrative structures and new administrative forms that they should be looking for something which would help weld together the essential elements of an emerging society. Those who have worked in the field of administration have not fully seen the dignity of this broader task, which is not simply to create a new Taylorism but to help build the framework of a culture.

We all know that the swift economic change of the past century has produced social disintegration. But this is only a meager half-truth. What we do not see so clearly is that economic change in and of itself is incapable of either destroying or building a way of life. It is economic change undirected and unchanneled by social controls that has been so destructive; and it is a redirection and re-channeling of economic change which may yet restore for us the conditions of a society in which an ordinary man can feel that he has a place. We have a chance to use administration for rebuilding the pattern of our lives. In a new conception of labor-relations services, in a more affirmative attitude toward public health and education and social security, in a more determined effort toward public housing, in a clearer organization of the strategic centers of our economy such as investment and the credit system, lies an opportunity for the administrative services to go beyond mechanism to what is organic in a society.

For unless we can give to our millions of people a sense of being securely riveted to a way of life, our economic efforts and our political contrivings can do little to save us from cultural doom.

Brooks Adams once said that "it has been on administrative difficulties that revolutions have for the most part supervened." One may add that it is only through new administrative structures that revolutions have been consolidated, as witness the Soviet bureaucracy after Lenin and the German corporative system under Hitler and Göring. But one may add also, and more pointedly for our purposes, that the meaning of administrative change lies not only in preceding and supplementing revolution but also as an alternative to revolution. Ultimately the only effective alternative to a revolution of violence is an administrative revolution that builds within a culture the organic framework, strong and yet elastic, by which that culture may change and grow and therefore survive.

1940

8

Notes on the Two-Front War

Harold Laski and the Two-Front War

MORE than any other English intellectual, Harold Laski has risen to the demands of England's greatest crisis. He has not allowed the tyranny of past dogmas to betray him into opposing a war whose successful conclusion is a condition of any future democratic hope. Neither has he allowed his profound anti-fascism to betray him into accepting the war merely on the conditions of the British ruling class. Like other Labor Party intellectuals he has had to do his thinking, as also his fighting, on two fronts—facing the enemy of fascism abroad and the enemy of capitalist privilege at home. It is a measure of his humanity that he has known which is the greater enemy. But it is also a measure of his democratic realism that he has been unwilling to abandon his struggle against the lesser.

This little book [1] of his proclaims that the two struggles are linked: there can be no chance for economic democracy unless fascism is overthrown, but neither can there be any chance for a victory against fascism except through the extension of the democratic revolution.

All of Mr. Laski's books are part tract, part treatise. In this, one of his briefest and surely his most moving, the tract predominates. But this is not to say that it is, like most tracts, compounded of wishful thinking and reckless urging. Its fire burns the more fiercely because of the compactness of the logic that feeds it. If it expresses the dignity of suffering and the resoluteness before the enemy that England's plain people feel, and the whole political outlook of the Labor Party, it does so in language that belongs to no party or

---

[1] *Where Do We Go from Here?* New York, Viking, 1940.

class but to the whole English intellectual tradition. It is by all odds the most important book that has issued from England since the outbreak of the war.

I shall have some quarrels to pick with Mr. Laski's analysis before I am through. But I must confess that the book is beautiful in structure. It is in effect a long essay divided into three sections. The first traces the victories of fascism thus far to the weaknesses of the capitalist democracies, and these in turn to the central contradiction between capitalism and democracy. The second gives an analysis of fascism from which the fascist leaders emerge as adventurers who have built their power by exploiting the contradiction I have mentioned, and as outlaws who can neither tolerate nor survive a regime of law and freedom anywhere, who must drive on to complete world power and who are therefore utterly unappeasable. The third argues that the effort to overthrow them will be both impossible and fruitless except by a "revolution by consent," through which the capitalists will accommodate themselves to the needs of democracy and thus resolve the central contradiction of our society.

Note how each of these sections is, in effect, addressed to a different group. The first is an attempt to assess the blame for what happened in the two decades between wars and is an indictment of the Baldwin-Chamberlain-Hoare tories of the past. The second is an urgent plea to the tories of the present—the residues of the Munich men—to have done with the dream of appeasing Hitler, and incidentally a plea to the labor groups to push the war relentlessly. The third is addressed to the tories of Mr. Churchill's type, who want the war won but at the minimum cost to the basic structure of economic power. "When the leaders of a nation ask the masses to die for a dream," Mr. Laski writes, "the men who risk their lives are entitled to know on whose behalf those leaders dream." And again, "if we want the winds of democratic doctrine to blow through Europe, we must first set them in play in Great Britain."

The book is filled with insights. One is the author's emphasis on the way in which Hitler's rearmament program fitted beautifully into his whole strategy: it gave the masses a modicum of security, satisfied the demands and pride of the army (thereby driving a wedge between the generals and the capitalists), and gave the capitalists hope of heaven by the promise of the spoils of conquest. Another insight is that while Hitler uses planning techniques in the Nazi economy, it is not thereby a socialist economy, but rather a return to mercantilism: its aim is not living standards or abundance but state-power, which in effect means the power of the Nazi leaders.

What bothers me in this book is what has always bothered me in Mr. Laski—the rift between his analysis and his program. When he talks of the past, it is to say that the contradiction between capitalism and democracy is an inherent one, and that when the capitalists sabotaged democracy they followed the whole logic of their experience. But when he speaks of the future, he speaks as if the contradiction could be resolved and the capitalists lose their class blindness. He is careful to say not that they *will* see the light, but that in this war crisis they have a *chance* to.

I wish he had written another section exploring the psychology of capitalists in this crisis, which might lead them to this "accommodation," and the internal nature of a democratic collectivism which, through the certainty of economic expansion by planning, might prod their sense of humanity.[2]

1940

Defense and Slave-Men

THIS is the winter of our discontent. The massive effort we must now make to prepare for a war from which we have consistently kept our gaze will shake our social frame until every potential weakness is revealed. In the end that is healthful for a nation, and in the end we shall come through. But the process is a grim one. And any number of us, including the big names in journalism, muff its meaning. I wish, perhaps irrelevantly, that William Bolitho were alive. He could approach a topic by the most casual indirections yet somehow lay bare its marrow. Alone among the columnists of our time he had an untamed mind that avoided the snares of our everyday thought. I have been wondering what he would make of the current pother over labor and defense. That it is a convulsive question may be judged from its having sent all

---

[2] Laski's line of thought has since been elaborated with more detail in two books by Francis Williams, *War by Revolution*, New York, Viking, 1940; and *Democracy's Battle*, New York, Viking, 1941.

sorts of maggoty things crawling from the halls of Congress. I suppose I have by now read a hundred-odd pronouncements on it from columnists, editors, labor leaders, industrialists, politicians, and other bigwigs. We have bandied pro-labor and anti-labor arguments back and forth until our minds have become prisoners in the grooves they have made.

Let us start with first things. There can be little doubt that in a war or "national defense" economy labor generally gets the run-around. The task of the ruling groups in maintaining their rule is always made easier in a war emergency. This is as true in England and America as in the Third Reich or the Soviet Union. It means merely that in war, if the economic and political systems are not to crack, they must move more closely together. The lords of the earth become more lordly, their commands more imperative. In the name of patriotism they declare they will brook no opposition.

It is rarely, however, in a democracy that these lords deliver their commands in their own voice. They have to use a sort of political ventriloquism and speak through puppets. James Wechsler ran in *PM,* the New York daily, a remarkable series of interviews with the chief labor-baiters in Congress—Cox, Smith, Hoffman, Sumners. I shall not retraverse his ground. Even on their guard they revealed plenty. What was most interesting, however, was what was least sensational. For one thing, the labor-hatred of these men is an old story with them. The national-defense emergency is not the cause of their labor-hatred: it is rather the instrument.

But it is a peculiarly effective instrument. And the reason is that modern war has become a war of factories. As the recognition of that sinks into the middle-class mind it bears a bitter fruit of opinion. In a war of factories, men reason, industrialists are the generals. Hence the strategic position of Knudsen, the flattery heaped on him, the most recent honor and power that are being accorded him as head of the proposed new defense super-board, although his ability as administrator is still a matter of faith, and not of record. And in a war of factories, men reason again, workers are the soldiers. That is why the demand for decent wages and hours in the defense industries becomes to the middle-class mind sheer arrogance, collective bargaining becomes insubordination, and the right to strike becomes treason.

Let us make no mistake: this sort of outlook can be a powerful and dangerous force in public opinion. When Mr. Knudsen speaks before the National Association of Manufacturers and complains of the "blackout" of industry from Friday to Monday, the effect on middle-class opinion may be to further the movement for the longer work-week without overtime pay. When the newspapers play up a Vultee or an Aluminum strike, and forget to mention that for two instances of production-stoppage in defense there have been hundreds of disputes settled without any stoppage, they are playing on a panic-sense whose source is the idea of workers as soldiers. And when Representative Leland Ford of California gets up in the House and shouts that the CIO must be "abolished" and its leaders "put in concentration camps," he is not merely a Congressional primitive. He is, knowingly or not, repeating on American soil the strategy and outlook that have made out of the soil of continental Europe one vast concentration camp.

Every worker, like every other citizen, must be a soldier in a battle against barbarism. But the barbarians are inside the gates as well as outside. And to apply the techniques of militarism to the production of defense materials is to run a war in the fatally wrong way. France tried it and failed. Britain has learned that economic war requires economic techniques to be successful, and that when workers are offered a share in the organization of production and its control by the state, they become by that very fact better economic soldiers. It is as foolish to try to run labor relations by army methods as it would be to run an army by collective bargaining. Even from the military man's viewpoint this is true. For he must recognize that war today is not only a war of factories: it is also a war of morale. Or better, it is a war of morale *because* it is a war of factories. And the problems of production-morale cannot be resolved by using tin-hat methods and hurling around the term "treason."

I will not even dignify the viewpoint of Representative Leland Ford by calling it military. It is in the deepest sense feudal. It proceeds from the seigneurial attitude of corporate capitalism toward the serfs that compose its labor market: they must do the maximum of work with the minimum of expense and trouble. And it looks toward an even more restrictive society, in which—as under the Nazis—the workers are considered only as beasts of burden useful to the state. It is notable that Mr. Cox comes from Georgia, Mr. Smith from Virginia, Mr. Hoffman from Michigan, Mr. Sumners from Texas, Mr. Leland Ford from California. These are all states with either an old tradition of slavery or a new tradition of industrial feudalism. To be sure, these men may be sincere and even benevolent. Willa Cather tells us, in her novel *Sapphira and the Slave Girl*, that Sapphira too was benevolent. The good intentions of labor-baiters do not affect the status of the slave-men.

I have said above that in a war period the economic and political systems must move closer together. Our hope of heaven, like Britain's, lies in effecting that fusion not by making the state a vassal of business but by subjecting business to the control of the people. This must not and need not mean tyranny. It must mean, as Philip Murray has suggested, that we run our war industries by industrial councils in which management, labor, and the government will each have a share. It may be some intimation of that which has caused Mr. Prentis, in his speech to the NAM, to warn against war. It is just possible that the dog beneath the skin of the appeasement movement answers to the name of fear of democratic controls of business.

1940

Meeting the Blitzkrieg *on Labor*

WITH the ending of the Ford strike, the successful mediation of the Allis-Chalmers strike, and the steel agreement, we have come to the end of a phase of the problem of labor-management relations in the defense industries. Although at the present writing the great tension has, at least for the time, been relieved, it is the lull between two storms. For there can be little doubt that the campaign that has been waged against labor for months is not over, and that the near future will see a revival of it in a somewhat new form.

Up to now that campaign has been a three-pronged affair. One prong has been the stubborn resistance of some of the corporate industrialists, who seem to learn nothing and forget nothing, to all demands for collective bargaining and efforts at union organization. The second has been the attack on labor in Congress on the ground of the defense emergency. The third has been the campaign, in the press and in the newsreels, to stir public indignation against the interruption of the defense effort. All three attacks have been correlated with the skill of a Nazi General Staff planning a diplomatic, economic, and military *Blitz*.

It is still too early to say the attack has failed. All one can say is that it has not yet had the desired results. Why? One reason is that the President, despite the incitement of the reactionaries in Congress, has on the whole kept his head and refused to join the hysteria. Another reason is that the union leaders, for all their militancy and determination in defense of their rights, have also kept their heads pretty well. The widely advertised violence has not materialized. The labor movement is now reaping the fruits of its great organizing campaign of 1936 and 1937. It has an initial strength, a skill in organization and maneuver, a sense of confidence, and a quiet morale which have been of the greatest importance. The union leaders have made it clear that they are striking not against defense but against that very corporate tyranny which is the real enemy of democracy everywhere; and they have been willing in many instances to allow workers to remain on the job on actual defense contracts. But most important is the fact that even the usually gullible newspaper reader has begun to understand that many crimes can be committed in the name of defense; and that the American common man cannot defend democracy unless at the same time he has some democracy to defend.

And yet, among many of the lower-middle-class groups, as well as in the higher income brackets, the press campaign has taken its toll. All of us have encountered people who, because there have been a few jurisdictional strikes in the building trades, believe that all strikes are over jurisdictional squabbles. Or people who, because in a few instances there have been communists in the unions, argue that the defense strikes are communist plots. Or people who point to the fall of France and ascribe it to labor troubles, and argue a similar doom for us unless we crack down on unions. Or people who argue that while boys are giving up jobs to be drafted and get $21 a month, the workers are not content unless they get wage increases.

The arguments are familiar. One can answer them in detail to the point of exhaustion: that only a few strikes are jurisdictional, and none of the important ones; that men like Philip Murray, R. J. Thomas, Walter Reuther not only are not communists, but have consistently been fought by the communists; that the fall of France was due far more to the blindness of industrialists who wanted to smash labor at any cost than it was to any complaisance toward labor; that if the draftee's pay is allowed to depress wages of workers outside the army, the whole nation will become one vast draft camp.

And yet the attempt to give such answers in detail, as compared with the glaring press headlines about strikes, is like the attempt to retract on page sixteen a libel in the previous day's editions on page one. The retraction never catches up with the libel. So long as the same economic power group controls both the armament industries and the opinion industries, one cannot rely on reason and persuasion to fight corporate aggression.

That is why we must perfect the machinery we have begun to set up for minimizing and settling labor-management troubles (this is the better term—they are not simply labor troubles) in the defense industries. To that end I should like to propose a brief and summary program:

1. Proceed on the premise that strikes are a normal, not an abnormal, part of the process by which the less privileged groups in our society can get some increase in living standards and some social advance from the possessing groups. To treat every strike as an outbreak of leprosy is to stifle at the start any chance for progress. But proceed also on the premise that strikes are not an end in themselves; and that if wisely handled they can be settled and even, for the most part, avoided.

2. Differentiate between jurisdictional strikes and those in which the employer is not caught helplessly between two unions. Set up a separate mechanism for dealing directly with jurisdictional strikes.

3. Differentiate between strikes (such as the Bethlehem and Ford strikes) that are called for the purpose of winning collective bargaining, and those (such as that in coal and the threatened strike in General Motors) that are called to win a better contract after collective bargaining has already been in force.

4. In the first type of strike, a waiting period would be fatal to the workers; and the best that can be done is to insure orderly

picketing on one side and no violence on the other, to offer mediation by the government, and to enforce the National Labor Relations Act.

5. In the second kind of strike, adopt increasingly in all industries the principle of the Railway Mediation Board—the principle
of a waiting period or "breathing spell," during which there is to
be neither strike nor lockout. But there are two provisos of the
utmost importance. The waiting period is of no use unless during
that time there are actual negotiations going on between management and workers. And it is of the greatest efficacy when the provision for it is written directly into the labor agreement.

6. Use to the full the machinery of the new National Mediation
Board. It is a board with first-rate personnel. But we may as well
recognize that this is more than an emergency, and give the board
a more permanent character. The conciliation functions of the Department of Labor should be merged with it; it should not have to
wait until a case has been certified to it; and it should be given a
greater administrative spread and staff.

7. Empower the Mediation Board, if its efforts fail, to go to the
country with a report of what caused the failure. Because of the
danger that the press will ignore or distort the report, place at the
disposal of the board the full radio facilities of the national net-
works in order to direct the white light of publicity upon those
really to blame.

This program is no cure-all. Since strikes are an organic part of
our social system, they will be cured only when that system is really
democratized. Meanwhile, however, the program offers us a chance
to minimize economic frictions and concentrate our energies on the
political and military problems of our generation.

1941

The Burning of the Textbooks

THE National Association of Manufacturers, not content with
acting as a whip for reactionary business men in the area of
economics and government, has now laid its heavy hand on
American education. Several months ago it hired Ralph Robey,
who teaches banking at Columbia, to conduct a survey of un-
American attitudes in high-school textbooks in the social sciences.

Now, through the generous front-page space accorded him by the New York *Times* and other papers, Mr. Robey announces his results. One gathers that they make him despair of his country, because they are "derogatory of the American form of government and critical of free business enterprise."

What are the subversive doctrines? Extracts from seven of the books are given in the *Times*. Here are some of the un-American doctrines that our high-school students are reading: that there are a small number of powerful corporations in America; that there are trusts and monopolies; that there are sharp differences in living standards; that vast amounts of money are spent in advertising to break down consumer resistance; that the press has enormous power and speaks in general for a minority; that in actual operation the guarantees in our Bill of Rights are often infringed; that politics is not always clean; and that (most subversive of all subversive doctrines!) the NAM has itself been guilty of subsidizing propaganda against social legislation.

We do not doubt the right of Mr. Robey or those for whom he works to express opinions on our school system. But when a powerful employers' association like the NAM levels its big guns at the free expression of ideas, more is involved than criticism by private citizens. For the members of the NAM are, in their local communities throughout the country, men of substance and power. Mr. Robey says that the NAM does not propose to publish either a black list or a white list of textbooks. Yet the fact is that the NAM is placing in the hands of its members and school authorities everywhere a book containing abstracts of supposedly dangerous passages from six hundred textbooks. What can this mean except the victimization of the more liberal—or less reactionary—books? What can it mean in actual practice except a glorified burning of the textbooks?

Actually it is well known that American textbook writers are likely to be mild men who, by the very nature of the limits within which they work, suffer from an excess of caution. The excerpts from the seven books that the *Times* has publicized are thoroughly innocuous to anyone who knows the facts of American life or anyone who has studied the reports about our economic system issued by government agencies themselves. Read the reports of any of the Congressional investigating commissions from the Pujo committee to the TNEC, and they will make what the professors say seem pale in comparison. In fact, the crime of which the NAM is accusing the textbook writers is that they dare say that American democracy and capitalism are not wholly perfect, and that there is still some unfinished business before us.

What will happen if the NAM is allowed to have its way? Pressure will be applied by local reactionaries and intellectual vigilantes upon any school board that dares buy textbooks that mention the unfinished business of American democracy. What sort of reign of terror this will mean has already been revealed in the campaign carried on by Merwin K. Hart and others against the books of Harold Rugg. Neither the drive against Rugg nor that of the NAM is an isolated affair. They are parts of a concerted campaign to censor and suppress free thought in the social sciences, and to turn the school system into an arm of the reactionaries in imprinting stereotypes on the minds of our children.

When the holders of economic power in any society grow panicky because they are bewildered at the forces loose in our world, their first impulse is toward suppression of thought. They hit out against the ideas whose truth they cannot face. It is well known that the NAM has in the past sought to introduce its own propaganda into high-school textbooks. Finding its propaganda attempts not wholly successful, it now turns to censorship. To be sure, Mr. Robey speaks in lofty terms of the skepticism which is undermining the morale of our youth. But that is an old dodge by now. It is not hard to infer that the real intent of the NAM is to use the defense emergency to force an entrance into our educational system that it has thus far not been able to effect.

What then can be done? Our first reliance must be on what Mr. Justice Holmes called "the power of the thought to get itself accepted in the competition of the market." Whatever may be said about particular textbooks, the school authorities have many varieties to choose from, without the intimidation of the NAM. But Mr. Robey charges that the general level of the textbooks is amazingly low. That may or may not be true. Who is Mr. Robey to say so? He teaches banking and has been a financial writer for the newspapers. We have never known him to be considered an authority of any sort on educational methods or an authority on the matters on which he is sitting in judgment.

If we are worried about our textbooks we can have recourse for judgment, not to the NAM or its employees but to those who, because of their knowledge and objectivity, have an undisputed standing in the social sciences. We are happy therefore that the American Committee for Democracy and Intellectual Freedom has chosen a group of men like Professors Wesley C. Mitchell, Robert M. MacIver, Robert S. Lynd, Carl Wittke, to examine the textbooks in question and report on their factual accuracy and their scholarly temper. Our chief regret is that a committee of this caliber was not chosen to do this job several months ago, as soon as the National Association of Manufacturers fired its first threatening gun.

The same issue of the New York *Times* which carried the textbook excerpts carried also a tiny news item from Vichy. The Education Department of the French government, it seems, has banned from the French schools a long list of history books which emphasized the French Revolution at the expense of the many centuries of French monarchy. The moral need not be underlined. Hail the Pétain mentality of the new American censors!

1941

Teacher-Hunt

THE most striking aspect of the Rapp-Coudert investigation of New York City colleges is its capacity for digging up unpleasant things in unpleasant ways. No one with a respect for the procedure of due process can approve of the summary investigating methods of the committee, which has convicted a number of men at the bar of public opinion on the testimony of one or two, and without giving the accused a chance to clear themselves publicly. Neither can anyone with a respect for the integrity of teaching fail to be profoundly disturbed by charges that a number of teachers in New York's municipal colleges are avowedly Communist Party members, using two sets of names, carrying on a dual existence as teachers and party members, and subject even in their teaching to party discipline.

Here surely is one of the most painful choices for those who believe genuinely in democratic processes and in freedom of teaching. For it is too late in the twentieth century to be naïve about either the objectives or the tactics of the communists. Neither can be described as democratic. Such charges as those made recently by Mr. Canning, a history instructor at the College of the City of New York, naming some fifty-odd staff members as communists, may in particular instances be false. Yet there is little doubt on the whole that the Communist Party has sought deliberately to use its faculty members to further party purposes.

But there can be equally little doubt that the present drive against the communists is not a disinterested attempt to further freedom of teaching or restore its integrity. There are three horsemen riding with unbridled fury through the ranks of American teachers today. One is the movement, always with us but now pressed with renewed strength, for paring educational expenditures to the bone. It is significant that immediately after the Canning testimony the head of a taxpayers' committee called for the closing of CCNY until all the "Reds" had been ousted. The second is the drive (revealed by the questioning of Assemblyman Page) against the teaching of the social studies in colleges and high schools. The third is the drive to terrorize liberal teachers of every persuasion, in public and private institutions alike.

These three horsemen are realities, so much so that genuine democrats must not allow their unfaltering opposition to communist methods to make them the unwitting victims of these campaigns. There is a movement on foot to oust from their teaching posts those who have been named as communists. This would be a tragic mistake. Quite apart from questions of evidence and proof, and quite apart from the doubts of its legal power, it would be unwise in the extreme for the Board of Higher Education to follow such a course. For, although only a very small proportion of either teachers or students are communists, the drive against them would destroy the morale of the whole teaching staff and the whole student body. The art of teaching is a difficult one at best; the context in which creative thinking can be done by teachers and pupils alike is fragile. The hand either of a legislative investigating committee or of the courts is too heavy and clumsy to be applied to the teaching process without destructive results.

What follows? That nothing need be or can be done? By no means. Here we must go back to some first principles about teaching. The purpose of teaching in a democracy is to develop a nation of people who can think for themselves. This means that the touchstone of democratic teaching is whether it makes possible a competition of ideas. This means objective teaching, but not "objective" in the sense that the teacher becomes a mere mechanism, a cipher without views or convictions. He may be Republican, Democrat, Socialist, Communist, or independent; and whatever he is, it is desirable that he be above-board about it. He will inevitably and often unconsciously allow his convictions to influence his teaching. But the test of whether he is objective is whether on any subject he is fair in summarizing conflicting viewpoints, and whether he presents fairly the "facts" on which students in colleges must ultimately form their own judgments.

From this viewpoint a political witch-hunt or a legal inquisition is the last way in the world by which to get good teachers and get rid of bad ones. From this viewpoint the only way to do it is for teachers to be judged by their peers. For teaching is one of the most complex and exacting of all arts. It takes brains, judgment, guts. And there can be no mechanical and ready-made tests, such as membership in the Communist Party or the Republican, as to whether teaching is being performed well. The trouble with a communist, much more than that he is "subversive," is that he is likely to be a soldier taking party orders and subject to party discipline in his teaching as in his other activities. But that must be judged in the individual case, as must also the timidity and closed-mindedness which may equally paralyze a teacher's usefulness.

The Board of Higher Education of New York City is, as school boards go, of very high caliber. We respect the ability and judgment of its members. Yet we feel it would be best for them, if they are to make any decisions leading to ousters, to set up first a committee of educators—perhaps professors from other universities—whose unquestioned standing will give their recommendations force and authority. A group of scholars such as that suggested for the scrutiny of high-school textbooks by the American Committee for Democracy and Intellectual Freedom, or a group such as the committee on academic freedom of the American Association of University Professors, would command assent from the whole teaching profession. They would not make the mistakes that laymen, however well intentioned, would inevitably make. And they could not be used as part of a reign of terror against liberal teaching. Their job would be a pragmatic one of judging individual cases not by membership, reputed or real, in any political party, but by performance in objective and creative teaching.

Even this, in the long run, will not solve the problem without aid from other factors. One is a strengthened teachers'-union movement, freed wholly from minority control by communists, and able to fight the threats against education. The second is the further development of a fierce integrity among teachers and a real pride of craftsmanship. And the third (with the aid of a better press) is a lay opinion which respects the art of teaching, and knows not only how to scrutinize it but also how to leave it alone.

1941

Planned Defense

READING Thomas Hardy's poems the other day, I was struck by the vivid relevance for our own age of his use of the Biblical phrase in the title of his poem "In Time of 'the Breaking of Nations.' " Hardy wrote in *The Dynasts* something like a Homeric epic of the wars of Napoleon, from a perspective of a century. We today need no such long perspective to see that we are living similarly not only in a time of the dissolution of the accepted European order, but in a time of the passing of the sovereign nation-state and the transformation of economies and governments everywhere. We may have to wait long for the poets to celebrate (as from Stendhal to Hardy they celebrated Napoleon) the impact of the heroic-diabolic Hitler symbol upon the people's consciousness. But the political commentator cannot wait that long. Writing with an eye to action, he must measure the reach of world events upon the American mind and the American frame of government.

First of all, let us understand that we are now about to pay the reckoning we have so long postponed. That applies both in our foreign policy and in our internal affairs. If we had taken collective security seriously over the seven years that have elapsed since both Hitler and Roosevelt came to power, we would today have a different world. But that is now past, and neither recriminations nor assessments of blame will do us much good. We still use the phrase "if Hitler wins." We refuse to face the fact that so far, because of our blunders in the past, he has won, and that even a concerted effort now by Britain, Russia, and the Americas—so necessary and so unlikely—would still leave him to be dislodged from Continental Europe. We shall have to reckon for a time with a Nazi domination of Europe which will seek to strangle America and establish a fascist government here.

For some years a group of writers have been stressing the urgency of economic reorganization to save democracy. They were ignored. And today the very people who scoffed at such a planned economy are the ones who are calling most loudly for military expenditures on so large a scale that only a collectivized economy could possibly meet the economic drain. We may now do under the stress of a military crisis what we should have done long ago under the conditions of peace. What was not done when it could have been done easily may have to be done now in haste, under conditions of danger and difficulty.

My thesis is that the problem of national defense in America is inseparable from the problem of economic reorganization and governmental revision. Hitler's victory represents the triumph of military planning, welded to the functioning and the habits of a planned economy, in the service of a cause fervently believed in. Until the Churchill Cabinet came in, the British not only had not planned their war machine; they had not even begun to lay the foundation for such a war machine by an industrial plan. Their industrial life still followed the pattern of a planless corporate capitalism, with all that this implied for munitions, aviation, equipment, transport, military engineering. About the French it would be too harrowing to make any comment.

Do we as Americans understand the full import of this? We keep debating whether we shall go to war or not, and in immediate terms it is an important question. But for the crucial question of our survival over the next decade, we are to all intents and purposes already at war. We are at war because survival dictates enormous military preparations carried out at a hitherto unheard-of speed. We are at war because this means a war economy and a war psychology, an enormous drain upon our national income which will inevitably come to a great extent from the standard of living of ordinary people. We are at war because a Hitler victory would leave us shorn of foreign markets, isolated economically and politically in a world in which the twin impulses of submission to a conquering power through fear and joining that power through bandwagon appeal will predominate. We are at war because we may from now on have to carry on the democratic effort, heart-breaking at the very best, in the context of Nazi prestige and our own disenchantment.

There is no need for us to yield to this disenchantment with democracy; no need to overestimate Hitler's power. One thing at least we have gained: we know now what it is that we have to face, and such knowledge should prove the beginning of militancy. But this knowledge will be of little avail if we do not understand that all our preparations for national defense must be an organic part of a wider economic plan, that any reorganization will not mean much unless it is part of a wider administrative reorganization, and that sacrifices by the people will be far less important in American survival than sacrifices by the present holders of economic power.

There are three paths open to us in the immediate future, and each of them will have its advocates. One will be the attempt to build a massive military machine without making any essential economic or administrative changes or any transfer of the locus of decision. It will masquerade under such slogans as "Preserve the Democratic Way" and "Do the Job through a Business Man's Administration." It will mean, as it has always meant in the past, that the job of building and equipping an army, a navy, and an air force will be ill done, done expensively, done with huge profits for a few and a great diminution of living standards for the many, done with the least effect upon unemployment and vested interests. It its hard to tell from the initial steps taken by the Roosevelt administration whether even it may not follow this plan, but sometimes I think so. I have as yet seen no recognition in this country of what the British have finally learned, although perhaps too late: that one cannot make up, even in military terms, for the lost time of the past and still have "business as usual."

The second path is that of a frank corporate and military dictatorship. It will not be called fascism, but it will be fascism nevertheless. If it comes at all, it is likely to come as the result of the panic following the collapse of the first method. It would use the international crisis as the occasion for setting up on American soil a home-built replica of the Nazi citadel. It would use all the slogans of Americanism, yet destroy completely the civil liberties, the rich cultural and religious divergences, the labor standards, the relative intellectual freedom of American life. It would be run by military men and business men in the service of what would start as a business dictatorship, but would become, as it did in Germany, an outright and cynical oligarchical control.

The third path I have called a democratic collectivism. But, one may well say, do not the adjective and noun cancel each other out? I do not think so. The thesis that a democratic collectivism is contradictory in terms has in the past had the distinguished sponsorship of Walter Lippmann and Dorothy Thompson. I have been scanning the columns of both recently with great eagerness for some light on their present views of how America can revitalize the democratic dogma effectively, other than through their suggestions for coalition cabinets, the suppression of fifth columns, and the suspension of party government. I am not speaking now of foreign policy, on which they have both had a good deal to say that has been always vigorous and generally valid. I refer to our domestic policy. Do they not know that administrative effectiveness, whether in England or in America today, can be achieved only by a vast effort of planning and co-ordination, by the concentration of power in the hands of a small group of individuals, by a rigorous system of priorities and exclusions in the use of natural resources, by a drastic trenching upon the concepts of free corporate decisions and corporate profits? [3]

I use Mr. Lippmann and Miss Thompson as symbols of the lag, even among our liberals, between international realism and internal realism. We are in the position of having to raise the national income, re-employ millions of people, turn out monstrous quantities of war supplies; and we are in the position of having to do this without scrapping the very things that alone can give our effort any meaning. To say that this cannot be done forces us back on one or the other of the two paths I described earlier. To say that it can be done means, unless we wish to hide our previous confusion behind words, an acceptance of the proposition that democracy is compatible with the socialization of industry and that democracy is also compatible with the concentration of governmental power.

---

[3] I must add that since this was first printed both Miss Thompson and Mr. Lippmann have been in the forefront of those advocating a planned defense economy.

But this does not mean that the task of making them march side by side is an easy one. I agree with Lewis Corey when he says that the lesson of the recent Soviet experience is to show us that socialism and dictatorship are also compatible. The task becomes, in other words, one of hammering out an economic plan which will integrate military with non-military uses of our resources and national income, which can combine administrative decentralization at the bottom with the concentration of power at the top, which can shift the axis decisions from the corporations to the government, and which will nevertheless be subject at crucial points to popular responsibility.

Let us not underestimate the immediate costs. Labor rights will be endangered, civil liberties will suffer. Governmentally as well as economically, America is on the threshold of changes vaster than any since the Civil War, vaster even than in the first years of the New Deal. Today's textbooks on the national government may well sound antiquated five years from now. If we enter on these changes with our eyes open, if we govern greatly and imaginatively, with the proper personnel, with the ultimate safeguards of Congressional debate and the rule of law and the two-party system, we shall be able to keep our democracy and even strengthen it in the long run. Our real danger lies not in the dangers of a democratic collectivism. It lies in the chance that corporate tenacity and popular hysteria will prevent us even from making the attempt, and that again in Lloyd George's phrase, we shall have dared "too little and too late."

1940

Dollar-a-Year Defense

THE papers [4] are full of the feud between the OPM forces under William Knudsen and the OPACS forces under Leon Henderson. The Henderson office has been in two serious tangles recently: one with Congress, over the question of giving Henderson explicit and adequate powers for price control; the second with the OPM over the Henderson order, which Mr. Roosevelt has thus far backed up, for a fifty per cent cut in automobile production. These tangles illustrate the two phases of the work of the OPACS—controlling runaway prices, and adjusting the rela-

---

[4] This was written in August 1941.

tion between civilian supply needs and the national defense economy. They illustrate also the resistances that are likely to be met by any real effort to prepare us in time for the war to come.

On both issues I hold with Mr. Henderson. If we are to have adequate price control, our Administrator must have adequate powers; you cannot run an economy by indirection and exhortation. And a drastic cut in automobile production would have the triple effect of easing up on raw material shortages, transferring auto production to aviation production, and bringing home finally to the American people that they are right in the midst of a war economy.[5]

But the issue that has been dramatized in the tilt between Mr. Knudsen and Mr. Henderson is an issue that goes beyond both of them. It concerns two alternative methods of organizing and prosecuting the economic phase of the American war effort. Michael Straight, in his Washington article in a recent [6] issue of the *New Republic,* well characterized the OPM effort thus far as "the mirage of production." If Mr. Knudsen can be taken not as himself, but as a symbol of how the OPM has thus far run our war economy, and if Mr. Henderson can be taken as a symbol of how our war economy could be run, the resulting analysis might be more fruitful than a *Time* write-up of the economics and histrionics of an administrative feud.

Behind Knudsenism [7] is the year-long history of wishfulness in thought and action as to what will be required to organize a war economy and how tough a job it will be. The men of the OPM have consistently overestimated what we have been producing, the extent of our effective spending, and contract awards. They have consistently underestimated the time it will require us to get into the full swing of war production. Their reports have lacked frankness, their speeches have been delivered with the cheerfulness of a doctor in his best bedside manner. Their calculations about raw material shortages have been wrong, and their reassurances monstrous under the circumstances. They have either themselves been

[5] Since this was written, another reorganization of the defense set-up has been made (September 1941), with the creation of the Supply Priorities Allocation Board. It has not yet resolved the difficulties indicated here, although Henderson's viewpoint seems to have won out with respect to the cut in automobile production.

[6] July 28, 1941.

[7] In what follows I owe much to I. F. Stone's first-rate analysis in his *Business as Usual,* New York, Modern Age, 1941.

blind or ignorant, or else they have treated us as adolescents to whom the facts of life had better be revealed warily and by easy stages. Contrast this with Mr. Henderson's recent speech before a trade association meeting, when he said frankly that the defense honeymoon was over. Even the conservatives of our country could learn from Mr. Churchill that the best tactic in a war situation is to speak to people in a democracy on the assumption that they are grown up.

In another area, that of economic techniques, they have been equally short-sighted. They have failed to evoke the energies of the small business units in the defense effort. They have not organized industry democratically from the bottom up. Business men in search of the niche in the defense economy where they could make their contribution have notoriously been given the Washington run-around. They have bungled the problem of farming-out. Because they have not wished to reveal or face the facts of monopoly in our economic set-up, they have allowed an intolerable situation in bauxite and aluminum; with the result that we find ourselves today in the pathetic situation, so far as aluminum is concerned, of appearing in a full-dress rehearsal for war, decked out like a wandering ministrel in the shreds and patches of a house-to-house collection of pots and pans. In fact, if it were not for the Truman committee and the work of Thurman Arnold and his staff, we would not even know why the aluminum shortage has arisen. Fortunately the force of the exposure has blasted the men of the OPM out of their complacency, so that finally we have set in motion an expansion of aluminum, steel, and power capacity.

It can never be said often enough that it is not the patriotism of these men that is at fault. The fact is that they are needed but they are in the wrong place. They have, as a business managerial group, a definite set of skills to contribute. But what Harold Laski once said about all experts should apply particularly to our dollar-a-year men: they should be on tap but not on top. In positions of government power men are what they are as a result of three sets of factors: their economic interests and political preferences, their technical training and experience, their mental conditioning and habituations. In all three respects the dollar-a-year men in the OPM are, with a few striking exceptions, unfitted for their present positions of power. Their economic interests are implicated in the decisions they have to make; their training fits them for intra-industrial rather than inter-industrial decisions; their habituations are against a planned and socialized economy which is necessary to win the war. "War," Clemenceau once said, "is too important a matter to be left to the generals." How much more truly could that be applied to the dollar-a-year men!

A final word about Mr. Roosevelt and his relation to this whole picture. The President, although he should have known better through his experience in fighting the depression, must have felt that the job of the war economy was merely a production job, involving few matters of economic complexity and social justice; and that it could be turned over to men like Knudsen and Biggers and Stettinius. The last year has proved how wrong he was. He made a good record under the New Deal because when he first came to the Presidency he came after someone else had flunked. He therefore introduced new methods and fresh conceptions. But it was he himself who started the defense effort. The consequences of failure did not seem so obvious: not jobs lost, only time. Now it is he who has flunked. And there is no one else to come in afresh. He must study all over again, take the make-up exam, and this time pass.

1941

The Common Man and a Fighting Faith

I SEE by that oracle of our time, the AP, that the Reuther plan for plane production has been called "impracticable" by un-named "high defense experts." If that is a news story, then I am a dadaist poet. It did not take much guessing to guess, when the plan was first publicized in I. F. Stone's articles, that it would meet the glacial hostility of those who will not and cannot think in terms of the planning of the unused resources of a whole industry. To be sure, the "experts" were not brusque. They made their cryptic statement "reluctantly," since the plan showed labor's desire to help with defense. It broke their hearts. But, heartbreak or not, the plan—not only in itself, but as a symbol of what labor can do—opens for us some long vistas.

Every culture needs a fighting faith. I do not mean a religion, which is (as the anthropologist views it) a product of fear; nor do I mean a crusading messianism, which is (as the psychiatrist views it) the product of the aggressive drives in us. I mean something that answers the question: who and what are there among us to keep our world going and moving forward?

We long ago lost our belief in kings and aristocrats. We were never much of a priestly country, and God forbid we should ever become one. We have had only intermittent enthusiasms for the generals; and it is an open secret that the politicians form our caste of untouchables. We pay the lawyers high fees and let them govern us; but if there is any purge that would command universal assent in America it would be a purge of lawyers. We have abandoned Jefferson's physiocratic belief in farmers. We never took much to Veblen's faith in the engineers. We have made half-gods of our scientists, but we view them uneasily as movie test-tube wizards who create Boris Karloffs that go berserk; and I will confess that even Bruce Bliven's series [8] on the new social vision of the scientists has not erased the Karloff image from my mind. As for movie stars and football heroes, we sit raptly in stuffy mosques gazing at shadows from Hollywood, or in windswept amphitheaters watching giants from Minnesota or Stanford show their prowess; but these are dream-wishes rather than our beliefs.

We have even lost our belief in the business men—the "lords of Creation." Louis Hacker [9] now tells us in retrospect that up to 1900, as long as they were real captains of industry, they were worthy of belief. Perhaps as a historian he is right. But it was in the 1920's, when they were only cardboard Humpty-Dumpties perched dangerously on walls of promises, that our belief in them and in their "new capitalism" reached its climax. They will never recover from their fall, and the class-blindness they have been showing in the past decades in Europe merely seals the coroner's verdict of death by suicide.

Since Nature abhors a vacuum of belief as well as any other, the faith of the ordinary American had to rush somewhere, and

---

[8] A series of articles in the *New Republic* during 1940 and 1941 on "The Men Who Make the Future."

[9] See his excellent book *The Triumph of American Capitalism*, New York, Simon and Schuster, 1940.

it sought out F.D.R. here, as in England the faith of the British common man has sought out Churchill. But such leaders hold the guardianship of belief by only the slenderest of threads—their own political lives. A culture cannot be safe, it cannot even get along, until it has gone beyond the individual leader to the creative group.

How about labor? It does not take much social sensitiveness to know that labor's stock has recently been very low. I am not now speaking of middle-class and agrarian hostility to labor, which is a problem in itself. A study of Gallup polls on labor shows that even before the hysteria over the sitdown strikes there was a body of bitter anti-labor opinion, with about the same percentage of die-hards (roughly twenty-five per cent) on either side of the fence, and the rest troubled fence-sitters. That means that in the minds of most people the problem of labor's place is an unresolved one. And it is well known that four out of five Americans think of them-selves as belonging in the middle class.

But more to the point is the feeling about labor that the young people have who are starting out on jobs or careers or the perilous voyage of the mind. We had for some time been building up for them a fighting faith in labor as a creative social force. Partly, I think, this came from the Marxian influence, partly from the demo-cratic American tradition, and partly it went further back than either of these to the Puritan sense of the poor as the inheritors of the earth. The recent collapse of the left carried with it a de-crease in labor's prestige. Those who had yielded so easily before the impact of Hitler's elite seemed no longer the stuff to fire our imagination or enlist our allegiance. And all that we have heard about labor's role in the fall of France, however false when ex-amined, did not help much.

And now the healing thing is how well, by and large, labor is standing up under the test of the war emergency. The workers in Madrid and Barcelona, in Warsaw, in Birmingham and Man-chester, in Pittsburgh and Detroit, have given a good account of themselves. Why should they not? They have a greater knowledge than anyone else of a war of factories, and a greater stake in what the fighting is for.

That is the context in which the Reuther plan takes on more meaning than just the technical one of plane turnout. Trade unionists have always been in a position to know what enters into production efficiency; but except in distressed industries like the garment trades their leaders have not been called in to share in the responsibilities of production. That Murray and Hillman for the CIO and R. J. Thomas and Reuther for the auto workers are ready now to assume a part of that responsibility is not merely a matter of labor tactic, nor is it merely a matter of war emergency. It represents the whole direction of trade-union striving. There is a real connection between the Reuther plan and Murray's proposal for labor representation in industrial councils. For labor is no longer to be seen as just a pressure group. Its stake in democracy is a stake in raising the whole national income. It is a stake in productive and social efficiency in the large.

I shall not pretend to discuss the technical accuracy of Reuther's 500-planes-a-day production estimate. I do know that the objections thus far raised against it by the "defense experts" are the piddling objections of those who want to run a war economy by the methods of "business as usual." Even if Reuther is only half right, he would still have justified his remark on the radio that the Battle of England will be won, if at all, not on the playing-fields of Eton but on the assembly lines of Detroit. He would still have justified my belief that labor has today more realism and more sheer social creativeness in approaching the problem of defense production than either business or the government group. When I speak of creativeness I do not want to leave the impression that this is fantasy. There is in the Reuther plan nothing of the hortatory or the desperate that makes war production a sort of national dervish dance. There is nothing in it of that haphazard wishfulness that is, under the present regime, trying to expand plane production by plastering the walls of a Detroit room with blueprints and asking the manufacturers to look at them and decide where they would fit in. No, it is not labor that is Utopian. It proceeds in calm engineering fashion by making inventories of unused production resources already available, and just as calmly going on to put them to use by a retooling method that embraces a unified plan.

Do I make a fetish of labor? I don't think so. Too many things have happened in the past few years to allow any of us the luxury of idealization. I am thinking of workers not as possessing any mystical virtue, but in their ordinary relation to production and their ordinary stake in democracy. And, even then, we shall have to extend our belief beyond workers as such. The future lies with the common man, whoever he be; and with the technicians of every sort, whether technicians of machine, brain, or administrative skills. It is industry that will give us the sinews of our strength, social intelligence that can alone keep that strength from destroying us, administrative skills that can organize that strength to be effective.

These are the elites for us, for as distant a future as we can pierce. They are democratic elites, recruited from the mass and always revitalized by the mass. Our belief in them can be a fighting faith.

1941

9

State, Class, and Party

The Broker State

I SHOULD hate to be in John Chamberlain's shoes. To have written in 1932, just before the New Deal, a book called *Farewell to Reform* is in itself an unenviable trick of fate. Chamberlain is as canny a reviewer as the craft contains, and he must have known that the boys would be lying in ambush for his next book, patient as redskins around a stockade. He waited, and they waited, for eight years. And when he finally came out plumping for reform and nothing else, it was inevitable that the reviewers should preface their columns with such barbs as "Farewell to Revolution" and "Hello to Reform." But a man has a right to shift his sights as he gets new insights. The test of consistency over time is less relevant to a critic than to a biographer. Let whoever has not eaten some of his words during the past decade cast the first stone.

A social historian in the future, seeking to describe the mood of 1940 intellectuals, will find *The American Stakes* [1] a first-rate starting-point. It is anti-Marxian, it is a "democracy book," it is pluralist in philosophy, middle-wayish in temper, nativist in emphasis, New Dealish in politics, realist in tactics, casual in its broken rhythms, and homely in the tang of its style. If intellectuals sat on cracker-boxes they would talk as Chamberlain does in this book. He flees what he calls "grand political theory" like the very devil. Along with a lot of theorizing there is the traditional American contempt for theory. He makes a fetish of never making a fetish of anything, and there runs through the book a monistic obsession with whatever is pluralist, pragmatic, full of loose ends, in the nature of

---

[1] John Chamberlain, *The American Stakes*, New York, Carrick & Evans, 1940.

compromise. Without seeking directly to describe the climate of our time, he illustrates it superbly.

In structure his book is loose: a series of essays on economics and politics, republished or rewritten from various journals. But common to them all are certain conceptions worth examining.

The central one is Chamberlain's conception of the state. One may say that there are today roughly three main schools of state theory: the philosophical idealists see the state as the embodiment of some idea of justice or order or creativeness, transcending group and class visions; the Marxians and their allies still cleave to a primarily class theory of the state; and the pragmatic liberals see the state as the arena in which various pressure groups contend for supremacy. Chamberlain belongs in the third school. One would have to be totally blind to ignore the enormous role of pressure groups in recent American politics. But while some of the idealists have deplored them because they obscure the larger national interest, and some of the Marxians because they obscure the class struggle, Chamberlain glorifies them. For him they *are* the state. His is the "broker" state, mediating between pressure groups with a shrewd eye for margins of difference, veering with the strength of the wind but always remaining distinct from the economic groups themselves.

Once given this central idea, the rest of the book is satellite and supplementary. For if ours is a broker state, then class theory loses its meaning. And (see the chapter "Whose State?") since the state is not a class instrument, it may be used as an instrument by whatever group has the heart and wit to use it. And (see "Whose Democratic Party?") they must work within the existing party machinery, however difficult that may be, and turn it to their own purpose. Political leadership becomes the art of skillful mediation between pressure groups, Roosevelt and La Guardia being described as "two master brokers." It follows also that the "blocked roads to freedom" are those of communism, syndicalism, anarchism, guild socialism, which were concerned with the state in the large as the subject of "grand political theory." The only one of these that Chamberlain still regards as somewhat fruitful is guild socialism, which obviously falls in with the broker-state conception. And on the same reasoning the "growing points" of our society are the co-operatives and the Borsodi experiments in decentralized living.

It is hard not to be attracted by the indigenous flavor of Chamberlain's thought, his lack of pretentiousness, his journalist's eye for the concrete, his nervous, alert, and occasionally vernacular style. Even so trivial a detail as his way of referring to the figures in the foreground of the American scene by their nicknames is not without meaning. For if Cohen is "Ben" and Corcoran "Tommy" and Tugwell "Rex," then even leftist democracy becomes a home-grown product. If Landis is "Jim" and Douglas "Bill," then surely the difficulties of the security exchanges and constitutional law cannot lie beyond the compass of the democratic process.

Yet I am not convinced that the broker theory cuts deep. Chamberlain restricts it to capitalist democracies. He agrees—all too uncritically, I fear—with the Oppenheimer thesis that the state originates in conquest and oppression and is the method by which the rulers exact a toll from the rest of the people. Yet the democratic state, he insists, is different. It may be, like all states, a "racket" for the governing group, but it is a "limited racket"—presumably because a truce has been called on class warfare, and various groups are willing to "divide the take." "It is the assumption of this book," he writes, "that no clear-cut victory of any class over any other class is immediately at hand as far as America is concerned. All the classes in the United States have either enough or the prospect of getting enough, to make totalitarian warfare on each other an inexpedient thing. Better to take a fall in the rate of profit than make the hazardous attempt to enslave the working-class and better to take a WPA job than raise the barricades."

What is at fault, of course, is that Chamberlain assumes as self-evident what it should have been his task to examine. If classes are real entities, what is their role in politics, as distinguished from pressure groups? Must class conflict be reckoned with as a more or less continuing force in any state, or does it operate only in the origin of the state? How can we assume that the democratic state represents a truce in class warfare? Were the German capitalists, faced by the falling rate of profit, afraid to attempt to enslave the working-class?

For all his allusions to the class-domination theory, Chamberlain nowhere squarely confronts the basic problem it presents. No class theorist of any subtlety has ever denied that the class-domination concept has plenty of room at the joints. It is not always, or even very often, a matter of the naked victory of class over class. Nor are the governing groups in Mosca's sense necessarily identical with the economic ruling groups in Marx's. One can easily ridicule the notion that Mr. Roosevelt and his brain-trusters and the present Supreme Court are the executive committee of the giant corporations. In a period of capitalist stress the state machinery may be and several times has been seized by non-corporate groups, to create a social-service state. Even in Lenin's rigorous *State and Revolution,* one finds the statement that "there are periods when the warring classes so nearly attain equilibrium that the state power, ostensibly appearing as mediator, assumes for the moment a certain independence." The real question is how long the New Deal can survive as a mediatory state.

The Popular Front and Labor Party interludes in France and England are not hopeful. They seem to show that a mediatory state is almost by definition transitory. Since it must remain umpire it cannot push a particular set of class claims or a particular vision of the good society; and it cannot therefore push its program to the point where it can make its reform stable. Whatever it does falls short of the transfer of basic economic decisions to socially responsible groups. And in the wake of this failure, and the failure to break the class monopoly of finance, the armed forces, and the major industries, the government machinery reverts to the accredited capitalist spokesmen.

What this amounts to is that we must avoid the liberal tendency, influenced by eighteenth- and nineteenth-century science, to see the state as an equilibrium, or as a parallelogram of pressures. We must recognize that the state cannot be considered apart from the structure of economic power; that to call our democracy a "limited racket" makes sense only if you go further and say that the limits are set by class power, and that so far as the national income is concerned the "division of the take" is effected only after the major part has gone into the pockets of the big shots; and that even within the limits in which the state acts as broker it does so only in periods of social peace. To recognize the existence of pressure groups is the part of realism; to make them the essence of democratic government is to confuse a necessary evil in a capitalist democracy with a creative principle.

It is difficult to reconcile Chamberlain's political theory with his economic program. The latter has three phases. One is the attack on over-all planning. Here he follows much the argument that Walter Lippmann does in his *Good Society*. His fear is that planning will crush economic freedom and that it will become tyranny. I cannot help feeling that he is demolishing a straw man. I know of few if any planning theorists in America who advocate completely uniform or centralized planning, and I know of few who would disagree with Chamberlain's contention that there must be room at the joints for an economy to function. The second phase is his economic pluralism, and his insistence that five economies (small enterprise, corporate enterprise, public utilities, government collectivism, co-operatives) can exist side by side. Here, too, there would be little difference of opinion, although we are indebted to Chamberlain for stating the case so clearly, and for insisting that "freedom dwells in the interstices of the five economic systems." Yet we must go further and inquire where the emphasis will lie and how the controls can be co-ordinated. Actually we already have the five economies that Chamberlain mentions, yet we have neither economic freedom for the masses nor economic efficiency for the nation as a whole.

Here we arrive at Chamberlain's third contention—the need for a NEP, in which small industry is left free and big industry is subjected to control. Excellent. But what sort of control? And by whom? And in a NEP, what happens to the distinctions between corporate enterprise, government collectivism, and public utilities? Here, where we should most welcome a specific program, there is silence. And another question. If there is to be an American NEP, it will involve a considerable transfer of power from the present economic ruling groups. How will that transfer be effected without a bitter conflict of classes, and what happens in such an event to the "broker state"? For Lenin's Russia to move from war communism to a NEP was one thing and relatively easy; but for America to move from democratic capitalism to a NEP would be quite another thing. "If a prime mover is not discovered," writes Chamberlain, "then youth will take on the Storm Troopers' mentality." True enough. But why not planning as a prime mover, with all that it involves?

There remains only to say a word about Chamberlain on American foreign policy. In one of the best chapters of the book—meaty,

factual, reasoned—he argues against any form of interventionism
and for the laudable policy of making democracy work at home.
I have a considerable sympathy with this attitude.[2] Yet even here
I cannot help feeling that his particularism and his sense of America's uniqueness have misled him. We want to stay out of this war
not because we feel we are unique or because of our continental
economy or because we want to secede from the world forces. We
want to stay out of it precisely because we understand the nature of
those forces. The same process that has made corporate monopolies
the center of the national anarchy has made the new huge corporate
empires—whether German, English, or Russian—the center of the
international anarchy. The world economy is as surely being organized by these corporate empires as our own national economy
has been organized by Big Steel or General Electric or Aluminum,
by the Morgans or the Mellons. A reluctance to face the problems
of power involved in corporate control and government planning
within America may lead to a similar reluctance to face the problems of power involved in imperial control and world economic
planning. Our interventionism or non-interventionism should be
the realistic sort that flows from the knowledge that the national
and international problems are similar and organic rather than
separate and unique. Only we shall never be able to face the problem of organizing the peace of the world until we have become masters in our own house.

1940

Tweedledum and Tweedledee

How far will party government be a victim of the war crisis
in America?
As long ago as last fall, when the war first broke out,
so fervent a believer in the two-party system as Walter Lippmann
proposed a coalition Cabinet, and Mr. Roosevelt has taken a step
in that direction. Dorothy Thompson's plea for a coalition Roose-
velt-Willkie slate in the election campaign received wide comment
in the press, and later she wrote scornfully of two-party govern-

---

[2] This was written before I understood the nature of the Nazi *Blitzkrieg*. Yet my shift
of emphasis toward foreign policy since then, which should now make me phrase this
differently, does not affect the basic analysis in this paragraph, with which I still hold.

ment as an out-worn notion and added that in Paris the term "politician" is greeted with bitterness. I have heard it said by men who probably regard themselves with sincerity as democrats that if only this were not an election year they would more freely urge American intervention. The people, yes—but to hell with them if they stand like ignorant clods in the way of the objectives which our elite have in their superior wisdom determined upon. The two-party system, yes—but not if it stands in the way of the kind of national unity desired by one particular group.

I am convinced that Pendleton Herring, for one, would not yield to these clamors. He does not discuss this problem except indirectly in a book [3] which was probably written in the main before the outbreak of the war. Nevertheless, his whole book may stand as an eloquent defense of two-party government in America. Therein lies its merit—and, in the face of an Iron Age to come, perhaps also its weakness.

It is in scope and temper the broadest discussion of the American party system that we have had. It does not possess the massiveness and originality of Ostrogorski or the magisterial quality of Bryce, but it has a quiet depth of its own. The author's mellowness of tone is notable for one who must still be classed in the younger generation of political thinkers. It draws for its material upon the best in American political literature. It is judicious and even-tempered, yet not lacking in sharp characterizations. It is objective and yet saturated with value judgments. Its weakness lies in its tendency to fall apart into a series of essays on various aspects of the American party system, each of them ending on pretty much the same note.

With the underlying thesis of the book—that the vitality of the American party system lies in the chance it offers for a vigorous opposition and for the clash of group interests—I can have no quarrel. But Herring goes beyond this. He sees the American party system primarily as a force blurring class, group, and sectional differences which might otherwise be intolerably sharp. He sees it as a balancing force against what might otherwise become absolute rule. "Power," he says, "must be finally identified with no one class

---

[3] Pendleton Herring, *The Politics of Democracy: American Parties in Action*, New York, Norton, 1940.

or group; it must be handled like a loving cup and passed about lest one of the company get drunk." He applauds, rather than deplores, the fact that neither of the major parties in America is an outright liberal or conservative party. He regards benignly the failure of third-party movements. And here I confess I do not follow him. I know that Mr. Herring is sincere in his belief that the party system, by blurring sharp divisions on social policy, has performed a service for the national interest. Nevertheless, if a totalitarian America should ever come it would be partly because of the way in which our party system has obstructed the relatively swift changes in economic organization necessary for national survival today.

Mr. Herring tries to hold the balance between innovation and conservatism in American life. He says that both are necessary. He even goes so far as to say, "I would cheer the [reforming] zealots on; they are an essential part of the democratic process." But this sideline cheering reminds me of Lincoln's story about the woman who stood watching the struggle between her husband and a bear and shouted encouragingly to both, "Go it, husband! Go it, bear!" I feel strongly that Herring, like many other commentators on the party system, should distinguish more sharply between the two-party system as a democratic essential and the heterogeneous composition of parties as a democratic brake. What is essential is that there should be a continually functioning opposition, scrutinizing and criticizing every act of a government; otherwise we shall find not only tyranny but also ineptitude entrenched indefinitely. But a party system which does not really represent divergent philosophies of social policy will mean that the necessary changes in government will always come too late to be effective. That this has been true of England and France the plight of both nations testifies today.

In short, I feel that Mr. Herring has gone too far in following the tradition of John Morley and writing an American version of *On Compromise*. The moderation of our party system was achieved, to start with, only by the extremism of our Revolution, and the chance for all of us to enjoy the amenities of American democracy in the future may depend upon the extreme vigor with which we pursue the imperatives of economic and social planning, whether in war or in peace. I have never wanted the 1940 elections scrapped in the interest of some putative national unity: an election is necessary to turn inefficient administrations out or to keep efficient ones from becoming inefficient. It is the mechanism by which one majority is succeeded by another majority. Since I believe that the essence of totalitarian control in both Germany and Russia lies in the one-party system, I have no patience with attempts to introduce that system here. Nevertheless, the party that wins should come into power with a clear notion of why it was elected and what it wants to do, and within constitutional limits it must be given all the power necessary to do it.

I have selected for discussion the phase of Mr. Herring's book that seems of most immediate relevance. But this review does not begin to suggest the wealth of comment and discussion in the book as a whole. The best thing about it is that it does not adopt a holier-than-thou attitude toward party government. It takes most of the things that men tend to rail at in our party system today and accepts them as part not only of its normal but of its desirable functioning.

On a psychological plane the book raises a question that our generation will somehow have to resolve. That question is the extent to which parties have ceased to be a focus for men's real loyalties. Mr. Herring says, speaking of the undesirability of introducing the concepts of left and right into party government: "What if our parties do at times resemble Tweedledum and Tweedledee? The pacific relations between these two would-be warriors offer an example that is not without point in an age where there is enough conflict." Yet he recognizes elsewhere in his book that if democracies are to survive, men must believe strongly in the democratic dogma. Traditionally in American life parties have engaged our very strong loyalties. This is becoming decreasingly true, largely because of Tweedledum and Tweedledee and the effort to avoid conflict. But loyalties that are drained away at this point are likely to be channeled in another direction. If parties become too colorless for real loyalties, what substitute will men come to believe in? One might perhaps answer, the nation as a whole; and the present efforts to whip up a factitious national unity testify to the probability that this will be the trend. But Mr. Herring and others would do well to note that unless a way can be found to give parties once more some real meaning, such a unity is likely to be achieved at the expense of the party system about which they care so deeply.[4]

1940

---

[4] For Professor Herring's sharp reply to this review, see the *Nation*, October 26, 1940, vol. 151, p. 403.

10

The Presidential Office

The Job in the White House

A FTER alternately worshiping and reviling particular Presidents, we now seem ready prayerfully to study the office. The book under review [1] is one of at least four that have appeared recently on the Presidency. If this augurs a minor boom in Presidency books, I like it much more than I liked the spate of "democracy" books; for if American democracy is to survive we shall have to make or keep it strong at particular strategic points. And who can doubt that the Presidency is today the nub of the matter, at least so far as political institutions go? Never in history has the success of a whole way of life depended to so great a degree upon a single office. I say "office" rather than "man," because what we are dealing with here is not some specific incumbent but the job itself, a continuing job in what is likely to prove a continuing crisis, a job so big that even the biggest men we have had have not been cramped in it.

There are two major ways of looking at the Presidential job. Professor Corwin takes one way—a constitutional study of the important aspects of the office (chief executive, administrative chief, commander-in-chief, foreign-affairs chief, popular and legislative leader), of the powers that have been claimed for it, and of the problems of selection and tenure that it raises. His approach merits comparison with that of Harold Laski's *American Presidency*, published a few months earlier. While Corwin's work is rich in marginal discussions of personalities, politics, and the history of ideas, they are definitely marginal, while the analysis of the legal limits

---

[1] Edward S. Corwin, *The President: Office and Powers,* New York University Press, 1941.

of power is kept central. The result is a book with an astringent and deflating quality. And a rather funereal quality too, especially in the discussion of the current Presidency; for Corwin sees it as resting on the ruins of three of the major constitutional principles —separation of powers, no Congressional delegation of power, and a balanced federalism.

In contrast, Laski's book was affirmative and almost optimistic. Laski saw the Presidency as the spearhead of the "positive" state, alone capable of furnishing the leadership to carry us without violence through the transition period. Where Corwin sees *powers* through the eyes of one who has steeped himself in Supreme Court decisions, Laski saw *power* through the eyes of a democratic collectivist. And here more than anywhere else, the whole (Presidential power) has been and must be more than the sum of the constituent parts.

I do not mean to decry Corwin's achievement, which is massive. His erudition (there are nearly 150 pages of notes) all but silences criticism, and he is one of the few writers whose notes I find meaty and often entertaining. The structure of the book, to be sure, seems loose and contrived rather than organic, and I suspect that more people are likely to consult it than read it. But Corwin's qualities —a critical yet far-roving mind, a combination of the magisterial and the charming in manner—shine through the apparatus of scholarship. He has made his book indispensable to the student of both American law and American politics. His sensitiveness to the danger zones of constitutional tension was shown when in 1935 he wrote *The Twilight of the Supreme Court*. It is notable that he now believes that "the center of gravity of our constitutional system" lies in the relation between the President and Congress, and —in order to make it a more workable one—suggests reshaping the Cabinet to include Congressional leaders, men "who could bring the Presidential whim under an independent scrutiny which today is lacking."

Where the book is disappointing is in its major assumptions about American government. I say "assumptions," because I will not quarrel with a constitutional scholar if he does not include cosmic discussions of political theory in his book. But even a constitutional discussion will often take its color from the "inarticulate major premises" of political theory. And what I miss in Corwin's book is the premise, articulate or other, of a democratic dynamism. It is not enough to say, "constitutionally, the President may go thus far and no further." The problem is rather, "given the huge job the President has, how can a flexible Constitution that is a real instrument of government enable him to get enough power to do the job? And how can an administrative system help him to pool intelligence and organize will on a nation-wide scale?" Corwin says the principal merit of his plan for a new Cabinet is that it will bring in men not dependent on the President. But it is not the crucial thing today to find no-men to check the President's will. We have plenty of those in Congress, in business, in the press. We have ample checks already on the President's power. What we want is a conception of the Presidency big enough for the job, and then the machinery to carry out the conception. This is not to argue for an opportunistic surrender of plenary power to the Presidency. There must be safeguards. Yet they should not be of the check-and-balance variety, but the safeguards provided by a majority will operating within a civil-liberties tradition.[2]

Corwin's present emphasis is curious in view of his *Twilight of the Supreme Court,* which was one of the most cogent statements of the proposition that the Constitution is an instrument for achieving positive values, and that the Court must not be allowed to interpose obstacles to the majority will. I miss a similar instrumental view in the present book. I wonder whether I am wrong in detecting in it a somewhat tired feeling, as if the writer, taking a long historical perspective of the attempts to achieve a strong Presidency, felt in confronting the present administration that this was where he came in. Actually, the historical perspectives are what give the book a good deal of its value. The analysis of the constitutional conceptions of the Presidency held by Jefferson, Jackson, Lincoln, T.R., and Wilson gives a new slant to the history of the Presidency as a story of "discontinuous aggrandizement." One might add also, discontinuous creativeness. It is worth noting, in passing, that Corwin does not consider F.D.R. as important a figure as Jackson,

---

[2] Professor Corwin has written me in comment: "I think you rather overemphasized the purpose of my proposed reform of the Cabinet to bring the President's discretion under some sort of control. I had equally in mind the idea of stabilizing and facilitating his direction of the legislative process."

Lincoln, or Wilson. His argument may depress or cheer, depending on the viewpoint.

At any rate, the President's job will more and more in the immediate future become a dual one—that of exercising overseership of a far-flung administrative network, the parts of which must be kept harmonious with each other; and that of leadership, of imparting will and energy and direction to a government. To accommodate both of these functions the constitutional limits of the President's power will be stretched in the years to come. Fortunately, as concerns the Presidency, the Constitution is not a straitjacket. Corwin gives a striking account of the way in which Lincoln as war President, knowing that the Union would not survive unless he tapped new sources of national powers for himself, found what he wanted in the President's role as Commander-in-Chief. He presented the Court with a *fait accompli,* and history has ratified it. It would be much better for us to envisage ahead of time the possibilities of other crises such as Lincoln's. If we take a flexible and creative view of the Presidency to start with, we may be able to minimize the shock of Lincoln's sort of constitutional dictatorship. For that is what the Presidency, a prisoner in peacetime of the press and Congress and the party system, tends to become in wartime.

1941

Hamlet and the Presidency

AMERICA is plunged into a vast collective Hamlet-reverie, set off by the question of the grant of Presidential power in the lease-lend bill. To give or not to give, to trust or not to trust. Of course, we screen our basic indecision by talking of the danger of "blank-check" delegation of power by Congress. And yet we know that if we are to have effective action we must look to the executive for it. But when it comes to the question of empowering him to use the full force of our nation we hesitate. We are caught between the will to act and the fear of mastery.

Ever since the struggle of Parliament against the Tudors and Stuarts, the English-speaking world has associated freedom with the legislature, security with the courts, and potential tyranny with the executive. And in the shadow of Nazism we are even more inclined to regard the reactionary Congress that we have as the bulwark of our liberty and the progressive President that we have as a potential Hitler.

This madness is not without its method, if you view it in terms of the struggle for control of the American state. For the Presidency has always been the great stumbling-block of the moneyed minority group in American life, and the great instrument of majority-rule democracy. Who have been the strong Presidents? They have been the people's Presidents, the champions of the democratic cause— Jackson, Lincoln, T.R., Wilson, F.D.R.

It is no matter of surprise therefore that your reactionary regards the strong President as anti-Christ—unless indeed the President be his own, which he has not been because the cue of reactionary Presidents has been to leave well enough alone and let corporate power take its course. And today the isolationist-appeasement-tory group sheds crocodile tears over the danger of dictatorship when it would like nothing better than a good whopping try at the same dictatorship. The aid-to-Britain conservatives are torn between two impulses. Their spokesman, the New York *Herald Tribune,* headed its lease-lend editorial "The Great Dilemma." As indeed it was for those who fear the collapse of Britain but fear equally in America an aroused people, believing in its own democracy and willing to use its majority-rule sanctions to fight for it.

For that is what the Presidency is: not our master, nor indeed, in any but an unctuous sense, our servant; but a weapon, the greatest majority-weapon our democracy has thus far shaped. Of course it is dangerous. All weapons are, if you do not know how to use them. That is why we keep in our own hands the actual fashioning of broad policy; that is why we watch hawk-like in Congress, in the press, on the radio, every move of the President. If you have followed the bitter day-to-day struggle of American foreign policy ever since Hitler wrote his will across the European skies, you will testify that nowhere in the world have the main outlines of policy been so insistently debated and so carefully shaped as here. Once that policy has been decided, the Presidency becomes the focal point of will and action.

Why don't the liberals know this? I have a letter from a professor in a great university saying that in a crisis the inevitable tendency is toward a strong Presidency, and therefore he intends to work critically in the other direction. But that is not so. Buchanan was a crisis President as well as Lincoln. There was nothing inevitable about Lincoln. Hoover was a crisis President as well as Roosevelt. The one thing "inevitable" in a crisis state is the strong drive for the suppression of civil liberties. I regard the present drive against "Reds," typified by the sub-mentality of the feudal Democrats in Oklahoma and the Irish Democrats in New York, as the most dangerous force in our country. At Albany Senator Coughlin has introduced a criminal-syndicalism bill which would clap you into prison for ten years for having dangerous thoughts; and Senator Dunnigan has introduced an anti-ism bill which would deny you the ballot for reading aloud one of Jefferson's speeches.

I think that this fear of repression underlies a good deal of the liberals' hesitation about an effective Presidency. Yet the great threat to civil liberties comes generally from the state legislatures and local police desperadoes. And the federal government has, up to now, done far more to control the flames than to fan them.

The basic reason, I think, for the indecision of the liberals is their Great Tradition of never being happy unless they are in the opposition. They want to see a good society created, but they dare not be in on the creation. They are most of them Villards or Flynns, whose loftiest dream stretches only to a sort of veto power over other people's actions. They are incapable in their twisted solitude of having a hand in those majority-rule revolutions that have been the glory of American history.

Actually the man in the street sees more clearly here than they do. He was not worried over the third-term issue, and he is not worried much about the present delegation of power. He knows that every scare the press has created about Presidential power in the past eight years has proved unfounded. He knows that in a time of lightning war the executive cannot be put into mental fetters in its conduct of foreign policy. There is in him little of the Hamlet death-urge, and little of the Hamlet indecision.

1941

11

Two Presidents in Wartime

Lincoln in the Civil War

WITH these four volumes [1] Carl Sandburg completes the life of Lincoln begun in *The Prairie Years*. Taking the total achievement, there is nothing in historical literature that I know quite comparable with it.

I generally distrust the meeting of perfect writer and perfect theme. There is a blueprint seemliness about such conjunctions that rarely issues in a creative product. The surprising thing about Sandburg writing on Lincoln is that in this case the results are good: the democrat, the poet, the storyteller, the earthy Midwesterner, the singer of the people has managed somehow to write about another democrat who was also something of a poet in his way and a vast storyteller and an earthy Midwesterner and a product of the popular mass. He has sought to depict him on a canvas broader than anything else in American biography: over 2000 pages of text, hundreds of illustrations, a hundred pages of index. Even the four-volume Beveridge *Marshall*, expanded by long discussions of cases and decisions, seems dwarfed. Sandburg has brought to his theme a brooding vigor and compassion, a precision of detail, a lyricism, a gusto for people and experience, that would be hard to match among American writers. And the work he has given us is not only a biography of Lincoln and a history of the Civil War. It is itself a battlefield, a sprawling panorama of people and issues and conflicts held together only by Sandburg's absorption with the central figure.

The historian's art has been narrowed by the academies to the

---

[1] Carl Sandburg, *Abraham Lincoln: The War Years*, New York, Harcourt, Brace, 1939.

point of making people believe that there is only one right way of setting down a history. Sandburg's way is as characteristically his own as Carlyle's was when he wrote of Cromwell. It is the right way for him because through it he can best express his own basic drives and outlook. He is in these books three things: reporter, poet, lover.

As reporter he sets down what happened with the athletic matter-of-factness that the best journalists put into their craft. But it is a reporter who has a million and a half words at his disposal, and so Sandburg empties his notebooks into his pages. But while nothing is too minute to be put in, there are no superfluous interpretations. The facts are allowed to speak for themselves, yet almost always they are so arranged (with a simplicity that almost conceals the cunning) that they do speak and have something to say. And Sandburg has the reporter's passion for concreteness. We always learn the exact numbers of everything, the exact look of everyone who enters the story. There is something even a bit frightening about the detail. I think I can understand Sandburg's intent: the Lincoln literature has grown so vast that a definitive factual work was needed to gather together everything available and valid. The result has one great flaw: the sense one gets of a curious one-dimensional plane, in which the detail gets the same loving attention as the big event, at a considerable sacrifice of perspective. Sandburg is a little like a painter in the primitive style. He is your true democratic historian. In his universe all facts, once they have been validated, are free and equal. Yet he gives his material thereby an unforced character that should cause the biographers who come after him to bless him. Unless I miss my guess, Sandburg's *Lincoln* will become an inexhaustible storehouse from which will be drawn a myriad of other Lincolns.

There is also Sandburg the poet. A poet turning to biography and history is likely to flaunt his Muse or, by an inversion, to be ashamed of it and suppress it. Not Sandburg. The America of Lincoln, the teeming years of suffering and battle and greatness, lie drenched in the moonlight of his lyricism. The Sandburg here is the Sandburg of the Chicago poems, celebrating America and the obscure ways of life, setting his words down with neither elegance nor precision but with a curious random obliqueness that nevertheless manages almost always to reach its object. "Out of the smoke and the stench, out of the music and violet dreams of the war, Lincoln stood perhaps taller than any other of the many great heroes." Thus Sandburg. What biographer who was not Sandburg's kind of poet would dare say "music and violet dreams" when describing war, or juxtapose "violet dreams" with "the smoke and the stench"? Yet while there are passages verging on the dithyrambic, particularly at the end of chapters, the whole tone of the book has a quietness and restraint that only one who has mastered his subject and is sure of it could afford.

I have mentioned Sandburg the lover. I know of no other word that will describe the twelve years spent in wooing the material, the care lavished on every detail; or the complete identification with the subject that allows him to analyze Lincoln without once raising his voice in shrillness, and with the effortlessness of what might almost be a reverie. Nor do I know of any other word to describe the deep and shrewd tenderness for common people throughout the book, such as one might expect from the author of *The People, Yes.*

Sandburg has evidently taken care not to write the sort of contemporary book that underlines the parallels between yesterday and today. He has given us Lincoln the man, Lincoln the war President, America in the war years. If there are morals to be drawn for today, he has left it to us to draw them.

I am not averse to drawing my own. But one does not need the stimulus of the modern instance to find excitement in the task of human interpretation that every Lincoln biographer has faced. Sandburg's *Lincoln* stands out not for its sharpness of thesis but for its very lack of the monistic view. It has a catholicity and an unforced quality that are rare in biography, without succumbing to mere straddling and the colorless. One gets the external man and the internal tensions. There is no attempt to prettify, to play down crudities and failings; neither is there any hint of exploiting them. All the lumbering awkwardness of the man is there, his gropings and fumblings, the way he entered the reception room at the White House and made people feel he was the man in the room who was least at home. But the simplicity of the man is also there—a simplicity which, in Emerson's phrase about him, was "the perfection of manners."

Throughout the book we find ourselves on the verge of the symbolic. To quote Emerson again on Lincoln, "He exerts the enormous power of this continent in every hour, in every conversation, in every act." Sandburg spells that out in detail, while he never lets us lose the sense of the symbolic relation between Lincoln and the American energies. And he manages also to convey Lincoln's tortured sense that there had been imposed on him a task too great for a human to bear. It is here that one strikes the deepest chord in Lincoln. The fatality of it: that he, with his tenderness for everything living, should become the instrument of death for tens of thousands; that he, who always saw the danger of men's control over men, should have in his hand the destinies of millions; that he, who always shrank from action, should at the peril of his people be galvanized into a train of actions with vast inscrutable consequences. From this viewpoint there are two peaks in the book: the chapter on Lincoln's laughter and religion, and the analysis of how Lincoln had to tell his stories in order to relieve the intolerable tensions within him; and the chapters on the assassination and the country's mourning. To the latter especially Sandburg brings his most complete gifts, telling the story with the subdued reverence of a passion play, and with a fatality as if the actors were moving in a dream. Here one reaches great writing.

It is a bit of luck for us that these volumes should appear just when the question of the conduct of the war by democracies is so much in our minds. One will not find here, as in the Baker volumes on Wilson, much discussion of the now frayed theme of American neutrality. But there is a store of stuff on the question of what happens to a democracy when it goes to war.

Lincoln has gone down in American history as one of the "strong" Presidents, who flouted constitutional restrictions and established a dictatorship in order to win the war. The view is not without its truth. Yet never has a government waged so fierce a war as Lincoln had to wage, and departed so little from the democratic spirit. Lincoln the war President, Lincoln the Commander-in-Chief of the national armies, Lincoln who suspended *habeas corpus* when it seemed an indispensable measure and who backed up the arrest and expulsion of Vallandigham by General Burnside —that Lincoln never ceased to be also Lincoln the humanist and

Lincoln the democrat. He was sore pressed as no American President has ever been. He made mistakes, but as one reads the Sandburg volumes they seem to have been mainly on the side of excessive tolerance rather than lust for power. He had to deal with all the plagues that beset a war government—the militarist mind, the messianic mind, the bureaucratic mind; with war passions and hysteria, with patrioteers, with the lynching spirit, with lethargy, with an opposition so bitter it verged continually on sabotage and treason. He had no genius for organization, little capacity for delegation, little administrative ability as it is generally understood. But with all these limitations he never once lost sight of the main chance. He had a way of cleaving to the heart of a problem that baffled subtler and more expert and sophisticated minds. There were men around him with more powerful wills, men with a greater commitment to humanitarian and radical values. But there was no one who saw better than Lincoln the dilemma and task of a democracy at war: how to win the war with the minimum sacrifice of traditional liberties and democratic values.

In a world in which there have been so-called war leaders like the Daladiers and the Chamberlains, we have reason to be proud of Lincoln. We have reason to be proud that with every opportunity for setting up a dictatorship, he did not succumb; with every opportunity for betraying democratic values under the guise of war necessity, he did not succumb. Long before the end of the war he was giving his best thought to the problem of a humane peace and a constructive plan for rebuilding the defeated states. I have no intention of saying that Lincoln was wholly consistent in the strength of his humanism. There were forces in American life that proved too powerful for him, for the cause of the North was tied up with the cause of a predatory capitalism, and the Reconstruction that followed Lincoln's death was almost devoid of either democratic or human values. Yet there was never a time when it was more important for us than now to know the capacity of a democracy to turn up greatness of Lincoln's sort from its humblest sons—a greatness that will survive the grime and savagery of war.

If I read my own Lincoln somewhat into Sandburg's pages, there is room for others as well. He has given the coming generations the material out of which to construct a succession of Lincoln images. All the material is there—from the day that Lincoln

boarded the train at Springfield to ride to his inauguration, down
to the day when his coffin was placed in a flower-heaped vault in
the Springfield he had left. What four years were crowded between
those two boundaries! The hordes of people, office-seekers, hand-
shakers; the jokes and stories, deep, illimitable stories, lighting up
what was comic and contradictory in life; the grim wild humor of
a President-elect conferring with his advisers as to how he might
travel through Baltimore on his way to his inauguration without
being lynched; the Cabinet officers, with their intrigues and jealous-
ies; the vast decisions and petty details; the generals, and the heart-
breaking search for military leadership that would be confident
and firm and aggressive; the violent attacks in Congress and the
press; the drama of emancipation, and the harrowing uncertainty
of its consequences; Father Abraham; the see-sawing of war's fortunes; the draft riots, the desertions, the Copperheads; the unending delegations of politicians and ministers and zealots and cranks;
Jay Cooke and the financing of the war; the profiteering and poverty, at one extreme costly furs bought with war profits, at the
other the starving families of soldiers; the European diplomats and
statesmen puzzled by this ungainly fellow who told crude stories;
the faith of the masses, growing and deepening every year; the rows
of hospital cots, the faces pleading and rebuking; the dream of
sudden death and the deep inner conviction that it would come;
the unerring course of Booth's bullet; Whitman's threnody; the
grief of the people. And then the legend.

1939

I Thought of Lincoln

THERE will be many political dinners this year, as always, to
celebrate Lincoln's greatness. Wendell Willkie is scheduled
to speak at one, Thomas Dewey will contribute his Lincoln-
ism to another, and Clare Boothe hers to a third. The orators will
orate, the well-fed and sleekly dressed thousands will applaud.
There is nothing new in this. Yet this year as never before, in a
national crisis deeper than any since the Civil War, we must reas-
sert that Lincoln is not the monopoly of a party with whom today
he has nothing in common.

He belongs, as leader, to the whole American people. And he is today the most complete and satisfying symbol of leadership we have. Leadership has two facets. At any moment a people needs not only a leader for the present but a leader for the past as well. And the man in the past to whom a people turns is just as important a fact about it as the man to whom it turns in the present. There has been a vast amount of guff written about Lincoln, and he has grown to the proportions of a legend. Yet, legend or not, the fact is that with every year Lincoln has been emerging more clearly as our great historical leader.

There are reasons for that, reasons which reach down to our sense of equality and our will to live. For Lincoln was a democrat, a man out of the people who never tore the roots that bound him to them. And he was a humanist who felt deeply about inequality and inhumanity wherever he saw it. And he was a nationalist in whose mind the survival of the united nation came first. And he was a strong President who, when the time came for decisive action, knew how to act decisively. We tend to forget today that Lincoln's decision to risk a destructive war was a hard decision to make, and by no means as inevitable then as it seems to us now with the hindsight of history. All these qualities are the qualities that make great leadership in a crisis democracy. Whether he knows it or not, Mr. Roosevelt is being measured in our minds to that fit, as every leader will be measured as long as Americans have the task of making out of their democracy a strong state and out of their strength a living democracy.

There were many things wrong about Lincoln and the American democracy of his day. There were draft riots because the burden of service fell on those who could not buy their way out. There was bribery, inefficiency, appeasement. There were breadlines and banquets, profiteering and cowardice and criminal complacency. There were partisans to attack Lincoln from the political left and right, men who called him a baboon, accused him of selling out. But through it all, for all his veerings and indecisions, he clung tenaciously to his single-purposed course.

Given what the Civil War means to us, there are things also in our America of today for which we should apologize to those who died under Lincoln's leadership. I heard from a refugee just arrived from Marseille of the conditions in the prison camps for German and Spanish refugees in France; and then I looked at the obstacles our State Department is placing in the path of their coming to our country, and I thought of Lincoln. I read Leigh White's account of the butchery of innocent Jews in the slaughterhouses of Bucharest, and then I read the speeches of our appeasers, and I thought of Lincoln. I thought of Ford's fight now against his workers, and of the preparations being made by Bethlehem Steel to fight labor, and I thought of Lincoln. I read of the Jim Crowism still practiced in the American army, and of the fifteen Negro sailors dishonorably discharged from the navy because they had protested against discrimination, and I thought of Lincoln. I had a letter from a brilliant Negro professor who wrote that the vast body of his people saw the need for destroying Nazism: "How grimly ironic therefore that we should have to beg for our chance to help"; and I thought of Lincoln.

It is easy to idealize Lincoln and to read into him your own views and beliefs until they become his as well. But it is even easier to deflate than to idealize, to set him down as just a shoddy horse-trading politician. He was not that. If ever there was a man in our history who had the difficult stuff of heroism, this was the man. He was no absolutist and no program-builder. But neither was there any cant in him, as we know when we read his ironic letter to the delegation of ministers protesting as Christians against the war. He did a hard job well, with dignity, firmness, and—in the midst of desperate measures—with compassion. Always he had the distinguishing mark of greatness, the ability in any problem to get at the jugular. He saw when he came to office that the crux of adequate Presidential power in an emergency lay in the President's role as commander-in-chief. And, although a hard-bitten realist, he could know the meaning and the value of a dream.

He was no great leftist. Yet the American progressives have made a mistake not to claim him as one of them. Why have they, with a few exceptions, steered shy of him? Has it been some curious snobbishness—the knowledge that Lincoln is in the very stream of the American tradition, and the feeling that the left needs something more esoteric and marginal before it recognizes the stuff of heroism? If so, they have been cruelly wrong. For whether on a national or a trans-national plane, Lincoln, as the American common man raised to a heroic pitch, has in him the power to give meaning to the past and shape to the future.

1941

Roosevelt as Symbol

FROM the very beginning Franklin Roosevelt has been a crisis President, and there is little reason to suppose that he will cease to be President at a time when the crisis is deepest. This is bitter hemlock for reactionaries of every stripe to drink. But let us be clear at the outset: the chances are overwhelming that the next President of the United States will be that man now in the White House.[2]

He will be there for four more years, not because he wants to, but because the people want him there. I don't need the Gallup or *Fortune* figures to prove it, although they do help confirm something we would know without them. The people want him there, not because the New Deal has been a success, or because we fear to swap horses while crossing a stream. For the first, there is the persistent fact of some eleven million unemployed and the extremes of wealth and poverty as accented as ever. And for the second, in a democracy the time when you are crossing a stream is exactly the time when you are forced to swap horses—if the horse you are riding is not much good. Only the Hitler *Blitzkrieg* availed to force Chamberlain out and Churchill in. And to steer close to a grim play on words, without the change of horses the large part of the British army which crossed the Channel back to safety in England would today be mingled with the soil of Flanders and France. The point is that, for the people's purposes today, Mr. Roosevelt is a good horse. And they know it.

That knowledge goes deeper than party politics, deeper than political and economic experience. It reaches down to the pre-rational stuff in us out of which symbols are fashioned. It is the surge of these impulses that has already as good as swept aside the third-term tradition. I do not mean to be mystical: the events which have made the President the only possible Democratic choice are clear enough. They are the war in Europe, the onward thrust of

---

[2] This essay was first published in June 1940, on the eve of both the Republican and the Democratic nominating conventions. While I feel some satisfaction that the prophecies in it have proved true with respect to the nomination of both Mr. Willkie and Mr. Roosevelt and the outcome of the election, I have allowed them to stand in the tense in which they were written, not primarily on that account but because they are an integral part of the essay.

Nazi power, the new awareness of the revolution in war technology and of the nakedness of our defenses, the persistence of the world-wide forces out of which the Nazi revolution arose—all converging with the Presidential election. But this forms only the outer frame-work. Within it there have been our own inner tensions at work. With the crumbling of what had seemed the enduring bastions of the European order, our deepest political emotions have been re-leased. I mean the blank fear of our failure to survive as a tolera-bly democratic society; and the urge toward group cohesion, which means in this era the urge toward national unity; and—so rare in a democracy—the desire to submit to a leadership great enough to match the great times; and, finally, the longing for a symbol at once of security and of forward movement, of moderation and yet of ag-gressiveness.

Mr. Roosevelt comes closer to being such a symbol than anyone within our experience. Yet if he falls short of it—and how should he not?—measure by how much less he falls short than the other candidates. Their names have been successively before us during the past few months. Yet, in comparison with Roosevelt's, how far away and archaic some of those names already seem. Who was Garner? Was McNutt once taken seriously as Presidential timber? What graveyard crew will undertake to exhume Vandenberg and Taft? Was that Tom Dewey and Bert Wheeler that the Nazi tanks rolled over as they swept on to Paris? What are "Jedge" Hull's chances in a world that demands in its leaders, if not youth, then at least color and forcefulness? The fact is that Hitler and Stalin and Churchill now dominate our imaginations so monstrously, and the harsh age in which they have become leaders has so stretched our political horizons, that men of ordinary candidate stature seem puny. Roosevelt alone among the candidates can claim our atten-tion as a leader-symbol along with the Europeans.

Who will oppose him? It still requires, despite Dorothy Thomp-son, two to make an election. The Republicans, confronted by the clear probability of Roosevelt's nomination, have striven desper-ately to find the other man. But Roosevelt has had so big a lead that their hearts have simply not been in the effort. Even as I write, only a week before the opening of the Big Show at Philadel-phia, there is a funereal air about the preparations. The only real candidate the Republicans have is Willkie, and—despite his being

a former Democrat and a big public-utility man, both circumstances violating the outward political decencies—I would stake a
good deal that he will be the choice. Willkie has brought novelty
and freshness into Republican politics; his outward limitations
have been in themselves challenges; he has known the value of
mingling candor about his hopes with skepticism about his chances
—an irresistible combination whether in a lover or a candidate. If
it is Willkie who is picked to oppose Roosevelt in the election, it
will not be a wholly uneven battle. For Willkie has middle-class
"independent" appeal. His strategy will be to go along with Roosevelt on the intervention issue, but play himself up as the younger
and stronger man for the war crisis. The theme will be a dual one:
that the problem now is to organize American industry for defense,
and to do it without embracing economic collectivism—and who
could be more nearly ideal for both purposes, we shall be asked,
than a shrewd and successful utility executive? If Willkie is nominated, only Roosevelt can beat him. And there can be little doubt
that he would.

What sort of President would Roosevelt make? This is not a
whimsical question, despite our having had two terms of him. For
he would be President in a world half lost to Nazism, in which
whether or not we go to war we shall have a war economy and a
political organization of concentrated powers. How does the Roosevelt we know look in the light of the new world we can only dimly
discern?

The Roosevelt we know is a mirror of our own best energies, our
own possibly fatal confusions. Perhaps because of that fact no one
has yet taken the dimensions of the man in an enduring study. It is
not that our writers lack the art, but that in the face of so elusive a
figure they lack the confidence to use it. The political portraits,
whether done in bile or saccharine, are dismal things. Emil Lud-
wig's full-length study was pretentious as well as inaccurate. But
John Chamberlain, although working, as usual, within too limited
a medium, has done a canny job in his last book in showing Roosevelt as a master tight-rope walker. And Harold Laski's book *The
American Presidency,* while in form a study of the Presidential
office, is in effect a commentary on the most fateful American President.

I say "fateful" as applying both to the time itself and to the man's apprehension of it. Roosevelt has always had a sense of history. The well-worn story of his remark to newspapermen during the bank holiday of 1933—"I shall be either America's greatest President or its last"—is typical of a perspective few Presidents have had. One thing Roosevelt has said clearly: he has no intention of being another Buchanan. Which implies that all the basic conditions that characterize a country on the eve of a civil war are true of our period. But to avoid being a Buchanan in the face of impending civil war one must be something of a Lincoln. How much of Lincoln does Roosevelt have in him? More, I am convinced, than any President since Lincoln or before. I know that in externals they are poles apart. In the one an easy graciousness, in the other a clumsy grace; the one modern, alert, cosmopolitan, and the other a backwoodsman even for his own day; the one aristocrat, the other plebeian. Yet the resemblances are real. Each of them managed somehow to catch the accents and express the aspirations of the ordinary people of his day. But beyond these and more important, each was forced by the exterior tension of events to complete an interior crisis out of which his real greatness emerged. Lincoln was a brooding man of thought whom the Civil War compelled to action. Roosevelt is a man of action whom the crisis of the depression years and the international collapse have compelled to thought. The more memorable figure is undoubtedly Lincoln, the more effective President probably Roosevelt.

Yet Roosevelt has not been effective on the crucial question of unemployment, which is America's dynamite dump. Nothing can be clearer than his failure to translate his own deepening perceptions and his generous sympathies into a working program. I need not spell out that fact here. What needs, however, to be said is that while Roosevelt will no doubt be linked in history with the pragmatic and piecemeal reforms of the New Deal, he is at once smaller and bigger than the New Deal. Smaller because the New Deal is not one man's creation but the product of mass aspirations. Bigger in the sense that his personal stature has survived the relative failure of the New Deal and the scattering of its battalions. It may not be rational but it is true that many would vote for Roosevelt who would reject most of his works. His Presidential tenure offers an uncanny perspective: here is a man who lost or had to compromise on most of his goals, yet he has emerged with prestige and popular appeal probably as great as ever.

But to the unemployed and the disinherited, to WPA workers, and to youngsters just out of school and without a job, it is scant consolation to have symbol without substance. They still cling to the Roosevelt banner, partly because Europe has become a word of fear and bewilderment, partly because a war economy might make jobs for them, mainly because they are still convinced that Roosevelt will somehow keep moving forward without revolution or dictatorship. In short, the Roosevelt following today more than ever is a following based on fear, faith, and expectation rather than works. Nor have these people ever really been taught either the elements of the Roosevelt achievement or the sources of the Roosevelt failure. They do not know the great forward stride made in the development of the administrative agency; few of them understand that the President managed somehow to resolve a great constitutional crisis; many are forgetting the solid achievements in the protection of the worker, the farmer, the investor, against the more obvious harshness of capitalism on the decline. And as for the springs of failure, no one has pointed out to the people the role played by the opinion industries in bolstering every reactionary movement, by big-business sabotage, by the demoralizing anti-labor and anti-alien agitation, by the lack of audacity in genuine economic planning, by the failure to build enduring political support in a party realignment, by the crumbling of administrative morale.

When the people support a political leader through fear and faith, ignorant both of the sources of his past failure and of the conditions of his future success, that leader is in a dangerous position. He has as a politician encouraged expectations which as a policy-maker he will probably be unable to fulfill. I believe Roosevelt must know that. I think this insight, rather than the persistent rumors about physical exhaustion or some new ailment, goes far toward explaining the sense of tiredness the Administration conveys, and the very real and not feigned unwillingness of the President to stand for a third term. Being a political leader is at best one of the loneliest things in the world; but being one under the conditions Roosevelt has recently had to face must be desolating. Hav-

ing to cajole a hostile and often stupid Congress and handle a bitter and sometimes venal press, having to mend political fences
while building administrative structures, having to keep in sight
the forest of national welfare despite the trees of special interests,
having to see more clearly than most the logic and stakes of the
international scene, and finding oneself balked in translating that
insight into foreign policy—all that does not make a President's
lot a happy one.

I do not know whether Roosevelt himself is conscious that if his
past role as President has been difficult, his future role as President
would be even more so. Thus far he has relied mainly on two techniques. One has been the balancing of interests between various
groups, always with an eye to getting out of the trading of gains
and concessions as much as possible for the underprivileged. The
second has been the alternation of periods of swift legislative and
administrative advance with "breathing-spell" periods of consolidation. And usually there has been the understanding that even the
best army is as weak as its officers, and therefore a concern for filling
the key administrative posts with progressives. These standards
seem now in process of abandonment. If gains have come out of
the recent attempts to balance interests in Washington, they have
not been for labor and the low-income groups. The past two years
have been a long and continuous breathing-spell, with almost no
advance toward economic planning or social legislation. And the
key posts, especially in the new war-industry structures, are coming increasingly to be filled by men who can by no stretch of the
imagination be called New Dealers.

I think I can guess what rationale might be offered for these
moves. The important thing, we might be told, is the supreme national effort in the international emergency; party lines and class
lines must be transcended, and along with others the Administration must give up its pet preoccupations and its social hobbies; the
new powers the government is getting in the national-defense
economy are inherently mistrusted by the corporate capitalists,
and their consent must therefore be wooed; when we have met the
immediate emergency and can come back to interior problems, we
shall have an administrative plant that is a going concern and can
then be turned to the uses of economic democracy. And the New

Deal can then go on to its most daring phase—of attempting to run a peace machine with the same efficiency and the same sense of national welfare as a war machine.

I do not know that anyone in the Administration actually thinks this. I do know that the next President, if he is a liberal, will have to face the issue raised above. Mr. Roosevelt has always been a master of the strategic retreat. Perhaps the present New Deal doldrums fall under that category. But surely he must know that the world America faces in the next decade bears few resemblances to the world of the twenties or even of the thirties. He must know that whether we go to war or not we are already *at war* in the realest sense, because under any contingency we shall have to embark on a national-defense program which will channel from a third to a half of our national income into war preparations, reduce living standards and real wages, transform our economy into at least a semi-planned war economy, play ducks and drakes with our civil liberties, and sweep Latin America into the ambit of something approaching a good-neighbor imperialism. We have all been forced to grow up in the past months and can afford to call things by their right names. If, as seems increasingly clear, American survival depends upon such swift and heroic measures. I should rather have Mr. Roosevelt in the White House than anyone else who would stand a chance of being elected. (I assume Roosevelt has given up his hope of getting the political boys to accept Jackson or Douglas.) But I pray that it be a Roosevelt like the one who from 1934 to 1936 put through the basic program of New Deal social legislation, a Roosevelt who understands with Churchill that wars are never won by retreats and evacuations, no matter how brilliant. That applies to war on the social and economic fronts as well as the military. For there is as surely a world revolution today in economics and politics and social morale as there is in war technology, and the Liddell Hart defensive theory will not work in these areas any more than it did on the battlefields of Europe.

1940

12

Reflections on a Harsh Age

ERHAPS, in these roaring days, reflections of any sort are a luxury. The big questions are programmatic. As Harold Laski has put it, where do we go from here? And the answer eludes us. That may be a good reason, if reason I must have, for pausing in this harsh age for the irrelevancy of reflection. I hope that the Committee to Defend America and equally the America First Committee will wink at my dereliction. After all, even Dorothy Thompson can turn aside from her daily urgencies to write a column on "An American Love Story." And I have noted, when I talk with someone from whom I differ profoundly on the question of where we go from here, that I also differ from him profoundly on the questions of how we got here, and what the landscape "here" is like.

That it is a bleak landscape there will be general consent. But what is the special quality of its bleakness? And what is there to be learned, if anything, from our recent experiences about the social animal we call man?

First, and amazingly, that the animal is a far tougher and a far more variable animal than we had ever reckoned for. I do not pretend to know what historians and psychologists a century from now will say about our present age and its place in the human span, but I will gamble we will not be ignored. What the Spaniards, the Czechs, the Poles, the Norwegians, the English, the Greeks have suffered and done is not without importance in an estimate of one whom Shakespeare regarded as a "forked radish with a head fantastically carved." There is, of course, another column to the ledger; and if we were not prepared for the indestructible heroism of English housewives and Spanish workers and Greek peasants, neither were we prepared for the ungentle lengths to which men could go in the systematic destruction of their fellow-creatures. And yet, striking a trial balance, we are still in the black. Adam Smith once said that

407

there was a vast deal of ruin in a nation. As we watch cultures dislocated, sensitive artists transplanted but picking up their skills where the rough hands of the Nazis had interrupted them, we must conclude that there is a vast deal of ruin in the individual as well. All in all, the human ambit has been stretched, and that is, I think, good for the species, whatever its hardship for the single life.

I do not mean to glorify my fellows. There are many ugly things we have been learning about ourselves, even on this side of the Nazi fence. The one that seems to hurt most is that there is less of human sympathy in us than we had counted on. At the outbreak of the war we were predicting that the one thing Americans would not tolerate would be the systematic bombing of London civilians; and that two weeks after it happened it would find us at war. In the light of Guernica, Nanking, the Jews of Central Europe, we should have known better.

The experts tell us that what happens in an age of great suffering is that our sense of horror and sympathy is stretched too taut, until finally it snaps and goes dead. The moralists, among whom I count notably the Mumford-MacLeish school, tell us that our moral faculties have atrophied because we have been worshiping the false gods of materialism and creature comforts. Both may be right.

Yet I prefer a different view of the matter. I think we have come to the end of the era of the man of sensibility, as Richardson, Sterne, and Rousseau in the eighteenth century and Dickens and Mrs. Stowe in the nineteenth depicted him. Parson Sterne weeping over his prostrate donkey is as dead as Adam Smith squeezing the state out of his universe. The new hero in our literature is not the man of sensibility, or even the desperately translated version of him in the proletarian protagonist who feels for the injustices of his fellows. He is rather the man of an almost metaphysical intensity of spirit, such as Malraux achieved in *Man's Fate* and Hemingway, I think, aimed at in *For Whom the Bell Tolls*. He is more stoic than he is collectivist, though he has something of each. Most of all, he is fanatic, in the sense that he holds to an unshaken belief. But the important thing is that he is moved not by humanitarian impulses but by an inner passion. Actually, the Mumford-MacLeish group have themselves, for all their recoil from Nazi barbarities, come away far from the humanitarian tradition. Their moral values end by being absolutes, worth while because they are worth while, and not because of any human frame of reference or any operational truth. They have in the end a good deal of the fanatic. Which may be just as well, since the future belongs to the fanatics.

I find myself uneasy at this development. There was nothing wrong with humanitarianism except that it outstripped itself. It promised more than it could fulfill. Browning told his age that a man's reach should exceed his grasp. But when the distance between them becomes too great, and the man is jumping over a chasm, the result is not likely to evoke enthusiasm. A society that arouses in a nation a sense of injustice and a passion for equality must also organize the national will to erase the one and achieve the other. A society that encourages a sense of world brotherhood before it is willing to construct an international sovereignty is also headed for disillusion. What was at fault then was not the extent of our humanity but the defect of our social will and organization. And the remedy is not to recoil from social sensibility, but to steel our collective will.

That is what has plunged so many of our thinkers into a Spenglerian gloom. It is not merely that the efforts and dreams of the centuries of the great hope lie shattered like rubble. What ails us is that those centuries secularized our belief, shook us loose from the submission to blind forces, gave us the sense that society is a contrivance not of nature but of art, and that history can be fashioned by collective human effort. But with that sense has come the frustration of seeing the men in power unwilling or unable to mold history to the shape of our desires. And so, as we gaze at our world and compare it with the world we might have shaped but could not, our hearts and wills sink. It is the sense of falling short which, more than anything else, numbs the spirit.

This numbing of the spirit takes several forms—the indifference of those who have given up the fight, the myopia of those who feel there is nothing to choose between the contestants, the absolutism of those who want to perfect their world before they think it worth fighting for, the provincialism of those who believe that America would be out of her depth in any attempt to help in the organization of world peace and world order. These are the categories of numbness: fill in for yourselves the blanks where the names belong.

I do not blame these people: they may be right or wrong. I am writing reflections, not drawing up an indictment. I say merely that if they are right, we are sunk. For myself, I see no way of our surviving the harsh age except by further collective social effort— more dynamic than before, more sophisticated, determined to promise less and fulfill more.

I do not say we shall accomplish this. It is quite possible we shall not. But the path lies open for us. I recognize no inevitabilities that close it. Despite the current fervor in rejecting Marxian thought, the core of it is still useful: that men, working together to transform their social conditions, transform themselves in the process. The role of inevitability in Marxian thought has always been overplayed, as a convenient and useful myth. Marxism is a philosophy of social will in a context of maturing social forces. And here it fuses with the best elements of progressivism.

The immediate future is dark. The war will get worse before it gets better. It will, however, eventually be fought out and decided in three media: in the air, with engines of destruction; on the assembly lines, in making those engines; in men's minds, while enduring the extremes of destruction and suffering. If we are able, by planning our war industries, to help England capture control of the air, and by our morale to tip the scale of world prestige against fascism, then the long-run prospect brightens.

I have said above that the future belongs to the fanatics. The word is an unpleasant one, but let me illustrate. There are people today who say democracy is not worth defending unless it proves itself in action and not merely in words. In fact, that is an attitude so common as to tie together people as diverse as Robert M. Hutchins, Archibald MacLeish, Harold Laski, Norman Thomas. I have myself at times joined in the chorus. And yet it is really a bit meaningless. Democracy is worth defending because of our complete belief that by and large it offers human beings the only conditions on which life is tolerable. "Democracy in action" does not mean that we must wait passively to be shown a final thing of beauty before we stir ourselves. We may sit around sullenly, demanding from our society either guarantees or finalities before we act to transform it. But if we do, we shall find that our inaction has itself left the field open for those who do not share our paralyzing scruples.

The essence of democracy in action is the principle that if minorities obstruct the majority will, the majority moves on despite them. And the proof of this principle is up to the majority, whether in a harsh age or any other.

1941

13

The Left: End and Beginning

THERE can be little doubt that the left in America has come
to the end of a long phase of its history. There are clamant
voices all about us telling us so—confessions, repudiations,
accusations. But even more convincing is the deep inner voice that
tells us we must write finis to a chapter. But if there is an end, are
there also beginnings for us? To answer that question other than
wishfully, we must look backward to the past and with that perspective confront what may lie ahead.

There has always been an American left, under whatever name.
It is an honorable record—that of the vanguard movements in the
history of the democratic experience. There were the Committees
of Correspondence during the Revolution, then the Jeffersonians,
the Jacksonians, the early workingmen's parties, the Abolitionists
before the Civil War and the Knights of Labor after it, the liberals
and Mugwumps of the dreary decades, the populists, the single-
taxers, the muckrakers, the socialist and syndicalist labor forces of
the turn of the century, the trustbusters, the Wilsonians and Progressives, the Marxists of the post-war decades, the technocrats, the
New Dealers, the CIO.

It is a curious procession, so varied in the characters of its
individual elements that there is no one way to sum it up. The
now familiar classification into reformist and revolutionary movements, which entered American thought with Marxism and especially after 1917 with Lenin's influence, no longer seems fruitful.
On analysis there are very few of the movements I have cited
that do not yield both revolutionary and reformist elements. My
own impulse is toward a different division. Since left movements
are always concerned with power and its transformation, why not
separate the principal strains on the left in terms of their location

of the sources of power and their analysis of how to grapple with the problems of power in a capitalist democracy?

The first strain that emerges is the agrarian. Its great leaders were Jefferson and Bryan, its theorists John Taylor and some of the recent Southern agrarians. Even before the Civil War it had already a slightly anachronistic flavor. It cut athwart the laws of technological change and ultimately fell a victim to the march of the machines. Jefferson's states' rights doctrine, his fear and hatred of cities, his distrust of mechanics and bankers alike have remained the heritage of populist and agrarian movements since. In its own day it was a rousing creed, and carried much of the burden of democratic advance. But it proved a poor weapon with which to confront the developed capitalism of the turn of the century. It was militant enough, and even revolutionary at times, with a sporadic sort of twenty-four-hour violence. But with its eyes turned nostalgically to an agrarian past it had more meaning as a way of life than as an anatomy of power. It could not produce an analysis of American corporate capitalism, of its laws of growth, its strength and weakness, and its tenacity.

A second strain has been what, for want of a better name, I shall call a humanist liberalism. Its genesis was the post-Civil War period, although it had forerunners in the Concord school. Its prophet was Mill; its leaders were Godkin and Schurz. Yet it too set its face against the march of industrialism—against the crude energies of both capitalists and workers. It expressed the point of view of the cultured, middle-class left. It accepted the capitalist economy but was indignant against capitalists. It accepted democracy but feared and distrusted the popular energies and was never able to stomach the imperative of a mass base in a democracy.

There has been a third strain much harder to isolate. It drew much of its strength from the agrarians, shared the libertarian views of the liberals, was affected by Marxism. Basically, however, it was the strain of democratic socialization. Among its leaders are some of the great names in American thought. In economics it had Veblen, in law Brandeis, in journalism Steffens and the muckrakers, in politics La Follette, in its humanist phase J. Allen Smith, Beard, Parrington, Bourne. What distinguished these men was that they accepted the sweep of industrialism but sought to tame it to the purposes of mass welfare and cultural freedom and richness. On the whole they were tough-minded and experimental even when they were wrong. They confronted squarely, with the best knowledge at their disposal, the dual problem of power involved in capitalism and democracy. They influenced and were influenced by the course of the trade-union movement, the co-operatives, the left phases of the T.R. and Wilson administrations. The analysis of corporate capitalism in Berle and Means derives from them; the basic governmental investigations of capitalist power from the Pujo committee to the La Follette committee are linked with them; the TNEC is the product of their attitude; the techniques of economic control and planning owe much to them; the left New Dealers work in their spirit. They are, for all their weaknesses and lack of precise outlines, more squarely in the main line of the American left than is any other tradition.

It remains to speak of the Marxist tradition. With the exception of Debs and Reed, and perhaps De Leon and Upton Sinclair, this has produced no one in America even approximating first-rate stature. Yet it would be an error to underestimate its effect on American life and thought since the World War. It gave us a new emphasis on labor organization and new insight into labor's social role. It deepened our awareness of the democratic mass. It gave a more disciplined militancy to social action and taught us to think in terms of economic and political power. It taught us to see American life in the context of movements and forces world-wide in scope. Above all, it made us aware of society and social thought not in their fragments but as an individual whole—linking analysis and action, our perception of the past and our projection of the future.

It is important for us, particularly in the present revulsion against Marxism, to grasp these affirmative achievements. Nothing could be more dangerous than to equate the communist parties or Soviet international politics with the whole of the Marxian outlook. And nothing could be more foolish than the present tendency to view the recent influence of Marxism as merely a vast conspiracy, whether Stalinist, Trotskyist, or Leninist. A whole American generation cannot be summed up as the dupes of a clique in Moscow. The fact is that the Marxian influence was genuinely evocative. The revolutionary image and the image of men's control over their social destinies released energies in literature and art as in social action. Many were touched by it who never became Marxist in their thinking and never joined any of the Marxian parties or splinter groups.

But this phase of the American left had the defects of its qualities. Its intellectual rigor easily became rigidity. It produced a peculiar type of provincialism in thought which sought to measure the torrential flow of American life by the yardsticks of the Marxian books. It brought with it a concentration on the Soviet Union, whether by its apologists or its attackers, which allowed the reactionaries wide scope to stake out an exclusive claim to "Americanism." It gave the middle class a fear symbol and the fascist groups a hate symbol. It produced a bitter factionalism, always inherent in out-of-power left groups of absolutist tendencies in thought, but in this case intensified by the cross-fire of Russian and American sects and problems. And it led to an accent on faith which ultimately, in the context of the Soviet state structure and such maneuvers of international politics as the Nazi pact and the invasion of Finland, could result only in a drastic disillusionment.

We are now reaping the harvest of our sowing of provincialism, factionalism, hatred. And since what we sowed was the wind of doctrine, the harvest is the whirlwind of confusion and hysteria. If it has turned some to the sadism of a comprehensive red-baiting, it has turned others to the masochism of public confession. But the long-run importance of either of these trends is slight compared with a more characteristic trend—the sense of aloneness that has come to hundreds of thousands of progressives scattered over the country, young and old, in every walk of life, the terrifying sense of being left intellectually rootless, emotionally homeless.

And why should they not feel it? We have come to the end of a stage in our development, just as often happens in the growth of any creative person. It is futile to imagine that a culture or a movement does not have its biography, like an individual. The psychic crises, dead ends, transformations are as real in the one as in the other. The spate of repudiations and confessions is part of that crisis: they are heightened symbols of the inner revaluations that each of us must exact from himself because of what has happened in the world. It is no longer possible to go on as if nothing had happened.

Yet it is all too easy to take a catastrophic view. Individuals survive their psychic crises and grow because of them. Why should not groups and movements? One thing may be said: the air has been cleared of a good deal of cant and dream stuff. We can build more honestly and more realistically than ever before in our generation. If we cannot forget our rancors and find a common basis for comparing ideas and joining in action, then the suicide-urge is stronger in us than I think it is.

There are definite things we can learn from the whole course of our experience. Have we learned them? And can we adopt them as first principles in a reorientation of the American forces of the left? *Item:* that the obsession with Moscow, for or against, had better be abandoned. There can be no commitments that reach outside the boundaries of American life and obscure the impact of issues on our culture. *Item:* that the only possible focus for an American left is America. This does not mean seceding from the world or abdicating our judgment as observers of world events, but it does mean that we should think and act in the American grain. *Item:* that with all our disagreements, our continuing quest will be for some structure of industrial control and socialization that will provide full employment, the maximum national income, and economic democracy. *Item:* that Americans are in a better position than any other nation to achieve this without impairing the civil-liberties tradition and without sacrificing democratic controls. *Item:* that the meaning of economics and politics alike lies in the extension of the possibilities of human dignity for an ever-widening number of people.

On so much there can be agreement. Beyond that lie personal perspectives. My own preference is to follow the tradition of what I have called democratic socialization. The main lines of analysis as laid down in Veblen and Parrington and Bourne still offer tentatively a good starting-point for our own.

I say "tentatively" because the left must reject absolutes and be ready to re-examine its basic postulates. We must reconsider the values we attach to freedom, democracy, humanism. We must re-examine Marxism in the light not only of what has happened in the world of events but also of what has happened in the world of social thought. There are new insights and perspectives in anthropology, psychology, political theory, law, economics, the logic of language, and scientific method. No movement that seeks to subject the social energies to discipline and plan can afford to remain provincial in the sciences of society any more than it can afford to neglect the possibilities of technology.

But while we must use the utmost resources of rational analysis we must not repeat our past errors in assuming in men a greater rationality than they possess. The concepts and stereotypes on the left have too long clung to the eighteenth- and nineteenth-century belief in an ordered universe where men have only to discover the principles of order and then call upon their fellows to enact them. The course of events has had no tenderness for this fiction, nor can we afford to perpetuate it. Our efforts toward the reconstruction of the societies in which men live will have to take account of the whole person and not just half of him; of the fact that he is governed by passions, fears, and myths as well as by interests and ideals.

This will be a difficult insight for us to assimilate. We shall have to learn again things toward which the left has always adopted a lofty attitude—the imperatives of national cohesion and national survival about which Machiavelli wrote long ago in his *Discourses*. We shall have to learn to work within the framework of men's minds as we find them until we can extend their possibilities. But who is there among us that asks for or expects an easy task? Our hurdles will seem insuperable: to understand the mechanisms by which economies run while we are faced at the same time with the job of transforming them; to study the uses and limitations of power at the same time that we are getting ready for its responsibilities; to learn how the necessary power can be focused on our problems at the same time that we are decentralizing its administration; to resolve the paradox that while we must be single-minded in the pursuit of our objectives and enlist behind them belief and energy, every working system must be pluralistic and allow plenty of latitude at the joints.

It may be true, as I have heard again and again, that these paradoxes can never be resolved, and that in the present world a democratic militancy will never succeed. But the American nation has faced in other periods contradictions that loomed just as formidable at the time. We have the resources of a great people and a great heritage. If direction for the energies of the common people does not come from the left, it will mean the crushing of what America has stood for in world history.

1940

DGMENTS

D

EX

Acknowledgments

Where I have changed the title of an article or review, the original title appears in brackets.

PART ONE

1. The War as Revolution — *Nation:* 68–71, 88–92, 129–32, July 27, Aug. 3, Aug. 17, 1940

2. Letter on Democracy [Who Owns the Future?] — *Nation:* 41–4, Jan. 11, 1941

3. Democratic Ends and "Totalitarian" Means — *Virginia Quarterly Review:* 179–92, Apr. 1941

4. Economic Empire and Monopoly State — Introductory Critique in Guenter Reimann: *The Myth of the Total State* (Morrow, New York, 1941)

5. The People's Century — *New Republic:* 465–6, Apr. 7, 1941

6. If We Own the Future — *Antioch Review:* 270–90, fall 1941

PART TWO

1. Machiavelli and Machiavellism — Introduction to N. Machiavelli: *The Prince* and *The Discourses* (Modern Library, New York, 1940), xxv–xlv

2. The Mind and Faith of Justice Holmes — Unpublished

3. Randolph Bourne and Two Generations — *Twice a Year:* 54–78, fall–winter 1940

4. Franz Kafka and the Human Voyage — *Saturday Review of Literature:* 3–4, June 7, 1941

PART THREE

1. In the Time of the Great Debate
   Continentalism and World Leadership [In the Hour of Decision] — *New Republic:* 765–7, June 3, 1940
   The Daedalian Vision of Waldo Frank [Face the War] — *Saturday Review of Literature:* 1–2, June 3, 1940

2. Notes on the March of Fascism
   An American Yankee at Hitler's Court [Dodd's Diary] — *PM:* 42, Mar. 2, 1941

Hitler as Medicine Man   *New Republic:* 350–1, Mar. 11, 1940
Hitler's American Dream   *New Republic:* 790–1, June 9, 1941
Russia and the War of Ideas   *New Republic:* 17–8, July 7, 1941
3. Propaganda in Our Time   *New Republic:* 281–2, Aug. 26, 1940
4. Democracy for a War Generation   *Decision:* 7–11, Apr. 1941

PART FOUR

1. Case Studies in Democracy: Some Archaeological Notes
    The Case of the Corporate Surplus Tax [Corporate Tax Battle]   *Nation:* 669–71, May 27, 1936
    The Case of "Black Tuesday" [Notes on Black Tuesday]   *Nation:* 468–70, Oct. 30, 1937
    The Case of Governor La Follette [Phil La Follette, an Interview]   *Nation:* 552–5, May 14, 1938
    The Case of the Spanish Embargo [Behind Hull's Embargo]   *Nation:* 607–10, May 28, 1938
2. Constitution and Court as Symbols   *Yale Law Journal:* 1290–1319, 1937; republished in Douglas Maggs, ed.: *Selected Essays on Constitutional Law* (Foundation Press, Chicago, 1938)

3. Notes on the Supreme Court Crisis
    The Divine Right of Judges   *Nation:* 121–2, Jan. 29, 1936
    The Lawless Majority [The Lawless Supreme Court]   *Nation:* 213–5, Feb. 19, 1936
    The Fate of the Supreme Court   *Nation:* 379–81, Mar. 25, 1936
    The Supreme Court Revolution   *Nation:* 660–1, June 11, 1938
    Labor and Civil Liberties [The Supreme Court and Labor]   *New Republic:* 262–4, Feb. 24, 1941
    The Personnel of the Supreme Court   *National Lawyers Guild Quarterly:* vol. 2, 9–16, Apr. 1939
    Landscape with Judges   *New Republic:* 156–7, Feb. 3, 1941
4. Constitutional Crisis and the Crisis State   *William and Mary Bulletin:* Nov. 1941
5. Legalism and Legality   *Journal of Politics:* 336–42, Aug. 1940

6. Aspects of Economic Strategy
    TNEC: a New Technique [The New Trust Busters]   *Nation:* 59–60, July 16, 1938
    Trustbuster's White Paper   *New Republic:* 389–90, Sept. 16, 1940
    Keynes Meets Marx [Marxist-Keynesist Blend]   *Saturday Review of Literature:* 6, 15, Aug. 3, 1940
7. The Administrative Revolution in America [The Burden of Government Business]   Fritz Morstein Marx, ed.: *Public Management in the New Democracy* (Harper, New York, 1940), 3–13

8. Notes on the Two-Front War
    Harold Laski and the Two-Front War [Laski Tells Us Where to Go] — *PM:* 42, Nov. 17, 1940
    Defense and Slave-Men — *New Republic:* 897–8, Dec. 30, 1940
    Meeting the *Blitzkrieg* on Labor — *New Republic:* 598–9, Apr. 28, 1941
    The Burning of the Textbooks — *New Republic:* 296–7, Mar. 17, 1941
    Teacher-Hunt [Communist Teachers] — *New Republic:* 359–60, Mar. 17, 1941
    Planned Defense [America in a Totalitarian World] — *New Republic:* 23–4, July 1, 1940
    Dollar-a-Year Defense [Dollar-a-Year Democracy] — *New Republic:* 175–6, Aug. 11, 1941
    The Common Man and a Fighting Faith [A Fighting Faith in Labor] — *New Republic:* 51–2, Jan. 13, 1941
9. State, Class, and Party
    The Broker State — *New Republic:* 477–8, Apr. 8, 1940
    Tweedledum and Tweedledee [Party Government in Crisis] — *Nation:* 250–1, Sept. 21, 1940
10. The Presidential Office
    The Job in the White House — *New Republic:* 90, Jan. 20, 1941
    Hamlet and the Presidency — *New Republic:* 114, Jan. 27, 1941
11. Two Presidents in Wartime
    Lincoln in the Civil War [Lincoln as War Leader] — *New Republic:* 197–8, Dec. 6, 1939
    I Thought of Lincoln — *New Republic:* 177, Feb. 10, 1941
    Roosevelt as Symbol [FDR—Next President] — *Nation:* 752–5, June 22, 1940
12. Reflections on a Harsh Age — *New Republic:* 303–4, Mar. 3, 1941
13. The Left: End and Beginning — *Nation:* 164–6, Feb. 10, 1940

Index